An Introduction to Systemic Functional Linguistics
2nd Edition

An Introduction to Systemic Functional Linguistics

2nd Edition

Suzanne Eggins

continuum
NEW YORK · LONDON

To my teachers and my students

Continuum International Publishing Group
The Tower Building   15 East 26th Street
11 York Road   New York
London SE1 7NX   NY 10010

© Suzanne Eggins 2004

British Library Cataloguing-in-Publication Data
A catalogue record for this book is available from the British Library.

ISBN: 0-8264-5787-8 (hardback)
0-8264-5786-X (paperback)

Library of Congress Cataloging-in-Publication Data
A catalogue record for this book is available from the Library of Congress

Typeset by Servis Filmsetting Ltd, Manchester
Printed and bound in Great Britain by
MPG Books Ltd, Bodmin, Cornwall

Contents

Texts

Systems

Figures

Tables

Foreword to the Second Edition

As with the first edition, this second edition of *An Introduction to Systemic Functional Linguistics* offers an overview of systemic theory and some demonstration of how systemic techniques can be applied in the analysis of texts. Written for students who may have little or no formal knowledge of linguistics, it covers most of the major concepts in systemic linguistics (*semiotic system, genre, register, text, cohesion, grammatical metaphor* . . .). Taking Michael Halliday's *An Introduction to Functional Grammar* as its base, the book presents a functional grammatical description of the simultaneous metafunctional organization of the clause (its MOOD, TRANSITIVITY, THEME and CLAUSE COMPLEX systems) and introduces the basic techniques for analysing cohesive patterns in text (reference, lexical cohesion and conjunction).

In the ten years since the first edition, much has happened to systemic linguistics and to me. Since 1994, systemic functional linguistics (SFL) has moved from 'marginal' to 'mainstream' as an approach to language, at least in Australia. Systemic linguists now hold senior positions at universities in countries around the world, and SFL informs many postgraduate applied linguistics and TESOL programmes in English-language countries.

The past ten years have seen a corresponding outburst of publishing in SFL, from workbooks in the grammar and discourse, such as Martin *et al.* 1997, to major theoretical works, such as Halliday and Matthiessen 1999, and the progressive publication of Halliday's collected works edited by Jonathan Webster (Halliday and Webster 2002a, 2002b, 2003a, 2003b). Much fleshing out of systemic ideas has been published in journal articles and edited collections, and SFL contributions have also been published in many interdisciplinary collections about language.

These changes mean that a student new to SFL now has a wide range of resources to draw on to learn about the theory and its analytical methodologies. A new role for my book is to steer readers towards these other sources whenever possible.

Changes in my own institutional context have also affected how I approach this second edition. For the past dozen years I have held a position not in a Linguistics department but in an English (Literature) department, where I teach students who are majoring in literature, mother-tongue education or media and communication. Exposure to this context has broadened my own experience of texts and forced me to reflect on how systemic linguistics can be made accessible to students who have no prior linguistic training but want ways of talking about how texts work. As I hope I demonstrate in this second edition, I remain convinced that SFL is one of the most powerful ways of saying 'sensible and useful things about any text, spoken or written, in modern English' (Halliday 1994: xv).

Summary of changes in the second edition

Michael Halliday's *An Introduction to Functional Grammar* (IFG), first published in 1985 with a second edition in 1994, is the motivating text for this book. The third edition of *IFG*, substantially revised and extended, appeared as Halliday and Matthiessen 2004, just as this book was in production. Where possible, references have been updated to this third edition. Occasionally I have referenced earlier editions of *IFG*, as I am attached to the directness of some of Halliday's earlier explanations. The core grammatical chapters on Mood, Transitivity and Theme remain largely as they were in the first edition, but the book now includes one new chapter on the clause complex, positioned directly after Transitivity. All other chapters have been updated with recent references, and some have had new text examples substituted or added.

I have made only one theoretical modification to the first edition: in the 1994 edition I used Martin's (1992a) label of 'discourse-semantics' to refer to the stratum of language above grammar, and I devoted one chapter to Martin's methodology for the analysis of cohesive patterns as discourse-semantic systems. In this edition I have returned to Halliday's model, with the top linguistic stratum called **semantics**, and the cohesive analyses interpreted as non-structural grammatical systems (as in Halliday and Hasan 1976, Halliday 1994). For most students new to SFL, this change will be of no practical import at all. However, it has allowed me to devote one chapter to the fundamental question of *What is (a) text?* and to bring the sections on cohesion in line with Halliday 1994 (itself based on Halliday and Hasan 1976). Readers who wish to go further in theory and description are pointed towards Martin and Rose 2003.

In addition, the contents of some chapters have been substantially revised and chapter order adjusted, as follows:

Chapter 1 'An overview of systemic functional linguistics' has been updated, but is still organized around the three Crying Baby texts.

Chapter 2 'What is (a) text?' contains many new texts (all authentic), both fictional and non-fictional.

Chapter 3 'Genre' contains many new texts as well as some familiar ones.

Chapter 4 'Register' has only a new introductory section.

Chapters 5–8 and 10 on principles of grammatical analysis, systems, Mood, Transitivity and Theme remain largely unchanged.

Chapter 9 is a completely new chapter on 'The Clause Complex'. Positioned straight after its companion on the experiential system of Transitivity, the clause complex chapter presents the SFL understanding of the second, logico-semantic component of ideational meaning.

Chapter 11 discusses the complete analyses of the Crying Baby texts, now incorporating clause complex analyses. The analyses are in the Appendix.

I am indebted to Michael Halliday, whose way of thinking and talking about language captivated me from my first day as an undergraduate student at Sydney University. Special thanks also to Jim Martin and Clare Painter, first my teachers and more recently my colleagues, for encouragement over the years; and to my literature colleagues at the School of English at UNSW, who have helped me to broaden my awareness of texts and ways of talking about them.

Thanks also to the patient, loyal systemic linguistics community which has always welcomed me to conferences, despite my meagre and infrequent contributions. Thankfully, no one ever closed the door on me, and I realize now that the door never will be closed because SFL will forever inform how I think about language and life.

Suzanne Eggins
March 2004, UNSW, Sydney

Acknowledgements

I am grateful to the following conversationalists, authors, publishers and editors for allowing me to use copyright material in this book:

Gail Bell, for permission to reproduce an excerpt from a telephone interview in December 2003.

Pan Macmillan Australia Pty Ltd for permission to reproduce an extract from *Shot* by Gail Bell (2003).

Paul Marston and Richard Brightling for permission to reproduce an excerpt from *The Bridge Workbook for Beginners* (1985), Contract Bridge Supplies, Sydney.

The Editor, *The Bridge World Magazine*, for permission to reproduce an excerpt from *The Bridge World Magazine*, Vol. 63, No. 7, April 1992, pp. 4–5.

W. B. Saunders Co., Harcourt Brace & Company, Philadelphia, for permission to reproduce an excerpt from R. Behrman and R. Kliegman (1990), *Essentials of Pediatrics*, p. 32.

Harlequin Enterprises (Australia) for permission to reproduce an excerpt from *Fusion* by Cait London.

Pinter Publishers, London, for an excerpt from E. Ventola (1987), *The Structure of Social Interaction (Open Linguistics Series)*, pp. 239–40.

Martin Fallows (Publisher), Magazine House, Sydney, for an excerpt from *My Baby* magazine, 1991 edition, p. 24.

The School of English at the University of New South Wales for an excerpt from the *School of English Handbook* (1993), p. 4.

Carcanet Press Ltd, Manchester, for permission to reproduce 'The Grapevine' by John Ashbery.

'r-p-o-p-h-s-s-a-g-r' is reprinted from *Completed Poems 1904–1962* by e. e. cummings, edited by George J. Firmage, by permission of W. W. Norton & Company. © 1991 the Trustees for the e. e. cummings Trust and George James Firmage.

Penguin Books Ltd for permission to reproduce an excerpt from *The BFG* by Roald Dahl.

I am grateful to Val Noake and Arthur Easton for providing me with access to the Nestlé Write Around Australia archive at the State Library of New South Wales. Unfortunately, it was not possible to locate all copyright holders of texts used from that archive. Any contact information about copyright holders would be appreciated.

My thanks also to Stephen, Di, George, Simon and Marg for permission to reproduce excerpts from the 'Dinner at Stephen's' conversation, recorded in Sydney, April 1986.

Chapter 1

An overview of systemic functional linguistics

Aim of this book: explaining text

The aim of this book is to introduce you to the principles and techniques of the systemic functional approach to language, in order that you may begin to analyse and explain how meanings are made in everyday linguistic interactions.

In our ordinary, everyday lives we are constantly using language. We chat to family members, organize children for school, read the paper, speak at meetings, serve customers, follow instructions in a booklet, make appointments, surf the internet, call in a plumber, unburden ourselves to therapists, record our day's thoughts and activities in a journal, chat to our pets, send and read a few emails, sing along to CDs, read aloud to our children, write submissions. All of these are activities which involve language. Only for rare moments, perhaps when totally absorbed in a physical activity, does language drop out of our minds. In contemporary life, we are constantly required to react to and produce bits of language that make sense. In other words, we are required to negotiate *texts*.

The late twentieth century saw theorists from many approaches focus on texts and ask fundamental questions, such as: just how do texts work on us? How do we work to produce them? How can texts apparently mean different things to different readers? How do texts and culture interact? Answers have been suggested from disciplines such as literary theory (where the focus has been on the written texts highly valued, or 'canonized', by a culture) and cultural studies (where the interest has shifted to the written, visual and filmic texts of popular culture). Behind both perspectives lies a vast body of 'critical theory', proposed explanations about how we read texts, what texts are telling us, and how texts are (or should be) valued by the culture.

While the critical understanding of text is a fundamental goal we share with other text analysts, the approach taken in this book has different origins, orientations and methodologies. The systemic functional analysis presented here has been developed on the foundation of work by the social semiotic linguist Michael Halliday, whose extensive writings since the 1960s are currently being edited and re-issued in a ten-volume set of *Collected Works* (see Halliday and Webster 2002a, 2002b, 2003a, 2003b). Through the work of Halliday and his associates, systemic functional linguistics (often abbreviated to SFL) is increasingly recognized as a very useful descriptive and interpretive framework for viewing language as a strategic, meaning-making resource.

One of Michael Halliday's major contributions to linguistic analysis is his development of a detailed functional grammar of modern English (Halliday 1994[1]), showing how simultaneous strands of meanings (the ideational, interpersonal and textual metafunctions) are expressed in clause structures. Halliday's (meta)functional grammar is now accessible not only through Halliday's own substantial text (Halliday 1994 and now further extended in Halliday and Matthiessen 2004) but also through the many books which introduce and explore the grammar of the metafunctions and the relation of language to context (e.g. Halliday and Hasan 1985, Bloor and Bloor 1995, Thompson 2004, Martin *et al.* 1997, Halliday and Matthiessen 1999, Butt *et al.* 2001, Droga and Humphrey 2003, Martin and Rose 2003).

Michael Halliday prefaces the 1994 edition of his functional grammar with an open-ended list of 21 possible applications of SFL (Halliday 1994: xxix–xxx). These include theoretical concerns ('to understand the nature and functions of language'), historical ones ('to understand how languages evolve through time'), developmental ones ('to understand how a child develops language, and how language may have evolved in the human species'), and educational ones ('to help people learn their mother tongue . . . foreign languages', etc.). Underlying all these very varied applications is a common focus on the analysis of authentic products of social interaction (**texts**), considered in relation to the cultural and social context in which they are negotiated. Consequently, the most generalizable application of SFL, and the one which will provide the framework for this book, is 'to understand the quality of texts: why a text means what it does, and why it is valued as it is' (Halliday 1994: xxix).

Although Halliday's functional grammar deals in detail with the structural organization of English clauses, phrases and sentences, Halliday's interest has always been with the meanings of language in use in the textual processes of social life, or 'the sociosemantics of text'. As Halliday says of his functional grammar:

> The aim has been to construct a grammar for purposes of text analysis: one that would make it possible to say sensible and useful things about any text, spoken or written, in modern English. (Halliday 1994: xv)

Recent years have seen SFL used to say 'sensible and useful things' about texts in fields such as language education (Christie 1999, 2002, Christie and Martin 1997, Unsworth 2000), child language development (Painter 1998), computational linguistics (Teich 1999), media discourse (Iedema *et al.* 1994, White 2002), casual conversation (Eggins and Slade 1997), history (Martin and Wodak 2003) and administrative language (Iedema 2003), to name just a few. SFL has also been applied to interpret the 'grammar' of other semiotic modes, such as visuals (Kress and van Leeuwen 1996, 2001), art (O'Toole 1994) and sound (van Leeuwen 1999, Martinec 2000).

The field of SFL is now a substantial international one, as can be seen by the number and range of publications and conferences in SFL around the world. An excellent systemic linguistics website, maintained by Dr Mick O'Donnell, can be found at **http:www/ wagsoft/com/Systemics/**. The website provides information about systemic discussion groups (the international email list sysfling has over 500 subscribers), recent publications in SFL, bibliographies, theses, conferences and journals such as *Functions of Language* which publish work in SFL.

While individual scholars naturally have different research emphases or application contexts, common to all systemic linguists is an interest in *language as social semiotic* (Halliday 1978) – how people use language with each other in accomplishing everyday social life. This interest leads systemic linguists to advance four main theoretical claims about language:

1. that language use is functional
2. that its function is to make meanings
3. that these meanings are influenced by the social and cultural context in which they are exchanged
4. that the process of using language is a *semiotic* process, a process of making meanings by choosing.

These four points, that language use is functional, semantic, contextual and semiotic, can be summarized by describing the systemic approach as a *functional-semantic* approach to language. The purpose of this chapter is to outline and illustrate what this means.

A functional-semantic approach to language

The systemic approach to language is functional in two main respects:

1. because it asks functional questions about language: systemicists ask **how do people use language?**
2. because it interprets the linguistic system functionally: systemicists ask **how is language structured for use?**

Answering the first question involves a focus on authentic, everyday social interaction. This analysis of **texts** leads systemicists to suggest that people negotiate texts in order to make meanings with each other. In other words, the general function of language is a semantic one.

Reinterpreting the functional questions semantically, then, systemicists ask:

1. Can we differentiate between types of meanings in language?, i.e. **how many different sorts of meanings do we use language to make?**
2. How are texts (and the other linguistic units which make them up, such as sentences or clauses) structured so that meanings can be made?, i.e. **how is language organized to make meanings?**

As will become clear from subsequent discussion, Halliday (e.g. 1985b/1989, 1994) has argued that language is structured to make three main kinds of meanings simultaneously. This semantic complexity, which allows **ideational**, **interpersonal** and **textual** meanings to be fused together in linguistic units, is possible because language is a semiotic system, a conventionalized coding system, organized as sets of choices. The distinctive feature of semiotic systems is that each choice in the system acquires its meanings against the background of the other choices which could have been made. This semiotic interpretation of the system of language allows us to consider the appropriacy or inappropriacy of different linguistic choices in relation to their contexts of use, and to view language as a resource which we use by choosing to make meanings in contexts.

Each of these rather abstract points will now be illustrated in turn with concrete language examples.

How do people use language?

As soon as we ask functional questions such as 'how do people use language?' (i.e. 'what do people *do* with language?'), we realize we have to look at real examples of language in use. Intuition does not provide a sufficiently reliable source of data for doing functional linguistics. Thus, systemicists are interested in the authentic speech and writing of people interacting in naturally-occurring social contexts. We are interested, for example, in language events such as Text 1.1 below[2]:

Text 1.1: Crying Baby (1)

(1)A baby who won't stop crying can drive anyone to despair. (2i)You feed him, (2ii)you change him, (2iii)you nurse him, (2iv)you try to settle him, (2v)but the minute you put him down (2vi)he starts to howl. (3)Why?

(4)The most common reason baby cries is hunger. (5i)Even if he was just recently fed (5ii)he might still be adapting to the pattern of sucking until his tummy is full and feeling satisfied until it empties again. (6i)When he was in the womb (6ii)nourishment came automatically and constantly. (7i)Offer food first; (7ii)if he turns away from the nipple or teat (7iii)you can assume (7iv)it's something else. (8i)It happens that babies go through grumpy, miserable stages (8ii)when they just want (8iii)to tell everyone (8iv)how unhappy they feel. (9i)Perhaps his digestion feels uncomfortable (9ii)or his limbs are twitching.

(10i)If you can't find any specific source of discomfort such as a wet nappy or strong light in his eyes, (10ii)he could just be having a grizzle. (11)Perhaps he's just lonely. (12i)During the day, a baby sling helps you to deal with your chores (12ii)and keep baby happy. (13i)At night (13ii)when you want (13iii)to sleep (13iv)you will need to take action (13v)to relax and settle him. (14i)Rocking helps, (14ii)but if your baby is in the mood to cry (14iii)you will probably find (14iv)he'll start up again (14v)when you put him back in the cot. (15i)Wrapping baby up snugly helps to make him feel secure (15ii)and stops him from jerking about (15iii)which can unsettle him. (16i)Outside stimulation is cut down (16ii)and he will lose tension. (17i)Gentle noise might soothe him off to sleep – a radio played softly, a recording of a heartbeat, traffic noise – (17ii)even the noise of the washing machine is effective!

(18i)Some parents use dummies – (18ii)it's up to you – (18iii)and you might find (18iv)your baby settles (18v)sucking a dummy. (19i)'Sucky' babies might be able to find their thumbs and fists (19ii)to have a good suck. (20i)Remember (20ii)that babies get bored (20iii)so when he is having a real grizzle (20iv)this could be the reason. (21)Is his cot an interesting place to be? (22)Coloured posters and mobiles give him something to watch. (23i)You could maybe tire him out (23ii)by taking him for a walk . . . or a ride in the car – (23iii)not always practical in the middle of the night. (24i)A change of scene and some fresh air will often work wonders – (24ii)even a walk around the garden may be enough. (25i)As baby gets older (25ii)he will be more able to communicate his feelings (25iii)and you will be better at judging the problem. (26i)Although you might be at your wit's end, (26ii)remember (26iii)that crying is communication with you, his parents. (27)And you are the most important people in your baby's life.

This text, whose source will be disclosed shortly, serves to illustrate a basic premise of systemic linguistics: that language use is purposeful behaviour. The writer of this excerpt did not just produce this text to kill time, or to display her linguistic abilities. She wrote the text because she wanted to use language to achieve a purpose: she had goals that she was using language to achieve. We could gloss the overall purpose of Text 1.1 as being to 'educate parents', although it will be suggested in a moment that this overall purpose implicates a number of distinct goals.

In having a purpose, this instance of language use is typical, not exceptional: people do not 'just talk' or 'just write'. Any use of language is motivated by a purpose, whether that purpose be a clear, pragmatic one (such as needing to write a letter in order to apply for a job), or a less tangible, but equally important, interpersonal one (such as 'needing' to have a chat with friends after a long day at work).

Text 1.1 also illustrates a second consequence of asking functional questions about language: that we have to look at more than isolated sentences. If I had presented you with only one sentence from the text, chosen at random, for example *A change of scene and some fresh air will often work wonders – even a walk around the garden may be enough*, it would have been very difficult for you to determine the motivation for the writing. Similarly, from the writer's point of view, it would have been almost impossible for her to achieve the desired goals through a single sentence: perhaps *Babies cry for many different reasons and there are ways you can try to stop them* would be a start – but no more than a start. If the writer is to educate us to cope with babies' crying, then she needs to spend time (and language) explaining the variety of possible causes, and reviewing the possible solutions. In other words, to achieve successfully the overall purpose of educating parents, the writer must meet the implicated goals of explaining a problematic phenomenon (why it is that babies cry a lot) and suggesting possible solutions parents could try.

It is not just explaining why babies cry that takes time. Very few (if any) of our communicative goals can be achieved through single sentences. Even the simple goal of getting you to carry out an action that I want done will typically involve at least two communicative 'moves'. For example, the brief command *Close the door!* is inherently structured to elicit a response. That response may be verbal (e.g. *Why?* or *Shut it yourself*), or perhaps non-verbal (e.g. the closing of the door). In either case, if we are to understand what language is achieving in the situation, we need to describe the communicative behaviour as involving not just one sentence, but at least two: <u>both</u> the command and the response.

Typically, of course, getting something done using language will involve many more than two moves. As Text 1.1 shows, in order to explain why babies cry and what we can do about it, the writer has presented a discussion running to 27 sentences. She has in other words produced what systemic linguists call a **text.**

The term **text** (which will be explained in detail in Chapter Two) refers to a complete linguistic interaction (spoken or written), preferably from beginning to end. Comparing authentic texts, particularly those which have something in common, points us towards interesting dimensions of language use. Consider, for example, Text 1.2:

Text 1.2: Crying Baby (2)

(1)The compelling sound of an infant's cry makes it an effective distress signal and appropriate to the human infant's prolonged dependence on a caregiver. (2i)However, cries are discomforting (2ii)and may be alarming to parents, (2iii)many of whom find (2iv)it very difficult to listen to their infant's crying for even short periods of time. (3)Many reasons for crying are obvious, like hunger and discomfort due to heat, cold, illness, and lying position. (4i)These reasons, however, account for a relatively small percentage of infant crying (4ii)and are usually recognised quickly (4iii)and alleviated.

(5i)In the absence of a discernible reason for the behaviour, crying often stops (5ii)when the infant is held. (6i)In most infants, there are frequent episodes of crying with no apparent cause, (6ii)and holding or other soothing techniques seem ineffective. (7)Infants cry and fuss for a mean of 1¾ hr/day at age 2 wk, 2¾ hr/day at age 6 wk, and 1 hr/day at 12 wk.

(8i)Counselling about normal crying may relieve guilt (8ii)and diminish concerns, (8iii)but for some the distress caused by the crying cannot be suppressed by logical reasoning. (9i)For these parents, respite from exposure to the crying may be necessary (9ii)to allow them to cope appropriately with their own distress. (10i)Without relief, fatigue and tension may result in inappropriate parental responses (10ii)such as leaving the infant in the house alone (10iii)or abusing the infant.

As you read this text through, you will no doubt have realized that in some ways it is very like Text 1.1, and yet in other ways it is very different. The two texts share a focus on crying babies and what can be done about them, and yet each approaches the topic in ways that indicate that they are intended for different audiences, and would be found in different places. In comparing those two texts with Text 1.3, once again about crying babies, you might try to suggest the likely sources of each text, and consider what aspects of the texts are providing you with clues.

Text 1.3: Crying Baby (3)
(the symbol = = indicates overlap; . . . indicates pause; words in capitals show emphasis)

S   (1)Did your kids used to cry a lot? (2)When they were little?
C   (3)Yea
S   (4)Well = = what did you do?
C   (5)= = still do
S   (6)Yea? [laughs]
C   (7)Oh pretty tedious at times yea. (8)There were all sorts of techniques = = Leonard Cohen
S   (9)= = Like what [laughs] (10)Yea I used to use . . . (11)What's that American guy that did 'Georgia on your mind'?
C   (12)Oh yea
S   (13)= = Jim – James Taylor
C   (14)= = James Taylor
S   (15)Yea yea.
    (16)He was pretty good.
C   (17)Yea. (18i)No Leonard Cohen's good (18ii)cause it's just so monotonous
S   [laughs]
C   (19)And there's only four chords. (20i)And ah we used to have holidays (20ii)when we only had one kid on a houseboat. (21)And that was fantastic just the rocking motion of the houseboat
S   (22)Mmm
C   (23)Mmm
S   (24)Were there ever times . . . (25i)Like I remember times (25ii)when I couldn't work out (25iii)what the hell it was. (26)There just didn't seem to be anything = = you could do
C   (27)= = No reason or . . . (28)Yea
S   (29)Yea every night between six and ten!

C   (30)Yea yea. (31i)Luckily I didn't have that with the second baby (31ii)but the first one was that typical colicky sort of stuff from about five o'clock.

S   (32)Hmm

C   (33i)I remember (33ii)one day going for a um walk along the harbour (33iii)one of those you know harbour routes that had been opened up. (34i)And um he started kicking up from about five o'clock (34ii)and we were getting panic stricken. (35i)I had him in one of those um front strap things you know sling things (35ii)ah cause that use to work wonders from time to time (35iii)but it wasn't working this time. (36i)And as we sat on the foreshore of this Vaucluse area (36ii)these two women came down (36iii)and they'd both been working as um governesses or something like that – (36iv)very, very classy ladies. (37i)And they said (37ii)'Oh what's wrong with baby? (38)He's got colic?' (39i)You know, they really wanted (39ii)to take over.

S   (40)Yea

C   (41)And so I just handed the baby to them.

S   [laughs]

C   (42i)And LUCKILY he kept on crying – (42ii)they couldn't stop him.

S   [laughs]

C   (43)So I was really delighted. (44)They handed back this hideous little red wreck of a thing

S & C   [laughter]

In reading through these three texts, you have almost certainly been able to suggest the likely sources. You might now like to compare your suggestions with the actual source of each text, given at the end of this chapter[3]. You will probably be surprised at how accurately you were able to guess at the sources of the texts. How did you do it? How did you know where each text might be found?

Since you only had the words on the page to guide you, you must have worked out a great deal about the sources of each text from the way language is being used. You probably noted features like the following:

> Text 1.1: sounds 'chatty' because it is using everyday vocabulary (*baby, howl, grumpy, miserable, unhappy, twitching*, etc.) and is addressed to 'you'; but it isn't conversation because there's no interaction;
> Text 1.2: uses 'formal' or 'heavy' vocabulary (e.g. *compelling, prolonged dependence, discernible, suppressed, parental responses*, etc.) and sounds more 'academic' than Text 1.1; it's unlikely to be speech (no interaction);
> Text 1.3: seems to be a casual dialogue because the speakers take turns, use everyday vocabulary, even slang (e.g. *kids, guy, good, holidays, sort of stuff, hideous red wreck*, etc.), and seem to interrupt each other, etc.

What you have just done in an informal way is to deduce the context of language use from the linguistic patterns in a text. The fact that we can do this, that simply by reading or hearing a text we can figure out so much about its source, clearly suggests that in some way ***context is in text***: text carries with it, as a part of it, aspects of the context in which it was produced and, presumably, within which it would be considered appropriate. This example points to an issue which is of particular interest to systemic linguists: the relationship between language and context.

Language and context

Our ability to **deduce** context from text is one way in which language and context are interrelated. Our equally highly developed ability to **predict** language from context provides further evidence of the language/context relationship.

For example, if I were to ask you to predict both the overall structure and some of the specific words and sentences you would find in a recipe for scrambling eggs, you would have very little difficulty. If I asked you to write down the recipe text in a form publishable in a popular magazine or cookbook, you could almost certainly write the entire text with confidence that you were doing so in an appropriate way.

You would not, for example, give your recipe a title such as *Mowing Lawns*, nor would I find words such as *telephone, picture, jeans, swim* in your text, since such items would be quite blatantly inappropriate given that the topic of a recipe is food and its preparation. You would also be unlikely to find yourself writing sentences such as *If it is possible, you are strongly advised to take six eggs* or *Perhaps you should maybe mix the eggs and milk for about two minutes or so.* Such sentences express a degree of tentativity inappropriate to the role of 'recipe writer'. Nor would you find yourself writing *Hi guys! Cop this for a recipe!*, since the relationship between the writer and reader of the recipe is generally more formal than those greetings suggest. Finally, you are unlikely to have written *Take six of these. Break them, and put them in there. Then add this*, since there are a number of words which your reader, distant from you in time and space, would be unable to interpret. In our ability to predict accurately what language will be appropriate in a specific context, we are seeing an extension of our intuitive understanding that language use is sensitive to context.

Final evidence which emphasizes the close link between context and language is that it is often simply not possible to tell how people are using language if you do not take into account the context of use. One example of this was given above, when it was pointed out that presented with just one sentence chosen at random from Text 1.1 you would have found it difficult to state confidently just what the writer of that text was doing. Considered in its textual context (as a part of a complete linguistic event), that sentence clearly did have a function (to propose a possible solution). Taken out of context, its purpose is obscured, with at least part of its meaning lost or unavailable.

A similar point can be made with conversational examples. Consider the following sentence:

I suggest we attack the reds.

Taken out of context, this sentence is ambiguous in a number of respects. You might think, firstly, about what *reds* refers to. It could mean:

- playing a game: time to move out the red soldiers
- choosing from a box of sweets: take the ones with red wrappers

Without further contextual information, it is not possible to determine which meaning is being made. Technically, we can say that the sentence is **ideationally** ambiguous: we cannot be sure which dimensions of reality are being referred to.

The sentence is also ambiguous in other ways. Think, for example, about the meaning of the verb *suggest*. Just which meaning does *suggest* have?

- if your boss *suggests* something to you it usually means *Do this!* It is not a suggestion at all because you cannot refuse it.
- if a subordinate *suggests*, it is usually a plea
- if your friend *suggests*, it may be a real suggestion. You can refuse.

The pronoun *we* is similarly ambiguous. Does it mean *we* (as it would among friends) or *you* (as it might when a superior is talking to a subordinate)?

Taken out of context, then, the sentence is not only ideationally ambiguous, but also **interpersonally** ambiguous: we cannot be sure just what the relationship between the two interactants is.

Given some contextual information, such as the response made by the addressee (*Yea, I brought some French reds*), it becomes possible to understand what aspect of reality is being talked about (wine), and what the relationship between the interactants is (friends). In this case, the initiating sentence can be glossed as meaning 'let's both of us start drinking the red wines'.

Our ability to deduce context from text, to predict when and how language use will vary, and the ambiguity of language removed from its context, provide evidence that in asking functional questions about language we must focus not just on language, but on **language use in context**. Describing the impact of context on text has involved systemicists in exploring both what dimensions, and in what ways, context influences language. As we will see in Chapters Three and Four, systemicists have attempted to describe:

1. exactly what dimensions of context have an impact on language use. Since clearly not every aspect of context makes a difference to language use (e.g. the hair colour of the interactants is usually irrelevant), just what bits of the context do get 'into' the text?
2. which aspects of language use appear to be effected by particular dimensions of the context. For example, if we contrast texts in which the interactants are friends with texts where the interactants are strangers, can we specify where in the language they use this contextual difference will be expressed?

Questions such as these are explored within systemics through genre and register theory, which we will review in detail in Chapters Three and Four. As you will see there, systemicists divide context into a number of levels, with the most frequently discussed being those of **register** and **genre**.

Context: register, genre and ideology in SFL

Register theory describes the impact of dimensions of the immediate context of situation of a language event on the way language is used. SFL identifies three key dimensions of the situations as having significant and predictable impacts on language use. These three dimensions, the register variables of **mode** (amount of feedback and role of language), **tenor** (role relations of power and solidarity) and **field** (topic or focus of the activity), are used to explain our intuitive understanding that we will not use language in the same way to write as to speak (mode variation), to talk to our boss as to talk to our lover (tenor variation) and to talk about linguistics as to talk about jogging (field variation).

The concept of **genre** is used to describe the impact of the context of culture on language, by exploring the staged, step-by-step structure cultures institutionalize as ways of achieving goals. While we can sometimes achieve our goals by just a short linguistic exchange (for example, asking the time generally requires just two moves, a question and an answer: *A: What time is it? B: Five past six*), most linguistic interactions require many more moves than this. In fact, even this simple exchange is very frequently extended through politeness over a number of moves:

A: Sorry to bother you.
I was just wondering whether you knew the time?
B: Yea.
Just a sec.
It's um five past six but I'm generally a bit fast.
A: Oh OK.
Thanks a lot.
B: No problem.

Most often when we use language to do things we have to do them in a number of stages. For example, as we can see from the humorous narrative in Text 1.3, telling a story involves going through (linguistically) a number of steps. You have to set the scene (time, place, participants); develop the actions; relate the dramatic event; give the happy ending; express a judgement on the outcome; and wrap the story up.

When we describe the staged, structured way in which people go about achieving goals using language we are describing **genre**. It is to genre theory that we turn in order to explain the organization of Texts 1.1 and 1.2 as Explanation texts, with the steps of Statement of Problematic Behaviour, Explanation of Possible Causes, Suggested Alleviating Actions, and Statement of Outlook. Genre is the subject of Chapter Three.

A higher level of context to which increasing attention is being given within systemic linguistics is the level of **ideology**[4]. Whatever genre we are involved in, and whatever the register of the situation, our use of language will also be influenced by our ideological positions: the values we hold (consciously or unconsciously), the perspectives acquired through our particular path through the culture. For example, Texts 1.1 and 1.2 above illustrate the ideological claims:

- that we should write for parents in a very different way than we write for trainee medical personnel;
- that it is important for the medical text to foresee the possible negative outcomes of behaviour (parents will injure the baby), while the magazine article foresees the positive outcomes (things will get better).

In addition, while Text 1.1 embodies the claim that babies are motivated human actors (they are always crying for a reason, even if that reason is simply grumpiness or boredom), Text 1.2 suggests that babies cry because that is what babies do (i.e. that crying is frequently inexplicable and unmotivated, but conforms to statistical estimates!). It is easy to see that the ideology of Text 1.1 is more conducive to empowering parents to cope than is the ideology of Text 1.2, which in fact encourages the discounting of the behaviour as meaningful. However, since Text 1.1 also makes the parents responsible for their baby's behaviour, while Text 1.2 leaves it with the baby, it is likely that Text 1.1 will lead to frustrated parents, while Text 1.2 will lead to frustrated babies.

The identification of ideology in such apparently innocuous texts as the Crying Baby ones should alert us to the fact that just as no text can be 'free' of context (register or genre), so no text is free of ideology. In other words, to use language at all is to use it to encode particular positions and values. However, for reasons which are themselves ideological, most language users have not been educated to identify ideology in text, but rather to read texts as natural, inevitable representations of reality.

The implication of identifying ideology in text is that as readers of texts we need to develop skills to be able to make explicit the ideological positions encoded, perhaps in order to resist or challenge them. This means we need a way of talking about how language is not just representing but actively constructing our view of the world. This *semiotic* approach to language is explored more fully below. As ideology makes a very diffuse contribution to text, and is best approached once descriptive skills are mastered, we will return to it in Chapter Eleven.

How is language structured for use?

It was pointed out above that SFL does not only ask functional questions about how people are using language, but it also interprets the linguistic system itself from a functional-semantic perspective. Departing from the descriptions systemicists have made of how language is used in authentic texts, in this more abstract sense of functional, systemicists ask **how is language structured for use?**

In order to understand how systemicists answer this question, let us return to the statement made earlier: that the fundamental purpose that language has evolved to serve is to enable us to make meanings with each other. In other words, language users do not interact in order to exchange sounds with each other, nor even to exchange words or sentences. People interact in order to make meanings: to make sense of the world and of each other. The overall purpose of language, then, can be described as a semantic one, and each text we participate in is a record of the meanings that have been made in a particular context.

The choice of the word **meanings** rather than 'meaning' in the last sentence is a significant one, for systemic analysis seeks to demonstrate that linguistic texts are typically making not just one, but a number of meanings simultaneously.

Consider how you would answer the question 'What does Text 1.1 mean?' An immediate, and obvious, response would be that the meaning Text 1.1 is making is that babies cry, that there are a number of reasons for this, and that in some cases we can do things which will help to stop babies crying.

It is certainly the case that the text is making this kind of 'real world' or **ideational** meaning. In fact, if we fail to understand the ideational meaning the text is making (for example, we interpret it as a text about building fences, or we think it means that babies should be beaten when they cry), then we are likely to encounter serious problems in social life.

However, at the same time that it is making this strand of ideational meaning, the text is also making some other equally important meanings.

The text is, for example, making **interpersonal** meaning. There is a strand of meaning running throughout the text which expresses the writer's role relationship with the reader, and the writer's attitude towards the subject matter. The writer clearly wants to establish a friendly rapport with the reader, to be seen more as a 'fellow sufferer' offering useful advice based on her lived experience as a lover and carer of babies. This meaning of positive supportive solidarity is clearly separable from the meaning about the causes and solutions of babies crying, because in Text 1.2 we find similar ideational meaning being made (causes and solutions of babies crying), but the role taken by that writer is more one of a distant, unfeeling specialist who gives the impression of never having been moved to any emotion by the sight or sound of a baby.

Finally, while expressing both ideational and interpersonal meaning, a text also makes what we describe as **textual** meaning. Textual meaning refers to the way the text is organized as a piece of writing or speech. Text 1.1 has been organized as a message about two people: the baby (expressed as a male individual by the pronoun *he*) and the parents (expressed by the pronoun *you*). It is these pronouns which dominate first position in the sentences and clauses of the text. This organization of the text around people contrasts with the organization of Text 1.2, where the abstract noun of *reasons* is the focus for many of the sentences.

This example demonstrates that a text can be seen to be expressing more than one meaning at a time. In fact, this book will explore Halliday's claim that a text can make these different meanings because units of language (texts, sentences, clauses, etc.) are simultaneously making *three* kinds of meanings. These three types of meaning are expressed through language because these are the strands of meaning we need to make in order to make sense of each other and the world.

As the above discussion of Text 1.1 indicated, **ideational meanings** are meanings about how we represent experience in language. Whatever use we put language to, we are always talking about something or someone doing something. Take a familiar sentence:

I suggest we attack the reds.

This sentence makes meanings about bottles of wine and what we should do with them. It makes meanings that focus on the actions we, as human agents, should carry out, and the entities our actions will affect (the reds). Had the speaker said instead *I suggest the reds are very good* a very different reality would have been represented through language: a reality where one entity (*reds*) is ascribed with some quality (*good*) through a process merely of 'being'.

Simultaneously, we use language to make **interpersonal meanings**: meanings about our role relationships with other people and our attitudes to each other. Whatever use we put language to we are always expressing an attitude and taking up a role. To take our sentence example, *I suggest we attack the reds* makes a meaning of friendly suggestion, non-coercive, open to negotiation; the kind of meaning we might make with friends, whose opinions we are interested in and whose behaviour we do not seek to dominate. Compare it to *We have to attack the reds* or *Attack the reds* or *I wonder whether it might not be possible to attack the reds perhaps?*, each of which constructs a very different relationship between the interactants.

Finally, in any linguistic event we are always making **textual** meanings: meanings about how what we're saying hangs together and relates to what was said before and to the context around us. Whatever use we put language to we are always organizing our information. For example, the sentence *I suggest we attack the reds* takes as its point of departure the speaker's intention (only to suggest, not to impose) and the interactants (*we*). It is a possible answer to *What should we do now?* Compare it to *The reds should be attacked now, I'd suggest*, which would be more likely as an answer to *Which should we drink next?*, since it takes as its point of departure *the reds* rather than *we*.

At both a macro (text) and micro (sentence) level, then, it is possible to identify these three different types of meanings being made – and, most significantly, being made simultaneously. This leads us to ask: how? How can language accomplish this semantic complexity? Answering this question takes us into an exploration of language as a semiotic system.

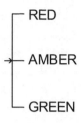

System 1.1   Traffic lights

Meaning as choice: semiotic systems

A classic demonstration of a simple semiotic system is that of traffic lights[5]. We can represent the set of traffic lights found at many urban Western intersections as follows in System 1.1.

This diagram represents the traffic lights as a system. A system (as we will see in detail in Chapter Seven) has the following basic attributes:

1. it consists of a finite set of **choices** or oppositions: this system contains only three choices since the traffic lights can only be either red or green or amber;
2. the choices in the system are **discrete**: when you drive up to the intersection, the lights can only be one colour at a time;
3. it is the **oppositions**, not the **substances**, in the system that are important: it does not matter exactly what shades of red or green or amber we use (deep red/light red, light green/dark green). All that matters is that red is not green – that each of the three coloured lights is different from the others.

However, although the diagram presented above is a system (in that it captures choice), it is not yet a *semiotic* system. To construct the semiotic system, we need to observe that each coloured light triggers different behaviours in the drivers who arrive at the intersection. When the light is red, drivers stop, when the light is green, they go, and when the light is amber, they prepare to stop.

In fact, as we well know, it is this ability to regulate drivers' behaviours that is what traffic lights are really all about. They are not provided merely to beautify the urban environment, but to act as signs which stand for a way to behave. A red light does not just mean 'here is a red light'; it means 'stop now'. In other words, the coloured lights are operating as part of a **sign system**, whereby the colour of the light is encoding, or expressing, which action from a set of possible 'behaviours at traffic lights' should be performed.

This semiotic dimension of the traffic lights can be captured by expanding our diagram to show the relationship between the behaviours and the lights, as in System 1.2.

This diagram has introduced some technical labels for the components of our semiotic system. You will see that we use the terms **content** and **expression** to refer to the two dimensions which together constitute a sign: meaning (content) and realization (expression). With the traffic lights, the content of the signs is the behaviour they are designed to trigger, while the expression is the particular coloured light. Ferdinand de Saussure (1959/1966), the Swiss linguist who was instrumental in formulating the theory of semiotic systems, used the terms *signifié* (signified) and *signifiant* (signifier) to label the content/expression sides of the sign.

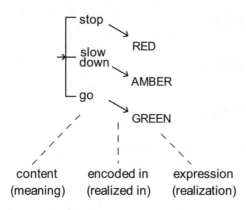

System 1.2   Semiotic system of traffic lights

System 1.2 also indicates that the relationship between the content and its expression is described as one of **realization** or **encoding**. This realization relationship is indicated by the downwards pointing arrow. Thus, the meaning STOP is realized by/encoded in the coloured light RED. Similarly, the coloured light GREEN realizes or encodes the meaning of GO. Thus, signs in a semiotic system are a fusion or pairing of a content (meaning) and an expression (realization or encoding of that meaning).

The traffic light system also illustrates the fact that semiotic systems are established by social convention. As Saussure pointed out, the fusion between the two sides of the sign is arbitrary. There is no natural link between the content STOP and the expression RED LIGHT in a traffic light system: we could just as easily train our drivers to GO when the light was RED and STOP when it was AMBER. Semiotic systems, then, are arbitrary social conventions by which it is conventionally agreed that a particular meaning will be realized by a particular representation.

In summary, then, a semiotic system can be defined as a finite collection of discrete signs. We have a sign when a meaning (content) is arbitrarily realized through a realization (expression).

Considering the traffic light system can also help to explain the function of semiotic systems. The function of sign systems like the traffic lights is to make meanings. Sign systems create meanings by ordering the world in two ways:

1. they order **content**: of all the possible behaviours that we could enact at intersections, the system sets up only three as being meaningful (i.e. going, stopping, slowing down);
2. they order **expression**: of all the possible coloured lights we could have at intersections, the system sets up only three as being meaningful (i.e. red, green, amber).

To describe a simple semiotic system such as the traffic lights, we need just a two-level model, as shown in Figure 1.1.

Two-level semiotic systems such as the traffic lights, with the conventional pairing of a representation with a meaning, are surprisingly common in social life. One obvious example is that of clothing (or, to use the label more indicative of its semiotic function, *fashion*). Originally, back in the cave for example, clothing would have been adopted for very practical reasons: to keep people warm, to protect vulnerable parts of the body. And the choice

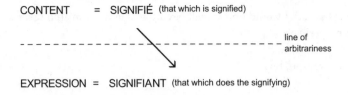

Figure 1.1   Content and expression in a two-level semiotic system

of materials out of which clothes could be made would have been largely determined by practicalities: what was to hand, what could be caught and skinned.

But very rapidly clothing went beyond its survival value and acquired a semiotic value in our culture. For example, some clothing has acquired meaning as 'male' or 'female' (e.g. trousers vs skirts); 'at home' vs 'going out' (e.g. jeans vs suits); 'dependents' vs 'independents' (e.g. schools and institutions that make their adherents wear uniforms vs situations offering choice in clothes). And of course think of the changing semiotics of denim jeans, once the working wear of the outdoor cowboy, now the uniform of a casual western lifestyle.

Sometimes it is a particular combination of items of clothing that carries meaning, such as a suit with a white shirt, silk tie and shiny patent leather shoes. At other times, individual items of clothing can carry very significant social meaning: for example, the doctor's white coat, which signifies the wearer as professional, expert, careful, trustworthy.

What we see with clothing is that what began as a 'natural' system has been developed by convention (in other words, by the unconscious agreement and enactment of us all) into a very potent semiotic system. If you ever doubt its potency, just think about the strong social expectations (which you most probably share) about how one should dress to go for a job interview – if one wants to get the job.

The clothing example may suggest to you other ways in which we live in a semiotic world. For example, the cars people drive, the layout of the houses they live in, the magazines they buy, the cigarettes they smoke: wherever people have the possibility of choice, there we find the potential for semiotic systems, as the choices we make are invested with meaning.

Language as a semiotic system

By far the most sophisticated and elaborate of all our semiotic systems is the system of language. What gives language its privileged status is that other semiotic systems can generally be translated into language. While we can use language to talk about the semiotic systems of clothing or cars, we cannot use clothing or cars to make *all* the meanings language makes.

We will see in a moment that language achieves this special status because it is a more complex semiotic system than the two-level kind we found in the traffic lights. However, just like the traffic lights, language can be described as a semiotic system because it involves sets of meaningful choices or oppositions.

Imagine that I am talking to a friend about the recent exploits of my five-year-old progeny. I want to say, for example, something along the lines of *When I got home from work yesterday, I could not believe what my* [progeny] *had done!* While the word [progeny] does capture the genealogical relationship between us, it is unlikely that I would use that word in a conversational context. Instead, I would find myself having to choose from among a set of possible words, including perhaps:

kid, child, brat, darling, son, boy . . .

My choice of one word or another from this list involves me in a meaning-making process, where I must choose which dimensions of contrast I wish to encode. One of the choices I face is whether to specify the progeny's sex or not: words such as *son* and *boy* specify sex, while *child, brat, darling* do not. Underlying the list of words, then, is a dimension of (ideational) contrast that can be systematized as in System 1.3.

Here then is one semiotic system in which my list of words is implicated. However, a further meaningful dimension of contrast among these words is that of attitudinal content. Some of the words make meanings about my attitude towards the child: either a negative attitude (*brat*) or a positive attitude (*darling*). Other words are neutral for attitude (*child*). This set of (interpersonal) semiotic oppositions can be diagrammed as in System 1.4.

These examples indicate that whichever word I choose from this list (and there are others we could add, for example *progeny, offspring, infant*), the meaning of each word comes in part from the fact that that word stands in opposition to the other words in the list. My choice, for example, of *brat* is made against the background of the fact that I could have chosen *child*: my conversational audience recognizes this, and thereby interprets my choice as encoding negative attitude (since I could have chosen to encode neutral attitude).

This example also indicates that we can describe the lexical items in a language (the vocabulary) as semiotic systems. Identifying systems of **lexical choice** involves recognizing that words encode meaningful oppositions, and that the process of choosing a lexical item is a semiotic process.

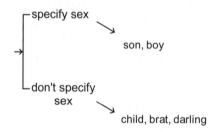

System 1.3   Lexical choice, specifying sex

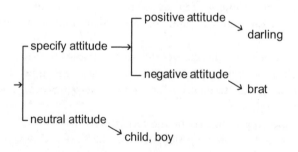

System 1.4   Lexical choice, specifying attitude

	Traffic Lights	Language
CONTENT	meaning	meaning
		words ↘
EXPRESSION	lighting ↘	sounds ↘

Figure 1.2   Content and expression in traffic lights and language

Just as with the traffic light system, so with the lexical systems we find that the relationship between a human infant of unspecified sex and the sound sequence **k-i-d** is an arbitrary one. This arbitrariness of the content/expression pair is easily demonstrated by noting that other languages will use different sounds to refer to their human infants.

And, like the traffic lights, we see that with linguistic signs it is the oppositions and not the substance that are important. Just as it was not important whether our traffic light was dark red, light red, or even pink, so it does not matter exactly how I pronounce the 'k' or 'i' or 'd' in *kid* so long as the sounds cannot be confused with other sound configurations, such as *kit* or *did* or *cot* which express different contents (i.e. which make different meanings).

However, there is a critical difference between language as a semiotic system and a simple semiotic system such as the traffic lights. For with our lexical system, we can break down our lexical items into component sounds. Thus, the word *kid* is itself realized by a combination of the sounds k-i-d. Note that with the traffic lights we could not break down the coloured lights into any smaller components. The coloured lights directly realized the contents of our sign system. However, with language, the realization of the meaning 'progeny no sex specified' is mediated through a word, itself realizing a sequence of sounds.

In language, then, we do not just have meanings realized by words, for the words themselves are realized by sounds. This means that to describe language we need three levels or strata, illustrated in Figure 1.2.

The function of language as a semiotic system

Not only do linguistic systems look quite similar to other kinds of semiotic systems, but they also function to do the same thing. Like the traffic lights, linguistic systems are also systems for making meanings. And, like the traffic lights, linguistic systems make meanings by ordering the world for us in two ways.

Firstly, they order **content**: of all the ways of talking about human offspring, our simple lexical systems above show us that English speakers organize this conceptual domain by recognizing sex of child and parental attitude as (two of the) relevant dimensions of contrast. That these dimensions are considered relevant is established not by nature but by convention. The system of choice which opposes *brat, child* and *darling* both recognizes and validates the right of parents to express attitudes about their offspring. We do not have in English lexical items which contrast offspring in terms of offspring's attitude towards parents (e.g. we do not have words for 'a child who loves his parents' vs 'a child who can't stand his parents' vs 'a child who is ambivalent about his parents'). Although such a contrast is linguistically perfectly feasible (we just need to think of three words to use), it is not culturally feasible, because it is not judged appropriate for the powerless (i.e. children) to express attitudes about the powerful (i.e. parents).

The system thus orders the conceptual world according to culturally established conventions about which dimensions of reality are meaningful. Since most of the lexical systems we use exist prior to us, we are often not conscious of the conventions on which they depend. As we tend to see language as a natural, naming device, it becomes very difficult for us to think about dimensions of reality other than those which are encoded for us in our linguistic systems. However, semiotic theory demonstrates that the world is not out there as some absolute, determined reality simply to be labelled (and therefore talked about) in only one possible way. Reality is constructed through the oppositions encoded in the semiotic systems of the language we use. It follows from this relativistic interpretation that not all languages will order experience in the same way. For example, not all languages will differentiate lexical items for children in terms of sex or parental attitude.

The second way in which linguistic signs order the world for us is by ordering **expression**. Thus, of all the possible sounds we are physiologically capable of producing, English recognizes only about thirty or so as being meaningfully distinct. For example, the difference between pronouncing the *k* in *kid* with little or no release of air (unaspirated) or pronouncing it with a rush of air (aspirated) is <u>not</u> a meaningful difference in English (we will hear the two versions as meaning the same thing). However, the difference between *kid* (where the final sound is produced by vibrating the vocal chords and so is *voiced*) and *kit* (where the final sound is produced without vibration of the vocal chords and so is *voiceless*) is a significant difference to English speakers, since it serves to differentiate between two different meanings. The fact that languages divide up the spectrum of possible sounds or expressions differently is brought home to you when you try to learn a foreign language. You will find that the inventory of meaningful sounds will be different for each language.

Grammatical systems in language

Systems of lexical choice are not the only kind of systems we find in language. We also have systems of **grammatical choice**. See, for example, System 1.5.

This system says that whenever I produce a clause it must be only one of these three:

- a declarative: The baby is crying.
- an interrogative: Is the baby crying?
- an imperative: Cry!

Note how the oppositions, or choices, in this kind of system are realized. Each choice is realized by a particular sequencing of a number of grammatical elements, here the elements of **Subject**, **Finite** and **Predicator**. The system says that the choice 'declarative', for example, is realized by the sequence of elements: **Subject** followed by **Finite** verb. For example, *The baby* (Subject) *is* (Finite verb) *crying* (Predicator), whereas the choice 'interrogative' has the elements of Subject and Finite in the opposite order: *Is the baby crying?* The imperative is realized by the omission of the Subject and Finite elements, leaving only the Predicator: *Cry!*

In a grammatical system, then, each choice gets realized not as particular words (I could change all the words to *my dog, was barking* and still have the oppositions), but in the order and arrangement of the grammatical roles the words are playing. That is, these choices are realized by **structures**. What linguists mean by **structure** will be explored more fully in Chapter Five. For now we need only note that the choice from a grammatical system is

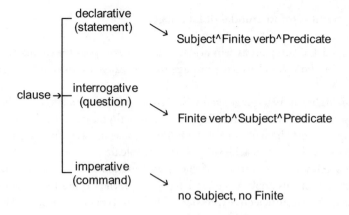

System 1.5   Grammatical choice

	Folk Names	**Technical Terms**
CONTENT	meanings	(discourse-)semantics
	wordings (words and structures)	lexico-grammar
EXPRESSION	sounds/letters	phonology/graphology

Figure 1.3   Levels or strata of language

expressed through the presence and ordering of particular grammatical elements. And of course these structures will eventually get realized as words, and then finally as sounds.

In order to incorporate these types of linguistic systems, our model of language as a semiotic system now looks like Figure 1.3.

This diagram presents the systemic model of the levels or strata of language, using on the left the 'folk' or non-technical terms, and on the right the technical terms that we will use from now on.

The diagram can be read as saying that in language, meanings are realized as wordings, which are in turn realized by sounds (or letters). Technically: **semantics** gets realized through the **lexico-grammar**, which in turn gets realized through the **phonology** or **graphology**.

When we compare this model of language with our traffic lights, we see that language is a different kind of semiotic system **because it has three levels**, not just two. That is, language has two meaning-making levels, an upper level of content known as **semantics** (or discourse-semantics for some systemicists), and an intermediate level of content known as **lexico-grammar**.

Because systemic linguistics is concerned principally with *how* language makes meanings, this book explores only the content level of the lexico-grammar – the level responsible for turning 'meanings' into 'wordings'.

Implications of a tri-stratal semiotic model of language

Having sketched out a model of language as semiotic system, it is now possible to link this back to our earlier question: how does language manage to make three kinds of meanings simultaneously?

Comparing the traffic lights and language, you will see that what makes language different is that it possesses an intermediate encoding level of lexico-grammar. In Chapters Five to Nine we will explore how the structure of the English clause involves the choice of elements which 'map onto' each other to achieve semantic complexity.

Introducing you to Halliday's descriptions of the multifunctionality of clause constituents is an important aim of this book, since as we have seen in the Crying Baby examples, the text itself reflects this simultaneous expression of different types of meanings. The three strands of meanings that run through any text get 'into' the text largely through the clauses which make it up. Thus, as Halliday points out, grammatical description is essential to text analysis:

> it is sometimes assumed that (discourse analysis, or 'text linguistics') can be carried on without grammar – or even that it is somehow an alternative to grammar. But this is an illusion. A discourse analysis that is not based on grammar is not an analysis at all, but simply a running commentary on a text. (Halliday 1994: xvi)

The notion of the semiotic system also gives a powerful way of interpreting language behaviour as choice. If language is a semiotic system, then the process of language use is a process of making meanings by choosing. In making a choice from a linguistic system, what someone writes or says gets its meaning by being interpreted against the background of what could have been meant (said or written) in that context but was not. Through this distinction we relate what people did write or did say on any particular occasion (their **actual** linguistic choices) to what they could have written or could have said (their **potential** linguistic choices).

We can illustrate this by returning to our linguistic systems outlined above. We look at the linguistic choices speakers did make (e.g. statement rather than command, *brat* rather than *child*, or saying *I suggest we attack the reds* rather than *The reds should be attacked next, I suppose*). And we ask: what is the function of that choice? Why didn't the speakers make the other choice?

In a functional-semantic approach, then, we are concerned to describe two dimensions of language use. Firstly, what are the possible choices people can make? In doing this we describe the linguistic system. Secondly, what is the function of the choice they did make? In doing this we describe how language is used in different social contexts, to achieve various cultural goals. It enables us to talk about linguistic choices not as 'right' or 'wrong', as in the traditional prescriptive approach to language. Instead, we talk about choices as 'appropriate' or 'inappropriate' to a particular context.

Summary of systemic functional linguistics (SFL)

This chapter set out to give an overview of SFL, introducing many of the terms and concepts which will be developed in detail in subsequent chapters. In summary, SFL has been described as a functional-semantic approach to language which explores both how people use language in different contexts, and how language is structured for use as a semiotic system.

As a linguistic approach to meaning in texts, systemic linguistics has (or has had) common ground with text grammarians and discourse analysts from a range of perspectives (e.g. Biber 1986, Brown and Gilman 1960, Brown and Levinson 1978, Chafe 1980, Labov and Fanshel 1977, Mann and Thompson 1986, van Dijk 1977). There have also been points of connection with research in areas such as sociolinguistics (e.g. Labov 1972a, 1972b, Labov and Waletzky 1967, Schiffren 1987) and the ethnography of speaking (e.g. Gumperz 1982a, 1982b, Hymes 1964/1972, Tannen 1980, 1989, 1991), exploring ways in which social and cultural context impact on language use.

As a semiotic approach, it has common ground with semiotic theoreticians and those, following Fairclough (1989, 1992), working in what has become known as the Critical Discourse Analysis (CDA) approach. For a comprehensive overview of critical discourse analysis, see Toolan's four-volume collection *Critical Discourse Analysis* (Toolan 2002a, 2002b, 2002c, 2002d).

However, what is distinctive to systemic linguistics is that it seeks to develop both a theory about language as social process *and* an analytical methodology which permits the detailed and systematic description of language patterns.

This book introduces you to both dimensions of the approach. Thus, we will explore the systemic model of language (what language is, how it works, its relation with context) and we will also acquire a set of techniques for analysing different aspects of the language system (e.g. analyses of transitivity, mood, theme, the clause complex). Learning these techniques requires the introduction of technical terms.

Discussion of how language works in this chapter has been limited because I have had to avoid using too many technical linguistic terms. Thus, for example, while we have noted some obvious differences between Texts 1.1, 1.2 and 1.3, it has not been possible to explore fully the contrasts between those texts since to do so we need to talk about patterns such as nominalization, choices of process type, mood and modality of the clauses, Theme/Rheme structure, reference chains, etc.

While this book will introduce you to the techniques and technical terms necessary for talking about basic lexico-grammatical dimensions of whatever texts are of interest to you, these techniques are more comprehensively described in Halliday and Matthiessen 1999, 2004, Martin *et al.* 1997, Martin 1992a, and Martin and Rose 2003, and it is suggested that you follow up this book by referring to those sources to develop your descriptive skills.

In the following chapter, we begin this technical exploration of language by asking just what a **text** is. With some understanding of the text's pivotal nature as the meeting point of contextual and linguistic expression, we then move out to explore levels of context and their encoding in language. In Chapter Three we look at techniques of generic description, and in Chapter Four, register. Chapters Five to Ten then develop the description of the lexico-grammar, covering the grammatical systems of mood, transitivity, theme and the clause complex, with a brief interlude in Chapter Seven to reconsider systems. Finally, in Chapter Eleven, equipped with a shared technical vocabulary and a shared perspective on language, we will consider how to go about systemic text analysis. A comprehensive discussion of the Crying Baby texts introduced in this chapter will be used to demonstrate ways in which the combination of theoretical model and practical analyses provides a powerful means of talking about how people use language to make meanings.

Notes

1. Halliday's influential *An Introduction to Functional Grammar* was first published in 1985, with an updated 2nd edition published in 1994 and a 3rd edition, substantially revised by C.M.I.M. Matthiessen, published in 2004. Wherever possible, references are to the 3rd edition.
2. Throughout the texts in this book, subscript numbers are used to show sentences (ordinary numbers) and clauses (roman numerals).
3. Sources: Text 1.1 is taken from a popular parenting magazine, *My Baby*, 1991 edition, p. 24 (unauthored article). Text 1.2 is taken from an introductory textbook for medical/nursing students, R. Behrman, and R. Kliegman (1990) *Essentials of Pediatrics*, W. B. Saunders Co., Philadelphia, p. 32. I am indebted to Yvette Slimovits at Sydney University for drawing these two texts to my attention. Text 1.3 is taken from a recording of a casual conversation between two female speakers, Carol, aged 38, and Sue, aged 32 (author's data).
4. For useful approaches to ideology in language, see the work of Critical Discourse Analysis, including Fairclough 1989, 1992, Fowler *et al.* 1979, Kress and Hodge 1979, 1988, Toolan 2002a.
5. I claim no originality for the use of the traffic light example. Like others (including Martin 1984, Allerton 1979, Kress and Hodge 1988, to name only a few), I have found the simplicity and familiarity of the traffic lights useful in introducing the notion of the semiotic system.

Chapter 2

What is (a) text?

Introduction

As stated in Chapter One, this book aims to provide you with concepts and analytical tools to explore how meanings are made in the texts that interest you. A useful first step in this exploration is to clarify just what our basic unit is. Accordingly, this chapter asks: What is (a) text? How do we know when we've got one? And what does the nature of text tell us about the organization of language as a text-forming resource?

As we progress through the examples in this chapter, we will see that to understand what a text is we must recognize that a text's **texture** derives not only from linguistic patterns of **cohesion**, but also from the text's **coherence** with its social and cultural context, which will lead us naturally into the following two chapters on genre and register. The examples will also show, however, that textness is best regarded as a continuum, with certain pieces of language displaying a high level of texture and others problematizing particular dimensions, either intentionally (for strategic purposes), or accidentally (perhaps due to lack of language expertise).

What is (a) text?

Right from page one of this book I've claimed that systemic linguistics concerns itself with the analysis of text. The term 'text' has been glossed as 'authentic products of social interaction', and I have assumed that we can unproblematically identify what a text is. But it's now time to take that assumption apart and ask just what a text is. How do we know when a piece of language is a **text** and when one is not (a **non-text**)?

In their pioneering analysis of spoken and written English, Halliday and Hasan (1976: 1) offer the following definition of text: 'The word TEXT is used in linguistics to refer to any passage, spoken or written, of whatever length, that does form a unified whole'. In describing how a text forms a unified whole, Halliday and Hasan introduce the concept of **texture** (Halliday and Hasan 1976: 2, Hasan 1985b: Chapter Five). Texture is the property that distinguishes text from non-text. Texture is what holds the clauses of a text together to give them unity.

Texture, Halliday and Hasan suggest, involves the interaction of two components: **coherence**, or the text's relationship to its extra-textual context (the social and cultural context of its occurrence), and **cohesion**, the way the elements within a text bind it together as 'a unified whole'. The result of the interaction of these two dimensions is a piece of language which is using linguistic resources in a meaningful way within a situational and cultural context.

Note that Halliday and Hasan refer to both spoken and written language as **text**. Some linguistic approaches differentiate between 'text' as written language and 'discourse' as spoken language, but in SFL **text** is a technical term for any unified piece of language that has the properties of texture. The term **discourse** is used in systemics to refer either (untechnically) to 'spoken text' or (more technically, following Martin 1992a, Martin and Rose 2003) to the level of meaning above the lexico-grammar, the level concerned with relations of meaning across a text.

Text as a semantic unit

To understand how Halliday and Hasan come to their definition of text, we can begin with an obvious point: not all uses of language constitute text. Consider Example 2.1.

U P X G

W E L I

A C F M

T R Z B

D J Q N

O K S H

Example 2.1

Although Example 2.1 is a language example regularly used in the culture (it is in fact an eye chart), we cannot read it 'as text', for the most obvious reason that the sounds or letters do not in sequence combine to give us words of the English language. What we have is no more than a sequencing of phonemes, sound units at the lowest level of the language system. But the phonemes represented by the letters are not functioning as units of meaning – they do not constitute words. Instead of letters, pictures could be substituted, though in a highly literate culture it is obvious why letters are used. Without those minimum units of meaning, words, the passage cannot be read as sequenced language constituents functioning together to communicate meaning.

The occurrence of letters arranged in words, however, is not sufficient to constitute text either, as the page from a handwriting textbook for primary school children shown in Example 2.2 demonstrates.

mean mad adder made because

Example 2.2 handwriting[1]

Although this page presents students with linguistic units (in this case, words) which individually convey (some) meaning, the words do not 'hang together'. The principle motivating the juxtaposition of the words is not a semantic one: the words are put together because the writer wants students to practise particular fine motor skills.

The following example, though at first disorienting, shows an important move towards textness:

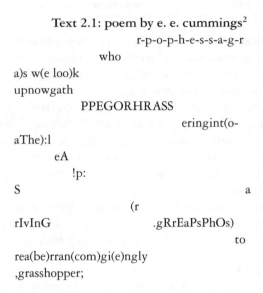

Text 2.1: poem by e. e. cummings[2]

This poem by the American poet e. e. cummings shows that we usually expect text to be presented to us in discrete words in sequence. But, as the Russian formalist Shklovsky suggested, like all art, literary art functions to *disrupt* our expectations:

> Art exists that one may recover the sensation of life; it exists to make one feel things, to make the stone *stony*. The purpose of art is to impart the sensation of things as they are perceived and not as they are known. The technique of art is to make objects *'unfamiliar'*, to make forms difficult, to increase the difficulty and length of perception because the process of perception is an aesthetic end in itself and must be prolonged. *Art is a way of experiencing the artfullness of an object; the object is not important.* (Shklovsky 1992: 18–19)

Thus, Shklovsky suggests, the purpose of art is to 'make strange' or **defamiliarize** our expectations. Cummings has defamiliarized this text so that it doesn't (initially, at least) offer us recognizable words. Unlike Example 2.1, however, this language can be re-constituted as text: the letters can gradually be unscrambled to give us recognizable English words. And unlike Example 2.2, the words are made 'meaningful' because the text uses them within (minimal) lexico-grammatical structures, also retrievable from the text.

By the term 'lexico-grammatical structures' you'll remember that we refer to the sequenced arrangement of constituents of the intermediate stratum of language, the stratum of 'words and structures'. As we will see in detail in Chapter Five, at the lexico-grammatical stratum there are several different units which carry patterns. The pivotal unit of lexico-grammatical structure, the unit at the highest 'rank', is the **clause**, with the upper boundary of grammatical relations the **clause complex** or sentence: only elements occurring within the same sentence can be grammatically related. The smallest unit which can

Table 2.1   The units of the lexico-grammatical rank scale

	Units of lexico-grammar
highest rank (largest unit)	clause, clause complex phrase, group word
lowest rank (smallest unit)	morpheme

enter into grammatical relations, the lowest 'rank' in the grammatical hierarchy, is the **morpheme**, as it is the smallest unit of meaning in language. Between the clause and the morpheme we have the units of **phrases** or **groups** and **words**, giving us the 'rank scale' of lexico-grammatical units seen in Table 2.1.

Lexico-grammatical analysis involves identifying the elements we find at each rank and describing the sequences and combinations in which they can occur to give us clauses accepted as 'possible' as well as 'usual' to users of the code of English. It is against this understanding of the potential of English grammar and its typical, unmarked usage that we can explain why e. e. cummings's poem both makes sense but is also a defamiliarized, or **marked**, use of the code.

When we try to unscramble Text 2.1, we find there are several possibilities – another characteristic of art is its preference for ambiguities and ambivalences, rather than single, straightforward meaning. One version we might come up with is:

> The Grasshopper
> A grasshopper who as we look up now gathering into leaps, arriving to rearrangingly become
> Grasshopper

Although this is not a standard vernacular sentence, there is enough lexico-grammar in cummings's poem for us to understand who is doing what. Unscrambled phoneme sequences give us recognizable words of English. Key grammatical constituents, such as the subject pronoun *who*, and the *-ing* morphemes on the verbs, signal that it is the grasshopper who is doing and becoming, simultaneous with our mental activity of watching it. While e. e. cummings troubles the orthographic structure of the poem, putting spaces and punctuation marks in odd places, he makes sure to leave us enough lexico-grammar to be able to make 'sense' out of what at first appears to be non-sense.

In cummings's case, the defamiliarization of English is a strategic move: he purposefully muddles things up in order to achieve a particular effect on readers. Among the effects achieved by the 'scrambling' in 'Grasshopper' we could list:

1. that it makes us slow down: as Shklovsky suggests, art defamiliarizes by slowing down our perception, de-automating the reading process so that we *really take in* what we're reading;
2. at the same time, the scrambling gives us a verbal approximation of what the grasshopper is doing physically (leaping), thus one semiotic code (language) is being used to try to evoke another (action);
3. as a result of (1) and (2), we may become aware of the conventions of poems and language, and may reflect on what there is to be gained by playing with language, stretching its conventional boundaries, to renew our experience of living and making meanings.

Grammar and the meanings of text

These first examples allow us to suggest that text depends on the 'meaningful' use of the codes of the two lower strata of language: the phonological and the lexico-grammatical codes. To make sense, a text has to either follow the codes or at least allow us to retrieve the code beneath surface challenges.

The following text, an excerpt from Roald Dahl's children's novel, *The BFG*, shows another form of challenge writers can offer us in text:

Text 2.2: excerpt from *The BFG*[3]

(1i)The BFG was still holding the awesome snozzcumber in his right hand, (1ii)and now he put one end into his mouth (1iii)and bit off a huge hunk of it. (2i)He started crunching it up (2ii)and the noise he made was like the crunching of lumps of ice.

(3i)'It's filthing!' (3ii)he spluttered, (3iii)speaking with his mouth full (3iv)and spraying large pieces of snozzcumber like bullets in Sophie's direction. (4i)Sophie hopped around on the table-top, (4ii)ducking out of the way.

(5i)'It's disgusterous!' (5ii)the BFG gurgled. (6)'It's sickable! (7)It's rotsome! (8)It's maggotwise! (9)Try it yourself, this foulsome snozzcumber!'

(10i)'No, thank you,' (10ii)Sophie said, (10iii)backing away.

(11i)'It's all you're going to be guzzling around here from now on (11ii)so you might as well get used to it,' (11iii)said the BFG. (12i)'Go on, you snipsy little winkle, (12ii)have a go!'

(13i)Sophie took a small nibble. (14i)'Ugggggggh!' (14ii)she spluttered. (15)'Oh no! (16)Oh gosh! (17)Oh help!' (18)She spat it out quickly. (19i)'It tastes of frogskins!' (19ii)she gasped. (20)'And rotten fish!'

(21i)'Worse than that!' (21ii)cried the BFG, (21iii)roaring with laughter. (22)'To me it is tasting of clockcoaches and slimewanglers!'

(23i)'Do we really have to eat it?' (23ii)Sophie said.

(24i)'You do (24ii)unless you is wanting to become so thin you will be disappearing into a thick ear.'

(25i)'Into *thin air*,' (25ii)Sophie said. (26)'A thick ear is something quite different.'

(27)Once again that sad winsome look came into the BFG's eyes. (28i)'Words,' (28ii)he said (28iii)'is oh such a twitch-tickling problem to me all my life. (29i)So you must simply try to be patient (29ii)and stop squibbling. (30i)As I am telling you before, (30ii)I know (30iii)exactly what words I am wanting to say, (30iv)but somehow or other they is always getting squiff-squiddled around.'

(31i)'That happens to everyone,' (31ii)Sophie said.

(32i)'Not like it happens to me,' (32ii)the BFG said. (33)'I is speaking the most terrible wigglish.'

(34i)'I think you speak beautifully,' (34ii)Sophie said.

(35i)'You do?' (35ii)cried the BFG, (35iii)suddenly brightening. (36)'You really do?'

(37i)'Simply beautifully,' (37ii)Sophie repeated.

(38i)'Well, that is the nicest present anybody is ever giving me in my whole life!' (38ii)cried the BFG. (39)'Are you sure you is not twiddling my leg?'

(40i)'Of course not,' (40ii)Sophie said. (41)'I just love the way you talk.'

(42i)'How wondercrump!' (42ii)cried the BFG, (42iii)still beaming. (43)'How whoopsey-splunkers! (44)How absolutely squiffling! (45)I is all of a stutter.'

The many children and adults who have chuckled their way through this book have little difficulty with the text, despite the BFG's frequent use of unusual vocabulary items (*snoz-zcumber, rotsome, slimewanglers, twitch-tickling, squibbling, squiff-squiddled, wigglish, whoospey-splunkers* . . .). These words make just enough sense to us because:

1. they conform to possible phonological combinations of English;
2. they exploit the phonaesthetic qualities of English sound combinations: sound symbolism and sound analogy make it possible for us to 'feel' what the words mean, even if we're not sure exactly what a *slimewangler* is, or what it's like to be *squiff-squiddled*;
3. they are incorporated into the grammar of English, through the attachment of conventional English morphemes of tense and word class. Thus the endings *-some* and *-ish* allow us to interpret *rotsome* and *wigglish* as adjectives; the *-ing* ending turns *squiffling* into a present participle; and *-ers* must make *slimewanglers* a plural noun indicating actors/agents. The morphemic structure is then reinforced by the incorporation of the words into clause structure: *It's* of *It's rotsome* sets up the kind of clause where the word after the *it's* we interpret as describing what *it* is. The placement of *twitch-tickling* before a word we know well means we read *twitch-tickling* as describing a type or kind of *problem*. We read *squiff-squiddled* as a verb of action, because we know the structure *x is always getting . . . -ed around*.

Thus, defamiliarization of words presents little problem, given that grammatical and phonological resources of the language are functioning conventionally. In much the same way Lewis Carroll's famous poem 'Jabberwocky' makes at least some sense.

And 'sense' is what we're always looking for in language. If text is a 'unified whole', it is a whole unified in terms of meanings, not in terms of form. As Halliday and Hasan (1976: 2) put it: 'A text is best regarded as a SEMANTIC unit: a unit not of form but of meaning'. More accurately, in systemic terms a text is a unit of meaning**s**, a unit which expresses, simultaneously, ideational, interpersonal and textual meanings. Examples like 'Grasshopper' and *The BFG* show us how important the grammatical level is if we are to be able to interpret these simultaneous meanings. In the cummings text, we can recover enough of these meanings by rearranging the orthography. In the Dahl example, some slight fuzziness in some of the ideational meanings in the text is far outweighed by the stacking up of retrievable ideational, interpersonal and textual meanings through the overwhelmingly conventional grammatical choices in the passage (and the book).

A piece of language that is more challenging for our pursuit of meanings is surely this one:

Text 2.3: excerpt from 'Stalin's Genius' by Bruce Andrews[4]

(1i) Stalin's genius consisted of not french-kissing: (1ii) sometimes I want to be in crud. (2i) Your spats of visibility – (2ii) o, crow fluke, genitally organized spuds, what can true work? (3i) Birth is skewed, anon., *capital*; (3ii) *lose* that disembowelment; (3iii) you must change it (3iv) by eating it yourself: (3v) don't pick your noses, (3vi) secrecy thrives on abuse. (4i) No, I don't mean the missile crisis, (4ii) cat goes backward (4iii) to suit international organization: (4iv) middle class families want the belly (4v) choose

(4vi) to obey authority – (4vii) waddle into arson (4viii) anything can be converted, (4ix) the accessories get you wet.

Since Text 2.3 has been widely published and its author is regarded as a writer of merit (if also of difficulty), we must assume that at least for some readers it constitutes (part of) a text. Yet most English speakers will find it a distinctly problematic piece of language. Although it uses mostly familiar English words, and has some recognizable grammatical structures, many readers complain that they 'can't make much sense' of it.

Our problem with it is that we cannot see the four sequent clauses as hanging together. As Halliday and Hasan suggest, text is more than just sentences in sequence:

> If a speaker of English hears or reads a passage of the language which is more than one sentence in length, he can normally decide without difficulty whether it forms a unified whole or is just a collection of unrelated sentences. (Halliday and Hasan 1976: 1)

When we say we have trouble seeing how the clauses hang together in Text 2.3, we are reacting to two dimensions of the paragraph. Firstly, its contextual properties: what we call its **coherence**. And secondly, its internal properties: what we call its **cohesion**.

Coherence refers to the way a group of clauses or sentences relate to the context (Halliday and Hasan 1976: 23). In fact, two types of coherence are involved in texture: **registerial** coherence and **generic** coherence. We will cover these in more detail in Chapters Three and Four, but the basic idea is that text usually exhibits contextual unity of these two types:

1. **registerial coherence**: a text has registerial coherence when we can identify one situation in which all the clauses of the text could occur. Technically, as we'll see in later chapters, this occurs when we can specify for the entire collection of clauses the domain the text is focusing on (its field), what roles the writer or interactants are playing (its tenor), and how closely language is tied to the experience it's commenting on (its mode).
2. **generic coherence**: a text has generic coherence when we can recognize the text as an example of a particular genre. Technically, generic coherence occurs when we can identify a unified purpose motivating the language (for example, it tells a story or accomplishes a transaction), usually expressed through a predictable generic or schematic structure, as we'll see in Chapter Three.

Text 2.3 appears to lack both these types of contextual coherence. Firstly, it lacks situational coherence, for we cannot think of one situation in which all these sentences could occur. There is no coherence of field (we jump from talking about *Stalin* to *sex* to *disembowelment* to *cats* and *fashion*), nor of mode (some clauses are obviously written language, others are apparently conversational dialogue), nor of tenor (we cannot determine what role the writer/sayer of this paragraph is playing).

Secondly, there is no immediately identifiable generic coherence. Ask yourself: just what is this text doing? What is it trying to achieve? What is its cultural purpose? I'd be surprised if you came up with a clear answer.

The lack of contextual coherence is reflected in, and is a reflection of, its accompanying lack of internal organization, its lack of **cohesion**. The term **cohesion** refers to the way we relate or tie together bits of our discourse. As Halliday and Hasan explain:

> Cohesion occurs where the INTERPRETATION of some element in the discourse is dependent on that of another. The one PRESUPPOSES the other, in the sense

> that it cannot be effectively decoded except by recourse to it. When this happens,
> a relation of cohesion is set up, and the two elements, the presupposing and the pre-
> supposed, are thereby at least potentially integrated into a text. (Halliday and
> Hasan 1976: 4: their emphasis)

The key notion behind cohesion, then, is that there is a **semantic tie** between an item at one
point in a text and an item at another point. The presence of the tie makes at least one of the
items dependent upon the other for its interpretation. For example, in the Dahl excerpt, Text
2.2, the BFG exclaims *'It's filthing!'*. The pronoun *it* is dependent for its meaning on the preceding noun *the awesome snozzcumber*. We have absolutely no problem establishing this semantic dependency and correctly decoding the meaning (or **referent**) of *it*. Compare this with the
situation in Text 2.3: clauses 3iii and 3iv each contain the pronoun *it*, but can we be sure just
what *it* refers to?

It is this absence of semantic ties between elements in Text 2.3 that prevents it from
hanging together internally as a piece of language, and which makes it difficult for us to
make much sense of it. And yet I'm prepared to bet that you will struggle very hard to find
meaning there, which leads us to an important insight into how we respond to language.

Sense in sequence: the sequential implicativeness of text

A basic property of text is illustrated by the following conversational excerpt between two
speakers:

> A: What time is it, love?
> B: Julie left her car at the station today.

Given these two turns at talk, presented one after the other, you will find yourself working
hard to make sense of the little exchange they apparently represent. You will try very hard
to find a way of interpreting B's turn as somehow an answer to A's question, even though
there is no obvious link between them *apart from their appearance in sequence.* Perhaps you
will decide that B has left his watch in Julie's car and so cannot tell A the time; or perhaps
both interactants are waiting for someone called Julie who is usually home by this time but
B can explain why she's late . . ., etc. You have no doubt constructed your own interpretation which allows you to 'understand' B's utterance. It is unlikely that you looked at the
example and simply said 'It doesn't make sense'.

From this example we can appreciate a point made some years ago by a group of conversation analysts (e.g. Schegloff and Sacks 1973/74, Sacks, Schegloff and Jefferson 1974,
Schegloff 1981). When these analysts looked at everyday conversations, they noticed that
'no empirically occurring utterance ever occurs outside, or external to, some specific
sequence. Whatever is said will be said in some sequential context' (Atkinson and Heritage
1984: 6). They developed this observation into the notion of **sequential implicativeness**
(Schegloff and Sacks 1973/74: 296). Sequential implicativeness arises from the fact that language is inexorably tied to linear sequence, so that one part of a text (a sentence or a turn at
talk) must follow another part of the text (the next sentence or turn at talk). The outcome of
this is that each part of the text creates the context within which the next bit of the text is
interpreted. And, as your own efforts with the example above will have demonstrated to you,
speakers or readers will go to enormous lengths to construct relationships between what is
said/written *now* and what was said/written a moment ago.

In the example above it is difficult (but certainly not impossible) to construct the links that would allow B's utterance to make sense coming as it does after A's question. There are no clues to the links provided in the speaker's talk. B could have been more helpful by saying:

> B: I know Julie's late, but we shouldn't get worried because she left her car at the station today and caught the train, instead of driving in to work.

But because of the context of situation shared by the interactants, it was not necessary to spell out the links explicitly. However, if most texts are to make sense to readers or listeners, the links between the parts have to be more easily recoverable. Making the links between the parts of a text recoverable is what the resources of cohesion enable language users to do, which is why we now need to look at cohesion in more detail.

Analysing cohesive resources

Following Halliday and Hasan, I'm suggesting that the texture of texts involves both the text's relation to its external context (which we will explore in Chapters Three and Four), and the text's internal cohesion. Texts like Text 2.3 which trouble either or both of these dimensions of texture are problematic for readers to make sense of, though we have a well-trained semantic orientation which leads us to try to find meaning in any sequence of language.

To see cohesive resources at work in their full power, let's look now at a famous (very) short story by American writer Kate Chopin.

Text 2.4: The Story of an Hour[5]

$_{(1i)}$Knowing $_{(1ii)}$that Mrs. Mallard was afflicted with a heart trouble, $_{(1iii)}$great care was taken $_{(1iv)}$to break to her as gently as possible the news of her husband's death.

$_{(2)}$It was her sister Josephine who told her, in broken sentences; veiled hints that revealed in half concealing. $_{(3)}$Her husband's friend Richards was there, too, near her. $_{(4i)}$It was he who had been in the newspaper office $_{(4ii)}$when intelligence of the railroad disaster was received, $_{(4iii)}$with Brently Mallard's name leading the list of 'killed.' $_{(5i)}$He had only taken the time $_{(5ii)}$to assure himself of its truth by a second telegram, $_{(5iii)}$and had hastened to forestall any less careful, less tender friend $_{(5iv)}$in bearing the sad message.

$_{(6)}$She did not hear the story as many women have heard the same, with a paralyzed inability to accept its significance. $_{(7)}$She wept at once, with sudden, wild abandonment, in her sister's arms. $_{(8i)}$When the storm of grief had spent itself $_{(8ii)}$she went away to her room alone. $_{(9)}$She would have no one follow her.

$_{(10)}$There stood, facing the open window, a comfortable, roomy armchair. $_{(11i)}$Into this she sank, $_{(11ii)}$pressed down by a physical exhaustion that haunted her body and seemed to reach into her soul.

$_{(12)}$She could see in the open square before her house the tops of trees that were all aquiver with the new spring life. $_{(13)}$The delicious breath of rain was in the air. $_{(14)}$In the street below a peddler was crying his wares. $_{(15i)}$The notes of a distant song which some one was singing reached her faintly, $_{(15ii)}$and countless sparrows were twittering in the eaves.

$_{(16)}$There were patches of blue sky showing here and there through the clouds that had met and piled one above the other in the west facing her window.

(17i)She sat with her head thrown back upon the cushion of the chair, quite motionless, (17ii)except when a sob came up into her throat (17iii)and shook her, (17iv)as a child who has cried itself to sleep continues to sob in its dreams.

(18i)She was young, with a fair, calm face, (18ii)whose lines bespoke repression and even a certain strength. (19i)But now there was a dull stare in her eyes, (19ii)whose gaze was fixed away off yonder on one of those patches of blue sky. (20i)It was not a glance of reflection, (20ii)but rather indicated a suspension of intelligent thought.

(21i)There was something coming to her (21ii)and she was waiting for it, fearfully. (22)What was it? (23i)She did not know; (23ii)it was too subtle and elusive to name. (24i)But she felt it, (24ii)creeping out of the sky, (24iii)reaching toward her through the sounds, the scents, the color that filled the air.

(25)Now her bosom rose and fell tumultuously. (26i)She was beginning to recognize this thing that was approaching to possess her, (26ii)and she was striving to beat it back with her will – (26iii)as powerless as her two white slender hands would have been.

(27i)When she abandoned herself (27ii)a little whispered word escaped her slightly parted lips. (28i)She said it over and over under her breath: (28ii)'free, free, free!' (29)The vacant stare and the look of terror that had followed it went from her eyes. (30)They stayed keen and bright. (31i)Her pulses beat fast, (31ii)and the coursing blood warmed and relaxed every inch of her body.

(32i)She did not stop to ask (32ii)if it were or were not a monstrous joy that held her. (33)A clear and exalted perception enabled her to dismiss the suggestion as trivial.

(34i)She knew (34ii)that she would weep again (34iii)when she saw the kind, tender hands folded in death; (34iv)the face that had never looked save with love upon her, fixed and gray and dead. (35)But she saw beyond that bitter moment a long procession of years to come that would belong to her absolutely. (36)And she opened and spread her arms out to them in welcome.

(37i)There would be no one to live for during those coming years; (37ii)she would live for herself. (38i)There would be no powerful will bending hers (38ii)in that blind persistence with which men and women believe (38iii)they have a right to impose a private will upon a fellow-creature. (39i)A kind intention or a cruel intention made the act seem no less a crime (39ii)as she looked upon it in that brief moment of illumination.

(40)And yet she had loved him – sometimes. (41)Often she had not. (42)What did it matter! (43i)What could love, the unsolved mystery, count for in face of this possession of self-assertion (43ii)which she suddenly recognized as the strongest impulse of her being!

(44)'Free! (45i)Body and soul free!' (45ii)she kept whispering.

(46i)Josephine was kneeling before the closed door with her lips to the keyhole, (46ii)imploring for admission. (47)'Louise, open the door! (48i)I beg, open the door – (48ii)you will make yourself ill. (49)What are you doing Louise? (50)For heaven's sake open the door.'

(51)'Go away. (52)I am not making myself ill.' (53)No; she was drinking in a very elixir of life through that open window.

(54)Her fancy was running riot along those days ahead of her. (55)Spring days, and summer days, and all sorts of days that would be her own. (56i)She breathed a quick prayer (56ii)that life might be long. (57i)It was only yesterday she had thought with a shudder (57ii)that life might be long.

(58i)She arose at length (58ii)and opened the door to her sister's importunities. (59i)There was a feverish triumph in her eyes, (59ii)and she carried herself unwittingly like a goddess of Victory. (60i)She clasped her sister's waist, (60ii)and together they descended the stairs. (61)Richards stood waiting for them at the bottom.

(62)Some one was opening the front door with a latchkey. (63i)It was Brently Mallard who entered, a little travel-stained, (63ii)composedly carrying his grip-sack and umbrella. (64i)He had been far from the scene of accident, (64ii)and did not even know (64iii)there had been one. (65)He stood amazed at Josephine's piercing cry; at Richards' quick motion to screen him from the view of his wife.

(66)But Richards was too late.

(67i)When the doctors came (67ii)they said (67iii)she had died of heart disease – of joy that kills.

Most readers find Text 2.4 a powerful and effective piece of language. Where we struggled with Text 2.3, we become absorbed and perhaps even moved by Text 2.4. We certainly have no trouble making sense of it. One reason is because in Text 2.4 Chopin has exploited with great craft the resources of the three main types of cohesion in written language: **reference**, **conjunction** and **lexical cohesion**. I'll now take you through how you can analyse these cohesive patterns in texts like Text 2.4. For more detail on these cohesive patterns, see Halliday and Matthiessen (2004: Chapter 9).

Reference

The cohesive resource of reference refers to how the writer/speaker introduces participants and then keeps track of them once they are in the text. Participants are the people, places and things that get talked about in the text. The participants in the following sentence are underlined:

> (1i)Knowing (1ii)that <u>Mrs. Mallard</u> was afflicted with <u>a heart trouble</u>, (1iii)<u>great care</u> was taken (1iv)to break to <u>her</u> as gently as possible <u>the news</u> of <u>her husband's death</u>.

Whenever a participant is mentioned in a text, the writer/speaker must signal to the reader/listener whether the identity of the participant is already known or not. That is, participants in a text may be either **presented** to us (introduced as 'new' to the text) or **presumed** (encoded in such a way that we need to retrieve their identity from somewhere). Contrast the following:

> (1i)Knowing (1ii)that <u>Mrs. Mallard</u> was afflicted with <u>a heart trouble</u>,
> (10)There stood, facing the open window, <u>a comfortable, roomy armchair</u>.
> (14)In the street below <u>a peddler</u> was crying his wares.

All these examples involve **presenting** reference: we are not expected to know anything about <u>Mrs. Mallard</u>, or <u>a heart trouble</u> or which <u>armchair</u>, or <u>peddler</u>, as all these participants are being introduced to us for the first time. Contrast those examples with:

> (11i)Into <u>this</u> <u>she</u> sank,

Here we have two **presuming** reference items: it is presumed that we know, or can establish, the thing and the person the *this* and the *she* refer to.

Only presuming participants create cohesion in a text, since ties of dependency are constructed between the presuming item and what it refers to (its referent). The commonest presuming reference items are:

1. the definite article: *the*
   ₍₆₎She did not hear <u>the</u> story as many women have heard <u>the</u> same
2. demonstrative pronouns: *that, these, those . . .*
   _(11i)Into <u>this</u> she sank,
3. pronouns: *he, she, it, they . . .; mine, his, hers, theirs . . .*
   _(11i)Into this <u>she</u> sank,

When the writer uses a presuming reference item, the reader needs to retrieve the identity of that item in order to follow the text. That is, if the writer has used the pronoun *she*, for example, the reader must be able to track down just who the *she* refers to. If presuming referents are not retrievable (i.e. if the reader cannot figure out who *she* refers to, or there are a number of possible candidates), the interaction will run into problems. For example, note the ambiguity in the following opening sentence from a story we'll be looking at in a minute:

<u>I</u> watched as <u>my companion</u> was attacked by <u>the polar bear</u>.

There are three presuming reference items in this sentence, none of which we can clearly decode because there is no prior text to tell us who the *I* is who has a companion, nor which polar bear we're talking about (let alone what it's doing there!).

The identity of a presuming reference item may be retrievable from a number of different contexts:

1. from the general context of culture: for example, when we talk about *how hot <u>the sun</u> is today* we know which sun we are talking about: the sun we share as members of this particular world. We call retrieval from the shared context of culture **homophoric** reference.
2. from the immediate context of situation: for example, if I ask you to *Put <u>it</u> down next to <u>her</u>*, and we're in the same place at the same time, you will be able to decode the *it* as referring to whatever object I am pointing to, and the *her* as the female in the room. When we retrieve from shared immediate context this is called **exophoric** reference.
3. from elsewhere within the text itself: frequently the identity of the participant has been given at an earlier point in the text. For example:
   ₍₆₎<u>She</u> did not hear <u>the story</u> as many women have heard the same
   Here we decode the identity of the presuming reference to *she* by referring back to *Mrs. Mallard*, and to *the story* by making the link back to the previous paragraph's mention of *the railroad disaster . . . with Brently Mallard's name leading the list of 'killed'*.

When the identity of a referent item is retrieved from within the text, we are dealing with **endophoric** reference. It is endophoric reference which creates cohesion, since endophoric ties create the internal texture of the text, while homophoric and exophoric reference contribute to the text's (situational) coherence.

Endophoric reference can be of three main kinds:

1. **anaphoric reference**: this occurs when the referent has appeared at an earlier point in the text. In the example given earlier (*<u>She</u> did not hear <u>the story</u> . . .*), both retrievals are anaphoric. Here is another anaphoric example:

(27i)When she abandoned herself (27ii)a little whispered word escaped her slightly parted lips. (28i)She said <u>it</u> over and over under her breath: (28ii)'free, free, free!'

We retrieve the identity of the pronoun *it* by referring back to the presenting referent in the previous sentence: *a little whispered word*.

Typically, anaphoric reference is to a participant mentioned nearby (one or two sentences previously), but sometimes it may refer back to an item mentioned many pages, minutes or even hours ago. When we read in sentence 64:

(64i)He had been far from <u>the scene of accident</u>, (64ii)and did not even know (64iii)there had been one.

we have no trouble working out *which* scene of accident: we link this presuming referent back to the mention of the *railroad disaster* in sentence 4.

2. **cataphoric reference**: this occurs when the referent has not yet appeared, but will be provided subsequently. For example, imagine Chopin had begun her story:

<u>The news</u> came as a terrible shock to <u>them all</u>, but most of all to Mrs. Mallard. It seemed her husband Brently had been killed in a railroad disaster. His friend, Richards, carried the sad tidings to Mrs. Mallard and her sister Josephine.

Here we begin with the presuming references to *the news* and *them all*, but it is only in the second sentence that we learn just what that news was, and only in the third that we can establish the referent for *them all*.

3. **esphoric reference**: this occurs when the referent occurs in the phrase immediately following the presuming referent item (within the same nominal group/noun phrase, not in a separate clause). For example:

(8i)When <u>the storm</u> of grief had spent itself

– here we learn *which* storm from the immediately following prepositional phrase *of grief*;

(12)She could see in <u>the open square</u> before her house <u>the tops</u> of trees that were all aquiver with the new spring life.

– we learn immediately *which* open square from the following phrase *before her house*, and the tops *of what* from the phrase *of trees*;

(15i)<u>The notes</u> of a distant song which some one was singing reached her faintly, (15ii)and countless sparrows were twittering in the eaves.

– here we see that an esphoric referent may be quite extensive. Which notes did she hear? The prepositional phrase tells us: *of a distant song which some one was singing*.

One further type of endophoric reference which can operate anaphorically, cataphorically or esphorically is **comparative** reference. With comparative reference, the identity of the presumed item is retrieved not because it has already been mentioned or will be mentioned in the text, but because an item with which it is being compared has been mentioned. For example:

(6)She did not hear <u>the story</u> as many women have heard <u>the same</u>

We interpret the comparative referent *the same* to refer back to *the story*, which itself anaphorically refers back to the whole of the preceding paragraph, where we have heard *the story* of Brently Mallard's death. This example shows us both comparative reference and also what we call **whole text referencing**. In **whole text referencing** the referent is more than a simple participant. It may be a sequence of actions or events mentioned previously; it may even be 'the whole text up to this point'. When a writer notes *This therefore proves that . . .*, the presuming *this* may refer to everything that the writer has been arguing to that point.

One special kind of reference is known as **bridging** reference. This is when a presuming reference item refers back to an early item from which it can be inferentially derived. For example:

> (10)There stood, facing <u>the open window</u>, a comfortable, roomy armchair.

There has been no previous mention of a window, yet we have no trouble bridging from the earlier reference to *her room* to work out that *the open window* refers to the window of her room. Similarly, in

> (15i)The notes of a distant song which some one was singing reached her faintly, (15ii)and countless sparrows were twittering in <u>the eaves</u>.

The reference item *the* signals that we know *which* eaves. In fact, no previous mention of eaves has been made, but we can 'bridge' from our assumption that she is in a room of a house to interpret *the eaves of her house*. And in the following example

> (67i)When <u>the doctors</u> came (67ii)they said (67iii)she had died of heart disease – of joy that kills.

we can bridge from earlier mention of her heart disease to figure out that *<u>the doctors</u>* are the ones treating her for her condition.

A common type of reference in narrative text is **possessive** reference. This is used throughout Text 2.4. Here's one of the simpler examples:

> (8ii)she went away to <u>her room</u> alone

We decode *her* in the possessive nominal group *<u>her room</u>* anaphorically to refer to *Mrs. Mallard*. In fact, *her house* is mentioned in a later sentence (sentence 12), so this could also be interpreted as cataphoric reference.

Possessive nominal groups may have even more participants, as this next example shows:

> (3)<u>Her husband's friend Richards</u> was there, too, near her.

The possessive pronoun *her* refers anaphorically to Mrs Mallard; *husband's* refers anaphorically to Brently Mallard.

There is one type of reference, known as **locational** reference, which involves not the identification of a participant in a text (a person or thing), but the identification of a location in time or space. In written text, locational referents such as *here, there, then, above, below* are usually retrieved endophorically, from surrounding text. For example, Chopin might have written:

She went away to her room alone. <u>There</u> she stayed for many hours.

There is a locational reference back to *her room*.

But in conversation, locational referents are frequently retrieved exophorically:

<u>Here</u> are some bikkies.
(retrieved exophorically: here where we are)
<u>These days</u> it costs a fortune.
(retrieved exophorically: these days that we live in now)

For more on categories of reference, see Halliday and Matthiessen (2004: 549–61), Martin (1992a: 93–158) and Martin and Rose (2003), where reference is treated under the category of **identification**.

Tabulating reference chains

A convenient way to capture the reference patterns in a text is simply to trace through mentions of the text's participants. This will give you a picture of how texture is created as **reference chains** develop across a text. Halliday and Matthiessen (2004) and Martin and Rose (2003) each suggest different ways of doing this. The main principle is the same: you identify presuming referents in a text, and then seek to link all mentions of that participant. You can do either a comprehensive analysis of reference, tracing *all* presuming referents, or you can concentrate on the major participants only, depending on the purposes of your analysis.

You can prepare a simple linear display of reference chains by simply listing all linked reference items alongside their sentence numbers throughout a text. If the identity of a presumed reference item is stated in the text (for example, it is introduced through a presenting reference), then simply include it in your list at the appropriate sentence number. If the identity of the presumed referent is never explicitly stated (i.e. it is not lexicalized in the text), then you may wish to write it in at the start of that reference chain [in parentheses]. Presenting reference items only need to be noted if they are referred back to by a presuming reference item at some point in the text. With possessive nominal groups containing presuming referents, list the group under each of the participants it refers to. You can use abbreviations to indicate from where the identity of the referent is retrieved (anaphorically, esphorically, bridging, exophoric, etc.). In the Appendix you can find reference chains for the three Crying Baby texts from Chapter One. Those analyses are discussed in Chapter Eleven. Here are 8 of the main reference chains in Text 2.4, followed by a brief discussion of what they show us about 'The Story of an Hour'.

Chain 1: Mrs Mallard
(1) Mrs Mallard – her – her husband's death – (2) her sister – (3) her husband's friend – her – (6) she – (7) she – her sister's arms – (8) she – (9) she – her – (11) she – her body – her soul – (12) she – her house – (15) her – (16) her window – (17) she – her head – her throat – her – (18) she – (19) her eyes – (21) her – she – (23) she – (24) she – her – (25) her bosom – (26) she – her – she – her will – her two white slender hands – (27) she – herself – her lips – (28) she – her breath – (29) her eyes – (31) her pulses – her body – (32) she – her – (33) her – (34) she – she – she – her – (35) she – her – (36) she – her arms – (37) she – herself – (38) hers – (39) she – (40) she – (41) she – (43) she – her being – (45) she – (47) Louise –

> **Key to reference analysis**
> Numbers refer to sentences (see Text 2.4, p. 31)
> Ties are anaphoric unless indicated by:
> C: cataphoric S: esphoric P: comparative L: locational B: bridging H: homophoric
> X: exophoric

(48) you – yourself – (49) you – Louise – (52) I – (53) she – (54) her fancy – her – (55) her own – (56) she – (57) she – (58) she – her sister's importunities – (59) her eyes – she – (60) she – her sister's waist – they – (61) them – (67) she

Chain 2: Brently Mallard
(1) husband's death – (3) husband's friend – (4) Brently Mallard's name – (34) (B) the kind tender hands – (B) the face – (40) him – (62) some one – (63) Brently Mallard – his grip sack and umbrella – (64) he – (65) he – him – his wife

Chain 3: her sister, Josephine
(2) her sister Josephine – (7) her sister's arms – (46) Josephine – her lips – (48) I – (58) her sister's importunities – (60) her sister's waist – they – (61) them – (65) Josephine's piercing cry

Chain 4: Richards
(3) her husband's friend Richards – (4) he – (5) he – himself – (61) Richards – (65) Richards' quick motion – (66) Richards

Chain 5: the news
(1) the news (S) of her husband's death – (4) (B) the railroad disaster – the list of 'killed' – (5) its truth – the sad message – (6) the story – the same (P) – its significance

Chain 6: 'something'
(21) something – it – (22) it – (23) it – (24) it – (26) this thing that was approaching to possess her – it – (27) (C) a little whispered word – (28) it – (32) it – (S) a monstrous joy – (33) the suggestion – (39) that brief moment of illumination – (43) this possession of self-assertion (S) which she recognized as the strongest impulse (S) of her being

Chain 7: the room/house
(8) her room – (10) (B) the open window – (12) (B) her house – (14) (L) the street below – (15) (B) the eaves – (16) her window – (46) (B) the closed door – (B) the keyhole – (47) the door – (48) the door – (50) the door – (53) that open window – (58) the door – (60) (B) the stairs – (61) (B) the bottom – (62) the front door

Chain 8: Mrs Mallard's eyes
(1) Mrs Mallard – (19) (B) her eyes - whose gaze – (20) it – (29) the vacant stare – her eyes – (30) they – (59) her eyes

This listing does not show *all* the presuming references in Text 2.4. There are many short chains that link just two or three participants to each other, but it's the longer, sustained chains that contribute most to creating cohesion in the text. What, then, can reference chains tell us about the text?

Firstly, reference chains show us who are the major human participants in a text, and their relative importance. It perhaps comes as no surprise to see just how dominant Mrs Mallard is as a participant in 'The Story of an Hour': there are 87 references to her, spanning the entire text. None of the other human participants even come close. Of the other three human participants, both Richards and Josephine feature only at the edges of the text, appearing as participants only as they intrude peripherally upon Mrs Mallard's life. More strikingly, Brently Mallard textually enacts his death and life: as her husband goes out of her life, he also goes out of her text, only to return to the text (and her life) at the very end. Despite his lengthy textual absence, his return enacts exactly the lack of freedom Mrs Mallard had been so joyous to escape: once he's back in the text, her reference chain dies.

But while this is very much a story about just one participant, Mrs Mallard, the text is less about what she *does* as a participant and more about what she *has*. Note that the Mrs Mallard reference chain contains a surprising number of possessive references: 42 of the 87, in fact. This again is a textual realization of the thematic concern of the story, as we see Mrs Mallard come into possession, achieving *self*-possession, only to have it snatched away again at the end.

And what does Chopin construe self-possession to mean? Judging by the reference chains, it means above all possession of one's own body. Most of the possessive references are to Mrs Mallard's body parts: her hands, her lips, her being, etc. Even though Mrs Mallard may whisper '*Free! Body and soul free!*', the text suggests that for Chopin it is a woman's physical freedom that matters most, or is most difficult to obtain.

There are so many references to Mrs Mallard's eyes that I've shown this as a separate chain. We'll see in a moment how it resonates with other lexical relations in the text. Here we can just note how these references to her eyes and gaze help to realize the metaphorical significance of *self-realization* in the story.

Aside from the human participants, the most extensive chains concern 'the news' and the elusive 'something' that is coming towards Mrs Mallard. The news chain is dense early on in the story, but this fizzles out once it has done its work of providing the catalyst for Mrs Mallard's movement towards her epiphany. The 'something' chain then takes over. Just what *is* the identity of the 'something'? All seems to point towards the referentially complex phrase *this possession of self-assertion which she suddenly recognized as the strongest impulse of her being*, but the referents in this chain are often as 'subtle and elusive' as is the something itself.

An extensive chain to do with place is realized, with 16 references (mostly through bridging) to Mrs Mallard's house, room and parts of the room. These references of course anchor the story in its setting, but they do more: notice how frequently open or closed windows and doors are referred to. Again, this chain contributes thematically, setting up the contrast between the closed and claustrophobic nature of Mrs Mallard's life (she is stuck within her marriage, within her house, within her room, behind a closed door) before her liberation (the realization of which comes to her through her open window).

If we consider now where most items are retrieved from we see that Text 2.4 is typical of written, fictional text: most referents are retrieved endophorically, from within the text itself, and most anaphorically. In this way the text creates its own fictional context, constructing itself as a largely context-independent use of language. This makes it possible for the text to 'travel' so successfully across time and space: though 'The Story of an Hour' was written in North America in the 1920s, we can read and understand the story now, wherever in the world we are. Pragmatic, non-fictional texts depend much more on the extra-textual context for exophoric and homophoric retrieval, as we'll see in texts analysed later in this book.

The combination of reference ties that span the length of the whole text, the consistent focus on a relatively small number of participants, the density of ties, and their endophoric retrieval together add up to create a highly cohesive, self-contained text. The reference chains are also cohesive in that they contribute to the thematic and metaphorical meanings the text is making. The patterns of reference chains help to realize Chopin's suggestion that conventional marriage deprives women of self-possession of their own bodies.

Kate Chopin makes it look easy, but constructing well-textured narratives can be a challenge for most young writers. Consider Text 2.5 below, a short story written by a 12-year-old Australian boy and submitted to a national creative writing competition.

Text 2.5: Fatal Alaska[6]
(spelling and punctuation as in original)

I watched as my companion was attacked by the polar bear. Then he fell to the ground and didn't move. I knew he was dead. My other companion was still in the plane, looking like it was he who had been attacked. I tried to ignore the body but two hours later could stand it no longer. I made a whole in the ice and left it for whatever actic creature was hungry.

My journey to Alaska consisted of two reason, finding the two men who set off from Canada to study penguins and to give the two Canadian mountys some experience in Alaska.

My name is Samual Jacobson, I am a 17 year old Canadian piolot who was assigned to this mission. At first I was proud to do it, then nervous and now I'm terrified. The snow storm last week is said to have covered their plane in ice and snow. I am told they were proffsianals.

I had to get my live companion to refrain from losing his mind. I could not afford to lose another friend or I might lose my own mind. It took a great deal of shaking to bring my friend to his senses, then I urged him to get moving, which he reluctantly did. We moved for several hours getting colder by the minute, and less confident.

Just when I feared we would have to turn back, I saw a light, that looked like a fire. I don't think my partner saw it so I steered him towards it. We saw then what it was, a fire, recently lit, in the middle of a cave.

We ventured into the cave and saw nothing inside but a rack with bones and body parts in it, a billy with meat in it and blood! Then a shadowy figure loomed at the entrance of the cave.

I stared at my partner, who once again had not noticed the happenings around him. I froze, I know its stupid but as the figure advanced, I just froze. My heart was a straight six motor for that ten or so seconds, and it was revving its guts out. Then, when the figure stepped into the flickering light of the fire I felt relief, as I recognized him from the photo of the explorers as Captain John, the leader of the expidition, and the brains.

I knew the bones and body parts and meat were not animal, they were his crew! Just then he pulled a hatchet from his coat and ran at me. That confirmed to me that he had canaballised on his men. I ducked sending him over my back and into the fire, he set alight. I watched as he frantically jumped up, ran outside and rolled in the snow, all the time holding his hatchet. He got up, furious and I knew he wouldn't miss again . . .

TO BE CONTINUED . . ..

This young writer is struggling with many narrative skills, of which referential cohesion is one – we'll return to another in the next chapter. Note how the writer creates confusion for the reader by the excessive use of presuming reference in the first paragraphs (presuming referents underlined):

I watched as <u>my companion</u> was attacked by <u>the polar bear</u>.
– we don't yet know who the I is, or which polar bear

Then <u>he</u> fell to the ground and didn't move.
– the companion or the polar bear? We make the conventional cultural assumption, but it's always possible we're wrong.

I knew <u>he</u> was dead. <u>My other companion</u> was still in <u>the plane</u>, looking like it was <u>he</u> who had been attacked.
– comparative reference now tells us that the 'I' has two companions, but we don't know who any of them are yet, nor how it is they're in a plane, wherever.

I tried to ignore <u>the body</u> but two hours later could stand it no longer. I made a whole in <u>the ice</u> and left it for whatever actic creature was hungry.
– *the body* bridges back to the dead companion, and when we get *the ice* we can link this homophorically with *the polar bear* and subsequently the *actic*. But why are we there? And who are we?

My journey to Alaska consisted of two reason, finding the two men who set off from Canada to study penguins and to give the two Canadian mountys some experience in Alaska.
– through esphoric reference we learn we're in *Alaska* (not quite the *actic*, after all), but we're still confused because we don't yet know who *the two men who set off from Canada to study penguins* are (we need some presenting reference, such as their names), or who *the two Canadian mountys* are. Could they be the two companions mentioned in the first paragraph? Perhaps, but we can't be sure.

It's only in the third paragraph that the *I* discloses his identity, along with some very necessary information about *this mission*, but not all ambiguities are cleared up.

While this young writer is struggling with reference, professional writers can sometimes deliberately problematize referential cohesion. Consider Text 2.6, a well-known poem by John Ashbery. Notice what you stumble over as you try to 'make sense' of the poem.

Text 2.6: The Grapevine[7]

(1)Of who we and all they are
You all now know. (2)But you know
After they began to find us out we grew
Before they died thinking us the causes
Of their acts. (3)Now we'll not know
The truth of some still at the piano, though
They often date from us, causing
These changes we think we are. (4)We don't care
Though, so tall up there
In young air. (5)But things get darker as we move
To ask them: Whom must we get to know
To die, so you live and we know?

Ashbery presents us here with what looks at first sight like a very conventional poem: the poetic style of the heading (article and noun), three four-line stanzas, poetic format (not complete lines), the use of poetic conventions such as running on, rhyme, the suggestion of metaphor, and the absence of narrative devices such as temporal sequence, characterization, dramatic event. The use of all these **genre** conventions triggers socialized reading practice and we set out to read the text *as a poem*, which means we're likely to work very hard at our reading. We expect poetry to be hard, its meanings to be ambiguous and many, its message(s) to be profound, moral and usually humanistic but also elusive. We'll probably read the text many times. And yet, try as you might, can you make much sense of this poem?

One problem with the text is that it's organized around the three presuming reference items *we, they, you*. But who do these pronouns refer to? There is no prior textual context from which we can retrieve the identity of the referents endophorically; nor can we retrieve them exophorically. Since we can never really know who the *you, they* or *we* refers to, the meanings of this text remain indeterminate. We can come up with quite a few possible interpretations of the poem, for all of which we'll have to suggest what those pronouns refer to. But we can never fully resolve the uncertainties, particularly of identity.

Lexical cohesion

Indeterminate reference is not the only problem you might have with Ashbery's poem. Not only are we in some doubt as to just *who* it's about, we're also confused about just *what* it's about. The title sets up multiple expectations: the word *grapevine* could be referring to the plant, in which case we wouldn't be surprised to find words like *wine, leaves, stalk, grow*, etc. Or it could be referring to *gossip, talk, stories*, etc. What it doesn't prepare us for, though, is the word *piano* right in the middle of the poem. Whatever slender lexical ties we were establishing to make meaning are likely to be shattered at that point, as we ask: just what is this poem about? Ashbery is frustrating our conventional expectations of lexical cohesion in text.

The cohesive resource of lexical relations refers to how the writer/speaker uses lexical items (nouns, verbs, adjectives, adverbs) and event sequences (chains of clauses and sentences) to relate the text consistently to its area of focus or its **field**. Lexical cohesion analysis derives from observing that there are certain expectancy relations between words. For example, if you read the word *mouse* in a text, you will not be surprised to come across the words *cheese, white, squeak, tail, rodent* or even *computer* in nearby text, while you would be much more surprised to come across the words *thunderstorm, shovel, bark* or *ironing board.* Lexical relations analysis is a way of systematically describing how words in a text relate to each other, how they cluster to build up lexical sets or lexical strings. Lexical cohesion is an important dimension of cohesion. When that cohesion is troubled, as it is in 'The Grapevine', and also in Text 2.3 'Stalin's Genius', so is our ability to take meaning from a piece of language.

Lexical cohesion operates between units which encode lexical content. These are what we call the *open-class* items of nouns, main verbs, adverbs and adjectives. Grammatical words, or *closed-class* items, such as prepositions, pronouns, articles and auxiliary verbs do not encode lexical content, and so do not contribute to lexical cohesion (though, of course, they contribute to the grammatical relations in a text).

There are two main kinds of lexical relations that we can recognize between words:

1. **taxonomic** lexical relations: where one lexical item relates to another through either class/sub-class (*rodent–mouse*) or part/whole (*tail–mouse*) relations. Although most frequently these relations link lexical items which refer to people, places,

things and qualities, and so are expressed in nominal groups, taxonomic relations can also link processes (verbs) (*eat–nibble*).

2. **expectancy** relations: where there is a predictable relation between a process (verb) and either the doer of that process, or the one effected by it (e.g. *mouse–squeak, nibble–cheese*). These relations link nominal elements with verbal elements.

Words which are taxonomically related may be related through either **classification** or **composition**.

1. **Classification**: this is the relationship between a superordinate term and its members, or hyponyms. Classification is the *x is a type of y* relationship. The main kinds of classification relations are:

a) **co-hyponomy**: when two (or more) lexical items used in a text are both subordinate members of a superordinate class:
influenza:pneumonia (both terms are members of the superordinate class *illnesses*)

b) **class/sub-class**: when two (or more) lexical items used in a text are related through sub-classification:
illness:pneumonia (here the relationship is superordinate term to hyponym)

c) **contrast**: when two (or more) lexical items encode a contrast relationship or antonmy:
clear:blurry; wet:dry; joy:despair

d) **similarity**: when two (or more) lexical items express similar meanings. There are two main sub-types:

i) **synonymy**: when two words essentially restate each other:
message:report; news:intelligence

ii) **repetition**: when a lexical item is repeated:
death:death

The second main type of taxonomic relation is that of **composition**:

2. **Composition** is the part/whole relationship between lexical items which are meronyms or co-meronyms. There are two possible types:

a) **meronymy**: when two lexical items are related as whole to part (or vice versa):
body:heart

b) **co-meronymy**: when two lexical items are related by both being parts of a common whole:
heart:lungs

The second main type of lexical relations, **expectancy relations**, may operate between a nominal element and a verbal element. The relation may operate between an action and the typical (expected) 'doer' of that action:
doctor/diagnose
baby/cry
sparrows/twitter
or the relation may operate between an action/process and the typical (expected) participant effected by that action:
whisper/word

Table 2.2 Simple and complex realizations of lexical content (adapted from Martin 1992a: 293)

MEANING EXPRESSED	SIMPLE REALIZATION (1 lexical item)	COMPLEX REALIZATION (2+ lexical items)
person	baby	human infant
action	embrace	have a cuddle
quality	desperate	at your wits' end
circumstance	sometimes	from time to time

> break/news
> play/piano

The predictability relationship between an event/process and the typical location in which it takes place may also be described as an expectancy relation:

> work/office

Expectancy can also be used to capture the relationship between the individual lexical items and the composite, predictable, nominal group they form:

> heart/disease
> child/care

So far all the examples given have involved single words. However, as Martin (1992a: 293) points out, sometimes two or more lexical items may be functioning to express one piece of lexical content. Some examples are given in Table 2.2.

Complex lexical items operating to encode one meaning can be treated as a single item for the purposes of lexical cohesion analysis.

We can capture the lexical cohesion in a text by listing all related lexical items, showing how they form **lexical strings** that add texture to text. A lexical string is a list of all the lexical items that occur sequentially in a text that can be related to an immediately prior word (if possible) or to a head word either taxonomically or through an expectancy relation. It often helps here to decide on the 'head word' for a string, and then bring together sequentially related lexical items. Sometimes you'll find that a lexical item can be linked in to more than one string. In that case, it's best to display the word in more than one string because the word is contributing texture through both semantic associations.

An analysis of lexical cohesion in the three Crying Baby texts appears in the Appendix and is discussed in Chapter Eleven. Here is a list of 11 major lexical strings in Text 2.4.

Key
Numbers refer to sentence numbers (see Text 2.4, p. 31)
Ties between items are classification unless otherwise indicated with:
C: composition
x: expectancy

String 1: death and life
(1) afflicted with x heart trouble – x death – (4) disaster – x killed – (12) life – (34) death – dead – (37) live – live – (48) x ill – (52) ill – (53) life – (56) life – (57) life – (64) accident – (67) died – x heart disease – x kills

String 2: news
(1) break – x news (2) sentences – hints – (4) x newspaper – intelligence – list – (5) truth – telegram – bearing x message – (6) story – significance – (27) (C) word – (28) x said – (32) ask – (33) dismiss x suggestion – (39) illumination – (45) x whispering – (56) prayer – (58) importunities

String 3: open/closed
(1) break – (2) broken – veiled – revealed – concealing – (10) open – (12) open – (18) repression – (19) dull x stare – x eyes – x gaze – (20) reflection – (26) recognize – (29) x vacant stare – look – eyes – (30) keen x bright – (33) clear x perception – (34) saw – looked – fixed – (35) saw – (36) opened – spread out – (38) blind – (39) looked – illumination – (46) admission – (47) open – (48) open – (50) open – (53) open – (58) opened – (62) opening – (65) screen x view

String 4: body
(1) heart – (6) x paralyzed – (11) physical exhaustion – body – (C) soul – (17) (C) head – (C) throat – (18) (C) face – (C) lines – (19) (C) eyes – (25) (C) bosom – (26) (C) hands – (27) (C) lips – (29) (C) eyes – (31) (C) pulses x beat fast – x coursing x blood – (C) body – (34) (C) hands – (C) face – (36) spread out x arms – (43) (C) being – (45) (C) body – (C) soul – (46) (C) lips – (59) (C) eyes – (60) (C) waist – (67) (C) heart

String 5: house
(8) room – (10) (C) window – (12) square – (C) house – (14) street – (15) eaves – (16) (C) window – (46) (C) door – (C) keyhole – (47) (C) door – (48) door – (50) door – (53) window – (58) door – (60) stairs – (62) front door – (C) latchkey

String 6: power, will, possession
(1) care – (5) careful – tender – (7) wild – abandonment – (8) storm – (17) x thrown back – (18) repression – strength – (21) fearfully – (23) subtle – elusive – (24) x creeping – reaching toward – (26) possess – beat back – x will – powerless – (27) abandoned – escaped – (29) x terror – (32) x monstrous – (33) exalted – trivial – (34) kind – tender – (35) bitter – (38) powerful will x bending – persistence – right – x impose – will – (39) kind – cruel x intention – crime – (43) mystery – possession – self-assertion – strongest impulse – (54) fancy – running x riot – (55) own – (59) triumph – (59) Victory

String 7: joy
(32) joy – (34) (C) love – (36) x welcome – (40) loved – (43) (C) impulse – (44) x free – (45) free – (53) elixir of life – (67) joy

String 8: time
(5) time – (12) (C) spring – (35) (C) moment – (C) years – (37) years – (39) (C) moment – (40) (C) sometimes – (41) (C) often – (54) (C) days – (55) spring days, summer days, all sorts of days – (56) x long – (57) (C) yesterday – long – (66) late

String 9: natural scenery
(12) trees x aquiver – new spring life – (13) rain – (15) sparrows x twittering – (16) blue sky – (C) clouds – (19) (C) blue sky – (24) (C) sounds – (C) scents – (C) color

String 10: cry
(5) sad – (7) x wept – x wild abandonment – (8) storm of grief – (14) crying – (17) sob x shook – cried – sob – (34) weep – (65) piercing x cry

String 11: extreme behaviour
(7) wild abandonment – (18) calm – (19) dull – (25) tumultuously – (26) x striving – (46) imploring – (48) beg – (50) x heaven – (54) running riot – (56) prayer – (58) importunities – (59) x feverish – goddess – (63) composedly

Again, remember that this is not an exhaustive analysis of *all* lexical cohesion in this text – there are other short strings not listed here. But these strings add depth to patterns we first detected through our reference analysis. Through the dense lexical relations in the text we see more clearly how Chopin weaves thematic meanings throughout the text.

There are, first of all, the strings that we perhaps 'expect' to find, given our surface reading of the story. For example, the string of life and death provides the background which gives the story its existence, but it is a comparatively short string. There is the string of 'news', but notice how this string is not just confined to the first couple of paragraphs of the story but in fact continues throughout the text, suggesting the surprising connection between the news of Mr Mallard's death and Mrs Mallard's own *illumination*. There is also the string of words to do with the setting, and the only surprise here might be just how limited the setting is. The furthest we go from home is to the square in the street. Again, the claustrophobia of Mrs Mallard's physical life is encoded linguistically. Contrast comes with the string of 'natural scenery', where it's the world *outside* Mrs Mallard's house, a world that awakens her awareness of her freedom, offering all that is positive – and that is momentarily within her reach.

But more surprising might be some of the strings which are not easy to notice from casual readings of the story. The open/closed string is strongly metaphoric, as we move from the *veiled* and *concealing* life Mrs Mallard lives at the beginning towards the openness of her freedom. All those *open windows* are cohesively linked to Mrs Mallard's *illumination*, until at the end the story returns to concealment, as Richards tries to *screen* Mrs Mallard again.

The dense string of 'body' words reinforces the pattern we first noticed in reference analysis: that Chopin is much concerned with a woman's control of her body as an essential component of her *self-possession.*

Alongside the short, positive string expressing the 'joy' this self-possession might bring is the much denser, more disturbing string expressing 'power, will, possession'. Through this string the story associates many negative, almost violent meanings with the criminal imposition of a husband's will within marriage.

This string is reinforced by another I have recognized, that of 'extreme behaviour', where we see the inscription of the powerful emotions at work in the story. One specific form of extreme behaviour, crying, constitutes a string on its own, with these negative emotions and responses far outweighing the number of positive lexis, giving the story its rather bleak tone despite the moment of self-realization.

Again, we see from cohesion analysis how Chopin builds up a dense web of lexical links throughout the text, not only binding the separate sentences and paragraphs together into a tight semantic unit but also leading us towards the meanings the story is making beneath (or rather through) its surface events.

We can also see now part of why Text 2.3 above, 'Stalin's Genius', is so difficult to read *as text*: it lacks lexical cohesion. Most of the lexical items in Text 2.3 do <u>not</u> enter into relations of predictability with other lexical items. Perhaps the only cohesively related items are *disembowelment – abuse* (class member to superordinate); *visibility – secrecy* (antonymy); and the two expectancy relations: *pick (your) nose* and *obey authority*. But these few examples demonstrate in fact how difficult it is to juxtapose language items and <u>not</u> have readers struggle to find cohesive links between them! There is thus no stable

ideational domain developed through the text, no one area of experience being represented as sentence follows sentence.

Similarly, we've seen how Ashbery's poem 'The Grapevine' throws all our lexical expectations out in line 6 when we encounter the word 'piano'. And yet, I suspect you find the
Ashbery text more meaningful, or at least easier to deal with, than 'Stalin's Genius' . Why?
One reason is the poem's adherence to generic conventions, giving us at least some orientation to its meaning (more on this in Chapter Three). But another reason is Ashbery's use
of a second type of cohesive device: that of conjunction.

Conjunctive cohesion

The cohesive pattern of conjunction, or conjunctive relations, refers to how the writer creates
and expresses logical relationships between the parts of a text. For example, if you come
across the sentence $_{(19)}$*But now there was a dull stare in her eyes, whose gaze was fixed away off yonder
on one of those patches of blue sky*, you can only fully interpret the meaning of the sentence if you
read it as standing in a contrastive logical relation with a previous sentence, such as $_{(18)}$*She
was young, with a fair, calm face, whose lines bespoke repression and even a certain strength.* In this
example, the logical connection between the two sentences is signalled explicitly through
the conjunction *but*.

Conjunctive cohesion adds to the texture of text, helping to create that semantic unity
that characterizes unproblematic text. Following Halliday and Matthiessen (2004:
538–49), we will recognize three main types of conjunctive relations: **elaboration, extension** and **enhancement**. When we reach Chapter Nine, you'll see that these three types of
meaning are part of the logico-semantic system of the English clause. We'll see there that
meanings of elaboration, extension and enhancement allow us to create semantically meaningful structural links between clauses as we chain clauses together to form **clause complexes**. But in our current discussion of conjunctive cohesion, we're looking at what
Halliday and Matthiessen (2004) sees as the non-structural use of these logico-semantic
categories: at how these meanings create conjunctive links between **sentences**, not between
clauses. This distinction between structural (i.e. grammatical) and non-structural (i.e. cohesive) relations will become clearer later on. For now, here's a brief description of each of the
meaning categories, with examples of conjunctions used to express each.

1. **Elaboration** is a relationship of restatement or clarification, by which one sentence is
(presented as) a re-saying or representation of a previous sentence. Common conjunctions
used to express this relation listed by Halliday and Matthiessen (2004: 541) include *in other
words, that is (to say), I mean (to say), for example, for instance, thus, to illustrate, to be more precise,
actually, as a matter of fact, in fact*.

> Mrs Mallard had heart trouble. <u>In fact</u>, it was her heart that killed her.
> Chopin's story is carefully crafted. <u>For example</u>, Chopin's opening sentence conveys
> an enormous amount of information about characters and events.

2. **Extension** is a relationship of either addition (one sentence adds to the meanings made
in another) or variation (one sentence changes the meanings of another, by contrast or by
qualification). Typical conjunctions listed by Halliday and Matthiessen include *and, also,
moreover, in addition, nor, but, yet, on the other hand, however, on the contrary, instead, apart from
that, except for that, alternatively*.

(39i)A kind intention or a cruel intention made the act seem no less a crime (39ii)as she looked upon it in that brief moment of illumination. (40)And yet she had loved him – sometimes.

– and yet expresses both addition (and) as well as variation (yet)

3. **Enhancement** refers to ways by which one sentence can develop on the meanings of another, in terms of dimensions such as time, comparison, cause, condition or concession. Common **temporal** conjunctions include *then, next, afterwards, just then, at the same time, before that, soon, after a while, meanwhile, all that time, until then, up to that point, now.*

> Mrs Mallard sat alone in her room for some time. <u>After a while</u>, she joined her sister and they went downstairs.
> Mrs Mallard sat alone in her room. <u>Meanwhile</u>, her sister and Richards worried about how she was taking the news.

Comparative conjunctions include likewise, similarly, in a different way.

> Her sister Louise told her the news carefully. <u>Similarly</u>, Richards was cautious and constrained in what he said.

Causal conjunctions include *so, then, therefore, consequently, hence, because of that, for, in consequence, as a result, on account of this, for that reason, for that purpose, with this in view.*

> She realized she now was free. <u>For that reason</u>, she felt suddenly filled with joy.

Concessive relations are expressed by *but, yet, still, though, despite this, however, even so, all the same, nevertheless.*

> (34i)She knew (34ii)that she would weep again (34iii)when she saw the kind, tender hands folded in death; (34iv)the face that had never looked save with love upon her, fixed and gray and dead. (35)<u>But</u> she saw beyond that bitter moment a long procession of years to come that would belong to her absolutely.
> – <u>but</u> links sentence 35 through a relationship of concession to sentence 34 (although she was sad, nevertheless she could see the positives)

> (1)The compelling sound of an infant's cry makes it an effective distress signal and appropriate to the human infant's prolonged dependence on a caregiver. (2)<u>However</u>, cries are discomforting and may be alarming to parents, many of whom find it very difficult to listen to their infant's crying for even short periods of time.
> – <u>however</u> is a more formal way to express a concessive relationship between sentences

As well as indicating different logical meanings, a less obvious dimension to conjunctive relations is that they may refer to **external** (real world) logical relations or to the writer's **internal** (rhetorical) organization of the events in his/her text. Compare the following examples:

> Mrs Mallard was very affected by her husband's death. <u>First</u> she cried in her sister's arms. <u>Next</u>, she sat alone in her room. <u>Finally</u>, she joined her sister to walk downstairs.

– temporal enhancing conjunctions, linking real world events. This is **external** conjunction.

> Mrs Mallard was very affected by her husband's death. <u>First</u>, it meant liberation from marriage. <u>Next</u>, it gave her financial independence. <u>Finally</u>, it allowed her to pursue her own interests.

– rhetorical elaborating conjunctions, itemizing the steps in an argument or exposition. This is **internal** conjunction.

In the first example, the three underlined conjunctions refer to the unfolding of the events in real time, to the external temporal sequencing of Mrs Mallard's actions. In the second example, however, the same three underlined conjunctions function very differently. The sentences are no longer related by temporal sequence (Mrs Mallard did not first become liberated from marriage and *then* get financial independence). Instead, the conjunctions here refer to the speaker's rhetorical organization of the information: *first* is 'first in the sequence of what I'm telling you', *next* is 'next in what I'm telling you', and *finally* is 'the last thing I'm going to tell you'. When conjunctions are used to relate sentences in this rhetorical way, we describe the relation as one of **internal** conjunction. The most common types of internal conjunctive relation are elaboration (in fact all elaborating conjunctions can be regarded as internal, since restatement by definition involves a rhetorical organization of information) and temporal (the *firstly, secondly, finally* type exemplified above). (For a more complete discussion of the internal/external contrast, see Halliday and Hasan 1976: 240–1, Martin 1992a: 207–30, Martin and Rose 2003: 120–27.)

Most conjunctive relations operate between two adjacent sentences. In this next example, the *But* links sentence 19 back to sentence 18:

> (18i)She was young, with a fair, calm face, (18ii)whose lines bespoke repression and even a certain strength. (19i)<u>But</u> now there was a dull stare in her eyes, (19ii)whose gaze was fixed away off yonder on one of those patches of blue sky.

However, the domain of a conjunctive tie can also stretch further, with a conjunction linking one sentence back to an earlier paragraph, a pattern more common in formal written texts such as expositions and arguments.

Finally, although in all the examples given so far the logical relation has been expressed through a conjunctive word or expression, not all conjunctive relations are in fact expressed **explicitly**. Conjunctive relations can also be expressed **implicitly**, through the simple juxtaposition of sentences. For example:

> (6)She did not hear the story as many women have heard the same, with a paralyzed inability to accept its significance. (7)She wept at once, with sudden, wild abandonment, in her sister's arms.

Here although there is no conjunction linking the two sentences, we can only make sense of the occurrence of sentence 7 in relation to 6 if we read in an extending relation (of contrast) between them. We could make this relation explicit by inserting the conjunction *Instead* at the start of sentence 7.

But Kate Chopin did *not* insert the conjunction *instead*, just as she did not repeatedly make explicit the temporal sequence of events with the conjunction *then*. Halliday warns us to be 'cautious' in reading in too much implicit conjunction when we're analysing a text:

> the presence or absence of explicit conjunction is one of the principal variables in English discourse, both as between registers and as between texts in the same register; this variation is obscured if we assume conjunction where it is not expressed. It is important therefore to note those instances where conjunction is being recognized that is implicit; and to characterize the text also without it, to see how much we still feel is being left unaccounted for. (Halliday and Matthiessen 2004: 549)

We can capture conjunctive cohesion in a text by listing sentences which are related to each other by conjunction, linked by a symbol that describes the type of link. The following symbols are widely used for logico-semantic relations in SFL:

= elaboration
+ extension
x enhancement

Here's an analysis of conjunction in Text 2.4, taking Halliday's caution about not reading in too many implicit conjunctive relations. (For sentence numbers, see page 31.)
1 = (more precisely) 2–5
6 + (instead) 7
18 x but 19
23 x but 24
24 x now 25 x (because) 26
32 x (because) 33
34 x but 35 + and 36
36 = (in other words) 37–39
37–39 + and yet 40 x (although) 41
53 = (more precisely) 54–57
56 x (yet) 57
65 x but 66
Compared to the other types of cohesion we've looked at there is relatively little conjunctive cohesion in Text 2.4: only 7 explicit conjunctive links, and another 8 implicit ones. The relative sparsity of conjunction can be explained by a number of factors, including the overarching generic structure of 'narrative' which carries with it certain logical implications. For example, because we recognize that we're reading a short story, we assume we're dealing with problematic events unfolding in a temporal sequence which will at some point go against our expectations. While Chopin does not need to make explicit much of the temporal logic of the text, she does build in more of the concessive, counter-expectancy relations through the enhancing *buts*. She needs to do this because 'The Story of an Hour' repeatedly confronts us with what we don't expect. We don't expect the grieving widow to be filled with joy as she realizes her freedom. We don't expect her to admit that she very often did not love her husband. And of course we don't expect her to die on his return. Just as this is a story primarily about going against cultural conventions, so the text itself is structured to help us follow Mrs Mallard's various surprises.

The text also uses elaborating relations, suggesting that Chopin is careful to make sure we fully grasp the counter-expectancies. In particular, the story gives us two key clarifications of the nature of Mrs Mallard's realization: in 37–39 and again in 54–57 we learn in detail just why Mrs Mallard would be so joyous to escape the *powerful will* of her husband, and what freedom will mean to her. In this way we cannot fail to empathize with Mrs Mallard, and in so doing perhaps accept Chopin's point that *a kind intention or a cruel intention made the act seem no less a crime.*

The structure of the text as a narrative will be considered more in Chapter Three, but we can see here how conjunction cohesion contributes to the successful staging of the narrative in ways that point us toward the story's thematic meanings.

Texts which accidentally or deliberately muddle conjunctive cohesion are usually difficult to interpret. With 'Stalin's Genius', Text 2.3, it is almost impossible to interpret conjunctive relations. There are no explicit conjunctions used in the first four sentences of the text, and it is very difficult to read in any implicit ones. It's thus difficult to construct logical relations between sentences with any confidence.

But with Ashbery's poem 'The Grapevine', we do have some markers of conjunctive cohesion. The cohesive links seem to be:

1 + 2 but (contrast)
2 x 3 now (temporal)
3 x 4 though (concessive)
4 x 5 but (concessive)

The logical relations here are those of an argument: this *but* that *however* something else *despite* that. We recognize the underlying textual strategy here, though it may not help us a great deal. There is just enough conjunctive cohesion in the text to give a sense of a logical structure, even if we can't quite figure out just what is being logically related to what!

Cohesion in spoken texts

So far we've looked at texture, and more specifically cohesion, in *written* texts. But texture is also what differentiates randomly juxtaposed spoken utterances from spoken text, sometimes called *discourse*. In describing the texture of spoken texts, we first of all describe the patterns of lexical relations, conjunction and reference, since all those patterns are drawn on dynamically to create texture in speech as in writing. However, texture in spoken interaction also comes from the patterns of **conversational structure**. Conversational structure describes how interactants negotiate the exchange of meanings in dialogue, and includes patterns of speech functions, exchange structure and ellipsis. Procedures for analysing conversational structure cannot be presented in detail here, but see Eggins and Slade (1997) and Eggins (2000). However, we will be analysing grammatical patterns in spoken language texts through this book.

Cohesion as continuity: the logogenesis of discourse

To fully appreciate how cohesion contributes to the texture of texts, it helps to think of cohesion from two different perspectives. When we look back at a text as a finished product, as we have done until now, cohesion looks like the 'glue' that sticks the elements and therefore meanings together in a text. But text really unfolds dynamically; text producers generate meanings in real time; and we apprehend those meanings in sequence, as we move from sentence to sentence. From this **logogenetic** or dynamic perspective, we can see that cohesion is fundamentally about the ongoing contextualization of meanings in terms of expectancy.

What lexical cohesion really does, for example, is that once the choice of one lexical item has been made (for example, *news*), it creates a context within which certain other words become more likely to occur than others. This probability of co-occurrence is experienced by readers as expectancy: having seen the word *news*, we are not at all surprised to soon come across the words *sentences, hints, intelligence, telegram, message.* We would be much more surprised to come across the words *flower pot*, or *metronome*, or *tissues*. In a highly crafted, cohesive text like Text 2.4, our expectations are met, and each successive mention of an 'expected' lexical item itself recalibrates the expectations for where the text will go next. In this way, the text can move forward, gradually expanding and shifting its meanings, without 'losing' us along the way by troubling or thwarting our expectations – until it does so in its strategic and spectacular dénouement.

This dynamic view also explains our problems with Text 2.3: lexical items in sentence 1 set up a particular context within the text. Having read *Stalin's genius*, we would perhaps not be surprised to read *powers, gift, strategem, Russia* or *revolution*, etc. What we do not expect – what has not been contextualized by the text – are the semantic domains of sexual behaviour (*French kissing*), appearance (*visibility*), fashion accoutrements (*accessories*) and rain (*get you wet*).

The same logogenetic contextualization occurs with the other systems of cohesion. Once a particular participant has been introduced into a text, the context is created for future references to that participant or to other participants somehow connected with it. We 'expect' to hear more about them. Once an opening sentence is 'on the table', all the possible ways of logically developing from that sentence become constrained, a few becoming more likely than others. For example, when we read a general statement (that *Knowing that Mrs. Mallard was afflicted with a heart trouble, great care was taken to break to her as gently as possible the news of her husband's death*), the text has created its own context for now providing us with specific elaborations (*Thus, her friends told her gently . . .*), extensions (*But she heard it abruptly from the maid . . .*) and enhancements (*So they waited for several hours . . .*) of the meanings realized in that sentence. If explicit or implicit conjunctive relations allow us to make sense of the following text in that way, we are not troubled. The text does what we expect it to. But when a sentence sets up confusing expectations (just what do we expect next, after *Stalin's genius consisted of not French-kissing?*), or when what we expect does not happen, we find the text troubling, its texture problematic.

As this dynamic perspective on text indicates, cohesion is a process through which each successive moment in a text can be linked to the moments that have gone before. As Halliday and Hasan put it: 'Cohesion expresses the continuity that exists between one part of the text and another' (Halliday and Hasan 1976: 299). As links are created through the use of cohesive resources, the text ongoingly recalibrates its context, making both continuity and change the defining characteristics of text. This logogenetic view of cohesion allows us to understand what Halliday and Hasan suggest is a general principle of how cohesion works:

> The continuity that is provided by cohesion consists, in the most general terms, in expressing at each stage in the discourse the points of contact with what has gone before. (Halliday and Hasan 1976: 299)

This general principle is useful in exploring longer passages of discourse, such as linked 'pages' of hypertext. Skilfully constructed websites ensure that hot linked pages are linked cohesively with preceding text. Navigational icons at the top or side of the page continually remind readers of the continuity possible within the text. Martin and Rose (2003) offer analyses of longer texts, demonstrating the ongoing recontextualizing role of cohesive choices.

Texture: from cohesion to coherence

In asking 'what is (a) text?', this chapter has explored one component of texture: the internal cohesion through which referential, lexical and logical ties bind passages of language into relatively coherent, unified semantic units. As examples of non-text and problematic text have shown, cohesion is not an optional add-on to the process of creating text, but an essential element in the process of meaningful communication: 'There has to be cohesion if meanings are to be exchanged at all' (Halliday and Hasan 1976: 300). But, as we saw earlier in this chapter, cohesion is not the only component of texture. Not only must a text ongoingly create its own cohesion, but so also a text must relate in relatively stable, coherent ways to the contexts in which it is functioning to mean. In the next chapter we explore one dimension of coherence: the functional-semantic relationship between a text and its generic purpose in the culture.

Notes

1. Example taken from p. 12 of *NSW Foundation Handwriting* Year 5 (J. Barwick (1996), Pascal Press).
2. Source: e. e. cummings in *The Norton Anthology of Poetry* 3rd edition (1983), p. 1044.
3. From *The BFG* by Roald Dahl (p. 51, Puffin Edition 1984).
4. Bruce Andrews 'Stalin's Genius', p. 531 in *Postmodern American Poetry – a Norton Anthology*, edited by Paul Hoover (1994), New York: Norton.
5. 'The Story of an Hour' by Kate Chopin (1851–1904), in S. Barnet and W. Cain (2000), *A Short Guide to Writing About Literature*, 8th edn, New York: Longman, pp. 13–14.
6. Source: David Wells, text held in the Nestlé Write-around-Australia archive, State Library of NSW.
7. From John Ashbery *Selected Poems* (1987), London: Paladin, p. 9.

Chapter 3

Genre: context of culture in text

Introduction

As we saw in Chapter Two, although a text is physically made up of grammatical units (clauses, phrases, words), text is more than just any collection of these units in a sequence. To be text, there must be patterns of cohesion tying the elements of the text together. But texture also involves the text's relationship with its context. Unproblematic texts are, as we saw in Chapter Two, coherent with their context.

This chapter explores the first dimension of contextual coherence, that of genre. We look at the systemic functional interpretation of genre as the 'cultural purpose' of texts, and examine how texts express genres through structural and realizational patterns. The chapter also touches on some implications and applications of genre analysis, including using knowledge of genre to help students write appropriately, genre in fictional and literary texts, and how to read genres critically.

An illustration of genre

To illustrate the principles of genre theory, let's turn to a short, published text:

Text 3.1: Threshold[1]

(1)You are on the threshold of a magnificent chapter in your private life, with substantial opportunities emerging after the new moon on the 5th. (2i)A man who is resourceful, good looking or born around November could be very helpful with your quest for a promotion, (2ii)and you could be celebrating a minor victory on the 9th, 24th or 28th. (3i)A trip, reunion or important talk that you could not fit in last month will be more straightforward or enjoyable $_{(3ii)}$if you wait until November. $_{(4i)}$If single, $_{(4ii)}$you may start dating a charming man whom you met briefly a few weeks ago. $_{(5i)}$Others may be startled by your apologetic actions $_{(5ii)}$as you seek a reconciliation. $_{(6i)}$Long-range ventures or people you have not met before should be avoided between the 12th and 17th, $_{(6ii)}$especially if your birthday is after the 12th. $_{(7)}$The pieces of a puzzle will fall into place in the last 10 days of the month or by early November.

Most readers have no problems identifying this bit of language as an example of a *type* of text, in this case a horoscope. Text 3.1 is doing something with language that we're familiar with. In its apparent claim to be able to predict events in our lives for the month ahead, we recognize that it's like other texts we've read in the horoscope section of magazines and newspapers.

When we state so comfortably that Text 3.1 is a horoscope text, what we are really stating is what <u>purpose</u> the text fulfils, what kind of job it does in its culture of origin. Identifying the purpose of a text clues readers in to how to 'read' and therefore interpret the (sometimes indeterminate) meanings of the text.

This apparently simple act of recognizing the **genre** of the text has important implications for text analysis, for it suggests that one aspect of the meaning of text is a text's relationship to types, its **generic identity**. It suggests that negotiating texts depends in part on identifying ways in which a particular text is similar to, reminiscent of, other texts circulating in the culture.

You can get a feel for the importance of genre to our understanding of text by comparing Text 3.1 to Text 2.3, 'Stalin's Genius', first presented in Chapter Two (page 28).

While Text 3.1 is 'easy to read', it's likely that you struggled to make sense of Text 2.3. All the individual words are fine; the grammar is apparently English. But it just doesn't all add up. We saw in Chapter Two that one of the problems with this 'text' is that it doesn't display much cohesion at all. The participants introduced in sentence 1 (*Stalin, I*) are not referred to again, and participants change from sentence to sentence; the lexical items are from a dozen different unrelated fields; and there are no interpretable conjunctive relations between sentences.

But perhaps even more disorienting than the text's lack of cohesion is its lack of purpose. Just what, you may wonder, is this text trying to do? How are we supposed to read this text? As a piece of fictional prose? But where's the narrative structure? Or as a poem? But where are the poetic conventions? Or as non-fiction? But of what kind? Different sentences in the text appear to come from different types of texts. For example, *No, I don't mean the missile crisis* appears to be an answer given in dialogue, but where is the question? *Cat goes backward to suit international organization* sounds like the clue to a cryptic crossword puzzle, while *the accessories get you wet* just might be from advertising.

What you're struggling with is the text's generic identity, and the example shows us that if a text can't easily be attributed to a genre, then it is in some ways a problematic text.

Genre is a term you'll come across in many disciplines, including literary studies, film studies, art theory and cultural studies. But we're using it here in a specifically systemic functional way, best captured by Martin's two definitions of genre. Firstly, 'a genre is a staged, goal-oriented, purposeful activity in which speakers engage as members of our culture' (Martin 1984: 25). Less technically, 'Genres are how things get done, when language is used to accomplish them' (Martin 1985b: 248). Defining genres in this way, we can see that there are as many different genres as there are recognizable social activity types in our culture. There are:

- literary genres: short stories, autobiographies, ballads, sonnets, fables, tragedies
- popular fiction genres: romantic novels, whodunits, sitcoms
- popular non-fiction genres: instructional manuals, news stories, profiles, reviews, recipes, how-to features
- educational genres: lectures, tutorials, report/essay writing, leading seminars, examinations, text-book writing

And there is also an extensive range of everyday genres, genres in which we take part in daily life, such as:

- buying and selling things ('transactional' genres)
- seeking and supplying information
- telling stories
- gossiping
- making appointments
- exchanging opinions
- going to interviews
- chatting with friends

But just how is genre signalled? For example, just how do readers recognize Text 3.1 as a horoscope text, even when it is presented (as in this book) without any explicit clues to its publication source?

Systemic linguistics suggests that the generic identity of a text, the way in which it is similar to other texts of its genre, lies in three dimensions:

1. the co-occurrence of a particular contextual cluster, or its **register configuration**
2. the text's staged or **schematic structure**
3. the **realizational patterns** in the text

We will briefly outline each of these areas.

Register configuration

To understand the relationship between register and genre, it helps to consider how genres come about. In an old but very useful exploration of social processes, Berger and Luckmann (1966: 70) suggest that 'all human activity is subject to habitualization'. You can see this in your everyday life. You probably eat breakfast every day. Although there is an almost infinite range of foods and food combinations from which you could constitute your breakfast, it's a fair bet that most days you eat the same things. You probably don't work your way around the 50 or so different cereals at the supermarket, or the dozens of breads, to say nothing of the rice, eggs, fish, meat and noodle alternatives.

As Berger and Luckmann point out, to simplify everyday life we quickly routinize the way we perform repeated activities:

> Any action that is repeated frequently becomes cast into a pattern, which can then be reproduced with an economy of effort and which, *ipso facto*, is apprehended by its

performer *as* that pattern. Habitualization further implies that the action in question may be performed again in the future in the same manner and with the same economical effort. (Berger and Luckmann 1966: 70–1)

Developing patterned ways of achieving tasks is useful to us as individuals, but it's even more essential when the tasks we face are social ones, such as using language to co-operatively achieve an outcome. The Russian linguist and literary theorist Mikhail Bakhtin pointed out that as language use becomes habitualized, we can recognize what he called 'speech genres'. Bakhtin claimed that speech genres develop as language patterns in particular contexts become predictable and relatively stable:

> We learn to cast our speech in generic forms and, when hearing others' speech, we guess its genre from the very first words; we predict a certain length (that is, the approximate length of the speech whole) and a certain compositional structure; we foresee the end; that is, from the very beginning we have a sense of the speech whole, which is only later differentiated during the speech process. (Bakhtin 1994: 83)

Why do we develop habits, patterns, genres? Theorists point out (and, again, you know this from your own everyday experiences) that doing something in pretty much the same way saves us time and energy. As Berger and Luckmann put it:

> Habitualization carries with it the important psychological gain that choices are narrowed. While in theory there may be a hundred ways to go about the project of building a canoe out of matchsticks, habitualization narrows these down to one. This frees the individual from the burden of 'all those decisions', providing a pyschological relief. (Berger and Luckmann 1966: 71)

In other words, eating the same things for breakfast day after day saves us from the psychological effort of having to make decisions so early in the morning, and the physical effort of having to spend more time at the supermarket.

On the subject of language genres, Bakhtin goes even further. He claims not just that genres are 'economic' but that they are essential:

> If speech genres did not exist and we had not mastered them, if we had to originate them during the speech process and construct each utterance at will for the first time, speech communication would be almost impossible. (Bakhtin 1994: 84)

In other words, if members of a culture did not jointly construct and maintain genres, meaningful interpersonal communication would be very difficult, if not impossible. Just imagine if every time you went to the café to buy your take-away latté you had to come up with a novel way of interacting with the person behind the cappuccino machine.

But what exactly do we habitualize when developing genres? As Martin and Rose suggest, the impetus for genres lies in the recurrence of the situations in which we use language:

> As children, we learn to recognize and distinguish the typical genres of our culture, by attending to consistent patterns of meaning as we interact with others in various situations. Since patterns of meaning are relatively consistent for each genre, we can

learn to predict how each situation is likely to unfold, and learn how to interact in it. (Martin and Rose 2003: 7)

In other words, as situations, or contexts, recur, so we develop recurrent ways of using language. But this begs two questions:

1. What aspects of situations need to recur for two situations to be felt by interactants to be 'similar enough' to call for the habitualized genre?
2. In what aspects of our language use do we see the 'relatively consistent' patterns of meaning in recurrent situations?

These two questions are what systemic linguistics deals with in its theory of register. As you will see in Chapter Four, register theory identifies three main dimensions of situations or context: field, tenor and mode. A genre comes about as particular values for field, tenor and mode regularly co-occur and eventually become stabilized in the culture as 'typical' situations. For example, the transactional genre of buying your coffee from the corner café involves the field of 'coffee', the tenor of 'customer/provider' and the mode of 'face-to-face'. Each of these situational dimensions can be related predictably to certain patterns in language: we see the field in the use of lexical items to do with requesting coffee (*latté, take away, no sugar*), the tenor in the request/compliance sequences of turns (*'Can I please have...', 'Right away'*), and the mode in the use of language markers of co-presence (*'Here you go'*).

Similarly, most horoscope texts bring together a field of 'predicting romantic, material, and career events'; a tenor of advice and warning; and a mode of direct address from writer to (generic) reader. We see these situational values realized in the predictable language choices of horoscope texts: nouns about love, marriage, physical appearance and acquisition of wealth and attitudinally loaded adjectives; the writer's use of imperatives (*avoid all men with blue eyes ...*); and the use of spoken language features (the pronoun *you*, elliptical structures) combined with written language techniques of nominalization.

We will return to these register implications for genre in Chapter Four, but for now the point to note is that genres develop as ways of dealing linguistically with recurrent configurations of register variables. In other words, as certain contextual combinations become stable, ways of interacting within those contexts also become habitualized and, eventually, institutionalized as genres. There come to be preferred, typical ways of negotiating such contexts.

We'll turn now to the most overt expression of genres: their tendency to develop into staged or structured linguistic events.

Schematic structure

Bakhtin suggested that we recognize speech genres because they have predictable 'compositional structure'. As he says: 'from the very beginning we have a sense of the speech whole'. Another way of saying this is that genres develop linguistic expression through a limited number of functional stages, occurring in a particular sequence. Horoscope texts, for example, typically involve the following stages, occurring in the following order:

General Outlook: a stage in which the astrologer makes a general statement about the period covered by the horoscope (e.g. *it's going to be a rosy month for you*)

Uncontingent Predictions: a stage in which general predictions are made about your immediate future (*you'll meet and marry a tall man*)

Contingent Predictions: a stage in which different advice is offered according to the salient category membership of readers (*if single, x will happen; if married, y*)

Advice: a stage in which the astrologer offers advice and warnings (*invest wisely*, etc.)

For example, here are these stages in Text 3.1:

General Outlook

(1)You are on the threshold of a magnificent chapter in your private life, with substantial opportunities emerging after the new moon on the 5th.

Uncontingent Predictions

(2i)A man who is resourceful, good looking or born around November could be very helpful with your quest for a promotion, (2ii)and you could be celebrating a minor victory on the 9th, 24th or 28th. (3i)A trip, reunion or important talk that you could not fit in last month will be more straightforward or enjoyable (3ii)if you wait until November.

Contingent Predictions

(4i)If single, (4ii)you may start dating a charming man whom you met briefly a few weeks ago. (5i)Others may be startled by your apologetic actions (5ii)as you seek a reconciliation.

Advice

(6i)Long-range ventures or people you have not met before should be avoided between the 12th and 17th, (6ii)especially if your birthday is after the 12th. (7)The pieces of a puzzle will fall into place in the last 10 days of the month or by early November.

As we habitualize our joint negotiation of communicative tasks, we establish a series of steps or stages. These stages are called the **schematic structure** of a genre. The term **schematic structure** simply refers to the staged, step-by-step organization of the genre, or, in Martin's terms:

> Schematic structure represents the positive contribution genre makes to a text: a way of getting from A to B in the way a given culture accomplishes whatever the genre in question is functioning to do in that culture. (Martin 1985b: 251)

Martin points out that the reason that genres have stages is simply that we usually cannot make all the meanings we want to at once. Each stage in the genre contributes a part of the overall meanings that must be made for the genre to be accomplished successfully.

Often as native speakers we only need to hear one stage to recognize the genre that it comes from. For example, when we hear *Once upon a time* we know that we are about to hear narrative of mythical events; when we hear *Can I help you?* we expect a transactional genre; *A funny thing happened to me on the way to the office* has us expecting a narrative of personal experience; and *Have you heard the one about the two elephants?* tunes us in for a joke.

Describing the schematic structure of genres brings us to two fundamental concepts in linguistic analysis: **constituency** and **labelling**. We will encounter both concepts again when we begin describing the lexico-grammatical organization of language, but they are also important for understanding how genres are structured.

Constituency

As the name suggests, constituency simply means that things are made up of, or built out of, other things. For example, a house is made up of bricks and mortar, a book is made up of a number of chapters, etc.

Most things are in fact made up of layers of constituents. For example, a book is made up of a number of chapters, and each chapter is made up of a number of paragraphs, and each paragraph is made up of a number of sentences, and each sentence is made up of a number of words, etc.

In the same way, a genre is made up of constituent stages – the steps discussed above. When we describe the schematic structure of a genre, what we are describing is its constituent structure – the structure by which the whole, complete interaction is made up of parts. In the most general terms, the constituent stages of a genre are a **Beginning**, a **Middle** and an **End**.

The aim of our description is both to identify the parts that constitute the whole, and, preferably at the same time, explain how the parts relate to each other in constituting that whole. This can be achieved by using **functional labelling** in our generic description.

Functional labelling

Once we begin thinking about dividing a text into its constituents we must consider on what basis we will establish that two parts of a text constitute separate stages. There are essentially two kinds of criteria we could use:

1. **Formal** criteria: we could divide the text into stages/parts according to the **form** of the different constituents. This approach emphasizes sameness, as we divide the text so that each unit/stage is a constituent of the same type.
2. **Functional** criteria: we could divide the genre into stages/parts according to the **function** of the different constituents. This approach emphasizes difference, as we divide the text according to the different functions of each stage.

Table 3.1 summarizes these differences in labelling.

If we took a formal approach to constituent analysis of genres, we could divide up the horoscope text into paragraphs, then each paragraph into sentences, each sentence into words and so on.

While this approach certainly tells us something about the class of linguistic items that occur within genres, it does not help us answer the sort of functionally-oriented question we are concerned with: how does each stage in the genre contribute towards achieving the overall purpose of the text?

For this reason we take the second approach to generic analysis and divide the text into functional constituents. That is, we recognize as stages only those sentences or groups of

Table 3.1 Formal vs functional criteria

FORMAL CRITERIA	FUNCTIONAL CRITERIA
asks: how does each constituent relate formally to the whole? i.e. what 'class' of item is it?	asks: how does each constituent relate functionally to the whole? i.e. what functional role is it playing?

sentences which fulfil a function relative to the whole. We therefore only call something a stage if we can assign to it a functional label.

In assigning labels, the aim is to describe what the stage is doing, relative to the whole, in terms as specific to the genre as can be found. 'Empty' functional labels such as Beginning, Middle, End, or Introduction, Body, Conclusion, should be avoided since they are not genre-specific (all genres have Beginnings, Middles and Ends). Instead, to find labels, ask, for example: 'what exactly is being done in this beginning of the text?' or 'what is being done in the body of an essay that is different from what is done in the body of a transactional genre?', etc.

As we have worked so far with written text, let us demonstrate schematic structure analysis on a spoken, interactive text. Text 3.2 below is a transactional or service encounter genre. In this interaction, our customer walks into the post office with the purpose of carrying out a transaction. In our culture, this particular register configuration regularly recurs, and it has become habitualized into a genre which most adult native speakers control quite effortlessly. Both our postal worker and our client have a sense (quite unconsciously, most of the time) of the script they need to follow to achieve the transaction successfully.

Both know that to accomplish this transaction it is necessary to go through a number of steps or stages. The customer cannot simply barge into the post office, throw her letters at the postal worker and rush out. Nor can the postal worker simply see the customer enter, grab her letters and disappear out the back into the nether regions of the post office. Habitualization of interactions like this has led to social conventions about which stages the interactants must jointly negotiate their way through in order to complete the transaction successfully.

Ventola (1987) identifies the following stages (the schematic structure labels are written with initial capitals):[2]

Text 3.2: Post Office Transaction[3]

Sales Initiation
   1 Salesperson   yes please
(Customer steps forward)
Sales Request
   2 Customer   can I have these two like that
(Customer hands over two letters)
Sales Compliance
   3 Salesperson   yes
Price
(3 secs – Salesperson weighs one letter)
   4 Salesperson   one's forty
(3 secs – Salesperson weighs the other letter)
   5 Salesperson   one's twenty-five

Sales Request

6	Customer	and have you got . . . the . . . first day covers of . . .
7	Salesperson	yes
8	Customer	(Anzac[4])

(2 secs – Salesperson looks for the stamps)

Sales Clarification

9	Salesperson	how many would you like?
10	Customer	four please
11	Salesperson	two of each?
12	Customer	what have you got
13	Salesperson	uh there's two different designs on the –

(5 secs – Salesperson shows Customer the stamps)

Purchase

14	Customer	I'll take two of each
15	Salesperson	Uhum

(6 secs – Salesperson gets the stamps for the letters and the covers)

Price

16	Salesperson	right . . . that's a dollar seventy thank you

(10 secs – Salesperson puts the covers into a bag; Customer gets out the money)

Payment

17	Salesperson	here we are

(2 secs – Salesperson hands over the stamps and the covers; Customer hands the money to Salesperson)

18	Customer	thank you
19	Salesperson	thank you

(5 secs – Salesperson gets the change)

Change

20	Salesperson	dollar seventy that's two four and one's five
21		thank you very much

Purchase Closure

22	Customer	thank you

(2 secs – Customer reaches for the letters)

23	Salesperson	they'll be right I'll fix those up in a moment
24	Customer	okay

(Customer leaves)

A more compact description of the generic structure of this text can be achieved by writing the stages out in a linear sequence, with the symbol ^ between stages to indicate that stages are **ordered** with respect to each other. Thus, a linear description of the schematic structure of the post office text becomes:

> Sales Initiation^ Sales Request^ Sales Compliance^ Price^ Sales Request^ Sales Clarification^ Purchase^ Price^ Payment^ Change^ Purchase Closure

This statement of schematic structure is a description of the schematic structure of the specific post office text reproduced in this chapter: i.e. it is the generic structure of an **actual** text. But you probably take part in transactions very similar to Text 3.2 on a regular basis, not all of them in a post office, not all of them even face-to-face. For example, Text 3.3 is a phone transaction. Notice how closely the stages of schematic structure from the post office interaction match the stages of this service transaction:

Text 3.3: Service Transaction over the Phone[5]

Sales Initiation

| 1 | Salesperson | Good morning. Sydney Opera House Box Office. How may I help you? |

Sales Request

| 2 | Customer | Oh, hallo. Um, I'd like to book three tickets to the Bell Shakespeare's *Hamlet*, please |

Sales Compliance

| 3 | Salesperson | Bell Shakespeare, yes, that's in the Drama Theatre |

Sales Clarification

4		Now what date did you want those for?
5	Customer (checking availability)	Saturday the 16th. In the evening
6	Salesperson	Saturday the 16th . . . Yes, I can give you three seats in row 'F' for the evening performance at 8pm. Fifty-six dollars per seat
7	Customer	Great, thanks

Purchase

| 8 | Salesperson | So you'll take those? Three seats for *Hamlet* at 8pm in the Drama Theatre |
| 9 | Customer | Yes, please |

Price

10	Salesperson	Is that three adults, or any concessions?
11	Customer	No, three adults please
12	Salesperson	That'll be three times fifty-six plus the booking fee, that's one hundred and seventy one dollars. Is that alright?
13	Customer	Whew, pretty pricey, but OK, yeah

Payment

14	Salesperson	Could I have your credit card details please?
15	Customer	Yes, it's a Mastercard. Number 3852 9483 1029 0323
16	Salesperson	That's Mastercard 3852 9483 1029 0323?
17	Customer	Yes
18	Salesperson	And the expiry date?
19	Customer	09 04
20	Salesperson	Cardholder's name?
21	Customer	Emily Rimmer. R – I – M – M – E – R

Purchase Delivery

22	Salesperson	And would you like us to post those tickets to you? Or will you pick them up from the Box Office?
23	Customer	No, post them please
24	Salesperson	The address?
25	Customer	25 Jellico J–E–double L – I – C – O Street, Mirameer Heights

| 26 | Salesperson | That's 25 Jellico Street, Mirameer Heights? |
| 27 | Customer | Yes |

Purchase Closure

28	Salesperson	Right, the tickets will be in the mail today. Is there anything else we can help you with?
29	Customer	Umm, no that's all, thanks
30	Salesperson	Thank you. Goodbye
31	Customer	'Bye

The similarity of structure between the post office and the box office transactions suggests that there are some elements of schematic structure that are somehow defining of the transactional genre, some elements which are keys to recognizing what a transaction is. To discover which elements of the schematic structure are the **defining** or **obligatory elements**, we can ask: what stages could we leave out and yet still have a transactional text?

We can use a variety of symbols to move from a description of schematic structure in a specific text to a general statement of schematic structure for a particular genre. By placing parentheses around a schematic structure stage ( ), we can indicate that a particular element is optional. The symbols < > placed round a stage indicate that a particular stage is recursive (can occur more than once); unordered stages can be indicated by being preceded by an asterisk *; and parentheses { } can be used to enclose a sequence of stages which are recursive as a whole. In summary, our schematic structure symbols are listed in Table 3.2. Using these symbols, we can refine our schematic structure description to give the more general description of transactional genres as:

> (Sales Initiation)^ < {Sales Request^ Sales Compliance^ (Sales Clarification)^ Purchase^ (Price)}>^ Payment^ (Change)^ (Purchase Delivery)^ Purchase Closure

This should be read as stating that a minimal transactional interaction could consist of only the stages of Sales Request, Sales Compliance, Purchase, Payment and Purchase Closure. Thus, imagine a situation in which you do not wait for the assistant to offer service, but initiate the interaction yourself, where you do not need to be told the price (as perhaps it is clearly displayed for you), where you skip the niceties of thank-yous, and where you do not require change. You would still have achieved a transaction, although the text you produce would look somewhat different from the post office or box office examples analysed above.

The formula also captures the fact that more than one Sales Request may occur within a transaction, and that each Sales Request will be resolved through the stages of Purchase and Price, while there will be only one Sales Initiation, Payment and Purchase Closure per transaction.

Table 3.2 Symbols used to describe schematic structure

SYMBOLS	MEANING
X ^ Y	stage X precedes stage Y (fixed order)
* Y	stage Y is an unordered stage
(X)	stage X is an optional stage
<X>	stage X is a recursive stage
<{X^Y}>	stages X and Y are both recursive in the fixed order X then Y

We use the distinction between obligatory and optional schematic structure elements to help us define what constitutes a particular genre. A genre is thus defined in terms of its obligatory elements of schematic structure, and variants of a genre are those texts in which the obligatory schematic structure elements are realized, as well as perhaps some of the optional ones. While any interaction realizing the obligatory elements only is therefore what we describe as a Transactional text, the inclusion of optional elements gives more extended variations of the genre.

We can therefore recognize the difference between what Hasan (1985a: 63–4) refers to as the **generic structure potential** of a particular genre, and the **actual generic structure** of a particular text.

As our description of schematic structure has indicated, the order of elements of schematic structure is a significant constraint. In many genres, such as the transactional one, most elements are fixed in their order of occurrence. For example, the stage of Payment can only come <u>after</u> the stage of Sales Compliance; and of course the stage of Change can only occur <u>after</u> Payment. As was suggested in Chapter Two, the linearity of linguistic interactions means order often carries dimensions of meaning.

Realization of elements of schematic structure

Although identifying the schematic structure of a genre is a major part of generic analysis, it cannot be performed accurately without an analysis of the **realizations** of each element of schematic structure. You will remember from Chapter One that realization refers to the way a meaning becomes **encoded** or expressed in a semiotic system. We need now to relate our elements of schematic structure to language.

Taking the step of relating stages of schematic structure to their linguistic realizations is the central analytic procedure in generic analysis. The analysis of the schematic structure of both our horoscope text (Text 3.1) and the post office text (Text 3.2) above might seem to you largely an intuitive and personal one. Perhaps you would argue for different stages, or different boundaries between the stages. If our generic analysis is to have any validity, it must be possible for us to establish objective justification for claims that, for example, horoscope texts may have stages of Uncontingent and Contingent Predictions; or that Sales Compliance is a different element of schematic structure from Sales Clarification, or that the stage Purchase begins and ends where it does.

It is obvious that all we have to go on in analysing genre is **language** – the words and structures speakers use. Technically, we can see that it is through language that genres get realized. It is through the discourse-semantic, lexico-grammatical and phonological patterns of the language code that the contextual level of genre is realized through, or expressed in, language.

For example, in our horoscope text, we only 'see' the field of 'romantic predictions' through the recurrent patterns of ideational meanings in the text: the choices of related lexical items to do with heterosexual relationship (*man, dating, private life*) and expressions of time (dates, months). We only see the tenor of advice and warnings through the recurrent patterns of interpersonal meanings: the use of modality and modulation (*could be, may, should be*). And the mode is only visible through the textual meanings: the patterns of direct address to the reader (the pronoun *you*).

The systematic hook-up we're suggesting here between dimensions of the context and types of meaning in language is fundamental to the functional approach to language. By suggesting that each dimension of social context is related in predictable and systematic ways to each type of meaning, functional analysis claims to show that language is 'naturally' related to the structure of social life.

There are two clear consequences of this. Firstly, if genres are different ways of using language, then we should find that the speakers make different lexico-grammatical choices according to the different purposes they want to achieve. That is, texts of different genres will reveal different lexico-grammatical choices – different words and structures. For example, the types of words and structures used in a transactional genre will not be the same as those used in an exchanging opinion genre, or in a narrative genre, or in a horoscope. Thus, *realization patterns will differ across genres*.

Secondly, if each genre is made up of a number of different functionally related stages, then we should find that different elements of schematic structure will reveal different lexico-grammatical choices. For example, we should find that the types of words and structures used in the stage Sales Initiation will not be the same as the types of words and structures used in the stage Purchase, and the language of both those stages will differ from the language of the stage Thanks. Thus, *realization patterns will differ across schematic stages*.

However, since we have only one language to use to realize all these different stages, it cannot be a question of stages using totally different words, or totally different structures, from each other. Rather, we would expect to find that different stages use different configurations of words and structures, different clusterings of patterns. Realization patterns can be exemplified by referring to a simple written genre: the recipe.

Schematic structure and realizations in the recipe genre

So far in our discussion of genre we have worked from the text to description. To demonstrate that genres (their schematic structure and their realizations) are something that as native speakers we unconsciously draw on in using language, we can now reverse the procedure. Instead of describing a text, we can <u>predict</u> schematic structure and realizations, and then compare those predictions against authentic examples.

You will remember that in Chapter One I expressed great confidence in your ability to produce an appropriate example of a recipe text for scrambled eggs. Part of that task involved your ability to predict the elements of schematic structure, in their likely order. Before you read any further, you might make a quick note of the schematic structure you would predict in a recipe for your favourite dish.

Here now is an authentic recipe text. Is your schematic structure appropriate to describe this text?

Text 3.4: Spinach Risotto[6]

This traditional dish of Greek-Cypriot origin offers an economical but substantial vegetarian meal.

3 tablespoons olive oil

2 onions, chopped

1–2 bunches silverbeet or English spinach

1 375 gr tin peeled tomatoes

2 tablespoons tomato paste

1 cup water

1 cup risotto rice

white wine (optional)

salt and pepper

Slice the dead ends off the spinach. Slice stalks off from leaves. Wash stalks and leaves. Slice stalks finely, and shred leaves.

In a large saucepan, heat the oil. Fry the onions till soft. Add the stalks and fry till soft. Add the shredded leaves and cook for several minutes. Then add the tomatoes and tomato paste. Turn low and cook for about 10 mins. Add water, wine, salt and pepper, and the rice. Cook until the rice has absorbed the liquid (10–15 mins).

Serve with Greek salad and crusty wholemeal bread.

Serves 4.

If we follow through the functional approach developed in this chapter, we would see that to describe this text we need to recognize the following stages:

Title: Spinach Risotto

This stage labels the name of the dish to be prepared. The stage obviously functions to differentiate individual recipes from each other.

Enticement: This traditional dish of Greek-Cypriot origin offers an economical but substantial vegetarian meal.

The purpose of this stage is to suggest why you should bother making this dish.

Ingredients:

3 tablespoons olive oil

2 onions, chopped

1–2 bunches silverbeet or English spinach

1 375 gr tin peeled tomatoes

2 tablespoons tomato paste

1 cup water

1 cup risotto rice

white wine (optional)

salt and pepper

This stage functions to tell you what you will need.

Method:

Slice the dead ends off the spinach. Slice stalks off from leaves. Wash stalks and leaves. Slice stalks finely, and shred leaves.

In a large saucepan, heat the oil. Fry the onions till soft. Add the stalks and fry till soft. Add the shredded leaves and cook for several minutes. Then add the tomatoes and tomato paste. Turn low and cook for about 10 mins. Add water, wine, salt and pepper, and the rice. Cook until the rice has absorbed the liquid (10–15 mins). Serve with Greek salad and crusty wholemeal bread.

This purpose of this stage is to tell you how to make the dish.

Serving Quantity: Serves 4.

This final stage functions to inform you how many the dish will feed.

Expressed linearly, the schematic structure of this text is:

Title^Enticement^Ingredients^Method^Serving Quantity

Now, the schematic structure you have established for this text might differ from the one I have offered. In particular, you might wish to include an additional stage to describe the sentence *Serve with Greek salad and crusty wholemeal bread*. After all, that sentence is presented as a separate paragraph in the original text, so it might seem that it should have a separate functional label – Serving Suggestions, perhaps?

To resolve the question of how many stages, we need to consider the lexico-grammatical patterns realized in each stage of the recipe. In other words, we need to look closely at the language of the recipe text.

We are somewhat hampered here by the fact that we do not yet share a common technical vocabulary for talking about lexico-grammatical patterns (we will by the end of this book). Using only some fairly common grammatical terms, we can see that each of the stages of the recipe genre can be associated with clearly distinct realizational patterns.

Title: this stage is realized by what we call a nominal group or noun phrase (a group of words where the main word is a noun), not by a complete clause or sentence. The type of nominal group typically contains a sequence of nouns (two in this case), rather than adjective and noun (e.g. the title is not Simple Risotto).

Enticement: unlike the Title stage, this stage is realized by a complete sentence. It begins with a 'be' clause, where *this dish* is described using positive attitudinal words *traditional, economical, substantial* (imagine how unenticing it would be to begin this stage with a clause like: *This revolting dish will take hours to cook.*).

Ingredients: here we return to only a nominal group as the pattern, but this time the nominal group does not have a sequence of classifying words, but of numbers and measuring words, e.g. *2, 375 gr, tin*. The head noun being modified by these measuring terms is of course the name of a food.

Method: this stage is expressed by clauses (not just phrases or groups), in the imperative mood (i.e. expressed as orders, rather than as statements). Circumstantial meanings of location (*in a large saucepan*), time (*for about 10 mins*), and manner (*till soft*) are expressed. The clauses are linked logically by time sequence (*Then . . . then*), although this is not always explicitly encoded (*then* only occurs once). The kinds of verbs are action-oriented: *slice, wash, heat, fry, cook*, etc.

Serving Quantity: this stage is realized by an elliptical declarative: i.e. a part of a clause. The full clause would be *This dish serves 4*. The clause is a declarative (statement), not an imperative: it gives information, but does not command us to do anything.

And it is this last realizational pattern that helps us to determine the schematic structure location of the sentence *Serve with Greek salad and crusty wholemeal bread*. Grammatically we see that the pattern of this sentence involves an imperative structure (a command), involving a verb of action (*serve*), and including circumstantial information about the manner in which the process should be carried out (*with Greek salad*, etc.). This pattern is the same as the other sentences of the Method stage. Therefore, on grammatical criteria we would consider that clause part of the Method stage, not a separate stage on its own, nor part of the Serving Quantity stage, where the pattern is for a different clause type altogether[7].

Although you may not understand all the terms used in the realization statements, you will be able to see that each stage of schematic structure is clearly associated with a number of grammatical and lexical features. By specifying in as much detail as possible the grammatical patterns of each part of the text, we can determine both how many stages we need to recognize and where to place the boundaries between the stages.

The same link between stages and realization applies to any text we care to analyse, whether spoken or written. With our horoscope text, we can clearly see that the language of the General Outlook stage is very different from the language of the Contingent Predictions stage: the first involves a relational process (the verb 'to be') with 'you' as Subject and general, abstract nouns, expressing your overall situation or quality, while the second involves conditional clauses (if . . ., then . . .), specific time references and process types, and modulation. Likewise, with the post office text, grammatical description would show that the patterns in the Sales Request stage (modulated interrogative clauses, i.e. questions using *could/can*) are different from patterns in the Sales Clarification stage (unmodulated interrogatives).

From the texts presented above we can note that there are different types of realization patterns. Some stages have ritualistic or conventional realizations. For example, the expressions which realize Thanks or Greeting stages are fairly limited and predictable. Other stages are realized by a limited range of linguistic structures. For example, the realization of a Service Request stage in a transactional genre can be through various (but limited) alternative structures: e.g. modulated declaratives (*I'd like 5 apples please*), imperatives (*Give me 5 of those apples, please*) or modulated interrogatives (*Would you have 5 of those apples, please?*).

Yet other stages are realized by the clustering of particular linguistic choices, rather than the simple choice of just one linguistic feature. One example is the Method stage of the recipe genre whose patterns were described above; a further example would be the Event or Action stage of a narrative, which is typically realized by the combination of temporal successive conjunctions (*then . . . then . . .*), action processes (e.g. verbs like *went, ran, caught, did, happened,* etc.), specific (usually human) participants and circumstances of time, manner, place (often in first position in the clause).

Finally, it is possible for some stages to be realized non-verbally. For example, the Payment stage of a transactional genre is very frequently realized non-verbally.

At the moment our discussion of the lexico-grammatical realizations of generic stages is very limited because we lack a common **metalanguage**, i.e. we do not share a common technical vocabulary, based on a shared approach to analysing language, through which we could specify realization statements in detail. The aim of Chapters Four to Ten is to equip you with that metalanguage, so that you are then able to complete the description of whatever genres interest you by specifying the grammatical and discourse-semantic patterns by which different genres, and different stages within genres, are realized.

At this stage the important point to grasp is that that schematic structure analysis is neither intuitive nor *ad hoc*. Every time we recognize an element of structure we have to be able to argue for it, and its boundaries, by finding its reflex in linguistic realization. Chapter Eleven will demonstrate generic analysis applied to the three Crying Baby texts introduced in Chapter One.

Short and long genres: the macro-genre

For reasons of space, the principles and procedures of genre analysis have been presented in this chapter using brief, everyday texts as examples. Generic analysis is of course equally applicable to much longer texts, both spoken and written. In these longer, more complex texts, Martin (1992b) suggests we may need to identify the entire text as an example of a **macro-genre**, within which it is possible to identify a range of other genres being used. For example, a university department's handbook is itself a macro-genre (the text as a whole fulfils a specific cultural function), but it typically contains sections exemplifying the genres of exposition (why you should study in particular faculties and disciplines), description (course outlines) and regulation (the student's rights/responsibilities/penalties). Martin uses Halliday's grammatical categories of logico-semantic relations (first encountered in our Chapter Two discussion of conjunctive cohesion, and revisited in Chapter Nine) to capture the relationship between the constituent genres in a macro-genre. For an example of macro-genre analysis, see the treatment of several very lengthy texts in Martin and Rose (2003).

The uses of genre analysis

Genre analysis is just a first step towards making explicit the cultural and social basis of language in use, but it can be a very powerful step. A systemic analysis of genre has three immediate applications. Genre analysis can help us:

1. to make explicit why some texts are successful and appropriate while others are not;
2. to contrast types of genres and their realizations in pragmatic contexts and interpersonal contexts;
3. to understand similarities and differences between non-fiction and fiction genres;
4. to carry out critical text analysis.

Space only allows a brief demonstration of these applications here. Those with more time will find Martin and Rose (2003) a useful – if demanding – extension.

Successful and unsuccessful examples of genres

One of the most useful applications of genre analysis for those of us who work in educational settings is that it can help us make explicit why some texts 'work' and others don't. Have another look at Text 2.5, 'Fatal Alaska', first presented in Chapter Two, page 40. We noted in Chapter Two that this story by a 12-year-old boy has serious cohesive problems. In particular, referential ties are ambiguous, with the writer presuming what should be presented. But the problems of cohesion are symptomatic of more general problems he's having achieving an appropriate realization of the genre of narrative.

   The sociolinguists Labov and Waletzky (1967) offer a functional analysis of the schematic structure of narratives. I'm using **narrative** in a technical sense here, to refer to a particular genre. Not all stories are narratives – see Eggins and Slade (1997) for discussion and exemplification of other story genres which occur in casual conversation and in written texts. Narratives can be defined as 'stories which are concerned with protagonists who face and resolve problematic experiences' (Eggins and Slade 1997: 239). Using the formalism identified earlier, the schematic structure of the narrative genre can be represented as:

(Abstract) ^ Orientation ^ <{Complication ^ Resolution ^ Evaluation}> ^ (Coda)

Abstract: this stage, if present, functions as a signal to prepare readers for the text that follows, often by orienting them to the kind of story that will be told or to the story's themes. For example, *Once upon a time* is a generic realization for folktale narratives.

Orientation: this stage provides readers with the information they need to understand the narrative and usually gives at least preliminary information about the participants in the story (who), the setting in space (where) and time (when), and the actions that were under way before things got sticky (what). This stage is typically realized by presenting reference and expressions of habitual actions.

Complication: this stage involves a problem culminating in a crisis. The events initiated in the Orientation somehow go wrong. There is a disruption to the usual sequence of events, and subsequent actions become problematic and unpredictable. This stage is typically realized by a shift from conjunction relations of temporal sequence (*and then . . . and then . . .*) to relations of concessive counter-expectancy and simultaneity (*but, all of a sudden . . .*).

Evaluation: Labov and Waletzky (1967) argue that the Evaluation stage is what gives the text its significance; it establishes the point of the narrative. As it occurs between the Complication and the Resolution, it creates a feeling of suspense and marks a break between these two action stages. Labov argues that this stage is obligatory as without it a narrative is incomplete:

> Evaluation devices say to us: this was terrifying, dangerous, weird, wild, crazy; or amusing, hilarious, wonderful; more generally, that it was strange, uncommon, or unusual – that is, worth reporting. It was not ordinary, plain, humdrum, everyday or run of the mill. (Labov 1972a: 371)

The shift from action to evaluation is realized by a shift from ideational into interpersonal meanings, expressed through some of the following patterns:

1. the expression of attitudes or opinions denoting the events as remarkable or unusual;
2. the expression of incredulity, disbelief, apprehension about the events on the part of the narrator or a character of the narrative, including highlighting the predicament of characters;
3. comparisons between usual and unusual sequences of events in which participants in the narrative are involved;
4. predictions about a possible course of action to handle a crisis or about the outcome of the events. (Rothery 1990: 203)

Although evaluative comments are often spread throughout a narrative (often 'embedded', Labov says, in other stages), a successful narrative will always also have a discrete Evaluation stage. The progress of the action will be interrupted while the narrator or characters explicitly offer an assessment of the emotional point of the story. (See Eggins and Slade 1997: 241–2 for further examples of Evaluations.)

Resolution: in this stage we are told how the protagonist manages to resolve the crisis. Through the Resolution, usuality returns and equilibrium is restored. Realizations include causal conjunctive relations (*so*) introducing the redemptive action, followed by a return to temporal sequential relations.

In extended narratives, there may be a sequence of {Complication^ Evaluation^ Resolution} sequences, in which case convention suggests that each Complication should be more dramatic than the one before. To build suspense, each Resolution will then also grow in difficulty, lack of predictability, and usually length.

Coda: this stage often refers back to the theme of the Abstract and makes an overall statement about the text. In conversational narratives, the Coda signals to listeners that the speaker no longer needs to hold the floor – her story is told. In written narratives, the Coda often creates a sense of finality by its circular return to the starting point of the narrative. This stage is often signalled by a shift in tense (from the simple past of the narrative events back to the present of the narration, for example), or by a shift from statements about specific participants, events and setting to generalizations about 'experiences like that'.

Applied to 'Fatal Alaska', this schematic structure allows us to identify several problems:

1. the sequencing of the stages is unhelpful: instead of beginning with an optional Abstract followed by the Orientation stage, David plonks us right into what is presumably one of several Complications. The Orientation seems to begin in paragraph 2, although paragraph 3 contains the most basic information and so should logically come first of all;
2. the successive Complications do not build gradually enough in intensity – we've already had one death in the first sentence – and so there is too little suspense created;
3. the writer ends his story with TO BE CONTINUED, instead of with a culminating Resolution and perhaps a Coda. While David is borrowing a device appropriate in other genres (e.g. TV or book series), this non-ending is really a cop-out in this case. He knows his story *can't* be continued, and it seems likely that he has simply 'lost the plot' and run short of time. Planning the stages of his narrative first could have avoided this problem.

Despite these problems, David's story has the skeleton structure for a well-formed narrative. Below I re-present his text with the stages reordered, and a suggested final Resolution. My contributions are shown in *italics*.

Text 3.5: Fatal Alaska[8]
reordered, with schematic structure labelled

(Abstract)
I've been in a lot of tricky situations, but I've never been as close to death as I was up north once.

Orientation
My name is Samual Jacobson, I am a 17 year old Canadian piolot who was assigned to this mission. My journey to Alaska consisted of two reason, finding the two men who set off from Canada to study penguins and to give the two Canadian mountys some experience in Alaska.

At first I was proud to do it, then nervous and now I'm terrified. The snow storm last week is said to have covered their plane in ice and snow. I am told they were proffsianals.

Complication 1
I watched as my companion was attacked by the polar bear. Then he fell to the ground and didn't move. I knew he was dead. My other companion was still in the plane, looking like it was he who had been attacked.

Evaluation 1

I tried to ignore the body but two hours later could stand it no longer.

Resolution 1

I made a whole in the ice and left it for whatever actic creature was hungry.

Complication 2

I had to get my live companion to refrain from losing his mind.

Evaluation 2

I could not afford to lose another friend or I might lose my own mind.

Resolution 2

It took a great deal of shaking to bring my friend to his senses, then I urged him to get moving, which he reluctantly did. We moved for several hours getting colder by the minute, and less confident.

Complication 3

Just when I feared we would have to turn back, I saw a light, that looked like a fire. I don't think my partner saw it so I steered him towards it. We saw then what it was, a fire, recently lit, in the middle of a cave.

We ventured into the cave and saw nothing inside but a rack with bones and body parts in it, a billy with meat in it and blood! Then a shadowy figure loomed at the entrance of the cave.

I stared at my partner, who once again had not noticed the happenings around him.

Evaluation 3

I froze, I know its stupid but as the figure advanced, I just froze. My heart was a straight six motor for that ten or so seconds, and it was revving its guts out.

Resolution 3

Then, when the figure stepped into the flickering light of the fire I felt relief, as I recognized him from the photo of the explorers as Captain John, the leader of the expidition, and the brains. I knew the bones and body parts and meat were not animal, they were his crew! Just then he pulled a hatchet from his coat and ran at me. That confirmed to me that he had canaballised on his men. I ducked sending him over my back and into the fire, he set alight. I watched as he frantically jumped up, ran outside and rolled in the snow, all the time holding his hatchet.

Complication 4

He got up, furious and I knew he wouldn't miss again . . .

Within seconds, he was running at me again, swiping at me with his lethal hatchet.

Evaluation 4

This time, I knew it was him or me! And I hadn't come all this way to be eaten.

Resolution 4

So I dodged around the cave, just out of reach of the crazy Captain, till I got close to a clump of loose rocks. Ducking down, I managed to pick up two really sharp, pointed ones. But it was a close thing – as I jumped away, his hatchet scratched down my arm, drawing blood.

I ducked back and took aim. I had only two chances, and he was moving all the time. I threw the first rock – it hit him on the shoulder, and slowed him for a second, but he recovered and came at me again.

I aimed the second rock carefully. This time I waited until he was really close. I knew if I missed, I'd be dead meat. When I could feel his smelly cannibal breath, I threw.

Crunch. Thump. He fell down, knocked out cold. My companion and I quickly tied him up and radioed out for help.

Coda

That was a really close call. And since then I've never eaten a mouthful of meat!

Explicit modelling of the target genre, with scaffolding of the generic structure and realizations, could help young writers like David produce much more successful texts. With better control of the genre, they give themselves the opportunity to then take the next step of playing creatively with its conventions. As literary biographies and autobiographies show, the writers we most admire began by mastering conventional realizations of genres. Only once they fully grasped the possibilities and constraints of a genre did they move on to defamiliarize and interrogate genre conventions.

SFL has been influential in promoting genre-based approaches to literacy. Christie and Martin (1997) and several chapters in Unsworth (2000) provide overviews of this work.

Genre in pragmatic and interpersonal contexts

For reasons of space and clarity in this chapter I have had to choose examples from a limited range of genres. But the spectrum of genres is of course vast indeed. Wherever language is being used to achieve a culturally recognized and culturally established purpose, there we will find genre. One application of genre analysis is to explore the ways genres from different contexts are similar to and different from each other.

Once we start looking at genre in spoken interactions, we find that not all interactions have the simple staged schematic structure of such texts as the post office or the box office. For example, in sustained casual conversation among a group of friends or workmates, although there may be moments with recognizable generic structure (when someone is telling a story, for example), there may be long segments of talk that do not seem to have a clear generic structure at all. This is not because the talk is unstructured, but rather that such talk is structured in a different way because it has different motivations.

We can in fact distinguish between two kinds of functional motivations for linguistic interactions: pragmatic motivation and interpersonal motivation. Pragmatically motivated interactions are those like the post office, the recipe, the narrative, even the horoscope: the interaction has a clear, tangible goal to be achieved. As Bakhtin would say, from the beginning of such texts we have a clear sense of an end. Interpersonal interactions, in contrast, do not have any tangible goal to be achieved. Instead these are interactions motivated by the exploring and establishing of interpersonal relations, the mutual creation of good feelings. The conversational texts presented in Chapters Six and Eight are examples of interpersonally motivated interactions.

When we compare interactions motivated in each of these ways, we find that the kinds of structure associated with each differs. Where the social goals to be achieved by talk are principally pragmatic (there are goods or services to be exchanged, information to be transmitted), talk and writing is organized with the kind of schematic structure we have seen in this chapter. Such schematic structure is entirely appropriate to interactions which have clear end points, and where in fact the goal of the interaction is to attain that end point. When we go into the post office to buy stamps for our letters, we don't wish to spend two hours in friendly chat with the salesperson in order to get that goal satisfied.

But where the social goals to be achieved by talk are principally interpersonal ones, to do with establishing and reinforcing social relations, then we find that other types of structure dominate. Thus, more open-ended structures tend to take over, as the talk develops dynamically, with no clear end point to be achieved, and few discrete steps or stage boundaries along the way. This more fluid structure of conversation can be captured by dividing a conversational text into **phases** rather than stages. The term phase (taken from Gregory 1985, Malcolm 1985) can be used to indicate a segment of talk (usually highly interactive talk) in which there is a certain stability of realizational patterns, but for which a functional schematic structure label does not seem appropriate (the talk is not a step on the way to somewhere else). An example of a conversational excerpt divided into phases on the basis of grammatical patterns is discussed in Chapter Eight, where it will also be seen that conversation typically involves an alternation between sections in which a phasal organization dominates, and sections which have clear schematic structure (for example, narratives).

Thus while the most common realization of genre is through staged, constituent structure, some genres are realized by different, more localistic types of structure. (For a detailed discussion of the structure of casual conversation, see Eggins and Slade 1997; for the use of phase as a text division in long texts, see Martin and Rose 2003).

However, recognizing different structural patterns does not in any way detract from the central claim of a systemic functional approach that all interactions are goal-oriented and purposeful. We never just use language – we are always using it 'to do something'. In putting a label on what it is that we are doing, and in analysing how we use language to do it, we are describing genre. In the following chapter, we will explore the fact that whatever we are doing with language, we are always doing it within a particular situational context.

Genre in fiction

Our concept of genres can also be applied and expanded by looking at genre in fictional texts. Genre has long been a foundational concept in literary studies. The traditional genre categories of poetry, prose and drama were then subdivided to give the different genres of poetry (ballads, sonnets, lyrics, epics . . .), prose (historical novel, crime novel . . .), drama (tragedy, comedy . . .). So central is genre identity to literary work that some categories of prose are known as 'genre fiction'.

An example from a 'genre fiction' sub-genre appears as Text 3.6 below. How long does it take you to work out what genre this excerpt is from?

Text 3.6: an excerpt from genre fiction[9]

(1i)When he placed a thermos on the wooden picnic table, (1ii)Taylor suddenly sensed (1iii)that Quinn was a deliberate man. (2i)His long fingers slid slowly away from the thermos, (2ii)and the movement reminded Taylor of a caress. (3i)His gaze ran down her body, (3ii)lingering, (3iii)touching, (3iv)seeking, (3v)and something within her stirred (3vi)and grew taut.

(4)'My mother sent potato soup. (5i)She's worried (5ii)you'll have a poor picture of the people hereabouts.'

(6i)Taylor pressed her lips together, (6ii)sensing (6iii)that Donovan's low voice shielded his real thoughts. (7i)She shifted uneasily, (7ii)disliking the leaping sense of awareness in her body, (7iii)uncomfortable with his eyes watching her carefully. (8i)'The thought was nice, (8ii)but I can find a restaurant.'

(9i)He took a few steps nearer, (9ii)and Taylor found (9iii)her hand locked to the back of the chair. (10)Donovan topped her five-foot-ten-inch height by half a foot. (11)His broad shoulders, narrow hips, and his carelessly combed hair only served to enhance his raw masculinity. (12i)He'd discarded the red bandanna tied around his forehead, (12ii)and his black brows and lashes gleamed in the sun, (12iii)shadowing his jutting cheekbones. (13i)His eyes caught hers – (13ii)a curiously dark shade of green that matched his daughter's. (14i)His dark skin gleamed as it crossed his cheekbones and his jaw; (14ii)a tiny fresh cut lay along his jaw, (14iii)as though he'd just shaved.

(15)Taylor jerked her eyes away from the grim set of his mouth. (16i)Despite his apparent dark mood, Donovan's mouth was beautiful, sensuous, (16ii)and her heart quivered (16iii)and flip-flopped just once. (17i)There was a beauty about Donovan, a raw male look – an arrogance, a certainty – (17ii)and beneath it lay a fine, grim anger that startled her.

(18)Taylor shifted her weight impatiently. (19i)Few men could intimidate her, (19ii)and she disliked the sense that this man – this Quinn Donovan – knew exactly what she was thinking. (20i)Despite her resolve not to give him another inch, when Donovan took another step toward her, (20ii)she released the chair and stepped backward.

(21i)A quick flare of satisfaction soared through Donovan's narrowed eyes, (21ii)and Taylor's throat tightened.

(23)She straightened her shoulders. (24)She refused to be intimidated by a towering bully. (25i)She caught his scent – (25ii)soap, freshly cut wood, sweat, and a dark, masculine tang that she knew she'd remember forever.

(26i)Taylor stepped back again, (26ii)then regretted the action. (27)Donovan was hunting her now. (28i)The dark meadow green eyes skimmed her mussed hair, the loose, untucked blouse open at her throat, (28ii)catching the fast beat of her heart, (28iii)then flowing down her body (28iv)to linger on bare toes locked in the grass.

(29i)The heat of his body snared her; (29ii)his inspection of her feet too intimate.

(30i)'I haven't invited you (30ii)to spoil my day. (31)Creeping up on me this way is trespassing.'

(32)'I don't creep.' (33)Donovan's flat statement cut into the clean spring air.

(34)His voice reminded her of the rumble of a storm, of a dark beast rising from his lair. (35i)From his narrowed eyes came the glittering thrust of a sword, (35ii)raised (35iii)and waiting.

It's likely that if you're a native speaker of English, resident in a western country, you very rapidly identified the source of Text 3.6 as 'romance fiction'. Romance fiction, like crime fiction, is referred to as one type of 'genre fiction' exactly because its texts adhere very closely to an almost inflexible schematic structure. In her pioneering work into this genre, Janice Radway (1991: 150) identified what she called a 'narrative logic' which successful romance novels follow. According to Radway, romances which experienced readers judged 'successful' generally work through the following 13 stages:

1. the heroine's social identity is thrown into question
2. the heroine reacts antagonistically to an aristocratic male
3. the aristocratic male responds ambiguously to the heroine
4. the heroine interprets the hero's behaviour as evidence of a purely sexual interest in her
5. the heroine responds to the hero's behaviour with anger or coldness
6. the hero retaliates by punishing the heroine
7. the heroine and hero are physically and/or emotionally separated

8. the hero treats the heroine tenderly
9. the heroine responds warmly to the hero's act of tenderness
10. the heroine reinterprets the hero's ambiguous behaviour as the product of previous hurt
11. the hero proposes/openly declares his love for/demonstrates his unwavering commitment to the heroine with a supreme act of tenderness
12. the heroine responds sexually and emotionally to the hero
13. the heroine's identity is restored

Not only does genre fiction have very fixed schematic structure, but also very predictable realization patterns. Realization patterns apply across three main dimensions of the narrative:

- **characterization**: in genre fiction a limited number of different character roles are realized, with the attributes of each role also limited and predictable
- **plot devices and sets of activities**: a limited and recurrent range of plot elements is used to realize each stage of the schematic structure
- **setting**: the events of genre fiction take place in predictable and limited settings

For example, Radway showed that successful romance fiction requires only four character-roles: the heroine and hero, and their opposites, a female foil and a male foil. The extreme focus on just two principal characters (heroine and hero) makes romance texts highly unrealistic, detached from social reality and claustrophobic. The foils function in the texts to exemplify negative female/male behaviour, in order to re-emphasize the qualities and behaviours of the desirable heterosexual couple.

Radway also identified the character attributes that must be realized by each role, and how, in the heroine's case only, these attributes change as the narrative progresses. The heroine, for example, must always be stunningly beautiful in a conventional western sense (slender not porky, and very sexually attractive to men but unaware of and uncomfortable with her 'thinly disguised sexuality'), while the hero must always display a 'spectacular masculinity' (Radway 1991: 128). This usually means he will be tall, dark, angular, and with a vast chest. But Radway points out that 'the terrorizing effect of his exemplary masculinity is always tempered by the presence of a small feature that introduces an important element of softness into the overall picture' (Radway 1991: 128). For example, he may have a loose curl of hair, or soft eyes. At the beginning of the romance, the heroine will be shown to be 'incomplete' in her femininity. This can be realized by having her wear business suits and other androgynous or at least not feminine clothes. She will often be hiding behind sunglasses, and her hair is often severely tied back or concealed. By the end of the novel, she will have changed her appearance to be more appropriately feminine: suits give way to dresses, her eyes glow, and her hair flows freely in the breeze. In other words, heroine and hero must exemplify patriarchal gender roles.

Similarly, the initiating stage of schematic structure which functions to throw the heroine's social identity into question is realized by plot devices that include: the heroine develops amnesia after an accident or illness; the heroine loses all family members through death or disaster; the heroine moves to an unfamiliar place in order to pursue her career (which she does to the exclusion of any romantic attachments).

Finally, the realization of settings of romance fiction limits the geographic, socio-economic and (until recently) racial options: many romances are set in semi-isolated, benign country villages, often after the heroine has fled from her unhomelike home in what is realized as an alienating western metropolis.

As our model of genre in relation to language implies, the predictability of realizations extends beyond these macro genre-level patterns through to micro lexico-grammatical patterns. Like our everyday genres of horoscope, recipe and transaction, romance texts are associated with particular preferred realizational patterns. For example, Text 3.6 displays the common preference in romance fiction for verbs of sensing, feeling and remembering (technically, mental processes, as we'll see in Chapter Eight). Every act of the hero – no matter how mundane – triggers an affective, mental reaction on the part of the heroine, whose viewpoint we are positioned to share: *When he placed a thermos on the wooden picnic table, Taylor suddenly sensed that Quinn was a deliberate man*. She may never have met the hero before, but his presence evokes cultural memories in her: the movement of his fingers *reminded Taylor of a caress* and his voice *reminded her of the rumble of a storm*. While the heroine's mental processes are reacting to his *raw masculinity*, her body often seizes up or behaves in involuntary ways in his presence: *He took a few steps nearer, and Taylor found her hand locked to the back of the chair*. She is construed as both mentally and physically powerless to resist the force of his *raw male look . . . Despite her resolve not to give him another inch, when Donovan took another step toward her, she released the chair and stepped backward*.

As well as emphasizing the heroine's involuntary physical and mental reactions to the hero's actions, romance fiction is also heavily concerned with the effect of his gaze on her, and her inability to control her perception of him. Both hero and heroine do a great deal of looking at each other, and the heroine is often reacting to *his gaze* and *his eyes* (*the dark meadow green eyes skimmed her mussed hair . . .*). Usually she dislikes his gaze (she feels *uncomfortable with his eyes watching her carefully*) but has trouble resisting the urge to gaze back at him (*Taylor jerked her eyes away*). In this emphasis on gaze, a vocabulary of disguise and deception is common, construing a barrier of misperception and lack of trust between the couple (*Donovan's low voice shielded his real thoughts*). Much of the plot of romance fiction involves the heroine learning to accept the hero's gaze, and respond to it in the way it invites her to.

And of course here we must note that a distinctive realizational pattern of romance is the way every action and comment between hero and heroine is imbued with a sexual meaning. The hero's every act is sexualized, but particularly his gaze (*His gaze ran down her body, lingering, touching, seeking*). This sexual gaze again produces an affective reaction in the heroine because her body responds despite herself (*She shifted uneasily, disliking the leaping sense of awareness in her body, uncomfortable with his eyes watching her carefully*).

Sexual innuendo colours all vocabularly choices. The hero's presence and physical attributes, described in detail, always trigger sexual mental associations for the heroine: *From his narrowed eyes came the glittering thrust of a sword, raised and waiting*.

Although sometimes the sexual connotations are softened into romance (*His long fingers slid slowly away from the thermos, and the movement reminded Taylor of a caress*), more often the hero's presence is construed as threatening, associated with verbs of fear and violence (*trespassing, creeping up*) and nouns with violent connotations (*a quick flare of satisfaction*). Figurative representations of the hero represent him as *a dark beast rising from his lair* who is *hunting her now*, and her body (against the wishes of her mind) experiences behavioural responses associated with fear (*Taylor's throat tightened*).

Fearful though they are, his actions or attributes trigger thinly disguised sexual response (*something within her stirred and grew taut*), and she is inevitably, despite herself, caught: *The heat of his body snared her*.

Again, we are hampered in what we can say about these realizational patterns because we don't yet share a technical vocabulary. But we can say enough to show that the heroine is consistently positioned through the grammar to **react to** the hero (rather than to initiate actions herself), and that her reactions are involuntary. The major drama of the plot comes from the heroine's ongoing conflict between what she desires mentally (*she refused to be intimidated by a towering bully*) and what she can actually do faced with this specimen of *raw masculinity*. The lexical and grammatical choices encode 'romance' as so overwhelming and fearful an experience for the heroine that she loses control of her own mind and body.

Crime fiction, another type of 'genre writing', similarly comes with a range of generic expectations in terms of characterization, plot devices and setting. The young writer of Text 3.7 below has already learnt many of the typical realization features of the 'hardboiled detective' genre: the hardened but philosophizing first-person detective-narrator; the thematic emphasis on death and mortality; the use of a bleak urban setting; the creation of a sense of doom and foreboding; and, of course, the clever twist in the tail.

Text 3.7: Inside Edge[10]

Death hung in the air. A tangible presence; a reminder of our own mortality. The body, of course, had been reduced to a blood stain and a chalk outline by the time I arrived on the scene, but still, it's never easy. I ran my fingers through my hair, feeling it suction onto my scalp, glued by my nervous sweat. This was the fifth murder in as many days – never a good sign – especially if they're all identical. I pushed away the proffered photographs. I knew what the body would look like.

I walked slowly over to the window, shoes echoing on the bare wooden floor. Outside, the street swarmed with television cameras and reporters. I'd face those jackals later. Inside, the rooms swarmed with uniforms and glove wearing forensics – the usual crowd. I walked around amongst them, gathering bits and pieces of information, taking notes, feeling sick. Nobody paid any attention to me, despite the fact I was in charge of the whole thing. I shrugged philosophically. My part would come later.

At the station that afternoon I added what evidence we had gathered on to the massive whiteboard. The smell of the whiteboard marker, and the emptiness of the air-conditioning made me feel dizzy and sick. The migraine that had begun at the scene that morning lapped around my neck and eyes. I pinched the top of my nose. I could taste the fumes of the marker, which had begun to leak, dribbling on my hands like black rivers of blood.

At home that evening I washed my hands carefully, scrubbing at my discoloured fingernails, watching as the stained water gurgles down the laundry sink. I think it gets harder every time. Another body, another uneaten lunch, another nightmare-filled sleep . . . If I can get to sleep at all. Sometimes I feel as if I bring death home with me. Can't escape what I do for a living. I can taste the bitter bile at the back of my throat. My thoughts rush chaotically around, chasing their tails. The phone will be ringing in a minute. It will be my partner. 'I hate to disturb you this late,' he'll say, 'but there's been another murder'. I'll have to act surprised. Again. It's not easy investigating your own crimes.

Genre in literary texts

Genre fiction is defined precisely by its predictability, its conformity to genre patterns. And, just as many of us find it 'economical' to interact in conventional genres, so we also derive much pleasure from reading genre fiction. Once we've identified a genre that we like, we can be pretty much guaranteed to find novels that please us under the relevant section in the bookshop.

But what about more creative writing, writing which falls outside the obvious predictability of 'genre fiction'? How is genre relevant to the analysis of the latest winner of the Booker Prize for fiction? Or to postmodern poetry? How, for example, can the concept of genre help us when we read the Kate Chopin short story presented in Chapter Two? Or 'The Grapevine' by John Ashbery, also presented there?

As I suggested in Chapter Two, Ashbery's use of conventional signals of poetry in 'The Grapevine' triggers our socialized reading practice and we read the text *as a poem*. Similarly, when you know that the text by Kate Chopin is a short story, rather than, say, a news story, you draw on certain ways of approaching the text: at the very least, you probably read it slowly. While we'll generally read a poem or short story many times (because we learn we have to work at it to understand it), we almost certainly won't re-read the same romance text over and over again, though we might go and buy another in the same imprint. We learn to expect that literary texts don't usually give up their meanings on a casual first reading. In other words, part of learning how genres mean is learning to read different genres in different ways.

Our deeper engagement with literary texts is partly the result of our apprenticeship into ways of reading. But that itself is a functional response to the different ways language is used in literary, as opposed to non-literary, texts. As Shklovsky and the Russian Formalists argued, the function of literary texts is to defamiliarize experience, and they generally do this by defamiliarizing the use of language. This defamiliarization then forces us to slow down. One of the dimensions of language that literary works often defamiliarize is genre. Literary works very often deliberately exploit the tension between the replication of genre conventions and their subversion. The literary text, some would say, is *always* and inevitably a comment on genre, as each text seeks to defamiliarize the genre in order to slow us down so that we can apprehend new meanings.

For example, we saw in Chapter Two how Ashbery frustrates our expectations about referential identity in 'The Grapevine'. Although poems are often difficult, most of the time we can figure out who is talking about what. In 'The Grapevine', we can't be sure.

Similarly, although Kate Chopin's short story appears to follow the expected stages of the narrative genre, she actually subverts conventional patriarchal realizations of the genre and confronts us with what would now be called a feminist interrogation. 'The Story of an Hour' falls into the following stages:

> **Orientation**: breaking the news to Mrs Mallard about the death of her husband
> **Complication**: her husband dies, so she is now alone
> **Evaluation**: she should be sad, but she realizes she is the opposite
> **Resolution**: he returns, unharmed; she dies
> **Coda**: how they explain her death

The subversion builds throughout the Evaluation, when Mrs Mallard (contrary to convention) realizes that she is not sad about her husband's death but in fact filled with joy at her unexpected liberty. Then in the Resolution, where a conventional narrative would have Mrs Mallard happy to have him back home (quietly packing back into the box any slightly risqué feelings she may have experienced), Chopin has his return kill his wife. The Coda is ironic, because what the doctors read as 'joy', we know to read as something akin to horror.

Through this generic structure and its realizations, Chopin offers a counter-narrative to texts such as Mills & Boon romance fiction. Chopin's evocation and then subversion of our expectations (that a wife without a husband must be very sad and incomplete) forces us to consider how women's experience of marriage is so often quite the opposite of the patriarchal ideal, so totally at odds with the representation relentlessly offered to women through romance fiction.

Literature exposes both our essential need for genre (we can only recognize meaning when it is expressed in largely conventional forms) and the necessity of creativity (we need to keep transforming genres if we're not to lose ourselves in a life (and world) of endless, deadening sameness). It is through playing with the system, stretching the genre boundaries both in structure and realization, that we open our lives up to meanings yet to be made.

Genre hybridity

Another form of creativity in fiction texts is to combine or blend different genres to produce 'hybrids'. While many texts confine themselves to a single genre, postmodern fiction is characterized by its interest in genre hybridity. The mixing and blending of genres is nowhere more apparent than in J. K. Rowling's *Harry Potter* series[11], where a novel combination of some very traditional children's literature genres is a large part of the series' success. Rowling blends genre elements from at least four children's genres:

1. high fantasy: Rowling takes the character roles of Fatherlike Chief Magician (Dumbledore) and Orphaned or Unlikely Apprentice with a special gift and unique destiny (Harry Potter); the theme of a perpetual battle between Good and Evil, Light and Dark (the wizarding world and Voldemort); the creation of a nostalgic secondary world under threat from the Forces of Darkness; and a 'natural' hierarchical social organization with rules and the compliantly ruled. Similar patterns are also present in other well known examples of this genre, e.g. J. R. R. Tolkien's *Lord of The Rings* and Ursula Le Guin's *The Wizard of Earthsea*.
2. low or domestic fantasy: from this genre, quintessentially represented by Roald Dahl (e.g. *Matilda, The BFG*), Rowling takes elements of humorous and unsympathetic caricature; the use of vernacular (rather than elevated) language; a mundane (rather than a fantastic) secondary world, and a reluctant anti-hero with an unlooked-for talent.
3. school story: a realist genre first realized by Thomas Hughes in *Tom Brown's School Days* (1857). From this genre Rowling takes what Hunt (2001: 139) identifies as the basic character types of: the basically upright hero (Harry himself), the best friend (Ron), the decent head of house or dormitory (Professor McGonagall), the small, frightened (but often highly religious) child (Neville), the bully (Malfoy), the God-like headmaster (Dumbledore). She also takes plot elements of: initiation into a new community, learning to cope with life, the idiosyncrasies of society (and especially restricted society). There's the use of conventional plot devices – bullying and the defeat of the bully, the hero who is nearly led astray but is saved by a good friend, and the moral role of sport as a means of proving character.
4. detective/mystery story: a realist genre. In 'rational' mysteries (e.g. Enid Blyton's *Secret Seven* and *Famous Five* series), mysteries are solvable (and are solved) through rational methods. The *Harry Potter* books fall very clearly into this rational mystery

sub-genre. At the local level, the mystery in each novel is resolved by the text's closure, while at the general level, the source of evil is clearly located within the character of Voldemort, who can only be defeated through the joint efforts of a tightly controlled, ever vigilant wizarding society. There is a validation of rational adult behaviour as the way to go about solving the problem of evil, with adults including Dumbledore and Sirius Black encouraging Harry and his friends to become detectives.

In blending fantasy genres with realist genres, Rowling sets up contradictions between the types of meanings her texts are making. In particular, fantasy and realist genres make very different meanings about destiny and self-determination. Fantasy genres generally suggest (through their schematic structure, characterization and settings) that we have little control over our destiny or social organization. Both are usually pre-ordained by god, tradition or some other transcendental force. Our task in life is to 'live up to our destiny' as best we can, accept our lot and – if we be 'chosen' – perform heroic tasks.

Realist genres, on the other hand, suggest that it is our own actions and decisions that create the world in which we live. Social structure and our own character is shaped by our specific socio-historical context and by our self-determined actions.

The blending of these two very different types of genres in the *Harry Potter* series results in a text which is postmodern in its method but traditional in its values. A text which appeals to those who like hierarchy, authority, security and compliance, as well as to those who want the risks of self-determination and change. See Eggins (in preparation). A genre analysis can help to explain, perhaps, why these texts really do seem to appeal to so many different groups of readers.

Another example of genre hybridity is the emergence of what's called 'new journalism' or 'creative non-fiction'. You can read an example of creative non-fiction in Chapter Nine, where I present an excerpt from Gail Bell's book *Shot*. In creative non-fiction we see a transfer of literary realizational techniques into the genres of journalism. For example, *Shot* recounts Gail Bell's experience of having been shot in the back when a teenager, so the book is based on real experience, and uses journalistic techniques such as interviews and factual reports to investigate the crime against her and the more general problem of guns in our culture. But *Shot* is also written in a very 'literary' way: Bell uses metaphor, intertextuality, polysemic vocabulary, subjective voice and unusual grammatical patterns. The language calls attention to itself, forcing us to slow down and work at the text. Creative non-fiction and other hybrid genres such as 'ficto-criticism' are functionally motivated responses to our endless pursuit of ways to move from the known and familiar towards the new.

Critical text analysis: reading genre

As I hope all the texts presented in this chapter have shown, the identification of genre is integral to how a text means. But there is more to genre analysis than just identifying the genre, analysing its schematic structure stages, and relating those to realizations. Useful genre analysis involves also reflecting critically on what cultural work is being done, whose interests are being served, by texts of particular genres.

With the genres of literary and genre fiction, the critical interpretation of genres is well developed, and books like Belsey's (2002) *Critical Practice* and Culler's (1997) *Literary Theory: A Very Short Introduction* give some idea of the range of post-structuralist literary and critical theory. But even so, the functional dimension of a systemic approach can often inflect these literary approaches in useful ways, as I hope my discussion of *Harry Potter* indicated.

Critical reading of genres is equally applicable and perhaps even more relevant for the genres of everyday life. When we analyse a genre, we should always ask: why is this genre useful for the culture? What does this genre tell us about the culture that uses it? For example horoscopes offer an interpretation of life as pre-destined to a large extent, in which material aspects (prosperity) and romantic (usually heterosexual) relationships are encoded as the most significant life concerns. These meanings reflect dominant cultural values, but values which are more useful to certain sectors of the culture than to others. Seeing life as predetermined not only removes our responsibility to act to change our circumstances, but it also implies the permanence of social inequities (such as class differences). Of course, such social differences are largely covered over by horoscopes (we don't get one lot of predictions for middle-class readers and another lot for working-class readers). Usually retained, though, is some recognition of the social dimension of married vs single, with its implicit claim that the goal of individuals is to be able to constitute a romantic (usually implicitly heterosexual) relationship, thus perpetuating dominant beliefs in (the myths of) romantic love. Encouraged to believe that happiness lies in acquiring (through luck/destiny) more wealth and perhaps more status (e.g. through promotion), readers are re-inscribed as competitive consumers in materialistic society. Determination by factors outside ourselves also removes anxiety; if it's 'in the stars', why worry? What can we do about anything, after all?

Horoscopes, then, encode meanings about life which support the maintenance of the social status quo, and the passivity of the individual. For many readers, they complement or replace other authorities no longer accessible or respected: ministers of religion, elders, doctors, etc. Their continued existence provides evidence of our craving for authority, guidance, dependence and social inertia.

Yet there is something very important that this critical analysis has to this point ignored: the fact most of us don't read horoscopes 'seriously'; we don't base our life decisions on them (and so we don't hold our breaths for the 12th of the month). Part of the generic identity of the horoscope text, then, is that it carries with it certain taken-for-granted assumptions about how it is to be read within dominant cultural practice (in this case, as 'not seriously'). Part of the generic coherence of a text is our willingness and ability to read the text 'unproblematically', in this naturalized, hegemonic way. We can only learn to do this through continual participation in the culture. So we grow up seeing many adults flipping to the 'Star Signs', but we do not see the majority of them living their lives based on the advice or predictions they find there. For most (compliant) readers, then, horoscope texts are largely entertainment, not direction. However, for a minority of readers, 'resistant' to the practices suggested by dominant culture, horoscopes can be read 'seriously'.

Yet although horoscopes are mostly read 'for fun', we may still want to question why we need to be spoken to in the form of such texts. Horoscopes may be highly unproblematic as texts, while being (for some of us) highly problematic as cultural processes.

This analysis also helps us to understand how a text like 'Stalin's Genius' (Text 2.3) could still be seen as a text, problematic though most of us will find it. Deliberately problematic texts like Bruce Andrew's 'poem' are just as functionally motivated in their use of language as conventional texts such as horoscopes. But they are motivated by political desire to *disrupt* meaning, to pull us up and make us think about how language works, and in doing that they also challenge us to reflect on how culture works. Once we know the generic identity it is claiming (as a postmodern poem), we have at least some handle on how to read it, if simply that we now cease to expect the text to 'make sense' in conventional ways. The classifiers 'high art' and 'postmodern', particularly juxtaposed, imply a suspension of everyday conventions of texture, and an expectation that whatever we expect, we will somehow be disappointed! As the text denies us the familiar comforts of referential stability, interpersonal consistency and textual continuity, it perhaps leads us to wonder if other things can be achieved through language than those currently recognized in dominant cultural practice. It suggests that the taken-for-granted can be purposefully disrupted, although with what outcome the text does not make clear.

To repeat a point made earlier, genres are about expectations, not about determination. Genres are open, flexible and responsive to users' needs. Thanks to the semiotic system of language, there is always the option of meaning the unexpected.

Summary: genre through language

Our ability to make predictions about genres illustrates that, as members of this culture, we have somehow acquired a knowledge about how people use language to achieve different things. When called upon, we find ourselves familiar with not only the schematic structure of many genres, but also the typical realizations: the typical types of meanings that get made in each stage of a genre, the typical words and structures that get used to express them. Genre theory is about bringing this unconscious cultural knowledge to consciousness by describing how we use language to do things, and reflecting critically on just what our cultural life involves. In the next chapter we extend this exploration of the dual predictability but also creativity of language when we look at the relationship between text and situation.

Notes

1. Source: *New Woman* magazine, September 1994.
2. See also Hasan (1985a: 59–69) for a detailed discussion of how to identify and label the structural stages of a genre.
3. Source: Ventola 1987: 239–40.
4. 'Anzac' is in parentheses because this is a guess by the transcriber.
5. Source: author's data.
6. Source: author's data (family recipe, written down for a school 'multicultural cookbook').
7. This analysis does not preclude later, more delicate (detailed) description, where the Method stage might be subdivided into the two sub-stages of Procedure and Serving Suggestion, with realizational patterns relating to the verb (*take/mix*, etc. vs *serve*).
8. Source: David Wells, text held in the Nestlé Write Around Australia archive, State Library of NSW.
9. Excerpt from *Fusion* by Cait London (1994), Silhouette Desire series (Harlequin Enterprises), pp. 20–1.
10. Source: Jacinda Smith, text held in the Nestlé Write Around Australia archive, State Library of NSW.
11. J. K. Rowling *Harry Potter and the Philosopher's Stone* and sequels, published by Bloomsbury, London.

Chapter 4

Register: context of situation in text

Introduction

In Chapter Two I introduced the concept of **texture** as the defining characteristic of text. We saw there that one aspect of texture is the text's internal **cohesion**, but that texts also display **coherence** with their extra-textual environments. In the previous chapter we explored how texts are coherent with respect to their cultural context, through the concept of **genre**. In this chapter we look more closely at how texts are coherent with respect to their context of situation, through the concept of **register**. The chapter is framed to explore the two questions:

1. What is meant by context of situation and the register variables?
2. How is register realized in language?

Why does context matter?

In our discussion of **texture** in Chapter Two, I pointed out that succeeding moments in the text project expectancies about what will happen next or later in the text. Some of these expectancies are to patterns *within* the text itself, as the unfolding text binds itself into a semantic unit through ties of cohesion. Through this process, later parts of a text display continuity with earlier parts.

But the expectancies on which texts depend to make sense may come not just from within the textual environment but from the extra-textual context. In other words, texts display continuity not just with elements within their boundaries, but with the contexts within which they take place.

The most obvious sense in which text has continuity with its context can be demonstrated by Text 4.1, a handwritten sign sticky-taped above the sink in the tea room at my workplace.

Text 4.1: Sign

You use it, you wash it!

The meanings of Text 4.1 are highly indeterminate in a number of respects. Firstly, the sign contains presuming reference items whose referents cannot be retrieved from the text itself (who is the *you?*, what is the *it?*). Secondly, the two key lexical items in the text are also vague: just what kind of *use* is meant here? And what kind of *washing?* Put it in the washing machine? Soak it in a bucket? Thirdly, the clauses are simply juxtaposed, so what is the intended link between them? Is it *you use it BECAUSE you wash it?* Finally, what is the meaning of the exclamation mark? Why not just a full stop?

And yet despite these indeterminancies, this short text is not at all problematic for the hundreds of people who see it daily for the simple reason that context, the environment in which the piece of language occurs, constitutes the text as a meaningful exchange. Context allows us to interpret *you* as 'you who are standing at the sink making your cup of tea or coffee or preparing your food'; *it* as 'the crockery you are using'. Context tells us that *using* here means 'having eaten off or drunk out of', and *washing* means 'washing up'. Context also suggests that the events referred to (*using, washing*) are being linked in a temporal cause/consequence sequence (*if you use it, then afterwards you wash it up*).

The exclamation mark is an explicit signal that the sentence is intended as an imperative (telling *you* what to do) and is not merely offered as a description of actions that might commonly occur around kitchen sinks. But even without the exclamation mark, readers are not likely to be confused because they correctly assume that language relates purposefully to its context, and there seems to be very little purpose achieved by merely appending a description of common activities above the sink, while there is a clear purpose achieved by commanding people to clean up their own mess (whether or not they comply with the command is beside the point).

This simple example suggests that context is an important dimension of texture, since context may function as the retrieval source to clear up indeterminacies of meaning. In fact in the washing up example we cannot interpret the text at all *except by* reference to context. Such highly context-dependent texts are risky: the less you spell out, the more chance there is that readers will (accidentally or intentionally) misinterpret your meanings (and use that as an excuse not to wash up their dishes). Such texts only work when there is a high level of shared understanding between the text users, which usually implies a high level of shared socio-cultural identity.

But it's not just signs and notices that depend on context for their meanings. *All* texts involve indeterminacies of meanings. As readers of texts, we learn how to tell when indeterminacies need to be resolved by reference to extra-textual context (as with our sign) or when indeterminacies are an integral feature of the genre and must be read for meaning *within* that genre.

For example, even in an apparently very self-contained text like Kate Chopin's 'The Story of an Hour' (Text 2.4, page 31), there are many aspects of meaning that are indeterminate. On the one hand, many details about characters, setting and plot are simply not supplied by the story. For example, what town or country is this story set in? At what period? What kind of house does Mrs Mallard live in? How old is her husband? How well off are they? Is Josephine, her sister, older or younger than her? How old is Richards? Does he live in the same town? What kind of work does Mr Mallard do? Why was he travelling by train? Part of learning to read the genre of the literary short story is learning that these details are not necessary. A short story is not a novel; there is no time for in-depth characterization or setting, and usually only one event can be represented. We learn to take the suggestive evocation of characters, setting and events from the brief schematic mention the short story writer provides. We learn not to need to know everything but instead to follow the writer's signals as she moves us rapidly past such unnecessary detail towards the main meanings of the text.

Then there are other indeterminacies created by meanings mentioned but not elaborated on in the text: what exactly were the *broken sentences* and *veiled hints* through which her sister told her the news? We know Mrs Mallard was *young*, but how young? What exactly is the nature of Richards' friendship with her husband? Again, we have absolutely no problem with these indeterminacies because they are signalled as peripheral to the main point of the story.

And finally there are the deliberate indeterminacies, the gaps the writer wants us to have to explore through the text. One we explore with Mrs Mallard as the text unfolds: just what is this *something coming to her*? Another, the nature of Mrs Mallard's *heart trouble* we must interpret for ourselves. If we read the text carefully, as a literary short story, we will have no problem with this and will appreciate retrospectively the double meaning the term has in the opening sentence.

Thus, both everyday and literary texts inevitably involve indeterminacies of meaning. Learning to tolerate a high level of indeterminacy is one of the skills we must acquire if we're to enjoy literary genres. But to negotiate more pragmatic, everyday texts, we generally try to reduce indeterminacies by anchoring a text firmly in its immediate context of situation. Register theory helps explain how this works.

How context gets into text

Just as all texts in fact point outwards, to context, and depend upon context for their interpretation, so also all texts carry their context within them. As we read texts, we are always encountering the traces of context in text, whether we are conscious of this or not. You will remember that in Chapter One you were asked to suggest the sources of the three Crying Baby texts. It is likely that you were able to do that quite accurately, deducing that Text 1.1 was taken from a popular magazine, Text 1.2 from an academic textbook, and Text 1.3 from casual conversation. It was suggested that your ability to deduce the source of a text merely from the text itself indicated that in some sense *context is in text*. Systemic linguists are interested in exploring just *how* context gets into text.

In the light of Chapter Three, you may now appreciate that one way in which context gets into text is through schematic structure. That is, one dimension of the three Crying Baby texts which would have helped you determine their sources was your (intuitive) analysis of the genres represented by each text. You might have noted that both Texts 1.1 and 1.2 are Explanation texts, sharing common goals to inform and educate by presenting information through a Problem ^ Possible Solutions schematic structure. The genre of explanation is a not uncommon one in textbooks or magazines. Text 1.3, on the other hand, is clearly an interactive genre, only the second half of which (the funny story) has an identifiable schematic structure. Such a pattern (interaction/narration) is common of conversational situations, rather than pedagogic/explanatory ones.

But generic considerations alone are not enough to explain how you identified the sources of the texts. Simply recognizing Texts 1.1 and 1.2 as Explanation texts does not explain how you deduced that such genres are more likely to occur in certain situations than in others. Similarly, how did you identify the fact that Texts 1.1 and 1.2 each explain to very different audiences? And how could you tell that the story told in Text 1.3 was not being told to someone the speaker had just met, or the Managing Director of the company she works for?

Observations such as these lead systemicists to argue that there is a second level of situational, as distinct from cultural, context which both constrains the appropriacy of using a particular genre, and which gives to the abstract schematic structure the 'details' that allow us to accurately place a text in terms of dimensions such as who was involved in producing the text, what the text is about and what role language was playing in the event.

It is of course easy to recognize that language use varies according to situations. We are well aware (consciously or unconsciously) that there are some situations in which the genre Lecture would be inappropriate. Similarly, we appreciate that we do not talk in the same way to an employment interview panel as we do to our best friends, that we do not talk in the same way about linguistics as we do about cooking, and that we do not write the same way we talk. However, it is much more difficult to formalize the nature of this relationship between language use and aspects of different contexts.

The question centres around the observation that although some aspects of situations seem to have an effect on language use, others do not. For example, although the different social statuses held by the interactants do seem to affect language use, it does not seem to matter much what the weather is like, what clothes the interactants are wearing, or what colour hair they have. Thus, some dimensions of a situation appear to have a significant impact on the text that will be realized, while other dimensions of a situation do not.

One of the first researchers to pursue this issue was the anthropologist, Branislaw Malinowski (1923/46, 1935). In transcribing the daily life and events of the Trobriand Islanders, Malinowski found that it was impossible to make sense of literal, or word-for-word translations from their language into English. In part, Malinowski argued that this indicated the need for the researcher to understand the cultural context in which the language was being used:

> The study of any language, spoken by a people who live under conditions different from our own and possess a different culture, must be carried out in conjunction with the study of their culture and their environment. (Malinowski 1946: 306)

In order for observers to make sense of the events being described in his attempted translations, he found he had to include contextual glosses, i.e. the linguistic events were only interpretable when additional contextual information about the situation and the culture was provided. Malinowski claimed that language only becomes intelligible when it is placed within its **context of situation**. In coining this term, Malinowksi wanted to capture the fact that the situation in which words are uttered 'can never be passed over as irrelevant to the linguistic expression', and that 'the meaning of any single word is to a very high degree dependent on its context' (1946: 307).

Although confining his argument to so-called 'primitive' (i.e. non-literate) cultures, Malinowski developed an account of language that is both functional (makes reference to why people use language) and semantic (deals with how language means). In the following extended quotation, you will see Malinowski making an important association, between the fact that language only makes sense (only has meaning) when interpreted within its context *and* the claim that language is a functional resource (i.e. language use is purposeful):

> It should be clear at once that the conception of meaning as contained in an utterance is false and futile. A statement, spoken in real life, is never detached from the situation in which it has been uttered. For each verbal statement by a human being has the aim and function of expressing some thought or feeling actual at that moment and in that situation, and necessary for some reason or other to be made known to another person or persons – in order either to serve purposes of common action, or to establish ties of purely social communion, or else to deliver the speaker

> of violent feelings or passions . . . utterance and situation are bound up inextrica-
> bly with each other and the context of situation is indispensable for the under-
> standing of the words . . . a word without linguistic context is a mere figment and
> stands for nothing by itself, so in reality of a spoken living tongue, the utterance
> has no meaning except in the context of situation. (Malinowski 1946: 307)

Malinowski thus considered that, at least in primitive cultures, language was always being used to do something. Language functioned as 'a mode of action' (1946: 312). In developing an account of the different functions to which language could be put, Malinowski differentiated between the pragmatic function (when language is being used to achieve concrete goals, as well as to retell experience) and the magical (the non-pragmatic functions). Even what appeared to be 'free, aimless social intercourse' (1946: 315) he considered to be a highly functional use of language. Labelling it 'phatic communion', he described such conversational uses of language as 'a type of speech in which ties of union are created by a mere exchange of words' (*ibid*.: 315). While Malinowski made an enormous contribution in identifying the fundamental semantic role of the **context of situation** and the **context of culture**, and in developing a functional account of language, he did not go on to formulate more precisely the nature of these two contexts, nor their relation to the functional organization of language. In addition, Malinowski restricted his observations by drawing an artificial distinction between 'primitive' and 'civilized' languages. Later theorists have argued that context is critical to meaning in *any* linguistic event in *any* language.

One scholar who developed a more general theory of meaning-in-context, influenced by Malinowski's work, was the linguist J. R. Firth (1935, 1950, 1951). With a life-long interest in the semantics of language, Firth extended the notion of context of situation to the more general issue of linguistic predictability. Firth pointed out that given a description of a context we can predict what language will be used. His rather quaint but exact formulation of this was to claim that learning to use language is very much a process of:

> learning to say what the other fellow expects us to say under the given circumstances
> . . . Once someone speaks to you, you are in a relatively determined context and you
> are not free just to say what you please. (Firth 1935/57: 28)

Predictability also works in the other direction: given an example of language use (what we would now call text), we can make predictions about what was going on at the time that it was produced.

In trying to determine what were the significant variables in the context of situation that allowed us to make such predictions, Firth suggested the following dimensions of situations:

> A. The relevant features of participants: persons, personalities.
>   (i)   The verbal action of the participants.
>   (ii) The non-verbal action of the participants.
> B. The relevant objects.
> C. The effect of the verbal action. (Firth 1950/57: 182)

This interest in specifying context was also pursued by researchers working within sociolinguistic and ethnography of speaking approaches (for example, Hymes 1962/74, 1964/72, Gumperz 1968, 1971), with significant contributions from early register theorists such as Gregory 1967, Ure 1971, Ure and Ellis 1977. The major contribution of Halliday's approach to context has been to argue for *systematic* correlations between the organization of language itself (the three types of meanings it encodes) and specific contextual features.

Register theory

Following in the functional-semantic tradition pursued by Firth, Halliday also asked *which* aspects of context are important, i.e. what aspects of context make a difference to how we use language? He has suggested (e.g. Halliday 1978, 1985b) that there are three aspects in any situation that have linguistic consequences: **field**, **mode** and **tenor**. As we saw in Chapter One, these can be briefly glossed as

field: what the language is being used to talk about

mode: the role language is playing in the interaction

tenor: the role relationships between the interactants.

These three variables are called the **register variables**, and a description of the values for each of these variables at a given time of language use is a **register description** of a text. A very brief register description of the three Crying Baby texts from Chapter One would be as follows:

Text 1.1

Field: childcare

Mode: written to be read

Tenor: specialists to general audience

Text 1.2

Field: childcare

Mode: written to be read

Tenor: specialist to trainee-specialists

Text 1.3

Field: childcare

Mode: interactive face-to-face

Tenor: friends

From this very limited register description we can suggest that the three texts are alike in field, but different in mode and tenor. (We will return to these observations in Chapter Eleven.)

In proposing these three variables, Halliday is making the claim that, of all the things going on in a situation at a time of language use, only these three have a direct and significant impact on the type of language that will be produced.

In order to test out his claim, we need to consider each register variable more closely, asking what exactly field, mode and tenor refer to (here we will be more specific about the dimensions of each register variable), and in what ways each variable impacts on language use (here we will illustrate briefly how each register variable makes a difference in text).

In asking why Halliday argues for these three register variables and not any others, we will review the systematic relationship set up in the systemic model between these contextual categories and the structure of language itself.

Mode

The general definition of mode offered above referred simply to 'the role language is playing in an interaction'. Martin (1984) has suggested that this role can be seen as involving two

casual conversation	telephone	email	fax	radio	novel

+visual contact	-visual	-visual	-visual	-visual	-visual
+aural	+aural	-aural	-aural	+one-way aural	-aural

+immediate feedback	+immediate feedback	+rapid feedback	+rapid feedback	+delayed feedback	

Figure 4.1 Spatial or interpersonal distance (simplified from Martin 1984: 26)

simultaneous continua which describe two different types of **distance** in the relation between language and situation:

1. **spatial/interpersonal distance**: as Figure 4.1 above indicates, this continuum ranges situations according to the possibilities of immediate feedback between the interactants. At one pole of the continuum, then, is the situation of sitting down to a casual chat with friends, where there is both visual and aural contact, and thus feedback is immediate. If you disagree with what your friend is saying, you say so straight away, or 'to her face'. At the other end of the continuum would be the situation of writing a book, where there is no visual or aural contact between writer and reader(s), and thus no possibility of immediate feedback, and even the possibilities of delayed feedback are limited. If you don't like a novel, how do you let the author know?

In between these two poles we can locate other types of situations, such as telephone calls (where there is aural but not visual contact, with slightly constrained feedback possibilities), and radio broadcasts (with one-way aural contact, but no immediate feedback). Modern communication modes (such as email, same-time internet chat rooms, fax, etc.) reveal complicated mode dimensions.

2. **experiential distance**: Figure 4.2 illustrates the second continuum of experiential distance, which ranges situations according to the distance between language and the social process occurring. At one pole of this continuum, we can put situations such as playing a game (of cards), where language is being used to accompany the activity interactants are involved in. We can describe the role of language here as almost a kind of action: as well as the action of dealing and playing the cards, there is the verbal action of making a bid, talking about whose turn it is, naming the cards to be played, etc. In such a situation, language is just one of the means being used to achieve ongoing action.

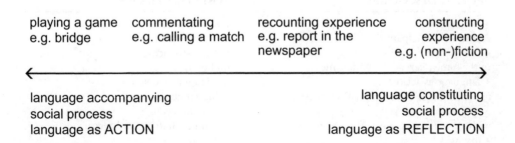

Figure 4.2 The experiential distance continuum (based on Martin 1984: 27)

Contrast this with the other polar extreme, for example writing a piece of fiction, where language is all that there is. There is no other social process going on: language is in fact creating, and therefore constituting, the social process. In these situations, language is being used to reflect on experience, rather than to enact it.

If we combine these two dimensions of mode (by taking the end points of each continuum), we can characterize the basic contrast between spoken and written situations of language use. Summarized in Table 4.1 below, we can see that situations where we use spoken language are typically interactive situations (we do not usually deliver monologues to ourselves, although we do often interact with ourselves by imagining a respondent to our remarks). In most spoken situations we are in immediate face-to-face contact with our interactant(s), and we are very typically using language to achieve some ongoing social action – e.g. to get the furniture positioned, the kids organized, etc. In such situations we usually act spontaneously, so that our linguistic output is unrehearsed. Because spoken situations are often 'everyday', we are generally relaxed and casual during the interaction.

Contrast this with a typical situation where we are using written language – for example, writing an essay for university. There we would typically find ourselves alone, not in face-to-face, aural or visual contact with our intended audience (the marker of our essay). Language would be being used to reflect on some topic – the lecturer does not want to read a commentary on our actions, feelings and thoughts of our essay writing process ('*now I'm picking up my pen, but I'm not really feeling like writing this essay . . .*'!). Written situations in our culture call for rehearsal: we draft, edit, rewrite and finally re-copy our essay. Finally, for most of us writing is not a casual activity: we need peace and quiet, we gather our thoughts, we need to concentrate. The two situations of language use, then, reveal very different dimensions.

To this point all we have done is suggest ways of analysing situations of language use. But you will remember that the SFL claim is much more than that: it is that this analysis of the situation tells us something significant about how language will be used. To evaluate that claim, what we have to do is to demonstrate that these dimensions of the situation have an effect on the language used.

In fact it turns out that there are some very obvious implications of the contrast between spoken and written modes. Certain linguistic patterns correspond to different positions on the mode continua.

Table 4.1   Mode: characteristics of spoken/written language situations

MODE: TYPICAL SITUATIONS OF LANGUAGE USE	
SPOKEN DISCOURSE	**WRITTEN TEXT**
+ interactive	non-interactive
2 or more participants	one participant
+ face-to-face	not face-to-face
in the same place at the same time	on her own
+ language as action	not language as action
using language to accomplish some task	using language to reflect
+ spontaneous	not spontaneous
without rehearsing what is going to be said	planning, drafting and rewriting
+ casual	not casual
informal and everyday	formal and special occasions

Table 4.2 Characteristic features of spoken and written language

SPOKEN and WRITTEN LANGUAGE the linguistic implications of MODE	
SPOKEN LANGUAGE	**WRITTEN LANGUAGE**
turn-taking organization	monologic organization
context-dependent	context independent
dynamic structure	synoptic structure
–interactive staging	–rhetorical staging
–open-ended	–closed, finite
spontaneity phenomena	'final draft' (polished)
(false starts, hesitations,	indications of earlier
interruptions, overlap,	drafts removed
incomplete clauses)	
everyday lexis	'prestige' lexis
non-standard grammar	standard grammar
grammatical complexity	grammatical simplicity
lexically sparse	lexically dense

Table 4.2 above summarizes the linguistic differences that correspond to our two polar extremes of a spoken and a written language situation. Here we can see that the language we use in a spoken situation will typically be organized according to the turn-by-turn sequencing of talk: first you speak, then I speak, then you speak again. Written language, on the other hand, will be produced as a monologic block. Because we are usually in the same place at the same time when we talk to each other, our language can depend in part on the context: when we're washing up, I can say to you *pass it to me* or *put it over here* or *don't do that*, because you will be able to interpret the *it* or the *that* from the ongoing context we share. But a written text needs to stand more or less by itself: it needs to be context-independent. It is not a good strategy to begin an essay with *I agree with this*, or *As it says here in this book*, as the reader will not be able to decode the *this* or the *it . . . here*. Because a spoken interaction tends to accompany action, so the structure of the talk will be a largely dynamic one, with one sentence leading to another to another to another (*Well if you don't pass me that I won't be able to get in here and then we'll be stuck because what will they say?*). Written text, however, because it is intended to encode our considered reflections on a topic, will be organized synoptically, i.e. it will have the Beginning ^ Middle ^ End type of generic structure that we discussed in Chapter Three. The structure will be determined before the text itself is complete. So, regardless of the specific essay question, the (good!) student will try to follow the stages of Statement of Thesis, Evidence, Summary, Reiteration of Thesis.

Further, if we recorded the spoken text, we would find that it contained a range of spontaneity phenomena such as hesitations, false starts, repetitions and interruptions, whereas the written text will (ideally) have all such traces removed. The spoken text will contain everyday sorts of words, including slang and dialect features (e.g. *youz*), and often sentences will not follow standard grammatical conventions (*I usen't to do that; I seen it yesterday*). In the written text, however, we will choose more prestigious vocabulary, and use standard grammatical constructions.

To this point the differences we have noted between the language of spoken and written situations are no doubt quite familiar to you. It is important to appreciate that these linguistic differences are not accidental, but are the functional consequence (the reflex) of the situational differences in mode.

However, there are two more linguistic features that are highly sensitive to mode variation: the degree of grammatical complexity, and the lexical density of the language chosen. As these features are responsible for perhaps the most striking differences between spoken and written language, we will spend a moment exploring them. As both can be related to the process of **nominalization**, we will begin there.

Nominalization

Let us imagine that you are behind in your university work and have to explain to your tutor why your essay has been handed in after the due date. When speaking to your tutor, you might say something like:

> i) I handed my essay in late because my kids got sick.

But imagine now that you have to write a letter of explanation, accompanying your essay. In that letter you will probably write something like:

> ii) The reason for the late submission of my essay was the illness of my children.

When we compare these two sentences we see that the same content, the same set of actions and events in the real world, get related in two very different linguistic forms according to whether we are speaking or writing.

In sentence i), we have one sentence made up of 2 clauses (*I handed my essay in late// because my kids got sick*). The two clauses are linked with the logical connective (conjunction) *because*. Each of the two clauses describes the concrete actions (*hand in, get sick*), expressed by verbs, performed by different human actors (*I, my kids*), with the actors occupying first position in each clause.

In sentence ii), however, we find that our message has somehow been condensed to fit into only one clause. This has been achieved by turning the actions of *handing in* and *getting sick* into nouns: *submission, illness*: the traditional category of abstract nouns. The only verb we now have is the non-action verb *is*. By turning what were verbs into nouns, sentence ii) is now able to express the logical relation between the two events also through a noun, *reason*, which now becomes the point of departure for the message. Finally, our human actors from sentence i) have been dramatically demoted in sentence ii): both the *I* and the *my kids* are no longer pivotal actors in the clauses, but only possessors (*my*), positioned now as qualifiers to nouns (*essay, children*). Here we also note also the lexical change from the slang form *kids* to the standard form *children*. (See Eggins *et al.* 1992 for more extensive discussion and exemplification of nominalization.)

We can summarize the differences between sentences i) and ii) as in Table 4.3.

This simple example illustrates the major differences between spoken and written language: that spoken language is concerned with human actors, carrying out action processes, in dynamically linked sequences of clauses, whereas written language is concerned with abstract ideas/reasons, linked by relational processes (verbs of being), in condensed sentences. A summary is in Table 4.4.

As we move from the spoken to the written version, the main means of achieving these changes is through the process of **nominalization**: turning things that are not normally nouns into nouns, with consequences for other parts of sentences.

Table 4.3   Contrasts between spoken and written examples

features of example i)	features of example ii)
two clauses	one clause
linked explicitly with *because*	no link
human, personal actors	abstract actors (reason, illness)
action processes	'being' process
	logical relation now a noun
	actors now possessors
	action processes now nouns

Table 4.4   Summarizing differences between spoken and written examples

spoken language	written language
human actors	ideas, reasons linked by
action processes	relational processes
dynamically related clauses	in condensed, dense sentence

The main parts of clauses that get turned into nouns are verbs (e.g. *to hand in, to get sick* become *submission, illness*) and conjunctions or logical connectives (*because* becomes *reason*). The following sentence exemplifies how other parts of clauses can also be nominalized:

> The increased complexity of tasks will lead to the extension of the duration of training programmes.

If we compare this written sentence with its spoken equivalent (*because the jobs are more complex, programmes to train people will take longer*), we can see that not only has the process *extend* been nominalized, but so also has an adjective (*complexity*) and an adverb (*duration*).

Although heavily nominalized language can sound pretentious and may make the meaning obscure, the real motivation for this grammatical process is a functional one: by nominalizing we are able to do things with the text that we cannot do in unnominalized text. Nominalization has two main textual advantages: rhetorical organization and increased lexical density.

Rhetorical organization

Nominalization allows us to get away from the dynamic and usually real-world sequencing that goes with speaking, where we relate sequences of actions in which we featured as actors. By nominalizing actions and logical relations, we can organize our text not in terms of ourselves, but in terms of ideas, reasons, causes, etc. Consider this short text from a university department handbook, detailing policy regarding late essays. The nominalizations have been underlined, and clause boundaries have been indicated with double slashed lines:

Text 4.2: Late Essays[1]

<u>Formal extensions</u> of time are not granted as such,// but if, through <u>misfortune</u> or bad <u>planning</u>, an assignment cannot be submitted on time,// it may be submitted within the next 14 days . . . If it is late because of some <u>unforeseen disability</u>// it will

not be penalised,// provided that (i) <u>documentary evidence</u> of the <u>disability</u> is attached to the essay and// (ii) the nature of the <u>disability</u> and of the <u>evidence</u> is <u>acceptable</u> to the Late Essay Committee. Full <u>details</u> of <u>penalties</u> are provided in the 'Submission of Essays and <u>Assignments</u>' <u>document</u>.

Compare Text 4.2 with Text 4.3, a spoken rewrite (or **unpacked** version) of the text. When we **unpack** a text, we remove as many of the nominalizations as possible, changing nouns back to verbs or conjunctions, etc. Note that unpacking frequently demands making some vocabulary changes as well:

Text 4.3: Late Essays (unpacked)

We won't formally extend the time you have to do your assignments,// but if you can't hand your assignment in on time// because something has gone wrong// or because you didn't plan properly,// then you can submit it within the next 14 days . . . If it is late// because something happened to disable you// and you couldn't have foreseen// that that would happen,// then it will not be penalised,// provided that (i) you attach a <u>document</u> which proves what happened to you to the essay and// (ii) the Late Essay Committee accepts// what you say// you had wrong with you// and the way you prove that to us . . . Look in the booklet about submitting essays and <u>assignments</u>// if you want to find out more about how we penalise you.

While the clauses in the first text frequently begin with nominalizations (*formal extensions, misfortune or bad planning, documentary evidence, nature of the disability, full details of penalties*), those in the second text begin with human actors: either *you*, the student, *we*, the School or *the Late Essay Committee*.

Rhetorical organization of the kind made possible by nominalization only becomes an option because written text is rehearsed, polished, redrafted: with the time that writing allows, we can reorganize our sentences to give priority to different parts, whereas in speaking the pressure of the dynamically unfolding situation means we generally do not plan much beyond the clause we are speaking now.

Lexical density

Nominalization also allows us to pack in more lexical content per sentence. This relates to the potential of what we call the **nominal group** in English. The nominal group is the part of the clause that contains nouns and the words that can accompany nouns. For example, all the following are nominal groups:

spiders
the three spiders
the three redback spiders
the three shiny redback spiders
the smallest of the three shiny redback spiders
the smallest of the three shiny redback spiders in the corner
the smallest of the three shiny redback spiders spinning their webs in the corner
etc.

These examples illustrate that we can do many things with nouns in English: we can count, specify, describe, classify and qualify them. It turns out that these are all things we cannot do with other parts of the clause, for example with verbs. Although the verbal group (the part of the clause where we express the verb or doing word) does have potential to be expanded, the result of expansion is very different. For example:

spins

is spinning

has been spinning

will have been spinning

may have been going to have been spinning

etc.

Although we have expanded the verbal group considerably, you can see that we have not added any more content than we had to start with: the content of *spin*. The effect of expansion has to do with specifying non-content aspects: tense, number, aspect, voice, etc. Thus, unlike the nominal group, expansion in the verbal group does not add more content to our clause.

It is by turning verbs and other parts of speech into nouns, then, that we increase the possible content of our text, and thus increase its **lexical density**. The lexical density of a text can be calculated by expressing the number of content carrying words in a text/sentence as a proportion of all the words in the text/sentence. Content carrying words include nouns, the main part of the verb, adverbs and adjectives. Non-content carrying words include prepositions, conjunctions, auxiliary verbs and pronouns. Table 4.5 below compares the lexical density of the two sample paragraphs given above.

Table 4.5 Contrasting lexical density

	Text 4.2	Text 4.3
no. of content carrying lexical items	37	43
no. of lexical items in text	89	130
total lexical density	42%	33%

This example shows that the highly nominalized written text allows a far greater proportion of the words in the text to be content carrying. Thus, written language generally has a much higher rate of lexical density than does spoken text.

Halliday (1985b) points out that the corollary of this is that spoken language has a higher level of **grammatical intricacy**. Grammatical intricacy relates to the number of clauses per sentence, and can be calculated by expressing the number of clauses in a text as a proportion of the number of sentences in the text. Whereas in spoken language we tend to chain clauses together one after another, to give often very long sentences, in written language we tend to use relatively few clauses per sentence. For example, Table 4.6 below compares the grammatical intricacy figures for Texts 4.2 and 4.3.

Table 4.6 Contrasting grammatical intricacy

	Text 4.2	Text 4.3
no. of clauses in the text	8	17
no. of sentences in the text	3	3
grammatical intricacy score	2.6	5.6

Table 4.7   Density and intricacy in spoken and written language

spoken language	written language
low lexical density	high lexical density
• few content carrying words as a proportion of all words	• many content carrying words as a proportion of all words
high grammatical intricacy	low grammatical intricacy
• many clauses per sentence	• few clauses per sentence

Table 4.7 summarizes the associations noted in these examples.

Text example: Crying Baby texts revisited

It is revealing to relate this discussion of mode differences back to the Crying Baby texts presented in Chapter One. You will remember that we characterized Text 1.2 as 'formal' and 'abstract', and we can now demonstrate that much of what gave us that impression has to do with the fact that this text is heavily nominalized.

This can be demonstrated by **unpacking** the text as much as possible, turning it back into a more spoken version. An unpacked version of Text 1.2 might be:

Text 1.2 unpacked

When an infant cries the sound compels (people) because it signals distress, which makes it appropriate to the way the human infant depends for a long time on a person who cares for it.

However, when an infant cries people get discomforted and parents may get alarmed. Many parents find it very difficult to listen to their infant crying for even a short time. Sometimes infants cry because they are hungry or are uncomfortable or because they are too hot, too cold, ill, or lying in the wrong position. But infants cry because of many other things too. When infants are crying because they are hungry, uncomfortable, hot, cold or in the wrong position, then people usually recognize why infants are crying and alleviate them. Sometimes we do not know why infants stop crying but they do often stop crying when they are held. Most infants cry frequently but we don't know why, and holding the infant or soothing him seems ineffective . . .

If parents are counselled to understand how much a normal infant cries, then they may feel less guilty and they may be less concerned. But some parents are so distressed when their infant cries that they cannot logically suppress feeling guilty. Those parents may need to spend time somewhere away from where the infant is crying so that they can cope appropriately and not feel distressed. Unless they are relieved, they will get tired and tense and they may respond inappropriately when their infant cries and may leave the infant in the house or abuse the infant.

As this shows, unpacking a text often involves re-inserting human actors, often rendered unnecessary by nominalization. The ability of nominalization to condense meanings is also clearly shown when we simply compare the length of the original nominalized text with the length of the unpacked version.

Significantly, this unpacked version has lost much of its 'prestigious' sound: it now seems very much more ordinary (and perhaps more accessible) than the original text. If we also substituted more everyday lexical items for the academic vocabulary used (e.g. used *baby* instead of *infant*), the text would seem very much like Text 1.1.

And this begins to explain how Text 1.1 achieves its aim of pitching itself to a more popular audience: how it will meet what we will see below are tenor demands to create a more 'friendly fellow-sufferer' (rather than 'distant objective specialist') role for the writer. It does it by being more like talk. This can be demonstrated by **packing** the text, i.e. increasing the lexical density, by nominalizing more frequently. For example:

Text 1.1 packed

An infant's incessant crying can lead to despair on the part of caregivers. When feeding, changing, nursing and soothing techniques fail, the reasons for his crying are not immediately discernible. The most common reason for crying is hunger. Even following a recent feed the infant may still be experiencing adaptation to the pattern of satisfaction resulting from sucking until replete, followed by dissatisfaction due to the subsequent experience of emptiness. As a foetus, nourishment came automatically and constantly. Food should be offered first. In the event that the infant declines nourishment from either breast or teat, another cause can be assumed for his crying . . .

The effect of nominalization here is to make Text 1.1 sound very much like Text 1.2: heavy and serious. We thus see that Texts 1.1 and 1.2, while both written texts, exploit the potential to nominalize quite differently: Text 1.2 uses heavy nominalization to make it quite clear that it is a reflective, authoritative text; Text 1.1 keeps nominalization to a minimum in order to retain some of the immediacy and personalization typical of speech.

Nominalization is one type of what Halliday identifies as **grammatical metaphor**, situations where meanings typically (**congruently**) realized by one type of language pattern get realized by other less typical (**incongruent**) linguistic choices. The concept is explained and exemplified more fully in Halliday (1985a: Chapter 10, 1985c), Eggins *et al.* (1992), Martin (1992a: 406–17) and Martin and Rose (2003: 103–9).

To this point, we have used nominalization to demonstrate very briefly some of the effects that the mode of a situation has on language use. The different types of linguistic patterns found in spoken as opposed to written situations are the realization of the impact of mode on language.

It would seem then that we can justify the claim that mode is an important aspect of context, for mode clearly has an effect on how we use language. We can now turn to consider tenor.

Tenor

Our initial definition of tenor was 'the social role relationships played by interactants'. For example, roles such as student/lecturer, customer/salesperson, friend/ friend.

Instinctively you can no doubt recognize that the kind of social role you are playing in a situation will have an effect on how you use language. For example, you do not talk to the greengrocer the same way as you talk to your mother. However, we need to get more precise about just what aspects of the tenor of situations are important, and in what ways.

Building on early studies of language variation and role relationship variables such as formality, politeness and reciprocity (e.g. Brown and Gilman 1960/1972), Cate Poynton (1985) has suggested that tenor can be broken down into three different continua: **power,**

contact and **affective involvement**. What this means is that the general notion of 'role relationships' can be seen as a complex of these three simultaneous dimensions:

1. **power**: Figure 4.3 schematizes the power continuum, which positions situations in terms of whether the roles we are playing are those in which we are of equal or unequal power. Examples of roles of equal power are those of friends; examples of roles of unequal (non-reciprocal) power would be those of boss/employee.
2. **contact**: Figure 4.4 schematizes the contact continuum, which positions situations in terms of whether the roles we are playing are those that bring us into frequent or infrequent contact. For example, contrast the frequent contact between spouses, with the occasional contact with distant acquaintances.
3. **affective involvement**: Figure 4.5 schematizes the affective involvement continuum, in which situations can be positioned according to whether the roles we are playing are those in which the affective involvement between us is high or low. This dimension refers to the extent to which we are emotionally involved or committed in a situation. For example, friends or lovers are obviously affectively involved, whereas work associates are typically not.

Halliday's identification, and Poynton's sub-classification, of tenor is proposed as more than just an interesting description of the interpersonal aspects of situations. It is proposed as a direct claim about the link between language and context. The claim, then, is that these aspects of our role occupation in a given situation will have an impact on how we use language.

Following the approach we used to discuss mode, we can draw a contrast between two situation types, the **informal** and the **formal**, according to their typical tenor dimensions. Thus, as summarized in Table 4.8, an informal situation would typically involve interactants who are of equal power, who see each other frequently, and who are affectively involved (e.g. close friends). A formal situation would be one where the power between the interactants is not equal, the contact is infrequent, and the affective involvement low (e.g. a first-year university student meeting the Vice Chancellor).

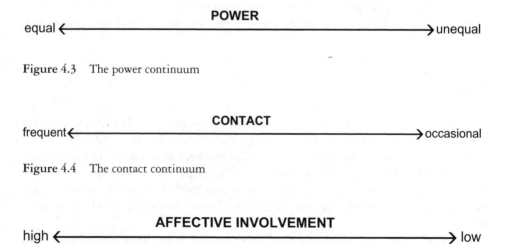

POWER

equal ⟵————————————————————————⟶ unequal

Figure 4.3   The power continuum

CONTACT

frequent ⟵————————————————————————⟶ occasional

Figure 4.4   The contact continuum

AFFECTIVE INVOLVEMENT

high ⟵————————————————————————⟶ low

Figure 4.5   The affective involvement continuum

Table 4.8 Formal vs informal situations

TENOR: typical situations of language use	
INFORMAL	**FORMAL**
equal power	unequal, hierarchic power
frequent contact	infrequent, or one-off contact
high affective involvement	low affective involvement

Just as we did with mode, so with tenor we can establish that language use will vary quite significantly from the informal to the formal situation. These differences, summarized in Table 4.9 below, include different vocabulary choices. In informal situations (e.g. chatting with our friends) we tend to use words that express our attitude (*fantastic, shitty, unbelievable*). Attitudinal lexis can express either a positive or a negative evaluation, and we often refer to these as 'purr and snarl' words. In a formal situation, on the other hand, we tend to keep our attitudes to ourselves, or to express them in apparently objective language (*unfortunate, surprising*). Lexis will also differ in terms of its degree of standardization: in informal situations, we frequently use slang and abbreviated forms of word (*chockies*). In the formal situation we use the complete lexical item (*chocolates*), and avoid slang. Other lexical differences will be that in formal language we find many politeness expressions (*please, thank you, you're welcome*, etc.), often absent from informal language. Swearing, while common in informal settings, is taboo in most formal situations.

One area of considerable interest that differentiates the informal from the formal is that of **vocatives** (see Poynton 1984 for a detailed discussion). Vocatives, or terms of address, are the words that people call each other when, for example, they wish to get each other's attention. The choice of which vocative to use reveals important tenor dimensions. Compare: *Sir John! Mr Smith! John! Johnno! Darl! Idiot Features!* As these examples indicate, vocatives are a very potent area for the realization of interpersonal meanings, an area very sensitive to these contextual constraints of tenor.

Poynton's study of vocatives in Australian English has suggested that there are correlations between the dimensions of power, contact and affect and the choice of vocatives. It appears that:

- when power is equal, vocative use is reciprocal: if I call you by your first name, you will call me by my first name. Or if I use title plus surname, so will you
- where power is unequal, vocative use will be non-reciprocal: you may call your doctor *Dr Bloggs*, but he may call you *Peter*
- where contact is frequent we often use nicknames: *Johnno, Pete, Shirl*
- where contact is infrequent, we often have no vocatives at all (e.g. the clerk at the post office, or the bus driver)
- where affective involvement is high, we use diminutive forms of names and terms of endearment: *Georgie-Porgie, Petie-Pie, Honey Bunch, Darl*
- where affective involvement is low, we use formal 'given' names: *Peter, Suzanne*.

Aside from vocatives, there are many other very significant ways in which these dimensions of tenor impact on language use. For example, in casual conversations (where you are talking not to achieve any clear pragmatic purpose but are just chatting), we can see a clear correlation between the tenor variables and both the length and type of interaction:

- where both affective involvement and contact are low (e.g. a conversation with your neighbour), conversations tend to be fairly brief; whereas with high affective involvement and frequent contact (e.g. with friends), conversations can go on for hours.
- in addition, where affective involvement and contact are low, the conversation will emphasize consensus and agreement; whereas where contact and affect are high, the conversation is likely to be characterized by controversy and disagreement (Eggins 1990, Eggins and Slade 1997).

These correlations help explain both why we find 'polite' conversation so difficult to sustain, and also why we spend most of our time with our friends arguing!

One further area in which tenor differences impact on language use concerns the grammatical systems of **mood** and **modality**. These systems will be explored in detail in Chapter Six. Briefly, what we find is that just as the variable of mode can be related to nominalization (one kind of grammatical metaphor), so the variable of tenor can be related to a different kind of grammatical metaphor: metaphor where we play with what we call the mood structure of the clause. Imagine you need help moving some furniture. In an informal situation (e.g. at home) you might turn to your partner/kids/friends and say:

> Hey, Freddie! Get off your butt and give me a hand here. Shove that chair over closer to the desk.

Now imagine that you are moving furniture at work, and that the only available helper is your boss. This time you might say:

> Oh, Dr Smith. I'm just trying to tidy my office up a bit and I wondered if you'd mind maybe giving me a quick hand with moving some furniture? If you've got time, I mean. It won't take a moment. Now if we could just move this chair over a bit nearer to the desk there. Thanks very much.

If we compare these two examples, we can see a number of the differences we have already discussed: the choice of vocatives, use/avoidance of slang and politeness phenomena. But another major difference between the two concerns the choice of clause structure. In the informal version, we see that to get an action carried out by somebody else we would use an **imperative** clause (*get off your butt, shove that chair*). This is the typical choice of clause type we use when commanding family and friends. But in the formal situation, although the speaker is still making a demand of the other person, this time the clause type is the **interrogative** or question (*would you mind . . . if we could . . .*). The interrogatives also involve the use of words like *would, could, mind*, words we describe as functioning to **modulate** or attenuate the request. Clauses which package requests indirectly, using structures other than imperatives, are examples of grammatical metaphor. Thus, one of the realizations of the tenor of the situation can be seen in the choice of mood and related grammatical areas. These differences are summarized in Table 4.9 below.

It seems, then, that we can establish that as well as mode having an effect on language patterns, so do the values for tenor. The last situational variable we need to consider is field.

Table 4.9   Formal vs informal language

FORMAL and INFORMAL LANGUAGE: the linguistic consequences of TENOR	
INFORMAL language	FORMAL language
attitudinal lexis (purr and snarl words)	neutral lexis
colloquial lexis	formal lexis
– abbreviated forms	– full forms
– slang	– no slang
	politeness phenomena (Ps and Qs)
swearing	– no swearing
interruptions, overlap	careful turn-taking
first names	titles, no names
nicknames	
diminutives	
typical mood choices	incongruent mood choices
modalization to express probability	modalization to express deference
modulation to express opinion	modulation to express suggestion

Field

We initially defined field as the situational variable that has to do with the focus of the activity in which we are engaged. Sometimes field can be glossed as the 'topic' of the situation, but Martin's (1984: 23, 1992a: 536) broader definition in terms of institutional focus or social activity type is more useful to capture the field in situations where language is accompanying action.

The effect of field on language use is perhaps the easiest register variable to demonstrate convincingly. Consider the following text:

Text 4.4: PC Care

A PC which won't stop crashing can drive anyone to despair. You boot it, you format your CDs, you create a file, you try to protect your edits, but the minute you try to save your file to a CD, the PC crashes. Why? The most common reason computers crash is faulty CDs. Even if the CD is brand new, it might still have a faulty track and so the CD won't accept any messages from the CPU. When the CDs are packaged, they pass through often lengthy transportation, and may be damaged in the process. Try another CD first; if the PC still crashes you can assume it's something else. It happens that PCs sometimes crash for inexplicable reasons – perhaps they are just overloaded. Perhaps you have inadvertently entered an unacceptable control code, or have accidentally pressed too many keys at once. Perhaps the CPU is faulty . . . etc.

You will no doubt have quickly recognized this text as very similar to Text 1.1, our first Crying Baby text from Chapter One. In fact, this text is exactly the same as Text 1.1, but for one thing: the field has changed, from childcare to 'PC care'. As you can see, changing the field has had a very immediate and significant impact on the text, particularly on the content words used.

But there is more to field than these obvious changes of topic. Consider now Texts 4.5 and 4.6 below:

Text 4.5: The Bermuda Bowl[2]

After three 16-board segments of the quarterfinals of the 1991 Bermuda Bowl. Iceland was well ahead of US-2 but the other matches were more competitive.

Fourth Segment

Board 52 furthered both the Brazilian and Polish rallies.

South dealer

Both sides vulnerable

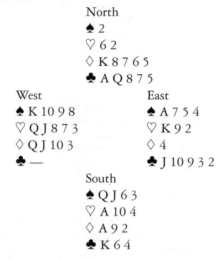

North
♠ 2
♡ 6 2
♢ K 8 7 6 5
♣ A Q 8 7 5

West
♠ K 10 9 8
♡ Q J 8 7 3
♢ Q J 10 3
♣ —

East
♠ A 7 5 4
♡ K 9 2
♢ 4
♣ J 10 9 3 2

South
♠ Q J 6 3
♡ A 10 4
♢ A 9 2
♣ K 6 4

US-1 vs BRAZIL

Table 1

South	West	North	East
P. Branco	*M'stroth*	*Mello*	*Rodwell*
1 ♣	Double	3 ♣	Pass
Pass	Pass		

Table 2

South	West	North	East
Miller	*Chagas*	*Sontag*	*M. Branco*
1 ♣	1 ♡	2 ♡	3 ♡
Pass	Pass	4 ♣	Double
Pass	Pass	Pass	

Rodwell's decision to pass out three clubs seems wise, and was justified by the layout – he went plus and had no obvious making contract of his own – but this led to the lowest East-West score on this trouble deal. Declarer won the diamond lead with the ace, cashed the club ace, recoiled, and led a spade to the jack and king. West tried the three of diamonds, but declarer deep-finessed, suffered a ruff, won the trump return with dummy's queen, cashed the club king, and gave up another diamond ruff. West had pitched hearts on the early trump leads, so the defense had to let declarer make his spade queen for an eighth trick, minus 100.

At Table 2 the final contract was not bad, the layout was awful. Declarer won the diamond lead with dummy's king to lead a spade: queen, king. Declarer won the heart shift with the ace, and led to the club ace to lead a diamond towards the ace in the closed hand. East discarded, so the declarer took his diamond ace, ruffed a spade, and exited with a heart. A further major-suit ruff in dummy could not be prevented; declarer had five clubs, two diamonds and a heart, eight tricks, minus 500, 9 imps to Brazil.

ICELAND vs US-2

Table 3

South	West	North	East
Ornstein	*Bald'sson*	*Ferro*	*Jorgensen*
1 ♣	1 ♡	2 ♡	3 ♡
Pass	Pass	4 ♣	Double
Pass	Pass	Pass	

Table 4

South	West	North	East
Arnarson	*Bramley*	*Johnsson*	*Feldman*
1 ♣	1 ♡	2 ♡	3 ♡
3 NT	4 ♡	Double	Pass
Pass	Pass		

At Table 3, declarer won the diamond ace, led to the club queen, ducked a diamond to West's ten. Then, he won the heart shift with the ace and finessed in diamonds, East ruffing. The defense cashed two major-suit winners, then tapped dummy, but declarer was in control – he took two high clubs ending in dummy and continued diamonds. Nicely played, but only the same eight tricks, minus 500.

Text 4.6: excerpt from Marston's *Bridge Workbook for Beginners*[3]
How Bridge is played

In this lesson you will learn the basic rules of the game. You will learn which bids you are allowed to make and those that you are not. You will also learn that the number of tricks you must take is dependent upon the bidding. The basic mechanics of whose turn it is to play, whose turn it is to lead and so on will be covered.

Bridge is a game for four players who form two partnerships. An ordinary deck of cards is used without jokers or bowers. The cards are ranked from the ace (highest), king, queen, jack, ten, nine, eight and so on down to the two. The full pack is dealt, one card at a time, in a clockwise direction, starting with the player on the dealer's left, so that each player begins with 13 cards.

Tricks

The cards are played out one at a time. One card from each of the four players is called a 'trick'. Each player plays in turn in a clockwise direction around the table and each player must follow suit if he can, that is if a spade is led (the first card played in a trick) each player must play a spade if he has one. If he cannot follow suit a player may play any card he wishes. The player who plays the highest card in the suit wins the trick, unless a trump has been played, but more about that in a moment. The player who wins the trick leads to the next trick. There is no need to keep track of the individual who has won the trick, only which partnership. Let's look at a sample trick:

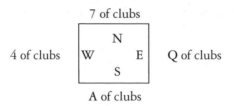

You may be wondering what the W, E, S, N is. In bridge diagrams, for easy reference, the four players are referred to by the four cardinal points. Assume that West was the first to play and led the four of clubs, North followed with the seven, East tried to win the trick for his side with the queen but South won the trick with the ace. South would then lead to the next trick.

Naturally each player works in with his partner. For example, if your partner led the king of spades you wouldn't top it with the ace unless you had to. If, however, one of the opponents led the king of spades you would play the ace because you would know that your partner could not possibly beat the king.

Trumps

A trump suit may be named in the bidding. When that happens that suit takes precedence over the others. When a trump is played on a trick it wins the trick no matter what is led. Here is an example:

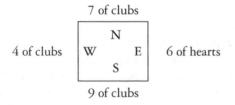

Imagine that hearts are trumps and West leads the four of clubs. North plays the seven of clubs and East who has run out of clubs plays a small trump. South must follow suit with a club so East's six of trumps wins the trick. If South was also out of clubs he would have won the trick by playing a trump higher the six.

The auction

A hand of bridge is played in two stages. First there is the auction to determine which suit, if any, is to be trumps and how many tricks must be won. Then comes the play of cards when the side that won the 'contract' tries to fulfil their obligation while the opposition are doing there best to take enough tricks to defeat them. The contract is the name of the last bid in the auction.

After the cards have been dealt the dealer has the right to make the first bid. He will pass with a weak hand and bid with a hand of above average strength. A bid in bridge is an undertaking to win the stated number of tricks plus six with the nominated suit as trumps, or no trumps. No trumps is as you would think – the highest card in the suit that's led ALWAYS wins the trick since there are no trumps to interfere. A bid of say 3 ♣ is an undertaking by that partnership to take at least nine tricks with clubs as trumps; a bid of six no trumps means your side must take at least 12 tricks without a trump suit.

As in other sorts of auction the early bids are usually made at a low level. After the dealer has made his bid or passed, the player on his left has a turn.

Both these texts have the same field: both texts are about the game of bridge. However, it is very clear that the situations which gave rise to each of these texts were very different: while Text 4.5 is written for experts (serious competition players), Text 4.6 is written for beginners. It seems, then, that we need to recognize that situations may be either technical or everyday in their construction of an activity focus. In other words, field varies along a dimension of technicality, as is schematized in Figure 4.6.

A situation which we would describe as technical would be characterized by a significant degree of assumed knowledge among the interactants about the activity focus, whereas in an everyday (or commonsense) situation, the only assumed knowledge is 'common knowledge'. The knowledge that constitutes a field can be represented in **taxonomies,** by asking 'how do people who act in this field classify and sub-classify the areas of the field?' When we construct field taxonomies, we find a striking difference between the depth and complexity of a technical taxonomy and that of a commonsense taxonomy. For example, part of the taxonomy of bridge which specialist bridge players share is represented in the following taxonomy, in Figure 4.7.

We can see that this taxonomy is complex: it involves initial classification of *bridge* into three main aspects, each of which is further sub-classified. The extent of the sub-classification involves up to five steps. Sub-classification to this degree produces what we describe as a **deep taxonomy**. This particular deep taxonomy represents a detailed, in-depth organization of the activity focus of bridge, and the taxonomy can thus be seen to encode the expert's understanding of the field of bridge.

Compare this to the layperson's taxonomy, in Figure 4.8.

As we can see, the commonsense taxonomy has a larger number of initial cuts (the basic classification of the activity into constituent aspects is more diverse, less generalized), but each aspect is only sub-classified a further one or two times. Thus, this **shallow taxonomy** captures the layperson's encoding of the field of bridge, which can be seen to be significantly different from the technical construction of that same field.

Table 4.10 summarizes the differences between technical and everyday situations.
As Texts 4.5 and 4.6 demonstrate, there are a number of linguistic implications to this variation in field. The most striking feature is that in a technical situation we find a heavy use of technical terms: not just technical nouns (*contract, ruff, layout, tricks*) but also verbs (*to pass out, to go plus, to cash a trick, to deep-finesse, to suffer a ruff*). These terms are usually drawn from the 'deep' end of the taxonomy, and of course no explanation for the terms is given. Even more inaccessible to the layperson are technical acronyms (IMPs). This use of 'jargon' is not designed to impress the outsider, although it can be used in that disempowering way. Its principal motivation is to allow the elaboration of the deep taxonomies of the field.

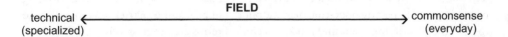

FIELD

technical ←————————————————————————————→ commonsense
(specialized)   (everyday)

Figure 4.6   The field continuum

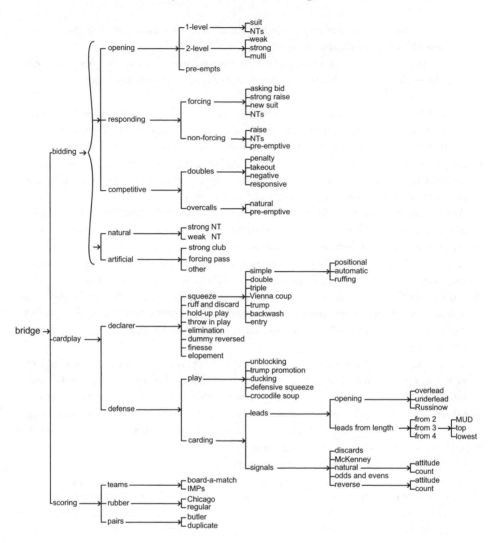

Figure 4.7   Bridge player's taxonomy of bridge

Technicality is not only encoded in the lexis, however. Technical texts frequently use abbreviated, non-standard syntax, although Text 4.5 does not. Instead, it exploits another common technical technique: the use of a visual representation of a type particular to the field (e.g. the bidding sequence diagrams in Text 4.5). The types of verbs used tend to be of technical processes (*trump, squeeze, finesse*), or of attributive (descriptive) processes (*the final contract was not bad*). These grammatical choices reflect the focus of a technical situation, which is to relate, comment on and evaluate an already shared knowledge base.

Language in an everyday field is more familiar to us: the lexis tends to consist of everyday words. Where a term is used technically, it will usually be signalled as such by being printed in bold or having quotation marks around it (e.g. Text 4.6: a 'trick'). Verbs will tend to be of the identifying (defining) kind, as technical terms are progressively introduced and defined (e.g. *bridge is a game for four players; one card from each of the four players is called a 'trick'*). The grammatical structures will be standard, and acronyms and visual representations will

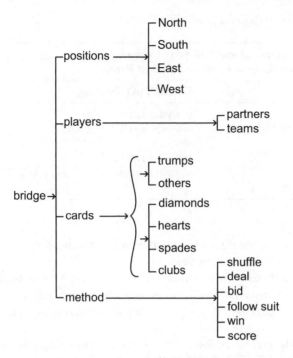

Figure 4.8 Non-player's taxonomy of bridge

Table 4.10 Technical vs everyday situations

TECHNICAL situation	EVERYDAY situation

assumed knowledge of an activity/
  institution/area
	'common knowledge'
	  no (or little) assumed knowledge

deep taxonomies	shallow taxonomies
– detailed sub-classification	– limited sub-classification

only be used if they are first introduced and explained. Text 4.6 provides a clear example of how readers are moved from the everyday understanding of bridge towards its technical construction. These differences in technical and everyday language are summarized in Table 4.11 below.

Since we can find clear linguistic implications corresponding to situational variation in the focus or topic of an activity, we are thus justified in claiming that field is a linguistically relevant dimension of the context of situation.

Register and types of meaning in language

If the claim that field, mode and tenor are the significant situational variables were the full extent of register theory, then it would have the same limitations identified for Firth's contextual description. But Halliday differs from Firth in that he pushed the analysis one step further and asked: *why these three variables?* Why are field, mode and tenor the three key aspects of situation? And he suggests that the answer lies in the structure of the semiotic system of language itself.

Table 4.11   Technical vs everyday language

<table>
<tr><td colspan="2" align="center">Technical and Everyday Language:
the linguistic implications of FIELD</td></tr>
<tr><td>TECHNICAL language</td><td>EVERYDAY language</td></tr>
<tr><td>technical terms</td><td>everyday terms</td></tr>
<tr><td>– words only 'insiders' understand</td><td>– words we all understand</td></tr>
<tr><td>acronyms</td><td>full names</td></tr>
<tr><td>abbreviated syntax</td><td>standard syntax</td></tr>
<tr><td>technical action processes
   attributive (descriptive) processes</td><td>identifying processes (defining terms)</td></tr>
</table>

Halliday claims that these are the three variables that matter because they are the three kinds of meanings language is structured to make.

He reaches this conclusion by analysing (in much more detail than we have been able to do here) exactly how each register variable affects language use. It turns out to be possible to identify parts of the language system that are concerned with realizing each type of contextual information.

Consider, for example, the variable of field. When I changed the field of Text 1.1 from childcare to PC care, I clearly did not change every linguistic feature of the text (you would not have recognized it as 'like Text 1.1' if I had).

This suggests that field is realized through just some parts of the grammatical system – in fact, through the patterns of processes (verbs), participants (nouns) and circumstances (prepositional phrases of time, manner, place, etc.). These types of grammatical patterns, expressing 'who is doing what to whom when where why and how', can be collectively described as the **transitivity** patterns in language. Describing these transitivity patterns is the focus of Chapter Eight.

With tenor, by contrast, we find interpersonal meanings of roles and relationships realized not through the transitivity patterns, but through patterns of what we call **mood**. As we will see in Chapter Six, mood refers to variables such as the types of clause structure (declarative, interrogative), the degree of certainty or obligation expressed (modality), the use of tags, vocatives, attitudinal words which are either positively or negatively loaded (the 'purr and snarl' words mentioned above), expressions of intensification and politeness markers of various kinds.

Mode is realized through yet a further area of the language system, that of **theme**. These textual patterns, to be explored in Chapter Ten, are patterns of foregrounding and continuity in the organization of the clause. Figure 4.9 schematizes this link between the register variables and their lexico-grammatical realizations.

It would seem, then, that there is a correlation between the situational dimensions of context and these different types of lexico-grammatical patterns. However, a further stage in this link between context and language comes from the SFL claim that the lexico-grammatical organization of language is itself a realization of the **semantic** organization of language.

You will remember from Chapter One that when we asked what a text means, we were able to identify three different strands of meaning: the **ideational**, the **interpersonal** and the **textual**. In identifying these three main types of meaning, Halliday is suggesting that of all the *uses* we make of language (which are limitless and changing), language is designed

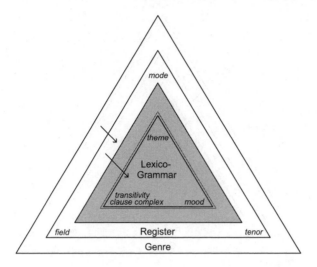

Figure 4.9   Context in relation to language

to fulfil three main *functions*: a function for relating experience, a function for creating inter-personal relationships, and a function for organizing information.

Halliday suggests that these types of meaning can be related both 'upwards' (to context) and 'downwards' (to lexico-grammar).

The upwards link is that each register variable can be associated with one of these types of meanings. Thus, field is expressed through patterns of ideational meaning in text, mode is expressed through textual meaning, and tenor through interpersonal meaning.

The downwards link is that we 'see' the types of meanings being realized through the associated lexico-grammatical patterns. Thus, putting this all together, Halliday claims that:

- the **field** of a text can be associated with the realization of **ideational** meanings; these ideational meanings are realized through the **Transitivity** and **Clause Complex** patterns of the grammar.
- the **mode** of a text can be associated with the realization of **textual** meanings; these textual meanings are realized through the **Theme** patterns of the grammar.
- the **tenor** of a text can be associated with the realization of **interpersonal** meanings; these interpersonal meanings are realized through the **Mood** patterns of the grammar.

These relationships are represented in Figure 4.10.

Thus, the claim Halliday makes is that each type of meaning is related in a predictable, systematic way to each situational variable. It is therefore no accident that we single out the three register variables of field, mode and tenor as the aspects of the situation significant to language use. Their status derives from the fact that they are linked to the three types of meaning language is structured to make: the ideational, the textual and the interpersonal. We can see that language is structured to make these three kinds of meanings because we find in the lexico-grammar the main grammatical resources of Transitivity, Clause Complex, Theme and Mood.

As this is a complex picture, one final restatement may be useful. Language is structured to make three kinds of meanings. And these are the three kinds of meanings that matter in

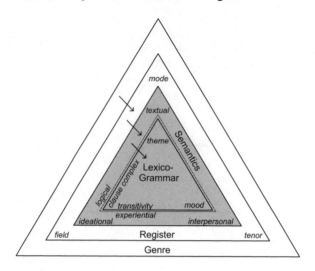

Figure 4.10   Context, semantics and lexico-grammar

any situation. It is this non-arbitrary organization of language that Halliday means when he states that:

> The internal organization of natural language can best be explained in the light of the social functions which language has evolved to serve. *Language is as it is because of what it has to do.* (Halliday 1973: 34: my emphasis)

We have thus reached a point where exploring our initial functional question (how is language used?) has led us to explore the more abstract dimension of 'functional' in the systemic approach: how is language structured for use? It is this second question which will be explored in Chapters Five to Ten, as we pursue an approach that is functional not only in relation to language use, but also in relation to the organization of the linguistic system itself. The core of the linguistic system is the lexico-grammar, and Chapter Five begins our exploration of the lexico-grammatical level of language by asking what grammar does and how we can analyse its patterns.

Notes

1. Source: *School of English Handbook* (1993), School of English, University of New South Wales, p. 4.
2. Source: *The Bridge World*, Vol. 63, No. 7, April 1992, pp. 4–5, 'The Bermuda Bowl III'.
3. Source: P. Marston and R. Brightling *The Bridge Workbook for Beginners* (1985), Contract Bridge Supplies, Sydney, pp. 1–3.

Chapter 5

Introduction to the lexico-grammar

Introduction

While Chapters Two, Three and Four have looked at how people use language in texts and how those texts make meanings in cultural and situational contexts, this chapter begins our exploration of the lexico-grammatical level of language by asking: what is the function of grammar? That is, why does language have this intermediate level of grammatical coding? The chapter then examines some basic principles of SFL grammatical analysis, and presents the multifunctional perspective on the clause that will be developed in subsequent chapters.

The traffic lights revisited: extending the system

In Chapter One, traffic lights were described as a two-level semiotic system, involving a level of content realized through a level of expression. Language, on the other hand, was seen to involve three levels: two levels of content (semantics and lexico-grammar), encoded in phonology. The difference between the simple and the complex semiotic systems, then, was the presence of this level of wording, the lexico-grammar.

The lexico-grammatical level was described simply as an intermediate level of linguistic coding. We must now consider in more detail what the function of this level is. What, for example, does it allow us to do in language that we cannot do with a two-level semiotic system like the traffic lights?

We can approach this question by considering how we could extend the traffic light system. The red/amber/green system that was described in Chapter One has two limitations:

1. it does not allow us to mean very much: in fact, we can only make three meanings.
2. it only allows us to mean *one thing at a time*: there is a one-to-one (**bi-unique**) relationship between content and expression, as each expression (coloured light) stands for one and only one content (desired behaviour), so each content is realized by one and only one expression.

Two strategies could be used to develop the system so that it could *make more meanings*. Firstly, new contents could be added to the system – we could simply increase the number of meanings the system can make. Alternatively, contents could be fused – we could try to use the system to make more than one meaning at a time. Each strategy rapidly becomes problematic.

Adding new contents

If we wish to extend the system so that we can mean more things (for example, we want to add the meaning 'reverse' to the system), we will have to find a new light to stand for this meaning. For each new content we must invent a new expression. For example, we could introduce a PINK light to encode this new meaning, giving us System 5.1.

To economize on the number of coloured lights we need to use, we could start using variations or combinations of expressions to realize new contents. See, for example, the realizations in System 5.2.

Thus, for each new content we can either come up with a completely new expression (a new coloured light), or we can combine the existing coloured lights in various ways.

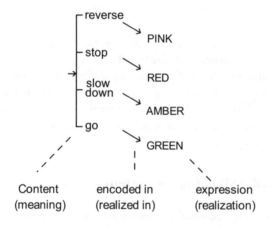

System 5.1   Extending the traffic light system

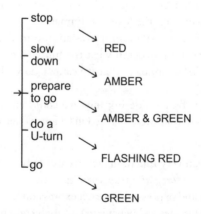

System 5.2   Combining expressions in the traffic light system

Very quickly this system will become far too cumbersome, both to remember and to distinguish. By the time we add 20 new meanings to our system, we are likely to be having trouble both finding new colours that can be clearly differentiated by our drivers, and remembering what each particular combination means.

Thus it seems that the traffic light system has a very significant drawback: its **creative potential** is very limited. It cannot mean much, and it cannot mean many new things.

Simultaneous meanings

An alternative strategy is to extend the system so that it is able to *mean more than one thing at a time*. Thus, an expression is to realize more than one content. This can be done through the use of complex signs, or sign sequences. For example, if we want to mean both 'stop' and 'danger ahead', we could:

1. introduce a new **complex sign**, e.g. a RED LIGHT with a BLACK DOT. This expression is complex as it can be broken down into two parts: a part meaning 'stop' (the colour red) and a part meaning 'danger ahead' (the black dot). Such complex signs are in fact like many of our normal road signs.
2. introduce a **sequence** of signs, e.g. alternating a RED LIGHT followed by a flashing AMBER light would mean both 'stop' and 'danger ahead'.

However, again it would not be long before the system would become unmanageable. Again, the traffic light system appears very limited. As soon as we try to extend it to make more meanings, we run into problems with remembering and distinguishing different lights or sequences of lights.

In real life this does not become a problem, because we only want traffic lights to make a very few meanings. We use traffic lights to make perhaps half a dozen meanings (stop, go, prepare to stop, go if turning right/left, stop if turning right/left, etc.). Even the more elaborate sign system of our road signs makes only a few dozen meanings altogether. It seems that these semiotic systems work quite well in those contexts, since we only need them to make a very limited number of meanings.

The demands we make of language

However, with the semiotic system of language, we want to make many many more meanings than that. In fact, the amazing demand we make of language is that we want to use it *to mean anything at all* – to make an infinite number of meanings. Language meets this demand, in that it has an unlimited **creative potential**. That is:

- language allows us to mean new things: you can say things that no one has ever said before, and you have no trouble understanding things that you have never heard before. So, while you could never hope to have heard every sentence it is possible to say in English, you will have no difficulty understanding any English sentence said to you (provided it conforms to the conventions of the system of English).
- language allows us to mean anything: it is very rare that, as a speaker of a language, you would come to a point where all of a sudden you cannot make the meanings

you want to because the system is too limited. (When this does sometimes happen, it is often because we are overcome with emotion or because we want to talk about ideas or beliefs which, being new to the culture, have not yet been encoded within the language.)

Since we are able to make infinite meanings in language, language is very different from the traffic lights. The explanation for this difference lies in the fact that language is not a bi-unique semiotic system. There is not a one-to-one correspondence between the content levels of language and the expression level.

If language were such a bi-unique system, one content would be paired with one expression, i.e. one meaning would equal one sound. Every time we wanted to make a new meaning, we would have to introduce a new sound. If language were based on this bi-unique principle, we would run into the same problems of memory and distinguishability that we found in extending the traffic lights.

This is clearly not the way language works. There is something about language that allows us to re-use sounds, so that individual sounds can be related to their occurrences in combinations. Perhaps, then, there is a bi-unique relationship between meanings and words, rather than between meanings and sounds?

But again we can quickly appreciate that language does not operate on such a principle. If there were a bi-unique relationship between meanings and words, language would be a system where every word in the language had one and only one meaning, and every meaning was realized by one and only one word.

In such a system, every time we wanted to make a new meaning we would have to invent a new word. The situation would not be very different from the one we just reviewed: the obvious problems of memory and distinguishability again arise. How could we ever remember all the words? How could we find enough new sound configurations to realize the meanings?

To avoid these impossible feats of memory and differentiation, there must be some economy principle operating in language that does not operate in systems like the traffic lights. We do not have one sound corresponding to one meaning, nor one word corresponding to one meaning. How is it, then, that language is different? How has language got away from this restriction of bi-uniqueness?

Lexico-grammar: the difference

What makes language different is that it has an intermediate level of **lexico-grammar**, what we more informally refer to simply as the **grammatical** level. The function of this grammatical level is to free language from the constraints of bi-uniqueness.

The effect of this freedom is that language can take a finite number of expression units (sounds) to realize an infinite number of contents (meanings). Thus, in language we use finite means to realize infinite ends.

The lexico-grammar allows us to do this by providing us with the means to combine sounds into words, which can then be arranged in different **grammatical structures** to make different meanings. For example, we can take the four words *John, eat, poached* and *eggs,* and by arranging them in different grammatical structures we get a range of different meanings, as shown in Table 5.1.

Table 5.1   Arranging words in structures

Expression	Meaning
John eats poached eggs.	statement about John's habitual behaviour vis-à-vis eggs
John is eating poached eggs.	statement about John's current behaviour regarding eggs
John ate poached eggs.	statement about John's past action
Poached eggs are eaten by John.	statement about something that happens to eggs
Did John eat poached eggs?	request for information about John's past action
Does John eat poached eggs?	request for information about John's habitual behaviour
John, eat poached eggs.	command to John to carry out action of eating
Poached eggs ate John.	statement about what John ate
Poach eggs, John.	command to John to carry out action of 'poaching'

One part of what these sentences mean is the words that are used (that we're talking about *eggs* and not *books, John* and not *the dog, eating* and not *running*). But a second part of their meanings is the arrangement of these words in **structures**. It is the structural differences that give us the meaning differences between making a statement or asking a question or commanding (technically, different **mood** choices). Similarly, structural differences are responsible for the meaning differences between talking about something that habitually happens, versus something happening now, or in the past (different verbal group patterns). (These structural differences underlie the need for slight modifications to the verbal element (*eat*) in order to express different meanings.)

Extending language

That the lexico-grammar provides language with an in-built creative potential can be demonstrated by attempting to extend language. As a first example, let us say that I want to make a new lexical meaning. For instance, I invent a machine that writes lectures automatically – you just feed in the topic, a list of the main points, and then you press a button and off it goes. How can I encode this new meaning in the language?

The first possible way is by inventing a totally new word, i.e. by creating a new sign, an arbitrary pairing of a content and an expression. For example, suppose I decide to call my machine a *boofer*. Now how did I get this new word? I took a certain number of sounds of English and arranged them in a novel way. However, it is important to note that I did not take just *any* sounds, nor did I arrange them in just *any* way. For example, I could not have called my new machine a *hvristu*, since HV is not an acceptable sound sequence in English.

Having 'coined' my new word in keeping with the phonological rules of English (the rules of the expression plane), it is now available for use in structures:

> Put it in the boofer.
> I'm just doing some boofing.
> Boof it for me will you?
> I boofed this lecture.
> She's a specialist in boofography.
> This material is not boofographic.
> She's a boofer programmer.

Although I only invented one word, I automatically have a creative potential to do a variety of new things with it. This creative potential comes from the grammar – the principles of coding for English which allow us to turn a noun into a verb, adjective, adverb, etc. and thus use it in a range of structures to make different meanings.

However, when I invented my new machine it is actually not very likely that I would invent an entirely new word. In fact, what I would probably do is to call my machine something like a *lecture-writer* or an *auto-writer* or a *lecturer's-aid*. In other words, I would exploit the in-built creative lexical potential of language to come up with a non-arbitrary name. Thus, instead of taking sounds to invent a whole new word, I would take words, pre-existing content units, and combine them in a novel way to express my new meaning. Again, as soon as I do that I gain access to the creative potential of language:

> This is lecture-written.
> He did it on a lecture-writer.
> Lecture-writers are on special at the moment.

Coining new words or combining existing words in novel ways represent the two most obvious ways speakers exploit the creative potential of language. Both are ways of using the finite phonological means of a language to achieve infinite semantic ends, and both are only possible thanks to the intermediate coding level of language.

However, the creative potential of language is not limited to the creation of new words and their automatic availability for use in grammatical structures. We can also use the grammatical repertoire of the language to make a meaning in an untypical, 'creatively different' way.

Imagine that my first-year students are restless and beginning to chatter among themselves during one of my lectures. One way I might achieve my desire for quiet in the room would be to say *Shut up* or *Stop talking please.*

What I would be doing there is using the grammatical structure of the imperative to realize the meaning of 'command'. That is the **unmarked** or **typical** way of expressing a command. And if my students are young, and if I'm feeling particularly annoyed, and if I get a kick from asserting power, that is probably the way I would express myself. But possibly I might wish to be more conciliatory with them:

> Would you mind not talking while I'm talking?

In this case I have used not an imperative structure but an interrogative structure, so that although what I am still meaning is the command 'shut up', I am 'borrowing' the grammatical structure we normally use to ask questions. You can tell that this is not a 'real' question by considering that *yes* or *no* are not acceptable answers here. The response needs to be compliance (or challenge) from the students: either they shut up, or they ignore me (thereby provoking conflict)! Another way I might make my command would be to say:

> It's so noisy in here I can't hear myself think.

Here I have used not an imperative, nor an interrogative, but a declarative: the kind of grammatical structure we typically use for giving information. Yet again it is obvious that I am not really out to give information, but to get the students to shut up. Yet another alternative is for me to say:

> What a racket!

Here I have used an exclamative structure, yet again it is obvious that I am not merely exclaiming about the state of affairs, but trying to command that the state of affairs be changed.

This pattern of playing with the system, of using non-typical structures to express our meanings in ways that can be highly sensitive to contextual constraints, is one kind of **grammatical metaphor** (nominalization, another kind, was discussed in Chapter Four). Grammatical metaphor is part of the creative potential that grammar offers language users.

Simultaneous meanings in language

Part, then, of what lexico-grammar does for language is to give it a creative potential: a way of creating new meanings, by inventing new signs which then get incorporated into the lexico-grammar of the language, by simply arranging existing signs in different ways, or by using existing structures in atypical ways.

However, there is significantly more to the role of the lexico-grammar than this. For not only does the grammar allow us to make *more* meanings, to create, it also allows us to **mean more than one thing at a time**.

A simple example of this is to take the single lexical item *John*. Any actual use of this lexical item will be overlaid with an intonation contour which will give the word not just the ideational meaning of 'the person called John', but simultaneously an interpersonal meaning of 'how I am relating to John'. For example, using Halliday and Matthiessen (2004: Chapter 8) descriptions of English tone choices, Figure 5.1 displays some of the meanings that *John* can make.

This is a very simple illustration of the fact that in language we can **mean more than one thing at a time**. (It also illustrates the important role intonation plays in making meanings – see Halliday and Matthiessen 2004: Chapter 8 for a discussion.) However, the situation is generally much more complex than this because we are usually dealing with sentences, not just isolated words. Nonetheless, the same principle of simultaneous meanings is at work. Take for example the clause:

> John eats poached eggs.

Part of the meaning of this sentence is the ideational meaning, the meaning of the words *John* and *poached eggs* (the participants involved), and the word *eats* (the process he is involved in). These ideational meanings are in contrast to a clause about *Peter reading books* or *the dog chewing a bone*.

But another part of the meaning of the clause is the structure Subject^Finite verb fused with Predicate^Complement, which gives us the meaning of 'declarative', a giving of information. Here, the clause contrasts with variants like *Is John eating poached eggs?* (a question, asking for information), or *Eat poached eggs, John* (a command, demanding the carrying out of an action).

A third kind of meaning conveyed in the same clause is that 'this is a message about John' – John is the Theme or departure point for this message, realized through the structural organization of putting *John* in first position in the clause. This is the clause's textual meaning. In this respect, the clause contrasts with *Poached eggs eats John*, where the focus would be on what he was eating, rather than who was doing the eating.

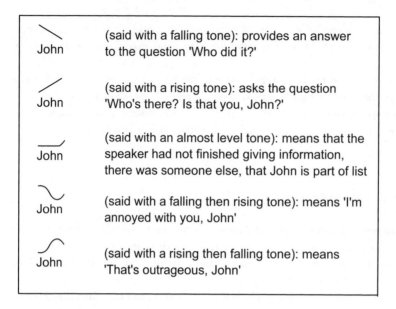

Figure 5.1 The meanings of *John*

In this one clause, then, we are actually making three kinds of meaning **simultaneously**. We are able to do so because there are three kinds of simultaneous grammatical structures working in any English clause. We can separate out each type of meaning, by varying the clause in only one respect at a time. So, compared to our initial clause of *John eats poached eggs*, we can see that:

> Poached eggs are eaten by John.

has the same ideational meaning (we are still talking about what action John performed on eggs), the same interpersonal meaning (it is still a declarative, a giving of information) but now it is a message about *eggs* – we have changed the thematic organization of the message, and so we have changed its textual meaning. In

> Did John eat poached eggs?

we have the same ideational meaning, and the same textual meaning (that this is a message about John), but this time a different interpersonal meaning: now I am no longer *giving* you information but *demanding* it, achieved through the structure of putting the Finite verbal element before the Subject, thereby splitting the verbal components of the clause into two (*did, eat*). With

> John, eat poached eggs.

we have changed the clause's interpersonal meaning. The clause is still ideationally about *John*, *eating* and *eggs*; and still textually to do with *John*; but it is now an imperative – not a giving or demanding of information, but a demand for action. This is realized through the structure of having *John* as a vocative element, having no Finite verb but only a Predicate element. Finally, with

> Pete, read your books.

the ideational meaning has changed, although textually and interpersonally the meanings remain the same as in the immediately preceding example.

These sentences demonstrate that a lexico-grammar enables language not only to make more meanings (to provide an unlimited creative potential) but also to mean several things at once. This is possible because the lexico-grammar enables language to have several simultaneous layers of structure. Chapters Six to Ten describe these simultaneous structural layers.

Principles of grammatical analysis: units and constituency

Having established that it is the lexico-grammar which gives language its creative potential, we will now focus on how the lexico-grammar is organized so that its creative potential can be exploited.

There are two preliminary observations that we can make of this level of lexico-grammar. The first is that we find a number of different kinds of **units**. The second is that these units are related to each other through **constituency** – smaller units make up bigger units, and bigger units are made up of smaller units.

We can begin to become aware of units of description and analysis by first of all considering the **expression plane** of language.

Consider Text 5.1 below, a partial version of which was presented in Chapter Four. Regarding this purely as a graphic representation (i.e. without any consideration of its meaning), we can ask what are the largest and smallest units we can recognize as physically distinct.

Text 5.1: Late Assignments

The School has a policy for the evaluation of late assignments which is fully explained in the document entitled 'Submission of Essays and Assignments', copies of which are available from any member of the School, or from the Departmental Office in Room 139 in the Woodstone Building.

Formal extensions of time are not granted as such, but if, through misfortune or bad planning, an assignment cannot be submitted on time, it may be submitted within the next 14 days. For each assignment, there are second and third collections on the following two weeks. Assignments in the second and third collections are divided into two categories. If the assignment is simply late it will be penalised. If it is late because of some unforeseen disability, it will not be penalised, provided that (i) documentary evidence of the disability is attached to the essay and (ii) the nature of the disability and of the evidence is acceptable to the Late Essay Committee.

Full details of penalties are provided in the 'Submission of Essays and Assignments' document.

Viewed as a piece of writing, this text is organized into a number of different units, each indicated by different spatial or graphological conventions, as summarized in Table 5.2.

When we arrange the units of the graphological expression plane in this way, it becomes obvious that the units are related to each other through **constituency**: each unit is made up of one or more of the units below.

Table 5.2   Units and criteria of graphological expression (rank scale of the graphological stratum)

Units	Criteria used to identify units
paragraph	double spacing
sentence	full stop
comma-unit	comma
word	spaces
letter	smaller spaces

We call this a **ranked constituent analysis**. In this case it's a ranked constituent analysis of orthographic expression. It is **constituent** because units at each level are made up of one or more of the units at the level below. It is **ranked** because we have organized it in terms of biggest to smallest. We can describe it also as a **rank scale**.

This ranked constituent analysis, or rank scale, indicates that the letter is the **ultimate constituent** of writing, i.e. it is the smallest unit of orthographic representation in English. It cannot be further divided (we do not have 'sub-letters').

Note that in establishing this rank scale of graphological units, we made no reference to the meaning or content of the passage, nor to its phonological properties. If someone were to read the passage aloud, we could go on to analyse the same passage from the point of view of its phonological expression. Still without making any reference to the meaning of the passage, we could analyse its phonological expression by asking what are the largest and smallest units of sound that we can recognize. We would be able to establish a ranked constituent analysis as given in Table 5.3.

This is a **ranked constituent** analysis of the **expression** plane in its phonological realization. It indicates that:

- tone groups are made up of feet which are made up of syllables which are made up of phonemes
- the phoneme is the smallest unit of sound that we can identify: it cannot be further subdivided. It is thus the **ultimate constituent** of the phonological expression plane.

The fact that the expression plane appears to be organized in constituent hierarchies suggests that this notion of constituency plays an important role in language as a whole. And in fact establishing the constituency hierarchy for the lexico-grammar is an important first step in examining grammatical structure.

Constituents of the content plane

In order to establish the rank-scale for the lexico-grammar, we need to consider language as content, not expression. We need to look again at Text 5.1, this time considering it as a piece of meaning. We need to ask: what are the largest and the smallest units of meaning that we can distinguish?

First of all, the entire passage can be seen to have meaning. We already have a name for this overall semantic unit: **text**.

The text as a whole can then be seen to be constituted of a number of different-sized units of meaning, most indicated by orthographic convention. The largest grammatical

Table 5.3 Rank scale of the phonological stratum

Unit	Criteria for identifying units
'verse'	silence either side (before we start and after we finish reading the text)
tone group	tonic (where the intonation movement is most noticeable)
foot	salience (where the rhythmic beat falls)
syllable	articulation of sound clusters
phoneme	articulation of discrete sounds

unit we can identify is the sentence, indicated by an initial capital letter and a full stop at the end. The sentence is a unit of meaning because it represents a coherent, structured packaging of information about something, but it is clearly smaller than the text itself. Here is Text 5.1, with // showing the boundaries between sentences.

Text 5.1: Late Assignments

The School has a policy for the evaluation of late assignments which is fully explained in the document entitled 'Submission of Essays and Assignments', copies of which are available from any member of the School, or from the Departmental Office in Room 139 in the Woodstone Building.//

Formal extensions of time are not granted as such, but if, through misfortune or bad planning, an assignment cannot be submitted on time, it may be submitted within the next 14 days.// For each assignment, there are second and third collections on the following two weeks.// Assignments in the second and third collections are divided into two categories.// If the assignment is simply late it will be penalised.// If it is late because of some unforeseen disability, it will not be penalised, provided that (i) documentary evidence of the disability is attached to the essay and (ii) the nature of the disability and of the evidence is acceptable to the Late Essay Committee.//

Full details of penalties are provided in the 'Submission of Essays and Assignments' document.//

Each sentence may in turn be made up of a number sentence parts, technically called **clauses**. Clauses, often indicated by colons, semi-colons or commas, make smaller chunks of meaning than the sentence. Here is Text 5.1, with / used to show clause boundaries:

Text 5.1: Late Assignments

The School has a policy for the evaluation of late assignments/ which is fully explained in the document entitled 'Submission of Essays and Assignments',/ copies of which are available from any member of the School, or from the Departmental Office in Room 139 in the Woodstone Building.//

Formal extensions of time are not granted as such,/ but if, through misfortune or bad planning, an assignment cannot be submitted on time,/ it may be submitted within the next 14 days.// For each assignment, there are second and third collections on the following two weeks.// Assignments in the second and third collections are divided into two categories.// If the assignment is simply late/ it will be penalised.// If it is late because of some unforeseen disability,/ it will not be penalised,/ provided that (i) documentary evidence of the disability is attached to the essay/ and (ii) the nature of the disability and of the evidence is acceptable to the Late Essay Committee.//

Full details of penalties are provided in the 'Submission of Essays and Assignments' document.//

Each clause can be further subdivided into groups of words, sometimes separated by commas, which we technically refer to as **phrases** or **groups**. Phrases or groups are collections of words doing a similar job in the clause: for example, a nominal group is a group of noun-like words, a verbal group contains the verb elements, a prepositional group realizes meanings about time, place, manner, etc. The phrases and groups in Text 5.1 are shown within parentheses[1]:

Text 5.1: Late Assignments

(The School) (has) (a policy for the evaluation of late assignments)/ (which) (is fully explained) (in the document entitled 'Submission of Essays and Assignments',)/ (copies of which) (are) (available) (from any member of the School,) (or) (from the Departmental Office in Room 139 in the Woodstone Building.)//

(Formal extensions of time) (are not granted) (as such),/ (but if), (through misfortune or bad planning,) (an assignment) (cannot be submitted) (on time),/ (it) (may be submitted) (within the next 14 days).// (For each assignment), (there) (are) (second and third collections) (on the following two weeks).// (Assignments in the second and third collections) (are divided) (into two categories.)// (If) (the assignment) (is) (simply late)/ (it) (will be penalised.)// (If) (it) (is) (late) (because of some unforeseen disability),/ (it) (will not be penalised),/ (provided that) (i) (documentary evidence of the disability) (is attached) (to the essay)/ (and) (ii) (the nature of the disability and of the evidence) (is) (acceptable) (to the Late Essay Committee.)//

(Full details of penalties) (are provided) (in the 'Submission of Essays and Assignments' document.)//

Part of the meaning of each phrase or group, however, is the individual words which make it up, so we need to recognize the unit **word**. The boundaries between words are clearly indicated orthographically by spacing, so that there is no need to display the text again. Finally, the meaning of a word in fact comes from a putting together of smaller meaning chunks, which we technically call **morphemes**. The word *misfortune*, for example, is made up of the following morphemes:

- content morpheme: *fortune* (this morpheme expresses the basic meaning of the word)
- grammatical morpheme: *mis-* (this morpheme functions to form the opposite, or antonym, of the content morpheme)

Similarly, the word *penalties* contains two morphemes:

- content morpheme: *penalty*
- plural morpheme: *-s*

Table 5.4   Initial list of content units in Text 5.1

content units	orthographic signals
text	paragraph
sentence	capital letter/full stop
clause	comma (often colon, semi-colon)
group/phrase	comma
word	spacing
morpheme	no signal (except that we tend to break words at morpheme boundaries when we need to hyphenate at the end of a line)

As we will not be pursuing morphemic analysis in this book, we will not take the division to this level. What we end up with, then, is the list of content carrying constituents given in Table 5.4.

Thus, in looking at Text 5.1 as a piece of meaningful language, we have been able to identify a number of different units of meaning, some of which correlate fairly closely with the units we identified when we looked at it as a piece of written expression. The close correlation between constituents of written expression and content constituents is explained by the fact that principles of orthography are derived from how we perceive language to be structured.

Grammatical constituents: the rank scale

Although we have now identified the meaningful units ranging from largest to smallest that realize our passage, there are certain problems with using the listing above as our set of grammatical units.

The first problem is that the unit the **text** does not belong in the lexico-grammatical rank scale. Text, as was discussed in Chapter Four, is a semantic unit and not a lexico-grammatical one. The relationship between text and everything below it is not one of constituency but one of realization. As Halliday and Hasan (1976: 2) explain:

> A text is not something that is like a sentence, only bigger; it is something that differs from a sentence in kind. A text is best regarded as a SEMANTIC unit: a unit not of form but of meaning. Thus it is related to a clause or sentence not by size but by REALIZATION . . . A text does not CONSIST OF sentences; it is REALIZED BY, or encoded in, sentences. (their emphasis)

One way to understand this difference between text and sentence is to consider how a sentence-by-sentence description of the text would fail to describe its texture. Cohesive patterns, as we saw in Chapter Two, may relate items that are not of the same kind (i.e. not the same type of constituents): for example, there may be a referential link between the single word/morpheme *it* and an entire two paragraphs of preceding text. Similarly, items cohesively linked do not have to necessarily be next to each other in the text: for example, a word in the first clause of a text may have a lexical link with a word or words used much later on.

These two features of cohesive relations point to an important distinction between what we describe as **text** or **discourse patterns** and what we describe as **grammatical patterns**.

Grammatical description is limited by two general characteristics:

1. it relates items of the same kind to each other (e.g. clauses to clauses, words to words, phrases to phrases, etc.)
2. it relates items that are adjacent, or nearly adjacent, to each other.

We will therefore remove **text** from our grammatical constituent scale. It *is* a unit of linguistic description, but at the semantic stratum, not at the grammatical stratum. This leaves us with the following content units: sentence, clause, group/phrase, word and morpheme.

For various reasons we will also remove the sentence from this scale, and instead add a new term, **clause complex**, next to, not above, the term clause. The term **sentence** refers to a unit of written expression, and is therefore biased towards the description of written language. Halliday (1994: 216) suggests that if we wish our grammatical description to deal equally well with spoken and written language, we need a unit that is neutral for mode. Hence, the use of the term **clause complex**, which refers to the association of clauses in sequence, in either written text (in which case clause complex boundaries are indicated by full stops), or in spoken text (in which case clause complex boundaries are indicated by a combination of rhythm, intonation and pauses).

The label **clause complex** is not, however, placed 'above' the clause on the rank scale, but rather next to it. This is because the relationship between two clauses in a clause complex is not considered to be a constituency relationship, but one which Halliday and Matthiessen (2004) describes as a **logical** structure. It is a relationship of (inter)dependency, more like the relationship between cohesively related items than the constituency relationship between stages of a text. We examine the clause complex in detail in Chapter Nine.

With these emendations made, then, we have established that the **rank scale at the grammatical stratum** is as listed in Table 5.5.

This **grammatical rank scale** defines for us the units of analysis and description at the grammatical stratum, and a complete grammatical description of a language would describe how each of those units is organized.

Remember that in identifying units of linguistic analysis we are trying to identify the units that carry different types of linguistic **patterns**. By **patterns** we mean different **structural organizations,** or different **structural configurations.** In separating out clauses from groups, and groups from morphemes, we are saying that each of these units carries patterns of different kinds; each unit is structured differently from the others.

At clause rank the kind of structures we find are those of participants carrying out actions in relation to other participants and situated in time or space. For example *The School has a policy for the evaluation of late assignments.* This is a structure we describe through such labels as Subject, Finite, Predicator, Complement.

At group rank, on the other hand, we find structures of expansion and modification, where there is one essential element to the group (the Head) with its various optional and functionally distinct Modifiers. For example, the structure of the nominal (noun) group *the*

Table 5.5   Rank scale at the lexico-grammatical stratum in a systemic approach

---

clause – clause complex
group/phrase
word
morpheme

---

three hairy redback spiders over there includes a number of possible elements before and after the head word *spiders* (the head word is called the Thing in the nominal group): Deictic (*the*), Numerative (*three*), Epithet (*hairy*), Classifier (*redback*), Qualifier (*over there*). (For the description of the nominal group, see Halliday and Matthiessen 2004: 311–35).

At morpheme level, our structures are concerned with the different combinatorial possibilities of **free** and **bound** morphemes. For example, the free morpheme *friend* can be followed by a number of bound morphemes, including -ship (*friendship*), -ly (*friendly*), -less (*friendless*), or preceded by be- (*befriend*), but it cannot be combined with other bound morphemes in English, e.g. dis- (*disfriend), or -ize (*friendize).

Thus, although each unit on the rank scale relates to the other units through constituency, we have to keep each unit distinct because each carries patterns of a different kind, and each unit requires a different structural description.

Bracketing

To this point, we have suggested the purpose of a grammar: to make infinite meanings from finite expression units, and to make meanings simultaneously. We have also seen that grammar is an intermediate level of coding, which breaks the bi-unique relationship between content and expression. Finally, we have suggested that the basic organization of a grammar is a constituent one, from which we are able to establish a rank scale, which gives us our different units of grammatical description. We now need to consider how we are going to uncover and describe the structures of the different units.

Since the grammar is composed of units which stand in a constituent relationship to each other, it is possible to reveal and describe part of how grammar works by looking at how grammatical constituents go together to make up structures.

One way of starting to think about describing structures, then, is to undertake what is called **constituent bracketing**. The technique we will use here is what is known as **minimal bracketing**, or bracketing according to the rank scale. (For a discussion of how minimal bracketing contrasts with the maximal bracketing tradition, see Halliday 1994: 20–4.)

Having decided that the highest unit of grammatical analysis we will be working with is the clause, a first approach to uncovering its structure comes from analysing it in terms of its constituents. For example, consider the clause:

All students must satisfy all assessment requirements.

One of the ways we can describe the structure of this clause is to consider quite simply how it is put together: how we get from the largest constituent (clause) to the smallest (in our case, words). By using graphical presentations in the form of **brackets** or **tree diagrams** (see below), we display how the clause is 'put together' at each level of the rank scale.

For example, the structure of the clause above can be analysed as follows, using a **tree diagram**, with **branches** (straight lines) and **nodes** (where lines meet)

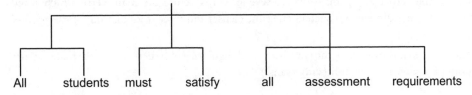

The same structural information can be captured using **brackets**:

((All) (students)) ((must) (satisfy)) ((all) (assessment) (requirements))

Both forms of representation are types of bracketing, and exemplify a minimal bracketing procedure. Minimal bracketing analysis involves taking the largest grammatical constituent (in our rank scale, this is the **clause**) and then progressively dividing the clause into the units which make it up *at each rank* (i.e. first phrases/groups, then words, then morphemes). By this procedure, each constituent is shown to be made up of one or more of the constituents of the lower rank, until the ultimate constituents of the grammatical stratum (morphemes) are reached. That is:

1. first, the clause is bracketed into the **phrases/groups** which make it up
2. then, each group/phrase is bracketed into the **words** that make it up

In a complete bracketing, each word would then be bracketed into the morphemes which make it up, but for our purposes we will only take the analysis as far as **words**.
    Here is another example of a minimally bracketed clause:

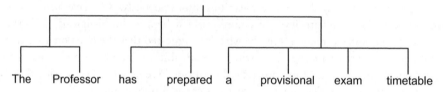

The	Professor	has	prepared	a	provisional	exam	timetable

Using parentheses, this example would be:

((The) (Professor)) ((has) (prepared)) ((a) (provisional) (exam) (timetable))

The purpose of bracketing the clause in this way is to give us an initial insight into how the clause is put together. The bracketing of the two simple clauses given above gives us the following information:

1. each clause is made up of a number of phrases or groups;
2. typically, these groups are sequenced so that we find a nominal group, followed by a verbal group, followed by another nominal group;
3. the nominal group can consist of a number of words of which the main word is (in these examples) the last word of the group, and is a noun (since we can substitute a pronoun for it). Various words (such as articles, adjectives, etc.) can come before the noun to give more information about the noun;
4. the verbal group may consist of a single word, where this word is a verb (a word which tells us what processes or actions are involved in the clause). Alternatively, the verbal group may involve several words before the main verb, which specify further dimensions such as the time (tense) and force (modulation) of the process.

Few clauses, however, have the simplicity and regularity of structure of these manufactured examples. Consider the following clause:

Application forms can be collected from the Secretary's Office on the first floor.

This clause contains two examples of **prepositional phrases**: *from the Secretary's Office* and *on the first floor*. Our first approach to bracketing these prepositional phrases may be to simply chop the phrase into the four words that make it up: *from, the, Secretary's, office*. However, it might occur to you that once you have chopped the preposition off, what you are left with is in fact a nominal group: *the Secretary's office* is a group of the same kind as *application forms*, since it has a noun as its head word. We note the same structure in our second prepositional phrase: preposition (*on*) and then nominal group (*the first floor*). It seems, then, that a prepositional phrase contains within it a nominal group, and this structural information can be captured in our bracketing as follows:

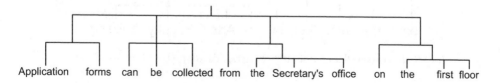

Note that what we are seeing here, then, is a variation on the typical constituent structure of the clause. Whereas we expect units of one rank to be made up of units of the next rank lower down, the prepositional phrase is an example of a unit of one rank being made up of a unit of the <u>same</u> rank, i.e. a phrase within a phrase. This is an example of **embedding**, or **rank shift**, and will be considered in more detail below. It is because the prepositional phrase has this more complex embedded structure that we call it a phrase rather than a group.

Now consider how you would bracket the following clause:

Application forms for postgraduate scholarships can be collected from the Secretary's Office on the first floor of the Arts Faculty building.

This clause now contains two additional prepositional phrases: *for postgraduate scholarships* and *of the Arts Faculty building*. However, these prepositional phrases do not seem to be functioning in the same way as the other two prepositional phrases in the clause. The following initial bracketing of the clause would <u>not</u> be satisfactory:

* (Application forms) (for postgraduate scholarships) (can be collected) (from the Secretary's Office) (on the first floor) (of the Arts Faculty building).

The reason this bracketing is unsatisfactory is that it does not capture the dependency that exists between *for postgraduate scholarships* and the nominal group *application forms*. The phrase *for postgraduate scholarships* is only 'in' the clause in order to give more information about which application forms. Similarly, *of the Arts Faculty building* is only in the clause to specify more clearly the first floor of which building. To capture the structure operating here we can initially bracket the clause as follows:

(Application forms for postgraduate scholarships) (can be collected) (from the Secretary's Office) (on the first floor of the Arts Faculty building).

The first and final constituents would then be bracketed as follows:

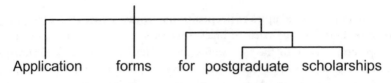

Application   forms   for postgraduate   scholarships

((Application) (forms)) ((for) ((postgraduate) (scholarships)))

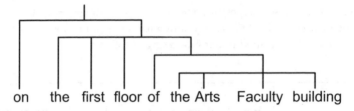

on   the   first   floor   of   the   Arts   Faculty   building

(on) (((the) (first) (floor)) ((of) ((the) (Arts) (Faculty) (building))))

These examples illustrate that sometimes a prepositional phrase can operate within a nominal group, to post-modify or qualify the head noun. Post-modifying prepositional phrases are not constituents at the first rank of the clause, but at the next rank down (the rank of phrase/group). In other words, your bracketing must capture that they are functioning *within* a unit at the rank of phrase/group, and not within the unit at clause rank.

This means that in dividing a clause into its constituents, you need to be able to decide just when a particular phrase or group is operating at the clause rank, and when it is operating at the phrase/group rank. There are a number of tests you can use:

1. **movability**: if an element is a clause rank constituent, it is likely to be independently movable. For example, in a clause like *For each assignment, there are second and third collections on the following two weeks*, you will find that you can move the phrase *on the following two weeks*:

> For each assignment, on the following two weeks there are second and third collections.
> On the following two weeks there are second and third collections for each assignment.

Where an element is *not* a constituent at clause rank but at group/phrase rank, you will find that it is generally not independently movable. For example, with *The School has a policy for the evaluation of late assignments* you can establish that the prepositional phrase *of late assignments* is not operating at clause rank by trying to move it to another position in the clause:

> * Of late assignments the School has a policy
> * The School has a policy of late assignments for the evaluation

2. **substitution**: elements which are acting together as a single clause constituent should be reducible to a single substituted item. For example, with a nominal group you should be able to substitute a pronoun, with a verbal group you should be able to collapse the verbal meaning into a single lexical verb (simple present or simple past tense). By asking just what your substitution item is standing for, you will be able to determine the bound-

aries of your constituents. For example, in *Formal extensions of time are not granted*, you can substitute the word *They*, to give you a rewritten clause *They are not granted*. This shows you that *formal extensions of time* is the nominal group, and not just *formal extensions*.

3. **probe questions**: constituents at clause rank will 'answer' to a range of probe questions. To probe the verbal group, ask 'What happened?', 'What did they do?' All the elements of the clause which respond to that probe represent your verbal group. For example, to determine the verbal group constituent in *it may be submitted*, ask 'What happens to it?' Answer: *may be submitted*. Nominal groups will answer to 'Who?' or 'What?' probes. Start with the verb, and ask 'Who did it?' or 'What did it do it to?' Again, all the parts of the clause that respond to the probe are your nominal group. For example, with *Documentary evidence of the disability must be attached to the essay*, determine firstly the verbal group *must be attached*, and then probe by asking 'What must be attached?' Answer: *documentary evidence of the disability*. With nominal groups after the verbal group, for example, *The School has a policy for the evaluation of late assignments*, again find the verbal group and then ask 'What does it have?' Answer: *a policy for the evaluation of late assignments*. With clauses in which the main verb is *to be*, you will often find that the following nominal group consists only of an adjective, rather than a noun: for example, *The exam timetable is ready now*. Use the same probe, asking 'What is the timetable?' Answer: *ready*.

Prepositional phrases and adverbial elements respond to a variety of circumstantial probes: when, how, why, in what way, with whom, of what, what about. Again, start by identifying the verbal group and then ask what seem the appropriate questions and remember to include everything in the response within the same phrase. For example, with *The exam timetable is ready now*, you need to probe with 'When is it ready?' which gives you *now* as a constituent, and since *now* and *ready* cannot be probed by the same question, you know they are each separate clausal constituents. A more complex example is *Copies are available from any member of the School, or from the Departmental Office in Room 139 in the Woodstone Building*. Here the probe test gives us *available* in answer to 'What are they?', and *from any member of the School or from the Departmental Office* in answer to 'Where from', and then *Room 139 in the Woodstone Building* in answer to 'Where?'

Embedding or rank shift

Very early in your bracketing career you will discover that sometimes a clause constituent seems to be a complex structure in itself. The case of the prepositional phrase considered above highlights one of the main complexities that bracketing can reveal, one that is important in understanding the structure of clauses. Consider how you would bracket the following clause, for example:

All students who are completing this year must submit their final essays.

If you apply the probe, substitution and movability tests suggested above, you will have no trouble identifying the verbal group (what must they do? they *must submit*) and the final nominal group (what must they submit? *their final essays*). However, when you probe the first part of the clause with the 'who' probe, you will find that the answer appears to be a very long nominal group *all students who are completing this year*.

That this is a nominal group is demonstrated, firstly, by the fact that the phrase is concerned with the noun *students*, and secondly (if you were not confident), by the fact that the entire phrase can be substituted with the pronoun *they*. Thus, the initial bracketing of the clause is as follows:

(All students who are completing this year) (must submit) (their final essays).

Bracketing this nominal group, however, reveals that it contains within it not just another phrase but *another clause*. This is a more complex example of **embedding** or **rank shift**. Here we have a unit of one rank (phrase/group) being made up of a unit of the rank above (clause). We deal with this by simply working through the minimal bracketing of the embedded clause (note that the embedded clause also contains a prepositional phrase, thus involving further embedding). The structure of the nominal group can be bracketed as follows:

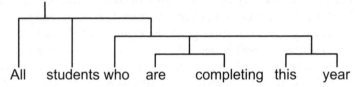

(All) (students) ((who) ((are) (completing)) ((this) (year)))

Embedded clauses (clauses functioning at group/phrase rank) occur commonly in the post-modifying position in nominal groups, where they function to specify more information about the head noun (e.g. which students?). However, they can also get into the clause directly, i.e. not through dependence on a head noun. For example:

Failing the course will mean exclusion.

Here we find that what answers our 'who/what?' probe is not a nominal group but in fact a clause: *failing the course*. This clause would be initially as follows:

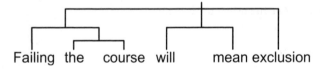

((Failing) (the) (course)) ((will) (mean)) (exclusion).

Note that we can get clauses filling the slot after the verb:

His excuse was that he had already failed the course.

Here the answer to the probe 'what was his excuse?' is the embedded clause *that he had already failed the course.*

It is also possible for clauses to fill the slots on both sides of the verbal group:

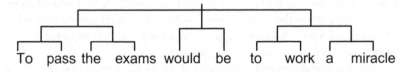

(((To) (pass)) ((the) (exams))) ((would) (be)) (((to) (work)) ((a) (miracle)))

As you will have realized as you study these examples, embedding is a way of boosting the content of a clause, by exploiting the clause's potential to recycle through the ranks. Once you have learnt to recognize embedding, then it need not present you with any problems. However, as systemic linguistics treats one kind of embedding slightly differently from many other grammatical models, one further explanation is necessary.

Embedding vs the clause complex

Many grammatical approaches would treat each of the following sentences as involving embedded structures:

i)   The Department believes that students have rights and responsibilities.
ii) The Examiner said that the candidate should pass.
iii) You will be advised of your results when the Examiner's reports have been received.

Many approaches would describe the 'that' clauses in i) and ii) as embedded noun clauses, while in iii) the clause introduced with 'when' would be described as an adverbial clause.

In a systemic analysis, sentences i), ii) and iii) are examples of **clause complexes**: they involve two clauses, with each clause having its own internal constituent structure. In i) and ii), the two clauses stand in a relationship Halliday calls **projection** (Halliday and Matthiessen 2004: 441ff.), whereby a process of mental or verbal action (e.g. *thinking, believing, saying, telling . . .*) is able to have a clause attached which either reports indirectly someone's speech or thoughts, or quotes directly someone's words or thoughts. In iii) the relationship between the two clauses is one of enhancement, whereby the second clause expands on the meaning of the first by contributing some relevant circumstantial information.

Systemic analysts would argue that clauses in such sequences (and sequences can be of any number of clauses) are not in a constituent relationship (neither clause is a 'part of' the other clause), but they are in a logical relationship: each clause is in an (inter-)dependency relationship with the other. A systemic bracketing of these clause complexes would therefore treat each of the clauses as having a separate structure, as follows:

i)   ((The) (Department)) (believes)// (that) (students) (have) ((rights) (and) (responsibilities)).
ii) ((The) (Examiner)) (said)// (that) ((the) (candidate)) ((should) (pass)).
iii) (You) ((will) (be) (advised)) ((of) ((your) (results)))// (when) ((the) (Examiner's) (reports)) ((have) (been) (received)).

Clause complex analysis is covered in Chapter Nine.

Labelling

We are now in a position to divide any clause into the constituents which make it up, and on the basis of our minimal bracketing we can make comments about the frequency and types of embedding that we observe. However, bracketing on its own is a very limited tool in grammatical analysis as it does not really tell us anything more about the structure than we already knew. We have, after all, known for some time that clauses are made up of groups, which are made up of words, and we also know that rank shift of various

Table 5.6   Examples of form/class labels at each rank

Rank	Form/Class Labels
clause rank	finite, non-finite, dependent clause, subordinate clause, relative clause . . . etc.
group rank	prepositional phrase, adverbial phrase, nominal group . . . etc.
word rank	noun, adjective, article, adverb . . . etc.

Table 5.7   Examples of function labels at each rank

Rank	Function Labels
clause rank	Main clause, Qualifying clause, Projected clause, etc.
group rank	Subject, Finite, Object, Agent, Actor . . . etc.
word rank	Deictic, Classifier, Thing, Head, Modifier . . . etc.

kinds is possible. In order to push our description of grammatical structure further, then, we need a more powerful descriptive technique.

Such a technique is **labelling**. If we can attach labels to the nodes of our structural trees, then the bracketing becomes very much more useful. However, there is an important distinction to be made between formal and functional labelling. You will remember from Chapter Three that formal labelling involves classifying an item in terms of its class membership (what it is on its own), whereas functional labelling involves classifying an item in terms of its role (what it does in relation to the whole). Formal and functional labels exist for grammatical constituents at each grammatical rank.

Some examples of **form** labels, often known as **class** labels, are provided in Table 5.6.

At word rank these labels are sometimes referred to as the **parts of speech**. Class labels like these tell us to which grammatical class an individual item belongs.

Function labels, on the other hand, tell us what grammatical function an item is performing relative to the whole. Some common function labels are exemplified in Table 5.7.

It is easy to demonstrate that class and function labels do not always match up. Items of the same class can perform different functions, and the same functions can be performed by items of different classes. For example:

Students don't like books.	The different functional roles of Subject (students) and Object (books) are both filled by items of the same class (nouns)
Students don't like doing exams.	The functional role of Object, filled by a nominal element in the first example, is here filled by a non-finite clause (doing exams)

In order to capture the possible range of correspondence and non-correspondence as part of an analysis of grammatical structure, a description that can label grammatical items at each rank for *both* class and function would seem essential.

However, in order to make this introduction to systemic grammar manageable, two limits on its comprehensiveness have had to be imposed:

1. Focus on the **clause**: of the various units of the rank scale, we will focus only on describing the structure of the clause. This is because the clause is generally

recognized to be the pivotal unit of grammatical meaning, and also because patterns which can be identified for the clause have parallels for units of lower ranks. Once you are familiar with clause structure, you should find it relatively easy to learn about phrase and group structure by referring to Halliday and Matthiessen 2004.

2. Priority to **functional labelling**: although both class and functional labelling of constituents is essential in a comprehensive description of the clause, we will concentrate on exploring functional labelling and its implications, leaving class labels in the background. This is because it is this functional perspective that allows us to make explicit how the clause functions simultaneously to express different meanings (see below). A rudimentary familiarity with the following class labels will be assumed: noun phrase (or nominal group), verb phrase (verbal group), prepositional phrase; noun, verb, preposition, adverb, adjective, conjunction. Many standard university grammars of English can familiarize you with these class labels.

Multifunctionality of clause constituents

Since we are focusing on the functional labelling of clause constituents only, the next issue we need to address is: what functional labels do we attach to the constituents? Rather than offering just one set of functional labels to be used in clause analysis, we will explore Halliday's claim that we need to develop *three* sets of functional labels to describe clause structure in order to reveal how the clause is a simultaneous realization of ideational, interpersonal and textual meanings.

We've seen that the lexico-grammar enables us to mean more than one thing at a time. This semantic complexity is possible because in nearly all cases the constituents of the clause are playing more than one functional role at a time. Because the systemic approach seeks to describe these distinct levels of functional organization, it might more accurately be described as a *multi*-functional approach to language.

This multifunctionality of the clause can be brought out, as Halliday suggests, by looking at what we usually think of as one functional role. He takes the role of Subject, as probably the most familiar grammatical role. In the following clause:

i) The redback spider gave the captured beetle a poisonous bite.

you probably have no trouble identifying *the redback spider* as Subject. But now look at example ii):

ii) A poisonous bite was given to the captured beetle by the redback spider.

If we ask now which part of the clause is Subject, we would identify *a poisonous bite*. What, then, has happened to *the redback spider*? Now look at iii)

iii) The captured beetle was given a poisonous bite by the redback spider.

Now the Subject is *the captured beetle*. How can we describe the roles of *the redback spider* and *a poisonous bite*? Now look at iv)

iv) A poisonous bite is what the captured beetle was given by the redback spider.

In this clause *the captured beetle* is the Subject, but what roles are being played by *a poisonous bite* and *the redback spider?*

These examples suggest that our notion of Subject is really a fusion of three different functional roles. In fact Halliday and Matthiessen (2004: 53–62) identifies three different types of 'subjects':

1. the **psychological subject**: the psychological subject is the constituent which is 'the concern of the message' (Halliday and Matthiessen 2004: 55), the information that is the 'point of departure' for the message. Halliday uses the functional label **THEME** to refer to this psychological subject.
2. the **grammatical subject**: the grammatical subject is the constituent 'of which something is predicated' (*ibid.*), the constituent we can argue about. Halliday retains the term **SUBJECT** to refer to this grammatical subject.
3. the **logical subject**: the logical subject is the constituent which is the 'doer of the action', the constituent that actually carries out the process. Halliday uses the term **ACTOR** to refer to this logical subject.

If we separate out these three functions, we can now capture the differences between our three clauses:

The redback spider	*gave its prey a poisonous bite.*
Subject/Actor/Theme	

In our first clause, we see that the three functional roles of Subject, Actor and Theme are 'fused' or **conflated** onto the same participant. This is what we refer to as the **unmarked** correlation between these roles.

A poisonous bite	*was given to the captured beetle*	*by the redback spider.*
Subject/Theme		Actor

Here we have the roles of Subject and Theme conflated in the constituent *a poisonous bite*, while the Actor, *the redback spider*, is now a separate constituent.

The captured beetle	*was given a poisonous bite*	*by the redback spider.*
Subject/Theme		Actor

Here Subject and Theme conflate in *the captured beetle*, with the Actor a separate constituent.

A poisonous bite	*the captured beetle*	*was given*	*by the redback spider.*
Theme	Subject		Actor

Here all three different 'subjects' are played by different constituents: the point of departure for the message is *a poisonous bite*, while the grammatical Subject is *the captured beetle*, with *the redback spider* as the doer of the action.

By the redback spider	*the captured beetle was given a poisonous bite.*
Theme/Actor	Subject

A final variation gives us Theme and Actor conflating on *by the redback spider*, which is not the same constituent as the grammatical Subject, *the captured beetle*.

What these examples demonstrate is that there are in fact three different types of meaning being made within the clause: a meaning about who grammatically is the argument of the clause, a meaning about who represents the doer of the action, and a meaning about where the point of departure for the message is. The examples also demonstrate that one clause constituent can play more than one functional role at a time: it may be both Subject and Theme, or Subject, Actor and Theme simultaneously.

In the **unmarked** (i.e. typical) case, there is a fusion or **conflation** of roles: the constituent which plays the role of Subject also plays the role of Theme and of Actor. As Halliday points out, grammars which tend to be based on 'typical' cases will tend to talk of only one Subject role because that is all they need to describe the typical case. However, once we start looking at how these typical cases can vary, we need to recognize that there are three simultaneous structures operating in every clause. A comprehensive analysis will need to separate these three types of meaning.

That a clause is expressing three different strands of meaning can be demonstrated further by exploring how a clause can be varied in three different ways. For example, consider the following set of clauses:

> The redback spider gave the captured beetle a poisonous bite.
> Did the redback spider give the captured beetle a poisonous bite?
> What did the redback spider give the captured beetle?
> Who gave the captured beetle a poisonous bite?
> Give a poisonous bite, redback spider!
> What a poisonous bite the redback spider gave the captured beetle!

In this set of clauses, some aspects are being varied – but not all aspects. The clauses are alike in some ways, different in others. In fact, while the ideational meaning (who the doer is, what reality is being represented) remains constant, the interpersonal meaning (how the clause constructs a dialogic role) has been varied. Now consider a second set of clauses:

> The redback spider gave the captured beetle a poisonous bite.
> It was the redback spider who gave the captured beetle a poisonous bite.
> By the redback spider the captured beetle was given a poisonous bite.
> A poisonous bite was what the redback spider gave the captured beetle.
> To the captured beetle the redback spider gave a poisonous bite.

In this set, the interpersonal meaning remains the same: each clause realizes the same Mood of 'declarative', thus all are interactively structured to give information. In addition, the ideational meaning is the same: all the clauses are still about the spider, the beetle and the bite. But the clauses differ in their textual meaning: what is taken as the point of departure for each message is different, ranging from the spider, to the beetle, to the bite. Now consider this final set of clauses:

> The redback spider gave the captured beetle a poisonous bite.
> The redback spider bit the captured beetle with poison.
> The redback spider sniffed the captured beetle.
> The redback spider thought about biting the captured beetle.
> The redback spider has a poisonous bite.
> The redback spider is the most deadly Australian spider.

In this set we see the same interpersonal meaning (all clauses are declaratives), the same textual meaning (the spider is the Theme in all clauses), but variation in the ideational meaning: the spider is not 'doing' the same thing in each clause. His actions range from *giving* (as if bites were separate from the spider), to the very concrete physical action of *biting*, through to behavioural action (*sniffed*), mental action (*thought*), possession (*has*) and finally being (*is*).

What these examples illustrate is that each clause is simultaneously structured in three ways, to realize the three different types of meaning with which we are now reasonably familiar: ideational meaning, interpersonal meaning, textual meaning.

Each kind of meaning is expressed by means of certain **configurations of functions**. Analysing just the Subject of a clause, for example, is not enough to capture variations in interpersonal meaning. We must also attach functional labels to all the other constituents of the clause:

Did	*the redback spider*	*give*	*the captured beetle*	*a poisonous bite?*
Finite	Subject	Predicator	Complement	Complement

Since we have to describe how three different types of meaning are expressed through grammatical structures, we will have to find three sets of functional labels:

Did	*the redback spider*	*give*	*the captured beetle*	*a poisonous bite?*
i) Finite	Subject	Predicator	Complement	Complement
ii)	Actor	Process	Beneficiary	Range
iii) Theme		Rheme		

Thus, in studying the structure of the clause we are actually studying three types of configurations of functions. This means we have to ask three questions:

1. How is language structured to enable interpersonal meanings to be made? Here we explore how different Mood structures allow clauses to realize different interpersonal meanings in text.
2. How is language structured to enable ideational meanings to be made? Here we describe how different Transitivity structures allow clauses to realize different experiential meanings in text.
3. How is language structured to enable textual meanings to be made? Here we examine how different Theme structures allow clauses to realize different textual meanings in text.

In the next chapter we will concentrate on the first of these questions. We are going to look at how language is structured to encode interpersonal meanings, by examining the structure of the clause to enable interaction. However, one final comment is needed as to the type of grammar we will be presenting.

Descriptive grammar and the notion of 'appropriacy'

Many people consider that in writing a grammar of English we are writing an account of how people *should* use English. For those people, the study of grammar equates with the study of how you should talk or write 'correctly'. Linguists, however, argue for a clear distinction between, on the one hand, the grammatical system of the language that enables people to use language the way they do, and, on the other hand, the moral and social judgements made by people about how the grammar of English should be used.

Grammars that impose moral judgements, that view grammar in terms of rights and wrongs, do's and don'ts, are **prescriptive** grammars. An account of how we should speak is a **prescriptive** or **normative** grammar. Such a grammar is interesting to linguists not for what it tells us about the facts of language, but for what it tells us about the values and prejudices of society at a given time.

The kind of grammars linguists write are **descriptive** grammars. A descriptive grammar makes no judgements about the goodness/badness, rightness/wrongness of language use. A descriptive grammar is an account of how speakers actually use the language. Linguists are not interested in making judgements about whether people should or shouldn't use particular structures. They simply describe the grammar that enables language users to do what they do.

Thus, for example, if we are writing a descriptive grammar of Modern Spoken Australian English, we might find that there is no need to describe what is usually called the subjunctive voice since it is almost never used: e.g. we rarely hear in the spoken language *I wish I were rich*, but always *I wish I was rich*, although in Modern Written Australian English we might still need to recognize the distinction.

Nor would we perhaps want to say that the WH-interrogative for asking about people is *Who* when Subject and *Whom* when indirect object, since in Modern Spoken Australian English you are unlikely to hear *Whom did you give it to?* but *Who did you give it to?*

But the fact that linguists do not make value judgements about language use is not to say that they do not assess usage at all. A linguist must be able to explain why saying *I seen the movie yesterday* or *What did youz all used to do?* is unlikely to impress a potential employer. While our descriptive goal means that we will not label such usages as 'wrong', a descriptive grammar must also allow us to explain the constraints on the use of such non-standard forms.

A descriptive grammar does this by making statements and assessments not about good/bad, right/wrong, but about **appropriacy** or **inappropriacy**. Degree of appropriacy is assessed not in terms of arbitrary blanket statements about inflexible grammatical 'rules', but as statements about grammar as a set of choices for use in context. Some choices are appropriate in certain contexts, but inappropriate in others. Part of what the grammar has to do is to specify the contextual dimensions of appropriacy for different choices.

Thus, our descriptive grammar would explain that the non-standard use of the past participle for the simple past (*seen*) or the form *youz* as a plural second person pronoun, while quite appropriate in situations of informality (e.g. among peers, where there is equal power, high affect, frequent contact), are inappropriate in formal situations (unequal power, etc.), as such forms have become carriers of certain socio-economic information (social class, ethnicity), and the overt display of such information interferes with an implicit ideological belief (fantasy) that we interact with others as equals.

The kind of grammatical description this book will be exploring allows us to make statements about the **appropriacy** of certain linguistic choices given the context of their use. It is a grammar by which we can relate the system of all possible choices (the total grammatical **potential** of a language) to the grammatical choices made when language is used within a particular context (how the potential is **actualized** in specific contexts of use).

Thus, although the following chapters plunge us into detailed grammatical analyses, the grammar is for us a means to an end. Being able to perform grammatical analyses, to understand how the lexico-grammar is structured, is an essential skill you must possess if you want to be able to describe, discuss, compare and understand how people use language to do social life.

The following chapter begins our excursion into the grammatical description of English in use by looking at the grammatical realization of interpersonal meaning through the Mood structure of the clause.

Note

1. Note that only phrases/groups operating at clause rank (i.e. non-embedded) are shown in this example, and discontinuous groups/phrases are not indicated.

Chapter 6

The grammar of interpersonal meaning: MOOD

Introduction

In the previous chapter we identified the two significant roles played by the lexico-grammar: to allow us to mean anything we like, and to allow us to make more than one meaning at a time. Since the constituents of each clause can be demonstrated to be playing more than one functional role at a time, it is necessary to develop three sets of functional labels to describe how the clauses in a text realize interpersonal, ideational and textual meanings simultaneously.

This chapter explores how the clause is structured to enable us to express interpersonal meanings. We will first establish a relationship between the semantic organization of inter-action and grammatical differences in the Mood structure of clauses. We will then identify the functional constituents and their configurations in clauses of different Mood types, and look at the role of modality (modalization and modulation) in interaction[1].

Interpersonal meaning and the structure of dialogue

The following authentic text can be used to introduce and exemplify many of the issues to be covered in this chapter. As you read the text through, consider whether you are able to specify the relationships between the interactants and how you are able to tell.

Text 6.1: Henry James

1	Simon	The whole point – it's like grammar, right, it's out the window, right, the whole thing is just up the shoot, right, it's just gone, really . . . some part of me. Everything you got taught, you know. It's hard to get
2	Sue	All those values you grew up with. They don't have them any more, do they, these young people?

3	Simon	I don't know. I don't know, like. There's so many – I have so much respect for the guys that could write. Like just Henry James, right. You read Henry James. This is a guy that can write.
4	Diana	Oh now he's talking about Henry James!
5	Simon	No?
6	Diana	What is this about Henry James?
7	Sue	It's so tortured. I think he had so much trouble coming to the point.
8	Diana	Henry James would do one sentence and it would go for a page and a half!
9	Sue	Page after page!
10	Simon	I loved him. I don't – I learnt the English language from this guy. He was – oh he was absolutely amazing.
11	Diana	Of course he's amazing, but he's not of this world. He's not contemporary. You can't do that these days.
12	Simon	Can't they?
13	Diana	Sometimes you get something to read and it's like Henry James. The sentence goes on for a page and a half.
14	George	Simon, what were those books you gave me to read?
15	Simon	So there they are. So poor old Henry's out the shoot too.
16	Diana	Well
17	Simon	(to George) Ever read a novel called 'The Bostonians'?
18	George	No. You know I haven't.
19	Simon	I will buy you a copy of this novel.
20	George	You know I won't read it.
21	Diana	Oh dear! What you should do is
22	George	Well what was that book that you gave me to read that I never read? It was some goddamn book.
23	Simon	Oh that was called the 'Wu Li Masters' or something.
24	George	I started reading that and it was
25	Simon	That was about quantum physics.
26	George	Yea. There was just no way that I could read that book, Simon.
27	Simon	It was quantum physics, George. That was Einstein.
28	George	Yea but
29	Simon	I was trying to appeal to you.
30	George	This guy, this guy was a big wanker, though, this guy that wrote that.
31	Simon	You read two sentences in the book and gave it up.
32	George	Because he wasn't – he didn't know anything about physics.
33	Simon	Oh he knew heaps about physics!
34	George	He did not.
35	Marg	Who?
36	Simon	It wasn't
37	Marg	Did you do physics, George?
38	George	I did a bit.
39	Simon	'The Wu Li Masters'. Its just – it's about Buddhism and quantum physics and Einstein.

40	George	He was trying to make me read it.
41	Simon	So I gave I bought George the book.
42	Sue	(surprised) Buddhism and quantum physics?
43	Simon	Yes. No it's really quite a nice analogy. He's really he's very lucid in explaining quantum physics, right, so that the layman can actually understand the Buddhist you know what Einstein
44	George	He was not
45	Simon	The whole rel – he explains relativity in
46	George	He wasn't a physicist, though, this guy.
47	Simon	I think in fact he was.
48	George	No.
49	Simon	What was he then?
50	George	He was nothing!
51	Simon	Who says? Well the book was great.
52	George	I didn't read it.
53	Sue	What do you read apart from bridge books, George?
54	George	I don't like books like that. I like adventure stories, you know, like I like – I've read a few of that guy um what's his name Wilbur Smith. I like his books. I think they're good fun to read. And I like some other science fiction stories. Oh it just depends, you know like, none of this bloody heavy literature and stuff. It's boring. You read stuff to enjoy it, not to read it after and say 'Oh yea that was deep and meaningful' you know like
55	Simon	It's like it's like going to a movie. You want to see something that's
56	George	Yea I mean I want to enjoy it. I don't want to find out the meaning of life or something like that from it.
57	Simon	Well god who wants to find out the meaning of life?
58	George	Oh you know what I mean.

There is little doubt that you would have decided that the five people interacting in this conversation were all 'friends'[2]. This is not, for example, the record of a first conversation among strangers, or the transcript of a staff meeting in the School of English. Among the clues you may have noted as indicating that between these people contact is probably very high, affective involvement is strong, and equal power operates might be that: the speakers interrupt each other freely, without the use of politeness formulae; there is frequent swearing and unselfconscious use of colloquial lexis and slang; strong attitudes are expressed very openly; speakers use each other's first names, etc. In other words, this text illustrates many of the characteristics of an informal tenor, as noted in Chapter Four. Again, we see evidence that the context (in this case, the social role relations or tenor) have been realized in the language of the text.

One major clue to the fact that this is a bunch of friends talking, rather than strangers, comes from the kind of dialogic exchanges that the speakers are engaging in. These people are not just talking, they are **arguing** with each other. Strong opinions are freely stated (*This is a guy that can write*), and equally directly shot down (*It's so tortured. I think he had so much trouble coming to the point*); claims are made (*Because he wasn't – he didn't know anything about physics*) only to be contradicted (*Oh he knew heaps about physics*); offers (*I will buy you a copy of this novel*) are abruptly rejected (*You know I won't read it*); and explanations (*I don't want to find* *out the meaning of life or something like that from it*) are challenged (*Well god who wants to find out the meaning of life?*).

It may seem contradictory to you to note that although these people are friends, what they are doing is arguing. We tend to think that 'friends' are people who will agree with each other, but in fact recordings of casual conversations suggest that Text 6.1 is a fairly typical example of how friends interact. So, why should friends want to argue?

The answer is that it is through engaging in sustained dialogue that we can establish and develop the social roles we are playing with other people. Establishing social identities such as 'friends', 'strangers', 'male', 'female', 'bossy', 'effusive' is not done by holding up a sign with a role label on it. Instead, it is done through talk. Being male and being friends, for example, means being able to dominate the talk, being able to argue in the direct and confrontational way of George and Simon. Being female and being friends means being willing and able to keep the conversation going, by making suggestions but giving up the floor without a fight (*Oh dear! What you should do is . . .*), by clarifying (*Did you do physics, George?*), and by finding out about people, especially males (*What do you read apart from bridge books, George?*).

The way that engaging in argument allows the participants in Text 6.1 to clarify their relationships with each other is just one specific demonstration of the general function of dialogue: that dialogue is the means language gives us for expressing interpersonal meanings about roles and attitudes. Being able to take part in dialogue, then, means being able to negotiate the exchange of interpersonal meanings, being able to realize social relationships with other language users.

The purpose of this chapter is to explore how dialogue is possible. Just how are clauses structured so that we can use them to challenge, assert, agree, contradict, offer, refuse, etc.? When we can describe the structure of clauses to enable dialogue we can uncover and explain how interpersonal meanings are being realized in interactive texts.

Semantics of interaction

Halliday (1984, Halliday and Matthiessen 2004: 106–111) approaches the grammar of interaction from a semantic perspective. He points out that whenever we use language to interact, one of the things we are doing with it is establishing a relationship between us: between the person speaking now and the person who will probably speak next. To establish this relationship we take turns at speaking. As we take turns, we take on different **speech roles** in the exchange. The basic speech roles we can take on are:

giving:

> Would you like to borrow my copy of 'The Bostonians'?
> 'The Bostonians' is a novel by Henry James.

demanding:

> Can I borrow your copy of 'The Bostonians'?
> Who wrote 'The Bostonians'?

At the same time as choosing either to give or demand in an exchange, we also choose the kind of *commodity* that we are exchanging. The choice here is between exchanging **information**:

Who wrote 'The Bostonians'?
'The Bostonians' is a novel by Henry James.

or exchanging **goods and services**:

Can I borrow your copy of 'The Bostonians'?
Would you like to borrow my copy of 'The Bostonians'?

By cross-classifying these two dimensions of 'speech role' and 'commodity', we can come up with the four basic 'moves' we can make to get a dialogue going. These are set out in Table 6.1.

These four basic move types of *statement, question, offer* and *command* are what Halliday refers to as **speech functions**. So we say that every starting move in dialogue must be one or other of these speech functions, and each speech function involves both a speech role and a commodity choice.

But, as Text 6.1 clearly illustrates, dialogue is inherently interactive: typically it does not involve simply one move from one speaker. We need also to recognize that after one speaker has initiated an exchange, another speaker is very likely to respond. Thus we need also to see that there is a choice between **initiating** and **responding** moves:

initiating	responding
Who wrote 'The Bostonians'?	– Henry James.
'The Bostonians' is a novel by Henry James.	– Yea, I know.
Can I borrow your copy of 'The Bostonians'?	– Sure.
Would you like to borrow my copy of 'The Bostonians'?	– OK.

Our choice of responding moves is constrained by the initiating move that has just been made. Every time I take on a role I assign to you a role as well. Every time I initiate an interaction I put you into a role of Responding if you want to interact with me.

The alternatives we face in responding can be broadly differentiated into two types: a **supporting** type of responding move, versus a **confronting** type:

initiating	supporting response	confronting response
Who wrote 'The Bostonians'?	– Henry James.	– How would I know?
'The Bostonians' is a novel by Henry James.	– Yea, I know.	– I think you're wrong there.
Can I borrow your copy of 'The Bostonians'?	– Sure.	– Sorry, I don't lend my books.
Would you like to borrow my copy of 'The Bostonians'?	– OK.	– What for?

Table 6.1 Speech roles and commodities in interaction (based on Halliday 1994: 69)

	COMMODITY EXCHANGED	
SPEECH ROLE	Information	Goods and Services
Giving	statement	offer
Demanding	question	command

In some registers, the expected response is a supporting move, but as Text 6.1 illustrates in other registers (such as casual conversation), the confronting responses are more common. Incorporating this interactive dimension, we can now summarize our picture of the semantics of dialogue as in Table 6.2.

This now gives us a list of eight speech function classes, which we can use to describe the move sequences in a simple dialogue involving three speakers, A, B and C:

A	Have you ever read 'The Bostonians'?	question
B	I really wouldn't know.	disclaimer
C	Yes, I have.	answer
A	It's by Henry James.	statement
C	Yea.	acknowledgement
B	No it's not!	contradiction
C	Would you like to borrow my copy?	offer
B	Well, OK.	accept
A	You'll enjoy it.	statement
C	Yea.	acknowledgement
C	Here, take it!	command
B	[takes book] Thanks.	compliance

Having established a basic picture of how dialogue works, we need to ask how this relates to the clauses we produce as we interact. In other words, what grammatical structure realizes these meanings? What is particularly interesting to us about these different speech function classes is that we can recognize a correlation between the semantic choice of speech function

Table 6.2 Speech function pairs (adapted from Halliday 1994: 69)

	SPEECH FUNCTION PAIRS (Initiations and Responses)	
initiating speech function	responding speech function	
	SUPPORTING	**CONFRONTING**
offer	acceptance (may be non-verbal)	rejection
command	compliance (may be non-verbal)	refusal
statement	acknowledgement	contradiction
question	answer	disclaimer

and the grammatical structure typically chosen to encode it. If, for example, you wish to make a statement, you will typically use a clause of a particular structure: a declarative clause:

A   It's by Henry James.   statement

If, on the other hand you wish to make a command, you will use an imperative:

C   Here, take it!   command

If you wish to offer something, you are likely to use a 'would like' interrogative (what we call a **modulated interrogative**):

C   Would you like to borrow my copy?   offer

And finally if you wish to ask a question, you will of course use the kind of clause we call an interrogative:

A   Have you ever read 'The Bostonians'?   question

There is also a correlation between the different structure of an initiating move and the structure of a responding move. You can see from the examples given above that most initiating moves are long, while most responding moves are short. Responding moves are short because they typically involve some kind of abbreviation or **ellipsis** or are what we call **minor clauses** (these terms will be explained below):

answer	Yes, I have.	instead of *Yes I have read it.*
acknowledgement	Yea.	instead of *Yea I know it's by Henry James.*
accept	Well, OK.	instead of *Well OK, I will borrow it.*
compliance	Thanks.	instead of *Thanks, I'm taking the book.*

The kind of differences we are uncovering here are not random. They have to do with what is called the Mood structure of the clause. The Mood structure of the clause refers to the organization of a set of functional constituents including the constituent Subject. The basic Mood types have already been mentioned. We can summarize these findings in Table 6.3.

Of course the examples of clauses presented above are not the only possibilities. These are only the typical correlations. Not all demands for goods and services have to be

Table 6.3   Speech functions and typical mood of clause

SPEECH FUNCTION	TYPICAL MOOD IN CLAUSE
statement	declarative Mood
question	interrogative Mood
command	imperative Mood
offer	modulated interrogative Mood
answer	elliptical declarative Mood
acknowledgement	elliptical declarative Mood
accept	minor clause
compliance	minor clause

imperatives. We need to consider the possibilities for both marked and unmarked correlations. Thus, while commands are typically expressed by imperative clauses (*Read Henry James*), they can also be expressed by declaratives (*I'm hoping you'll read some Henry James*), or modulated interrogatives (*Would you mind reading Henry James, please?*).

While offers are typically expressed by modulated interrogatives (*Would you like to borrow 'The Bostonians'?*), they can also be expressed by imperatives (*Take my copy of 'The Bostonians'*) or declaratives (*There's a copy of 'The Bostonians' here*).

While questions are usually expressed by interrogatives (*Is 'The Bostonians' by Henry James?*), they can also be expressed by modulated declaratives (*I was wondering whether 'The Bostonians' might be by Henry James*). And while statements are usually expressed by declaratives (*'The Bostonians' was Henry James' last novel*), they can also be expressed by tagged declaratives (*'The Bostonians' was Henry James' last novel, wasn't it?*).

We can now summarize our findings about dialogue in Table 6.4.

Table 6.4 begs the question of just when and why typical or untypical choices get made. Who uses the marked choices, and why? What are the implications of choosing to make a command through the structure of a declarative, for example, rather than through an imperative? These issues are obviously of considerable interest to functional linguists, as it seems likely that the choice between a marked or an unmarked structure will be influenced by contextual demands (what the register is and, specifically, what the tenor relationships are).

However, if we are to be able to explore this connection between clause structure and contextual dimensions, we need to first be able to describe the structures we are referring to. Just what is a declarative? What different types of interrogatives are there? We therefore need to study what Halliday refers to as 'the grammar of the clause as exchange'. What is the difference in structure between an imperative and an interrogative? Or an interrogative and a declarative? So, in this chapter we are going to look at the configurations of functions that constitute each of these structures.

But to do that we have to work out first of all what are the functional constituents that are involved. So in fact we need to address two questions:

1. What are the functionally labelled constituents we need to identify to describe the Mood structure of the clause?
2. What different configurations can they occur in? i.e. what different structures do they realize?

We will begin our exploration of the Mood structure by concentrating on how clauses are structured to enable us to exchange information. When the clause is used to exchange information, Halliday refers to it as a **proposition**. What we are looking at, then, is the

Table 6.4   Summary of dialogue

SUMMARY OF DIALOGUE		
speech function	typical clause Mood	non-typical clause Mood
command	imperative	modulated interrogative declarative
offer	modulated interrogative	imperative declarative
statement	declarative	tagged declarative
question	interrogative	modulated declarative

grammar of propositions. Later we will examine how the clause is structured to enable the exchange of goods and services when we look at the grammar of **proposals**.

Exchanging information: the grammatical structure of PROPOSITIONS

One of the commonest situations in which we exchange information is, as exemplified in Text 6.1, when we argue. By looking at an argument we can begin to work out the functional constituents we need to recognize in the grammar of the clause as exchange. Consider the following extracts from Text 6.1:

Diana	You can't do that these days.
Simon	Can't they?
. . .	
Simon	(to George) Ever read a novel called 'The Bostonians'?
George	No. You know I haven't.
. . .	
George	He wasn't a physicist, though, this guy.
Simon	I think in fact he was.
George	No.
. . .	
George	He didn't know anything about physics.
Simon	Oh he knew heaps about physics!
George	He did not.

In each of these excerpts, the first speaker's clause makes a statement, which is then argued with by the second speaker, with the first speaker sometimes coming back in again. When we ask how these arguments are carried forward, we can see that the clause appears to have two components. There is one component (*you can't/(you) ever read/he wasn't/he didn't know*) that gets bandied about, tossed back and forth, to keep the argument going, while the second part of the clause (*do that these days/a novel called 'The Bostonians'/a physicist/anything about physics*) disappears once the argument is under way.

The component that gets bandied back and forth is what we call the **MOOD** element of the clause (we use capital letters to differentiate the MOOD constituent of the clause from the general term, Mood, which describes the overall structure of the clause). The other component is called the **RESIDUE**. We can already, then, suggest that propositions can be divided into two functional constituents. For example:

He wasn't	*a physicist.*
MOOD	RESIDUE

To discover which part(s) of the clause constitute the MOOD element, we ask which part of the clause cannot disappear when the responding speaker takes up his/her position. The essential part of the clause contains the nub of the argument. Thus, we can continue the argument with:

He was. (leaving out *a physicist*)

But not:

> a physicist (leaving out *he was*)

The grammatical test Halliday uses to discover which part of the clause is the MOOD and which is the RESIDUE is to add a **tag**. A **tag** is what you can put at the end of any declarative to turn it into a question. We often do this to temper what we are saying. Compare:

> It's so torturous. (untagged)   versus   It's so torturous, isn't it? (tagged)

You will note that when we add a tag to a positive declarative, we usually change the tag to a negative form (using *not* or *n't*). When we tag a negative declarative, we typically make the tag positive:

> He wasn't a physicist, was he?

The elements that get picked up in the tag are the MOOD constituents of the clause. So, the first thing we can say about the grammar of the clause as exchange is that the clause consists of two functional constituents: a MOOD element, which functions to carry the argument, and a RESIDUE, which can be left out or **ellipsed**. Halliday describes the MOOD element as carrying 'the burden of the clause as an interactive event'. That is why it remains constant, as the nub of the proposition.

The components of the MOOD element that enable it to carry the nub of the proposition are revealed by examining responding moves in which the responder ellipses the RESIDUE. For example:

> He wasn't a physicist.
> – Yes he was.   – No, he wasn't.

These examples suggest that there are three main elements to the MOOD constituent:

1. an expression of **polarity**: either YES (positive polarity) or NO (negative polarity)
2. a nominal-type element, which we will call the **SUBJECT**
3. a verbal-type element, which we will call the **FINITE**

But since the polarity element can also be ellipsed without endangering the argument, there appear to be only two components that are essential to the MOOD: a Subject (always expressed by a nominal group in class terms) and a Finite (always expressed by a verbal group).

It is easy to demonstrate that we must have these two elements in a clause if we wish to argue. For example, imagine I walk into the room and simply say:

> is

we cannot proceed to argue, for you will have to ask me '*What* is? What are you talking about?' In other words, you will need to find out what the Subject of my clause is. Similarly, if I walk in and say:

> Henry James

we again cannot argue until you have established 'What *about* Henry James?', i.e. what Finite element I am attaching to the Subject.

Constituents of the MOOD

We have therefore identified two essential functional constituents of the MOOD component of the clause: the Subject and the Finite. Throughout our presentation of grammatical analysis for each Functional Role we recognize we will distinguish between the following:

> – what its Function is, what it does in the clause: the *definition* of the Function and
> – how we recognize the element filling that Function: the *identification* of the Function.

Definition and identification are not the same. The definition will be in terms of the role or contribution the element is making. Identification will be in terms of one or a number of grammatical tests you can apply to discover which part of the clause is filling the particular Function.

Subject

The definition of the Subject offered by Halliday and Matthiessen (2004: 117) is that it realizes the thing by reference to which the proposition can be affirmed or denied. It provides the person or thing in whom is vested the success or failure of the proposition, what is 'held responsible'.

The identification of the Subject can be achieved by the tag test: the element that gets picked up by the pronoun in the tag is the Subject. So, in order to uncover the Subject of any clause, you need simply to tag the clause. With a clause that is already a declarative, this is simple:

Henry James	*wrote 'The Bostonians'*	*(didn't **he**?)*
Subject		Subject

Although there will only ever be one Subject per clause, the class of items which can be Subject may vary. The Subject may be a single word (noun or pronoun), or it may be a lengthy noun phrase:

'The Bostonians', 'Portrait of a Lady' and 'Washington Square'	*were all written by Henry James*	*(weren't **they**?)*
Subject		Subject

There, a word empty of content, may also function as Subject, as the tag test will show:

There	*was just no way*	*(was **there**?)*
Subject		Subject

The Subject may even be a clause itself (an example of an embedded clause as Subject):

Actually,	*what I was looking for*	*was pink champagne*	*(wasn't it?)*
	Subject		Subject

As well as the tag test, another test which will help you detect the Subject is to change the verb from singular to plural (*was reading* to *were reading, likes* to *like*) or plural to singular (*were* to *was, like* to *likes*). The corresponding part of the clause that you will then have to change is the Subject:

> Only idiots **read** Henry James.

change *read* (plural) to *reads* (singular) and you will find that you must change the constituent *only idiots* to *only an idiot*. Thus, *only idiots* must be the Subject.

Finite

The second essential constituent of the MOOD element is the Finite. Halliday and Matthiessen (2004: 115) defines the Finite in terms of its function in the clause to make the proposition definite, to anchor the proposition in a way that we can argue about it.

The identification of the Finite again involves the tag test: the verbal part of the tag tells you which element the Finite is. For example:

George	*was*	*reading Henry James*	*wasn't*	*he?*
Subject	Finite		Finite	Subject

Where the verbal part of your clause consists of two or more words (*was reading, will be leaving, has finished*, etc.), you will have no difficulty identifying the Finite: it will always be the **first** of these verbal elements (*was, will, has*), as the tag test will clearly show you. Note that there will only be one Finite per clause. However, consider the tag test applied to the following clauses:

> I learnt the English language from this guy (didn't I?)
> He knew nothing about physics (did he?)
> The sentence goes on for a page and a half (doesn't it?)

Where does the 'did' in the tag come from? What happens is that with verbs in the simple present or simple past declarative, the Finite element gets fused with another element, known as Predicator. In earlier forms of English, and still in emphatic forms of contemporary English, the 'did' used to be present in the main part of the clause as well as in the tag.

I	*did*	*learn the English language from this guy*	*didn't*	*I?*
Subject	Finite		Finite	Subject

In unemphatic modern English, the *did* Finite has become fused in with the content part of the verb. But technically it is still there in the clause, as we see when we add the tag.

When the tag test shows you that *did* is the Finite, you simply write Finite under the first half of the verbal element as follows:

I		*learnt*	*the English language*	*from this guy.*
Subject	Finite			
MOOD				

With the verbs to be and to have (in the sense of 'possess'), the tag test will show the Finite. We will see below that with these two cases there is no need to write Finite only halfway under the verb as there is no other verbal constituent to be labelled:

He	*wasn't*	*a physicist*	*(was*	*he?)*
Subject	Finite		(Finite	Subject)

He	*has*	*a copy of 'The Bostonians'*	*(hasn't*	*he?)*
Subject	Finite		(Finite	Subject)

As mentioned above, the function of the Finite is to anchor the proposition, to bring it down to earth so we can argue about it. It does this through what Halliday and Matthiessen (2004: 116) refers to as Finite Verbal Operators, of which he identifies two kinds:

1. **Temporal Finite Verbal Operators**: these words anchor the proposition by reference to time. They give tense to the Finite – either past (*I learnt the English language from this guy*), present (*The sentence goes on for a page and a half*) or future (*I will buy you a copy of this novel tomorrow*).
2. **Finite Modal Operators**: these words anchor the proposition not by reference to time but by reference to Modality. Modality will be considered more closely later in this chapter. For now we can simply identify these as Finite elements which express the speaker's judgement of how likely/unlikely something is:

Henry James	*could*	*write.*
Subject	Finite:modal	

Henry James	*must*	*have written that.*
Subject	Finite:modal	

The Finite, then, carries either tense or modality to make the proposition arguable. The Finite also consists of the semantic feature of **polarity**, since to make something arguable it has to be either positive (something *is*) or negative (something *isn't*):

Henry James *was* writing 'The Bostonians'.   positive polarity
Henry James *wasn't* writing 'The Bostonians'.   negative polarity

Polarity is always present in the Finite, even though it does not appear as a separate element when polarity is positive. When polarity is negative, the *not* or *n't* morpheme has to be used. You can see that it is part of the Finite element because as soon as we need to negate a verb in the simple present or simple past, we are obliged to make the Finite element explicit (i.e. to reintroduce the *did*) so that we have a Finite to attach the negation to:

Henry James wrote 'The Bostonians'.   no *do* Finite

do reintroduced:

Henry James	didn't	write 'The Bostonians'.
Subject	Finite:negative	

Having identified the Finite, we are now in a position to understand the differences between the following clause types:

> I'm reading Henry James.
> Reading Henry James
> To read Henry James

The first clause is a **finite** clause: it contains a Finite element *am*. The second clause is an example of a **non-finite** clause. That there is no Finite element present becomes apparent if we try to tag the clause: not only do we not know who the Subject is (I, George, the Smiths), but we also do not know whether the Finite should be 'am', 'were', 'will be', 'might be going to', etc. Non-finite clauses are clauses which have not selected for a tense or modal verbal element. The third clause is also a type of non-finite clause, as it has no Finite element. We usually refer to it as an **infinitive** clause: the infinitive of a verb, its 'to' form, is the form in which verbs are listed in the dictionary.

These two elements of Subject and Finite link together to form the MOOD constituent. To capture their role as MOOD elements, we generally enclose them in the MOOD box, with the other constituents of the clause placed in the RESIDUE box:

I	learnt		the English language from this guy.
Subject	Finite		
MOOD		RESIDUE	

Simon	mightn't	have read 'The Bostonians'.
Subject	Fin:modal:neg	
MOOD		RESIDUE

Thus, a full analysis of the MOOD element includes not just labelling the Subject and Finite, but placing them within the MOOD box. We now need to identify and label the other elements of the clause: those in the RESIDUE.

Constituents of the RESIDUE

We have suggested that the RESIDUE component of the clause is that part of the clause which is somehow less essential to the arguability of the clause than is the MOOD component. For example, we noted that the RESIDUE could be ellipsed in the responding moves in dialogue. Just as the MOOD component contained the two constituents of Subject and Finite, so the RESIDUE component can also contain a number of functional elements: a Predicator, one or more Complements, and any number of different types of Adjuncts. We will review each of these in turn.

Predicator

The PREDICATOR is the lexical or content part of the verbal group. For example:

I	*'m*	*reading*	*'The Bostonians'.*
Subject	Finite	Predicator	
MOOD		RESIDUE	

The verbal group contains two elements: *am reading*. The first part of the verbal group, *am*, is the Finite as it carries the selections for number, tense, polarity, etc. The second verbal element, *reading*, tells us what process was actually going on. This element is the Predicator. The definition of the Predicator, then, is that it fills the role of specifying the actual event, action or process being discussed.

The Predicator is identified as being all the verbal elements of the clause after the single Finite element. Thus, in a clause with a lengthy verbal group:

Simon	*might*	*have been going to read*	*'The Bostonians'.*
Subject	Finite:modal	Predicator	
MOOD		RESIDUE	

might is the Finite, and all the remaining verbal elements (*have been going to read*) is the Predicator.

In clauses in which there is only a single verbal constituent (i.e. the simple present and simple past tense of verbs), we have the fusion of the elements of the Finite and the Predicator. These are the cases we saw above, where there was no distinct Finite element. In analysing these clauses, we align the Finite with one half of the verb, while the other half of the verb, which is carrying the lexical meaning, is labelled as Predicator:

He	*knew*		*nothing about physics.*
Subject	Finite	Predicator	
MOOD		RESIDUE	

Halliday and Matthiessen (2004: 122) points out that in addition to its function to specify the kind of process of the clause, the Predicator has three other functions in the clause:

1. it adds time meanings through expressing a secondary tense: for example, in *have been going to read* the primary tense (*have*, present) is specified in the Finite, but the secondary tense (*been going to*) is specified in the Predicator.
2. it specifies aspects and phases: meanings such as *seeming, trying, helping,* which colour the verbal process without changing its ideational meaning.

Simon	*was*	*trying to read*	*'The Bostonians'.*
Subject	Finite	Predicator	
MOOD		RESIDUE	

3. it specifies the voice of the clause: the distinction between active voice (*Henry James wrote 'The Bostonians'*) and passive voice (*'The Bostonians' was written by Henry James*) will be expressed through the Predicator.

'The Bostonians'	*was*	*written*	,	*by Henry James.*
Subject	Finite	Predicator		
MOOD		RESIDUE		

Although most non-elliptical clauses will contain Predicators, there are two verbs which have no Predicator in the simple past and the simple present tenses: the verbs *to be* and *to have* (in the sense of 'possess', not in the sense of 'take').

He	*is/was*	*a physicist.*
Subject	Finite	
MOOD	RESIDUE	

Simon	*has/had*	*a copy of 'The Bostonians'.*
Subject	Finite	
MOOD	RESIDUE	

The Predicator associated with these verbs appears immediately you use the verbs in a different mood (e.g. if you turn them into interrogatives) or if you use the continuous tense:

He	*was*	*being*	*a physicist.*
Subject	Finite	Predicator	
MOOD		RESIDUE	

Does	*Simon*	*have*	*a copy of 'The Bostonians'?*
Finite	Subject	Predicator	
MOOD			RESIDUE

A common occurrence in English is that of **phrasal verbs**, where the Predicator consists of a lexical verb followed by an adverb (*to run on*), a preposition (*to write up*) or both an adverb and preposition (*to look out for*).

Tests to determine whether a particular verb + adverb/preposition combination is a phrasal verb (and should therefore be treated as part of the Predicator) or whether there is a Predicator followed by a separate circumstantial Adjunct (considered below) include:

1. movability: if the preposition introduces a phrase which is independently movable, then it is not a phrasal verb; e.g. *He wrote on the page – On the page he wrote* (independently movable, so *on* is not part of the Predicator) versus *He wrote up the story – * Up the story he wrote* (so *up* is considered part of the Predicator). Similarly, if an adverb is independently movable, then it is not a phrasal verb;
2. substitution: frequently a single lexical verb could be substituted for a phrasal verb: e.g. *continue* for *go on*;
3. position: the adverbial component of a phrasal verb can be moved to the end of the clause: *He ran the sentence on* but not **He ran the race on*.

Complement

A second component of the RESIDUE is the Complement. A Complement is defined as a non-essential participant in the clause, a participant somehow affected by the main argument of the proposition.

It is identified as an element within the Residue that has the potential of being Subject but is not. A Complement can get to be Subject through the process of making the clause passive:

Henry James	*wrote*		*'The Bostonians'.*
Subject	Finite	Predicator	Complement
MOOD		RESIDUE	

'The Bostonians'	*was*	*written*	*by Henry James.*
Subject	Finite	Predicator	(Adjunct: see below)
MOOD		RESIDUE	

Clauses in which the Predicator is *give* or a synonym may contain two Complements:

Simon	*gave*		*George*	*a book.*
Subject	Finite	Predicator	Complement	Complement
MOOD		RESIDUE		

The passive test identifies both elements as Complements, as either could become Subject:

George	*was*	*given*	*a book*	*by Simon.*
Subject	Finite	Predicator	Complement	Adjunct (see below)
MOOD		RESIDUE		

A book	*was*	*given*	*to George*	*by Simon.*
Subject	Finite	Predicator	Adjunct	Adjunct (see below)
MOOD		RESIDUE		

The Complement is typically a nominal group, as in all the examples given above. It may at times be a whole clause, in which case we have an example of embedding:

Henry James	*is*	*a guy that can write.*
Subject	Finite	Complement
MOOD		RESIDUE

There is a particular sub-class of Complements which are called Attributive Complements, where the Complement is realized by an adjectival element (word or phrase):

He	*isn't*	*contemporary.*
Subject	Finite:neg	Complement:attributive
MOOD		RESIDUE

In these examples, the Complement functions to describe the Subject, to offer an attribute of it. Technically, Attributive Complements cannot become Subjects (they cannot form passives):

> * Contemporary is not been by him.

Adjuncts

The final constituents that we need to describe are Adjuncts. Adjuncts can be defined as clause elements which contribute some additional (but non-essential) information to the clause. They can be identified as elements which do not have the potential to become Subject – i.e. they are not nominal elements, but are adverbial, or prepositional. The Adjuncts in the following clauses are shown in bold:

> I learnt the English language **from this guy**.
> Camels always walk **like that**.
> **Actually**, I really wanted pink champagne.
> **Frankly**, I can't stand Henry James.

Although all Adjuncts share these characteristics, we can differentiate between three broad classes of Adjuncts, according to whether their contribution to the clause is principally ideational, interpersonal or textual. The different classes of Adjuncts are accorded different positions in the MOOD/RESIDUE analysis of the clause. At the end of the following discussion, a summary table covering all the Adjunct types is presented.

Adding ideational meaning: Circumstantial Adjuncts

Circumstantial Adjuncts add ideational content to the clause, by expressing some circumstance relating to the process represented in the clause. Circumstantial meanings may refer to time (probed with *when*), place (*where*), cause (*why*), matter (*about what*), accompaniment (*with whom*), beneficiary (*to whom*), agent (*by whom*). Here are some analysed examples:

TIME: when

They	*can't*	*do*	*that*	*these days.*
Subject	Finite:mod/negative	Predicator	Complement	Adjunct:circumstantial
MOOD		RESIDUE		

CAUSE: what for

You	*read*		*books*	*for fun.*
Subject	Finite	Predicator	Complement	Adjunct:circumstantial
MOOD		RESIDUE		

MATTER: of what, about what

Henry James	*writes*		*about women.*
Subject	Finite	Predicator	Adjunct:circumstantial
MOOD		RESIDUE	

AGENT: by whom

George	*was*	*read*	*'The Bostonians'*	*by Simon.*
Subject	Finite	Predicator	Complement	Adjunct:circumstantial
MOOD		RESIDUE		

Agent Circumstantials appear in passive clauses where the Agent has not been deleted. The Agent Circumstantial element (unlike other Circumstantials) can become the Subject of the clause, by changing the clause to active and deleting the preposition *by*: *Simon read George 'The Bostonians'*.

Circumstantial Adjuncts are usually expressed by either prepositional phrases or by an adverb of time, manner, place, etc. As Circumstantial Adjuncts do not contribute meaning which is part of the arguable nub of the proposition, although they are always available for querying, they are treated as part of the RESIDUE of the clause, and should be analysed in the RESIDUE box as shown above.

Adding interpersonal meaning: Modal Adjuncts

Modal Adjuncts are clause constituents which add interpersonal meanings to the clause. That is, they add meanings which are somehow connected to the creation and maintenance of the dialogue. They can do this either by impacting directly on the MOOD element (by adding some qualification to the Subject/Finite), or indirectly, by merely adding an expression of attitude or by making an attempt to direct the interaction itself. There are four main types of Modal Adjunct:

1. Mood Adjuncts
2. Polarity Adjuncts
3. Comment Adjuncts
4. Vocative Adjuncts

While the first two act directly on the MOOD constituent, and are therefore shown as being MOOD elements, the second two affect the clause as a whole and are therefore not included in either the MOOD or the RESIDUE boxes. Each sub-class of Modal Adjuncts will be considered briefly.

1. Mood Adjuncts
Based on Halliday and Matthiessen (2004: 126–9), the following categories of items can be classified as Mood Adjuncts:

  i) expressions of probability: e.g. *perhaps, maybe, probably*
 ii) expressions of usuality: *sometimes, usually*
iii) expressions of intensification or minimization: *really, absolutely, just, somewhat*
 iv) expressions of presumption: *evidently, presumably, obviously*
  v) expressions of inclination: *happily, willingly*

Camels	*probably/maybe/usually/ always/sometimes*	*walk*		*like that.*
Subject	Adjunct:mood	Finite	Predicator	Adjunct: circumstantial
MOOD			RESIDUE	

Mood Adjuncts expressing probability meanings are closely related to the Modal Operators considered above, and will be considered again under the Modality section below. They provide a second chance for the speaker to add her judgement of the probability/likelihood to a proposition. Note that many elliptical responses are classified as Mood Adjuncts: *Maybe, Possibly, Perhaps, Presumably.* In fact, a good test for recognizing Mood Adjuncts is that they are likely to be retained even in elliptical responses:
He was a great writer.

– Maybe
Adjunct:modal
MOOD

– Obviously
Adjunct:modal
MOOD

2. Polarity Adjuncts: Yes and No

Yes and *No*, and their common conversational alternatives (*yea, yep, na, nope*, etc.) may function in two different ways:

i) as Polarity Adjuncts: when YES or NO are standing in for an ellipsed clause, they should be analysed as Polarity Adjuncts. Since in this role they are taking the place of an ellipsed MOOD constituent, Polarity Adjuncts are classified as part of the MOOD constituent of the clause:

Henry James was a guy that could write.

– Yes.
Adjunct:Polarity
MOOD

In this Polarity role, they will always be stressed items, will realize an intonation choice, and the Subject and Finite ellipsed can be made explicit (e.g. *Henry James was a guy that could write. – He was.*)

ii) as Textual Adjuncts: when YES or NO (or more typically *yea* or *na*) occur in unstressed initial position, introducing a clause, they should be treated as continuity items and classified as Textual Adjuncts (see below).

3. Comment Adjuncts

While Mood and Polarity Adjuncts express meanings which are directly related to the arguable nub of the proposition (i.e. to the MOOD constituent), Comment Adjuncts function to express an assessment about the clause as a whole. For example:

Frankly,	*I*	*can't*	*stand*	*Henry James.*
Adjunct:comment	Subject	Finite:mod/neg	Predicator	Complement
	MOOD		RESIDUE	

Unfortunately	*I*	*'ve*	*never*	*read*	*'The Bostonians'.*
Adjunct:comment	Subject	Finite	Adjunct:mood	Predicate	Complement
	MOOD			RESIDUE	

Comment Adjuncts typically occur in clause initial position, or directly after the Subject, and are realized by adverbs. Halliday (1994: 49) identifies the following meanings as expressed by comment Adjuncts:

- admission: *frankly*
- assertion: *honestly, really*
- how desirable: *luckily, hopefully*
- how constant: *tentatively, provisionally*
- how valid: *broadly speaking, generally*
- how sensible: *understandably, wisely*
- how expected: *as expected, amazingly*

Comment Adjuncts are considered interpersonal elements in the clause, since they add an expression of attitude and evaluation. However, Halliday argues that because the scope of a Comment Adjunct is the entire clause (not just the Finite element), they should be seen to operate outside the MOOD/RESIDUE structure altogether.

4. Vocative Adjuncts

Vocative Adjuncts function to control the discourse by designating a likely 'next speaker'. They are identifiable as names, where the names are not functioning as Subjects or Complements, but are used to directly address the person named.

Like Comment Adjuncts, Vocative Adjuncts do not impact directly on the MOOD constituent of the clause, but affect the clause as a whole. They typically occur either initially or finally, although they may occur at a variety of different constituent boundaries in the clause. Because their effect is to organize the designation of the clause as a whole, they are not shown as belonging in either the MOOD or the RESIDUE box.

Did	*you*	*do*	*physics*	*George?*
Finite	Subject	Predicator	Complement	Adjunct:vocative
MOOD		RESIDUE		

Everyone	*knows*		*that,*	*Simon.*
Subject	Finite	Predicator	Complement	Adjunct:vocative
MOOD		RESIDUE		

Adding textual meaning: Textual Adjuncts

Textual meanings are meanings to do with the organization of the message itself. There are two main types of textual Adjuncts: **Conjunctive Adjuncts** and **Continuity Adjuncts**. The Conjunctive type, expressed by **cohesive conjunctions**, function to provide linking relations between one sentence and another. They typically occur at the beginning of the sentence, but they can occur at other points. They express the logical meanings of elaboration, extension and enhancement that we first encountered in Chapter Two when discussing conjunction. In written texts, Conjunctive Adjuncts are words like *however, moreover, nevertheless, in other words*. In conversation, however, speakers often use more informal conjunctions, such as *so, like, I mean*. Because these cohesive conjunctions are adding textual meaning but not interpersonal meaning. Conjunctive Adjuncts belong neither in the MOOD box, nor in the RESIDUE box and can be analysed as follows:

So	*poor old Henry*	*'s*	*out the shoot*	*too.*
Adjunct:conjunctive	Subject	Finite	Complement	Adjunct:conjunctive
	MOOD		RESIDUE	

Cohesive vs tactic conjunctions: making the distinction

Unfortunately for the newcomer to grammatical analysis, there's one further clarification to be made about Conjunctive Adjuncts: not all conjunctions are Conjunctive Adjuncts. As we'll see when we reach Chapter Nine, strictly speaking there is a grammatical distinction between **cohesive conjunctions** (which link sentences) and **structural** or **tactic** conjunctions (which link clauses within clause complexes). While cohesive conjunctions construct semantic ties between meanings that are not in the same clause, tactic conjunctions express structural relationships between clauses within a single sentence (clause complex). We're already familiar with cohesive conjunctions. Tactic conjunctions include *because, when, if, although, and, but, as, before, since.* Compare the following:

i) I don't read Henry James. <u>Therefore,</u> I can't comment on the length of his sentences.
ii) I don't read Henry James <u>because</u> his sentences are too long.

In i) we have two sentences. Each sentence consists of one clause. A cohesive tie of enhancement is established between the sentences by the cohesive conjunction *therefore*. Note that *therefore* is both optional and movable: it could be omitted altogether without affecting the structural completeness of the sentence (just weakening its explicit cohesion); and it could be placed elsewhere in the clause (*I can't comment, therefore, on the length of his sentences*). We capture this optional, textual role of *therefore* by analysing it as a **Conjunctive Adjunct** in our Mood analysis, leaving it outside both the MOOD and RESIDUE boxes:

I	*don't*	*read*	*Henry James.*
Subject	Finite	Predicator	Complement
MOOD		RESIDUE	

Therefore,	*I*	*can't*	*comment*	*on the length of his sentences.*
Adjunct:conjunctive	Subject	Finite	Predicator	Adjunct:circumstantial
	MOOD		RESIDUE	

But in ii) we have two clauses within one sentence (clause complex). The two clauses are linked by the tactic conjunction *because* which is neither optional nor movable: we cannot create this enhancing structural relationship without using a structural conjunction, and we can't move the *because* to anywhere else in the second clause. As we'll see in Chapter Nine, tactic conjunctions like *because* are really not adding textual meaning but logical meaning, which we capture through our clause complex analysis. For this reason, many analysts do not assign any label to tactic conjunctions (and other purely structural words) like *because*:

I	*don't*	*read*	*Henry James*
Subject	Finite	Predicator	Complement
MOOD		RESIDUE	

because	*his sentences*	*are*	*too long.*
	Subject	Finite	Complement
	MOOD		RESIDUE

Just as there is overlap in the meanings made by cohesive and tactic conjunctions, so also there is some overlap in the words used: *so* can function either cohesively (to link one sentence to an earlier sentence) or tactically (to link two clauses structurally within a clause complex). And to complicate matters even further, conversationalists often use tactic conjunctions to link their own comments to previous comments by other speakers, in which case we really have to treat their conjunctions as cohesive. For example, when George challenges Simon with:

Because	*he*	*didn't*	*know*	*anything about physics.*
Adjunct:conjunctive	Subject	Finite:neg	Predicator	Complement
	MOOD		RESIDUE	

George's *because* here creates an enhancing relation to Simon's earlier statement.

So, for the purposes of Mood analysis, cohesive conjunctions should be labelled as **Conjunctive Adjuncts** because they are indeed additional, non-essential components in the clause performing a textual role. But tactic conjunctions can be left unlabelled. However, if you find this distinction difficult to make at this stage, no great damage is done by labeling all conjunctions as Conjunctive Adjuncts. In fact, there is a drift in modern English for cohesive adjuncts (such as *however*) to be used as tactic conjunctions anyway, so this area of English grammar is currently in flux.

Continuity Adjuncts

The second sub-category of Textual Adjuncts is the Continuity Adjunct. This category includes the continuative and continuity items, particularly frequent in casual talk, such as *well, yea, oh*, where these items occur to introduce a clause, and signal that a response to prior talk is about to be provided. Unlike the Conjunctive Adjuncts, no specific logical relation (i.e. of elaboration, extension or enhancement) is expressed by a Continuity Adjunct. They merely signal that the speaker will be saying more. Again, these Continuity Adjuncts do not belong in either the MOOD or the RESIDUE boxes, as they contribute to the textual organization of the clause, rather than to dimensions of its arguability.

Well	*what*	*was*	*that book you gave me?*
Adjunct:continuity	Subject	Finite	Complement
	MOOD		RESIDUE

Continuity and Conjunctive Adjuncts may occur in sequence:

Oh	*now*	*he*	*'s*	*talking*	*about Henry James.*
Adjunct: continuity	Adjunct: conjunctive	Subject	Finite	Predicate	Adjunct:circ
		MOOD		RESIDUE	

It was pointed out above that when *yes* and *no* (or more typically *yea* or *na*) occur in unstressed initial (or near-initial) position, introducing a clause, they should be treated as textual items and classified as Continuity Adjuncts. The function of YES or NO in these situations is not primarily to express polarity (which is expressed in the Finite) but to signal that the speaker has taken a turn and is about to declare his/her position:

Yea,	*I*		*know.*
Adjunct:textual	Subject	Finite	Predicator
	MOOD		RESIDUE

The use of *yea* (often repeated at regular intervals) to signal continued listening by an addressee should also be considered a Textual Adjunct, since there is no ellipsed MOOD element involved.

Summary of Adjuncts

Unlike the other constituents we have looked at, Adjuncts are not limited in number of occurrence: a clause can contain an indefinite number of Adjuncts of different types. For example:

But	*unfortunately*	*Henry James' novels*	*can't*	*usually*	*be bought*	*in local bookshops.*
Adjunct: conjunctive	Adjunct: comment	Subject	Finite: mod/neg	Adjunct: mood	Predicator	Adjunct: circ
		MOOD			RESIDUE	

Table 6.5 summarizes the position and identification of these different types of Adjuncts.

Table 6.5 Summary of types of Adjuncts

		SUMMARY OF ADJUNCTS		
Type	sub-type	meanings	class of item	location in analysis
ideational	circumstantial	time, manner, location, etc.	prepositional phrase adverb	in RESIDUE
interpersonal (modal)	mood	intensity probability usuality presumption	adverb	in MOOD
	polarity	positive or negative	yes/no (elliptical)	in MOOD
	comment	speaker's assessment of whole message	adverb prepositional phrase	not in MOOD or RESIDUE
	vocative	nominating next speaker	name	not in MOOD or RESIDUE
textual	conjunctive	logical linking of messages	cohesive conjunction	not in MOOD or RESIDUE
	continuity	message coming	minor clauses adverbs (yeh/nah)	not in MOOD or RESIDUE

Summary: the Mood structure of declarative clauses

To this point we have identified and labelled all the constituents that appear in the Mood structure of declarative clauses. The labels we have introduced now allow us to make an important distinction between **major** and **minor** clauses. A **major** clause is a clause which has a MOOD component, even though that MOOD component may sometimes be ellipsed. Here are examples of major clauses:

non-elliptical (full) major clause

Henry James	*wrote*	*'The Bostonians'.*	
Subject	Finite	Predicator	Complement
MOOD		RESIDUE	

elliptical major clause (in answer to question: Did Henry James write it?)

Yes	*(he*	*did).*
Adjunct:Polarity	(Subject	Finite)
MOOD		

In an elliptical major clause, we know that a MOOD component has been selected because we can fill in the Subject and Finite.

Minor clauses, on the other hand, are clauses which have never had a MOOD constituent, for example, *Oh dear!, Well!, Eh?, OK.*

Minor clauses are typically brief, but their brevity is not the result of ellipsis. We cannot fill out a Subject and a Finite for a minor clause, for the simple reason that such clauses have never selected a Subject or Finite. *'OK'* does not mean *'I'm OK'* or *'It's OK'* or *'We'll be OK'* – it simply means *'OK'*. Consistent with the absence of the Subject and Finite, we find that minor clauses cannot be tagged – or rather, they can be tagged but in any number of ways, and we cannot decide which way is better as the clauses never had a Subject or Finite in the first place.

Major clauses, then, are clauses which have selected a Subject and a Finite. But so far we have only described one kind of major clause, the **declarative**, in which we have seen the typical structure is as follows:

Simon	*has*	*been reading*	*Henry James*	*lately.*
Subject	Finite	Predicator	Complement	Adjunct:circ
MOOD		RESIDUE		

where the Subject precedes the Finite, Predicator, Complement and Adjunct. This is the typical S^F^P^C^A structure of the declarative clause. We shall now explore the structure of other clause types. Although we will not need to identify any new constituents, what becomes important is how the constituents of Subject, Finite, Predicator, Complement, Adjunct are ordered with respect to each other.

Polar interrogatives

English offers two main structures for asking questions: **polar interrogatives** (yes/no questions) or **WH-interrogatives** (questions using who, what, which, where, when, why, how).

The structure of the polar interrogative involves the positioning of the Finite <u>before</u> the Subject. For example, we can derive a polar interrogative from a declarative as follows:

Simon	*is*	*reading*	*Henry James.*
Subject	Finite	Predicator	Complement
MOOD		RESIDUE	

Is	*Simon*	*reading*	*Henry James?*
Finite	Subject	Predicator	Complement
MOOD		RESIDUE	

In cases where the related declarative contained a fused Finite/Predicator (i.e. simple past and simple present of verbs), we need to introduce a Finite element to place before the Subject. This Finite element is typically the auxiliary verb *do*:

Simon	*learnt*		*the English language*	*from Henry James.*
Subject	Finite	Predicator	Complement	Adjunct:circumstantial
MOOD		RESIDUE		

Did	*Simon*	*learn*	*the English language*	*from Henry James?*
Finite	Subject	Predicator	Complement	Adjunct:circumstantial
MOOD		RESIDUE		

With the verb *to be*, which does not have a Predicator in the simple tenses, the structure of the polar interrogative is as follows:

Is	*he*	*a physicist?*
Finite	Subject	Complement
MOOD		RESIDUE

With the verb *to have*, which also does not have a Predicator in the simple tenses in the declarative, we find that to construct the polar interrogative we need to fill both the Finite and Predicator slots, usually by introducing the word *got* or *have* as the Predicator:

Simon	*has*	*a copy of 'The Bostonians'.*
Subject	Finite	Complement
MOOD		RESIDUE

Does	*Simon*	*have*	*a copy of 'The Bostonians'?*
Finite	Subject	Predicator	Complement
MOOD		RESIDUE	

Has	*Simon*	*got*	*a copy of 'The Bostonians'?*
Finite	Subject	Predicator	Complement
MOOD		RESIDUE	

Polar interrogatives as initiating moves are responded to by elliptical major clauses. The type of ellipsis that is common is to just get a Modal Adjunct of Polarity, or a Mood Adjunct expressing probability:

Does Simon have a copy of 'The Bostonians'?

– Yes.
Adjunct:polarity
MOOD

– No
Adjunct:polarity
MOOD

– Maybe
Adjunct:mood
MOOD

Or ellipsis may be of the RESIDUE:

Does Simon have a copy of 'The Bostonians'?

– He	*does.*
Subject	Finite
MOOD	

WH-interrogatives

In a WH interrogative, we need to recognize the presence of a WH element. This WH element is always conflated or fused with another element of clause structure. It may be conflated with either the Subject, the Complement or a Circumstantial Adjunct, and is shown as a constituent of the MOOD or RESIDUE according to the status of the element with which it is conflated.

WH element conflated with Subject (part of MOOD)

Who	*wrote*		*'The Bostonians'?*
WH/Subject	Finite	Predicator	Complement
MOOD		RESIDUE	

WH element conflated with Complement (part of RESIDUE)

What	*does*	*'quantum leap'*	*mean?*
WH/Complement	Finite	Subject	Predicator
RESIDUE . . .	MOOD		. . . RESIDUE

WH element conflated with Circumstantial Adjunct (part of RESIDUE)

When	*did*	*Henry James*	*write*	*'The Bostonians'?*
WH/Adjunct:circ	Finite	Subject	Predicator	Complement
RESIDUE . . .	MOOD		. . . RESIDUE	

The WH element specifies which element is to be supplied in the expected response. Typically responding moves involve ellipsis of all but the necessary information:
Who wrote 'The Bostonians'?

– Henry James
Subject
MOOD

When did Henry James write 'The Bostonians'?

– Late 19th century.
Adjunct:circumstantial
RESIDUE

When the WH element is used in a *be*-clause, it can sometimes be difficult to determine whether the WH element is conflated with the Subject or the Complement. For example:

> Who was Henry James?
> Who is the author of 'The Bostonians'?

To determine the structure of these clauses, provide an answer to the question and then analyse the structure of the answer:
Who was Henry James?

– *Henry James*	*was*	*the author of 'The Bostonians'.*
Subject	Finite	Complement
MOOD		RESIDUE

So, WH/Complement.
Which was Henry James' most famous book?

– *'The Bostonians'*	*was*	*Henry James' most famous book.*
Subject	Finite	Complement
MOOD		RESIDUE

So, WH/Subject. A further test is to change the form of the verb from the simple to the continuous form (*is* – *is being*). Where the WH is conflated with the Complement, the other clause participants will occur BEFORE the Predicator:
Who is Henry James?

Who	*is*	*Henry James*	*being?*
WH/Complement	Finite	Subject	Predicator
RESIDUE . . .	MOOD		. . . RESIDUE

Where the WH is conflated with the Subject, the other clause participants will occur *after* the Predicator:
Who is the author of The Bostonians?

Who	*is*	*being*	*the author of 'The Bostonians'?*
WH/Subject	Finite	Predicator	Complement
MOOD		RESIDUE	

Where the WH element is conflated with the Subject, the typical structure of the WH-interrogative is similar to the structure of the declarative, with the Subject preceding the Finite:

Who	*had*	*read*	*'The Bostonians'*	*at school?*
WH/Subject	^ Finite	^ Predicator	^ Complement	^ Adjunct

Where the WH element conflates with either the Complement or Adjunct, the typical structure is that of the polar interrogative, with the Finite element preceding the Subject:

What	*did*	*Henry James*	*write*	*about?*
WH/C	^ Finite	^Subject	^ Complement	^ Adjunct

When	*did*	*Henry James*	*write*	*'The Bostonians'?*
WH/A	^ Finite	^ Subject	^ Predicator	^ Complement

Exclamatives

Exclamative structures, which are used in interaction to express emotions such as surprise, disgust, worry, etc., are a blend of interrogative and declarative patterns. Like the WH-interrogatives, they require the presence of a WH element, conflated with either a Complement or an Adjunct:

WH conflated with a Complement (part of RESIDUE):

What a great writer	*Henry James*	*was!*
WH/Complement	Subject	Finite
RESIDUE	MOOD	

WH conflated with Attributive Complement (part of RESIDUE):

How amazing	*he*	*was!*
WH/Attribute	Subject	Finite
RESIDUE	MOOD	

WH conflated with an Adjunct (part of RESIDUE):

How fantastically	*Henry James*	*wrote!*	
WH/Adjunct:circumstantial	Subject	Finite	Predicator
RESIDUE . . .	MOOD		. . . RESIDUE

Structurally, the clause has the pattern of the declarative, with the Subject preceding the Finite: WH/C ^S ^ F ^P ^A

The typical response to an exclamative move is polarity (of agreement or disagreement), involving ellipsis of all but the Polarity Adjunct:
What great books Henry James was writing last century!

– Yep.
Adjunct:polarity
MOOD

Sometimes ellipsis may leave the Subject, a Mood Adjunct, and the Finite:
What great books Henry James was writing last century!

– He	sure	was.
Subject	Adjunct:mood	Finite
MOOD		

Often the responder will introduce a minor clause:
What great books Henry James was writing last century!

– Too right.
Minor

Modality: (1) modalization

We have now covered the structural elements involved in describing the grammar of propositions, the organization of the clause to give and demand information. We have suggested that when we exchange information, the clause takes the form of a **proposition**. A proposition is something that can be argued, but argued in a particular way. When we exchange information we are arguing about whether something *is* or *is not*. Information is something that can be affirmed or denied.

But these two poles of polarity are not the only possibilities. In between these two extremes are a number of choices of degree of certainty, or of usuality: something is *perhaps*, something isn't *for sure*. Something is *sometimes* or something isn't *always*. These intermediate positions are what we refer to as **modalization**.

Modalization is one half of the general grammatical area of **modality**, a complex area of English grammar which has to do with the different ways in which a language user can intrude on her message, expressing attitudes and judgements of various kinds. When modality is used to argue about the probability or frequency of propositions, it is referred to as **modalization**. When modality is used to argue about the obligation or inclination of proposals, it is referred to as **modulation** (which will be discussed later).

As Halliday and Matthiessen presents it (2004: 147–50 and 617–21), modalization involves the expression of two kinds of meanings:

 i) **probability**: where the speaker expresses judgements as to the likelihood or probability of something happening or being;
 ii) **usuality**: where the speaker expresses judgements as to the frequency with which something happens or is.

We have already come across these meanings of modalization in two places in our analysis: in the Finite category of modal operators, and in the class of Mood Adjuncts. The meanings made through modalization can therefore be present in the clause in three possible ways:
1. through the choice of a finite modal operator

'The Bostonians'	might	have been written	by Henry James.
Subject	Finite:modal	Predicator	Adjunct:circ
MOOD		RESIDUE	

2. through the use of Mood Adjuncts of probability, certainty, etc.

'The Bostonians'	was	possibly	written	by Henry James.
Subject	Finite	Adjunct:mood	Predicator	Adjunct:circ
MOOD			RESIDUE	

3. through both together: a modal Finite and a Mood Adjunct

'The Bostonians'	might	possibly	have been written	by Henry James.
Subject	Finite:modal	Adjunct:mood	Predicator	Adjunct:circ
MOOD			RESIDUE	

Both modal operators and Mood Adjuncts can be classified according to the degree of certainty or usuality they express: high (*must, certainly, always*), median (*may, probably, usually*) or low (*might, possibly, sometimes*). Thus, the same meanings can be realized in two ways: to each modal operator corresponds typically a modal adjunct which captures the same meaning:

LOW
Possibly Henry James might have written 'The Bostonians'.
Henry James sometimes wrote incredibly long sentences.

MEDIAN
Perhaps Henry James could have written 'The Bostonians'.
Henry James usually wrote incredibly long sentences.

HIGH
Certainly Henry James must have written 'The Bostonians'.
Henry James always wrote incredibly long sentences.

When the expression of modalization is negated, we can still distinguish the three degrees, although some verbs (can, could) change their position (from median to high):

HIGH
Henry James certainly did not write 'The Bostonians'.
Henry James could not possibly have written 'The Bostonians'.

MEDIAN
Henry James probably didn't write 'The Bostonians'.

LOW
Henry James possibly might not have written 'The Bostonians'.

HIGH
Henry James never wrote long sentences.

MEDIAN
Henry James did not usually write long sentences.

LOW
Henry James did not always write long sentences.

Modalization is the expression of the speaker's attitude towards what s/he's saying. It is the way the speaker gets into the text, expressing a judgement about the certainty, likelihood or frequency of something happening or being. Modalization is always expressing the implicit judgement of the speaker.

But, because people play with language, modalization can also be realized **explicitly**. Speakers can make it quite obvious that it is *their* judgement that is being expressed. Halliday points out that this can be done by using a particular type of Mood Adjunct:

low: I reckon, I guess

I reckon	*Henry James*	*wrote*		*'The Bostonians'.*
Adjunct:mood	Subject	Finite	Predicator	Complement
MOOD		RESIDUE		

median: I think, I suppose

I think	*Henry James*	*wrote*		*'The Bostonians'.*
Adjunct:mood	Subject	Finite	Predicator	Complement
MOOD		RESIDUE		

high: I'm sure

I'm sure	*Henry James*	*wrote*		*'The Bostonians'.*
Adjunct:mood	Subject	Finite	Predicator	Complement
MOOD		RESIDUE		

Mood Adjuncts like these are examples of what Halliday calls **grammatical metaphor**, in this case **metaphors of modality** (Halliday and Matthiessen 2004: 626–30). They are classified as metaphorical because a modality that would usually be realized either as a Finite modal operator or as an Adjunct in fact gets realized as a clause. *I think, I reckon, I'm sure* are technically complete clauses, with their own MOOD/ RESIDUE structure.

I		*think*
Subject	Finite	Predicator
MOOD		RESIDUE

Thus, what would usually be realized as a clause on its own comes out as a constituent of the clause, masquerading as an Adjunct.

We can see that these clauses are in fact functioning metaphorically as Adjuncts by applying the tag test. When we tag *I reckon Henry James wrote The Bostonians*, we find we do not pick up *don't I* (which would indicate that the subject of the clause was *I*), but instead *didn't he*, indicating that the grammatical Subject is in fact *Henry James*, and the *I* of *I reckon* is functioning as an Adjunct to the clause:

> I reckon Henry James wrote 'The Bostonians', *didn't he?* (not *don't I*)
> I'm sure Henry James wrote 'The Bostonians', *didn't he?* (not *aren't I*)

Because these pseudo-clauses are actually functioning as Adjuncts, we can also combine them with our other ways of expressing modalization in the clause, so that we can stack up the expression of modalization through clause-type Adjuncts, standard Mood Adjuncts, and modal Finite operators:

I reckon	*Henry James*	*might*	*possibly*	*have written*	*'The Bostonians'.*
I think	*Henry James*	*could*	*probably*	*have written*	*'The Bostonians'.*
I'm sure	*Henry James*	*must*	*certainly*	*have written*	*'The Bostonians'.*
Adjunct:mood	Subject	Finite:mod	Adjunct:mood	Predicator	Complement
MOOD			RESIDUE		

These clause-like Adjuncts make explicit the ownership or source of the modalization, through the pronoun *I*. However, speakers can also pretend that the judgement they are expressing is not 'just their own' but has some objective status:

> **It is possible** that Henry James wrote 'The Bostonians'.
> **It is probable** that Henry James wrote 'The Bostonians'.
> **It is certain** that Henry James wrote 'The Bostonians'.

Like the previous examples, this expression of modalization involves grammatical metaphor: a clause expressing the modalization is appended to the main clause. All these modalized pseudo-clauses really mean 'I think in my opinion that . . .', but the use of the '*it is . . . . that*' structure allows the speaker to hide behind an ostensibly objective formulation. Again, these objective expressions of modalization may be reinforced by the use of Finite modal operators and ordinary Mood Adjuncts:

It is possible that	*Henry James*	*might*	*conceivably*	*have written*	*'The Bostonians'.*
It is probable that	*Henry James*	*could*	*most likely*	*have written*	*'The Bostonians'.*
It is certain that	*Henry James*	*must*	*definitely*	*have written*	*'The Bostonians'.*
Adjunct:mood	Subject	Finite:mod	Adj:mood	Predicator	Complement
MOOD			RESIDUE		

Modalization is a very rich area of the grammar, allowing great subtlety in the expression of judgement of certainty and usuality. Paradoxically, however, it turns out that the more we say something is certain, the less certain it is. If we are sure of something, we do not use any modality, e.g. *Henry James wrote 'The Bostonians'.*

Thus, the use of any modality at all, however strong it appears, makes our proposition more tentative than it would be without any modality. For example saying *I'm absolutely convinced that Henry James certainly must most definitely have written 'The Bostonians'* is still less sure than saying *Henry James wrote 'The Bostonians'.*

Our analysis of how the clause is structured to enable interaction, then, needs to capture the fact that giving and demanding information involves both the choice of clause Mood (interrogative, declarative, exclamative) *and* the choice to express or not express modalization. If the speaker chooses to express modalization, this may be achieved grammatically in a number of ways: internally in the main clause through the choice of a Finite modal operator and/or one or more Mood Adjuncts; and/or externally by adding a pseudo-clause, which may be phrased subjectively or objectively.

We now turn to consider how language is organized to enable us to exchange goods and services.

Exchanging goods and services: the grammar of proposals

When we get together with people to interact we not only use language to exchange information, to argue about whether things are or are not. We also use language to influence each other's behaviour.

Our diagram of the semantics of interaction recognized two categories for using language to exchange goods and services: giving goods and services (which gave us the speech function **offer**), and demanding goods and services (which gave us the speech function **command**). What we want to examine now is how these two ways of interacting are expressed grammatically.

We can begin by noting that there is a very significant difference between proposals and propositions: they result in different types of exchanges, different types of give and take. Consider the following examples:

exchanges of information

Henry James wrote 'The Bostonians'.	*– Yea I know.*
Did Henry James write 'The Bostonians'?	*– Yes, he did.*

exchanges of goods and services:

Lend me your copy of 'The Bostonians'.	*(hands it over)*
	– OK.
Would you like to borrow my copy of 'The Bostonians'?	*– yes please*
	– no thanks
	– (takes it)

These examples indicate that in the exchange of information the response to an initiating move must nearly always be verbal, typically an expression of polarity accompanied by an elliptical segment of the initiating clause. With proposals, however, we see that the responding moves may very often be non-verbal: simply performing an action is often sufficient. Where a response to a proposal is verbalized, it is usually done with expressions that cannot be used to respond to propositions:

Did Henry James write 'The Bostonians'?	* *Yes please.*
Henry James wrote 'The Bostonians'.	* *Fine.*

With proposals, then, we see that words such as *please, thank you, OK* can be added to an optional verbal response.

This difference in the type of responses we get after an initiating proposal or an initiating proposition arises because we are engaged in a very different type of 'argument' when we exchange goods and services. While with propositions we are arguing about whether something *is* or *isn't*, with proposals we are arguing about whether something *happens* or *doesn't happen*. Such arguments cannot be affirmed or denied in the way information can be, but responses can be acted out: through acceptance or rejection, either non-verbal or verbal.

Since, then, the process of the exchange is different, you will not be surprised to find that the grammar of proposals is different from that of propositions. However, in order to describe the structure of the clause when it is used to exchange goods and services, we do not need to recognize any new functional constituents. What we need to do is look firstly at how different configurations of the constituents we are already familiar with are arranged to construct commands and offers; and secondly, at how goods and services meanings can be coloured by speaker judgements through the expression of modulation.

Demanding goods and services: the structure of imperatives

We suggested earlier in this chapter that demands for goods and services are typically (but by no means always) realized by imperatives. That is, we frequently use a clause of the Mood type **imperative** to make a command. Imperative structures may be of the following types: i) an imperative consisting of a MOOD element of Finite + Subject:

Don't	*you*	*take*	*my copy of 'the Bostonians'.*
Finite:neg	Subject	Predicator	Complement
MOOD		RESIDUE	

This imperative structure commonly uses the morpheme *let*, which functions to enable the expression of the Subject (we will therefore treat it as part of the Subject constituent):

Do	*let us*	*read*	*'Henry James'.*
Finite	Subject	Predicator	Complement
MOOD		RESIDUE	

ii) an imperative consisting of a MOOD element of Finite only (no Subject):

Do	*read*	*'The Bostonians'.*
Finite	Predicator	Complement
MOOD	RESIDUE	

iii) an imperative consisting of a MOOD element of Subject only (no Finite):

Let's	*read*	*Henry James.*
Subject	Predicator	Complement
MOOD	RESIDUE	

You	*read*	*Henry James.*
Subject	Predicator	Complement
MOOD	RESIDUE	

iv) an imperative consisting of only a RESIDUE (no MOOD element at all):

Read	*Henry James.*
Predicator	Complement
RESIDUE	

Note that although some imperatives do not contain any MOOD constituents, they are not minor clauses as they can be tagged (and are therefore considered to have ellipsed the Subject/ Finite elements, whereas minor clauses never selected a Subject/Finite in the first place).

Giving goods and services: the grammar of offers

The last major speech function class whose grammatical structure we need to explore is that of offers: when the clause is used to give goods and services.

In our earlier discussion where we listed the typical realization of each speech function, we stated that the offer is typically expressed by a **modulated interrogative**. As we have already described the structure of interrogatives in some detail, it would seem that unlike the other speech functions of command, question or statement, the offer is not expressed through a distinctive structural configuration. Rather, it 'borrows' the structure of questions: the interrogative mood, with the Finite positioned before the Subject. However, the verbal elements of the offer interrogative are distinctive, as they typically involve the expression of meanings both of modalization (probability) and of modulation (inclination and obligation). We will explore modulation in more detail below. First, however, here is the analysis of some common offer clauses:

i) modulation expressed in the Finite: the Finite *will* or *shall* expresses a meaning of willingness, i.e. positive inclination viewed from the speaker's perspective (Subject: I):

Will	*I*	*lend*	*you*	*my copy of 'The Bostonians'?*
Fin:modulated	Subject	Predicator	Complement	Complement
MOOD		RESIDUE		

ii) modulation expressed in the Predicator: the lexical verb is a verb of liking or desiring, and the clause addresses inclination from the addressee's perspective (Subject: you). The Finite element typically expresses a meaning of modalization (probability):

Would	*you*	*like*	*my copy of 'The Bostonians'?*
Fin:modalized	Subject	Pred:modulated	Complement
MOOD		RESIDUE	

iii) modulation in a complex Predicator: offers are also frequently expressed using a complex modulated Predicator, i.e. a Predicator involving a verb such as *like, desire, need* followed by a second verb in the infinitive form. The Finite is typically modalized:

Would	*you*	*like to borrow*	*my copy of 'The Bostonians'?*
Finite:modalized	Subject	Predicator:complex: modulated	Complement
MOOD		RESIDUE	

Modality: (2) modulation

Aside from the imperative and modulated interrogative structures we have examined so far, there are many other ways of using language to get people to do things for us, or of offering to do things for them. For example, all the following are ways of getting people to do things (or not do things) for us, getting them to behave in a particular way:

1. You shouldn't take my copy of 'The Bostonians'.
2. We must read 'The Bostonians'.
3. You are obliged to read Henry James!
4. You're required to read 'The Bostonians'.

Semantically, all these clauses have the meaning of commands – they are all demanding goods and services – and yet they do not have the grammatical structure of imperatives. Structurally, they are in fact declaratives, with structures of Subject, Finite, Predicator, Complement.

But it is not enough to simply describe them as declaratives, for each of these declaratives involves an additional semantic dimension. The difference is in the verbal elements of the clause. Examples 1 and 2 employ the Finite verbal operators *should, must*, operators which express meanings not of probability but of **obligation, necessity**. Such Finites are described by Halliday and Matthiessen (2004: 147) as modulated Finites:

You	*shouldn't*	*take*	*my copy of 'The Bostonians'.*
Subject	Finite:modulated	Predicator	Complement
MOOD		RESIDUE	

We	*must*	*read*	*'The Bostonians'.*
Subject	Finite:modulated	Predicator	Complement
MOOD		RESIDUE	

In examples 3 and 4, the same meanings of obligation and necessity are expressed through the Predicator constituent:

You	*are*	*obliged to read*	*Henry James!*
Subject	Finite	Predicator:modulated:complex	Complement
MOOD		RESIDUE	

You	're	required to read	'The Bostonians'.
Subject	Finite	Predicator:modulated:complex	Complement
MOOD		RESIDUE	

Consider now the following examples:

> I want to lend you 'The Bostonians'.
> I'd like to lend you 'The Bostonians'.
> I'm willing to lend you 'The Bostonians'.
> I'm happy to lend you 'The Bostonians'.
> I'm determined to lend you 'The Bostonians'.

All these clauses are ways of giving goods and services: each is functioning as an offer, but grammatically each has the structure of a declarative, with adjectives expressing **inclination**: how willing I am to do something for you. Such clauses can be analysed as follows:

I	'm	determined to make	you	a coffee.
Subject	Finite	Predicator:modulated:complex	Complement	Complement
MOOD		RESIDUE		

But just as I can act on you in these various ways, so I can ask you to act on my behaviour, for example by demanding direction, advice, permission, undertaking or capability, which can be analysed as follows:

Must	I	read	'The Bostonians'?
Finite:modulated	Subject	Predicator	Complement
MOOD		RESIDUE	

Can	I	have	a coffee?
Finite:modulated	Subject	Predicator	Complement
MOOD		RESIDUE	

Are	you	willing to make	the coffee?
Finite	Subject	Predicator:complex:modulated	Complement
MOOD		RESIDUE	

In all the examples we have considered above, we have needed to make reference to the semantic dimension of **modulation**. Modulation is the second dimension of modality, complementing modalization in propositions. With propositions you will remember that we did not just argue about *is* or *isn't* but about degrees of probability in between. Likewise with proposals, we do not just argue about *do* or *don't*. There is also a scale in between, but this time the scale is not of possibility or usuality, but of **obligation** and **inclination**.

Again, as with modalization, we can also recognize degrees of modulation (high: *must/required to*; median: *should/supposed to*; low: *may/allowed to*). And just as we found with modalization, so these meanings of modulation can be expressed in the clause in a number of different ways:

1. in the Finite, as a modulated verbal operator:

You	*shouldn't/must/have to*	*take*	*my copy of 'The Bostonians'.*
Subject	Fin:modulated:neg	Predicator	Complement
MOOD		RESIDUE	

As well as these straightforward ways of expressing modulation in the clause, we can also find, as with modalization, possibilities of subjective and objective expression that is external to the main clause. Thus, meanings of inclination may be expressed subjectively, by making the speaker's inclination an adjectival element, which is then followed by an infinitive clause. As exemplified above, we will analyse these clauses as follows:

I	*'m*	*willing to make*	*the coffee.*
Subject	Finite	Predicator:modulated:complex	Complement
MOOD		RESIDUE	

Meanings of obligation and necessity may be expressed objectively, through a passive expansion of the Predicator:

You	*'re*	*required to read*	*Henry James.*
Subject	Finite	Predicator:modulated:complex	Complement
MOOD		RESIDUE	

Modulation, then, is a way for speakers to express their judgements or attitudes about actions and events. When we are acting on or for other people, we do not only have the dogmatic choices of *do* or *don't do, I'll give you this* or *I won't give you this*. But between these two poles of compliance and refusal we can express degrees of obligation and inclination.

The parallels between modalization and modulation are very strong – which is, of course, why we draw them together under the label of modality. The two represent complementary resources speakers can draw on in achieving the exchange of information or goods and services. We can think of them both as grammatical resources for tempering what we say.

Of course in any exchange I can always turn the tables on you. One thing I can do is to challenge you, and when I do that it is usually by questioning your modalization or modulation:

> Henry James definitely wrote 'The Bostonians'.
> – Are you sure?
> Couldn't Henry James have written 'The Bostonians'?
> – How could he?

Will you have a coffee?
  – Why would/wouldn't I?
You should read Henry James.
  – Why should I?

Even when there is no apparent modality in your initiation, the fact that you have made an implicit choice *not* to modalize can be challenged:

Henry James wrote 'The Bostonians'.
  – Are you sure?
Will you have a coffee?
  – Why (do you want me to)?
Read Henry James.
  – Why should I?

Modalization and modulation are extremely complex systems, and interact in interesting ways. Both may occur in the same clause:

You should probably read 'The Bostonians'.
I think you could perhaps be obliged to read Henry James.
Will I sometimes have to read Henry James? – Yep, I think you'll have to occasionally.
Do I definitely have to read it? – You certainly do.

The fact that we can have both modalization and modulation going on within the one clause suggests that the line between propositions and proposals may not be as sharp as we have been assuming until now. In fact there are two main situations where it is difficult to decide whether what is being exchanged is information or goods and services:

The first is when you are talking to someone about the behaviour of a third person. Compare the following:

  i) Di to George: *You really have to start reading some Henry James.*
  ii) Di to Simon: *George really has to start reading some Henry James.*

In the first clause, Di has clearly made a demand for goods and services of George. She is making a command, realized through the structure of a modulated declarative. In the second clause, however, Di is expressing the same meaning of obligation, but this time it is not directed at the person implicated in the command, but at a third person. Since it is not up to Simon to comply with Di's command, and in fact since the appropriate response to ii) is not *OK* but *Yes, I agree*, we can see that what is really being exchanged in ii) is information. But the information exchanged is coloured by the speaker's attitudes of obligation, etc. In our culture we refer to information of that kind as **opinion**.

When we 'borrow' the grammar of proposals to exchange information, we express opinions. We use the modulation resources of proposals in an exchange where goods and services could not be provided. Opinions contrast with **facts** which we may define now as unmodulated clauses, such as *George is reading Henry James*.

This distinction has nothing to do with the truth or falsity of the information. It is a grammatical distinction. In casual conversation most of the information we exchange is not of the fact type, but the opinion type. We can of course be more or less sure of our opinions. For example, if Di said to Simon:

> *I think that George probably has to read some Henry James.*

she is expressing a degree of uncertainty about the force of her opinion.

So this is one example of where the grammar of proposals and propositions cross over. In such situations, resources typically used to modify goods and services exchanges get borrowed or transferred to exchange information of a particular kind. But they retain some of their goods and services meaning: if George overheard Di's remark to Simon, he would be likely to respond as if a command had been made of him (e.g. *OK, I will* or *No, I don't want to*).

The second situation in which the distinction is not so clear-cut is when we use modulation to demand direction, advice or permission.

> Must I read it now?
> Can I read 'Portrait of a Lady' first?
> Should I read 'The Bostonians'?

In these types of demands there is no tangible commodity being exchanged: what is demanded is a judgement, an opinion, as to the course of action to be carried out. They are thus like an intermediate step between an exchange of goods and services and an exchange of information. They lead to action, but the typical response is a verbal expression of opinion:

> Must I read it now?   – Yes, you must.
> Can I read 'Portrait of a Lady' first?   – If you like.
> Should I read 'The Bostonians'?   – No, you needn't bother.

So it seems as if things like advice and permission are encoded in the grammar not as types of information but as types of goods. Our everyday expressions capture this sense of permission and advice as goods to be traded:

> He gave me some advice.
> I got his permission.

Some interactions centre around the exchange of these intermediate commodities. For example, going to the doctor is typically an exchange of advice (not a reciprocal exchange, of course. Doctors do not take favourably to being advised to lose weight, clean up their waiting rooms, or lower their fees!).

Summary

Whenever we use language we are using it to interact, to exchange. Our first choice in an exchange is to decide whether we will take on the speech role of initiator or responder. If we choose to initiate an exchange, we must take on either the speech role of giving, or the speech role of demanding. However, in order to interact we must also have something to exchange: either information (an intangible, purely verbal commodity) or goods and services (tangible commodities or activities).

The choice of speech role and commodity type are expressed grammatically through choices in the Mood structure of the clause: i.e. choices about the functional constituents such as Subject, Finite, Predicator, Complement, Adjunct and their configuration (e.g. Subject before Finite; WH conflation; absence of MOOD element, etc.). The distinction between initiating and responding roles is associated with the structural difference between **full** and **elliptical** clause types. The distinction between giving and demanding can be associated with the different structures of **declaratives** and **imperatives**. And the distinction between information and goods and services can be associated with the Mood differences between **major** and **minor** clauses.

Although linguistic exchanges, whether of goods and services or information, are fundamentally arguments about **polarity** (is/isn't or do/don't), linguistic interaction is not usually a black and white exchange of absolute agreement/acceptance or contradiction/refusal. Through the two grammatical sub-systems of **modalization** and **modulation**, brought together under the label **modality**, language allows us to temper the exchange by expressing degrees of either probability/usuality or obligation/inclination.

What we have done so far in this chapter is to look at how the clause is structured to enable us to make the kinds of meanings essential for interaction to take place. We have uncovered a correlation between the semantic categories or **speech functions** of offer, command, statement, question and grammatical Mood classes. So when we ask 'how is language structured to enable interaction?' we find the answer lies (principally) in the systems of Mood and Modality. It is in describing the functional grammatical constituents of Mood, and their different configurations, that we are describing how language is structured to enable us to talk to each other.

The meaning of Mood: Mood, interpersonal meaning and tenor

The starting point for this rather lengthy and technical description of clause types was that in describing the Mood structure of the clause we would be describing how language is used to enable the expression of interpersonal meanings through dialogue.

And in fact it is by looking at how people use these systems of Mood and Modality in the clauses they exchange with each other that we can see speakers making meanings about such interpersonal dimensions as: the power or solidarity of their relationship; the extent of their intimacy; their level of familiarity with each other; and their attitudes and judgements. You will remember from earlier chapters that the systemic model claims that we can trace a direct link from the grammatical patterns of Mood in the clause, up to the semantics of interpersonal meanings, and out into context to the register variable of tenor.

One very simple way in which a Mood analysis can reveal dimensions of tenor is to simply consider who is doing the talking in a situation. The most striking indication of power is in who gets to be speaker in an exchange, and for how long. For example, in a typical classroom situation (primary, secondary or tertiary), the teacher gets to be speaker for most of the time. The relationship of unequal power that as a society we set up for many genres of classroom interaction is realized linguistically by the teacher's simple dominance of the speaker role. It is clear who is in charge in a classroom, because the teacher is the one who does the talking. In casual conversation, on the other hand, there is much freer access to the speaker role: the solidarity of the role relationships is acted out linguistically through a greater sharing of the role of speaker. No one has the intrinsic right to hold the floor.

And yet when you study casual conversation, even the short excerpt used at the beginning of this chapter, it is not hard to discover that some classes of people get to be speaker more frequently than others. In particular, men. In mixed casual conversation men get to be speakers more often and hold the role of speaker longer than women.

A second area of Mood choice in which Tenor dimensions are realized is seen by looking at what speakers do when they get the speaker role. For example, who gives? Who demands? And are these reciprocal rights?

When there is a lack of reciprocity, there we find status relations. For example, in spite of our folk attitude that teaching is all about giving people knowledge, linguistically we find that in pedagogic situations the teacher is very often demanding, and the student very often giving. The non-reciprocity of these roles is a clear indication of the unequal power relations between teachers and students. In a transactional encounter, we can see that the social role of salesperson means you take on the speech role of offer (giving goods and services), and therefore produce modulated interrogatives (*May I help you?*), whereas the social role of client means you take on the speech role of command (demanding goods and services), and therefore produce imperatives or modulated declaratives (*Give me six of those; I'd like six of those*). There is thus a clear relationship between the social roles we play in situations, and the choices we make in the Mood system.

In casual conversation, there are theoretically no intrinsic rights for people to give or demand. Anyone can do anything, as power is shared equally. However, the analysis of excerpts such as Text 6.1 suggests that women demand information but give goods and services; whereas men give information but demand goods and services. In the selection of speech roles, and their corresponding realization in the Mood structures, we see the linguistic realization of gender expectations of our culture: that women are conversationally supportive, while men just sit back and perform.

A further aspect of Mood choice which can be related to tenor concerns selections for modality: who modalizes? who modulates? This provides a realization both of relationships of power and of affective involvement.

Taking modalization first, we can distinguish here between the original or neutral meaning of modalization as tentativity vis-à-vis information, and a derived function to express deference. If, in casual conversation, I said *I think Henry James probably wrote 'The Bostonians'*, the *I think* and the *probably* express my lack of conviction: I am simply not one hundred per cent sure of my claim.

However, if my lecturer in English has just attributed *'The Bostonians'* to Jane Austen, I may find myself saying:

> That might not be quite right. I think Henry James might have written 'The Bostonians'.

In this instance the modalizations do not express uncertainty at all, but instead deference to the superior status of the lecturer. If I had said *You're wrong. Henry James wrote 'The Bostonians'*, I would have been perceived as speaking impolitely – because politeness in a hierarchic situation means speaking with adequate recognition of the superior's status. A related deferential use of modalisation is its use with people we do not know well, – i.e. where frequency of contact is low.

This use of modalization to temper speech also operates with proposals. In fact, one of the main motivations for switching from a command (demand for goods and services) to an opinion (modulated declarative/interrogative) is that this then allows the use of modalization. For example, while in the equal power situation Di might say to George:

> Read some Henry James.

when urging a superior to do so, she is likely to say:

> Perhaps you should read some Henry James.

with modalization used to soften the force of the 'should'. Or:

> Maybe you'd like to read some Henry James.

where deference is expressed in both the shift from obligation to inclination and the use of modalization to water down the opinion.

In many registers, then, the use of modalization has little to do with the speaker's judgements about probability, but is instead functioning to signal interactants' recognition of the unequal power or infrequent contact between them.

Even in casual conversation, where we would expect modalization to realize its neutral meaning, we find that women use it significantly more frequently than men. In Text 6.1, for example, you will see that George and Simon quite freely contradict each other in no uncertain terms (i.e. without any modulation), whereas the women frequently temper their speech with modalizations.

A further relation between modality in the clause and dimensions of tenor is illustrated in the use of objective modality. For example, compare two ways we might get students to read their set texts:

> It is required that all students read 'The Bostonians'.
> You must all read 'The Bostonians'.

In the first we see the agency of the command being obscured: depersonalization leaves the respondents (the students) with no one to argue with. Compare the responses they might make to the two alternatives:

> It is required that all students read 'The Bostonians'. – Who says?
> You must all read 'The Bostonians'. – No, we don't have to.

In the objectified version, the students must first establish who their interactant is. What the first example tries to do is to present an impersonal expression of personal attitude – a contradiction in terms. The reason why this pattern occurs so much in hierarchic situations seems to be that it is a covert attempt to get people to do things without having to take responsibility for issuing the command. Such faceless expressions of power leave interactants with no agent of the modulation to challenge.

Modalities also express affect, either positive or negative, towards what we are talking about. Compare, for example, the bubbly, effusive person who uses intensifiers (Mood Adjuncts) such as *absolutely, amazingly, unbelievably* all the time, versus the cold, rational, withdrawn, in fact IMpersonal person who never use these modalities at all. Thus, the choice of Modalities can also express the other side of interpersonal relations: the 'personal' rather than the 'inter'.

A final area in which Mood patterns relate to the expression of Tenor lies in the relationships of congruence or incongruence between Mood choice and speech functions. This chapter has suggested several times that typical correlations exist between the semantic categories of offer, command, statement, question and the grammatical structures of different Mood types. So typically a command will be expressed through the imperative structure, a question through an interrogative, etc. If these are the unmarked choices, the choices we make 'all other things being equal', then what is very interesting is to look at times when these choices are **not** made. What is the significance of a command that is **not** realized by an imperative? For example, the teacher who suggests *Shall we just have some practice doing that now?* instead of directly commanding *Get on with your work*. Or a question that is **not** realized by an interrogative. The choice of marked Mood structures typically functions to express tenor dimensions such as unequal power, deference or low contact and involvement.

In many interactive situations we do not in fact have many realistic choices to make. If we want to behave appropriately we have to accept the social definition of interpersonal relationships in that particular situation. So, for example, we have to accept that relationships between teachers and students are culturally construed as being of unequal power. We have to accept that in the greengrocers our roles are as unequal, distant acquaintances. The proof that we have accepted the social roles is found in our discourse roles, i.e. in the choices we make in Mood and Modality. In the types of clauses we use we see the acting out of conventionally established social roles.

Thus, in studying the grammar of the clause as exchange we are actually studying *how interpersonal meanings get made*. The systems of Mood and Modality are the keys to understanding the interpersonal relationships between interactants. By looking at the grammatical choices speakers make, the role they play in discourse, we have a way of uncovering and studying the social creation and maintenance of hierarchic, socio-cultural roles.

We are now in a position to validate a claim made in Chapter Four: that tenor is realized through interpersonal meanings, which are in turn realized through the grammar of the clause as exchange. Our analysis allows us to study how choices in Mood and Modality (as well as in some systems we have not had space to discuss, such as Vocation and Attitude) are the realization of tenor. By looking closely at the choices speakers make for Mood and Modality, we can uncover the interpersonal relationships that are being expressed in text. In the Appendix following Chapter Eleven I provide the Mood analysis of the three Crying Baby texts presented in Chapter One. The implications of those Mood analyses will be discussed in Chapter Eleven.

Throughout this chapter, frequent reference has been made to the notion of **choice** – choices in Mood or speech function, selections in modalization or modulation, etc. The following chapter will explain and develop this systemic emphasis on choice by examining the place and function of systems in SFL. That discussion will provide the context for our continued exploration of the grammatical systems of Transitivity, Theme and the Clause Complex in Chapters Eight, Nine and Ten.

Notes

1. For a more extended discussion of Mood analysis, see Halliday and Matthiessen (2004: Chapter 3).
2. The text is an excerpt from a dinner party conversation, 'Dinner at Stephen's' (author's data).

Chapter 7

Systems: meaning as choice

Introduction

The preceding chapters have explored in some depth what it means to take a functional approach to language. The purpose of this chapter is to explain the other major dimension of a systemic-functional approach: the **systemic**. In order to do this we will return to some of the concepts raised in the first chapter, exploring how a sign in a semiotic system gets its meaning through entering into both paradigmatic and syntagmatic relations with other signs. The chapter will discuss the systemic use of the **system** to capture paradigmatic relations between linguistic signs, with structure captured through realization statements. The chapter will introduce the conventions systemicists use for drawing systems, in order that future grammatical description can be presented both functionally and systemically.

Semiotic systems

You will remember from Chapter One that the signs in a semiotic system involve two dimensions: a **content**, or meaning, and an **expression**, or realization, and that the relationship between content and expression is arbitrary. Thus, with the traffic light system, the association between the meaning *stop* and the colour *red* is not natural, but conventional, and could therefore be changed by convention: for example, we could agree that henceforth the meaning *stop* will be realized by the colour *purple*. As the contrast between Systems 7.1 and 7.2 indicates, then, we can change the association between the signifié and the signifiant *without affecting the system itself*.

We could even decide that the meaning *stop* will henceforth be encoded by the colour 'green', so long as we now also change the association between *go* and *green* to avoid confusion. If we did not change the *go/green* association, we would no longer have the same sign system, as instead of three different signs, we would now have a system consisting of only two signs, as represented in System 7.3.

However, if semiotic systems are an arbitrary social convention, what can we really say about the 'meaning' of any light? How do the signs in a semiotic system get their meaning?

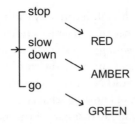

System 7.1   Original traffic light system

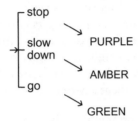

System 7.2   Changing a realization in the traffic light system

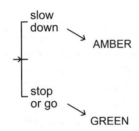

System 7.3   A two-sign system of traffic lights

With the traffic lights, we can see that the meaning of each sign comes largely **from what it is not**: what makes the association between *green* and *go* have meaning is that the *green/go* fusion stands in opposition to two other content/expression pairs: *red/stop* and *amber/slow down*. Thus, the meaning of any one sign is that it stands in opposition to two other signs: it means what it does because it does **not** mean what they do.

In the semiotic system of language, where the relationship between the content and the expression of a sign is also an arbitrary one, the same question arises: how do we know what any linguistic sign means?

Take the lexical sign *axolotl*. Imagine that you wanted to teach me, a foreigner, the meaning of this word. One way you might think of getting across to me what it means is to take me to the local aquarium and show me a fish tank containing ten different axolotls, of all different species. Pointing patiently at each you would say *axolotl*. Once I had had a chance to study this tank, you would be pretty confident that I would have figured out what *axolotl* means. So you are surprised when, moving on to look at the next tank, I point to the swimming creatures inside it and say *axolotl*. 'No,' you point out, 'those are gold-fish'. In the next tank I again claim the inhabitants as *axolotl*, but unfortunately they are octopuses. And so on, with me at each tank incorrectly calling all the inhabitants *axolotl*. In despair, you finally have to admit that your ingenious teaching strategy somehow failed.

It is quite obvious what has gone wrong: you showed me only the complementary possibilities of the word *axolotl*. You showed me only the things that **could** be called by that name. You forgot to show me what **could NOT**, i.e. what the oppositions were. From this example, we can begin to see that part of knowing what an *axolotl* is involves knowing what an *axolotl* isn't. More technically we can say that part of the meaning of a linguistic sign is in the oppositions it enters into.

These oppositions are established not naturally but by convention, and Saussure (1959/66) used a number of analogies to demonstrate the implications of the arbitrariness of signs[1]. One analogy was to compare language to a game of chess (Saussure 1959/66: 88, 110). Imagine, he said, that one of the chess pieces gets lost: a rook, for example. Is there any way we can keep playing? The answer is yes, of course. All we need to do is simply to find some object, for example a cigarette lighter, and agree between the two of us that this object is a replacement for the missing rook. So the cigarette lighter becomes by convention a rook, and we can keep on playing without any trouble as long as two conditions are met:

1. that the cigarette lighter performs exactly the same type of moves as the rook – as long as it moves only up or across the board, and not diagonally, and
2. that the cigarette lighter cannot be confused with any of the other pieces: we recognize that the cigarette lighter is not a queen or a pawn.

This analogy demonstrates two important points about chess. Firstly, that it is not the **substance** of the chess pieces that matter: their shape, colour or size are irrelevant, since any object can be substituted for them without affecting the game. The pieces are thus conventional. Secondly, it demonstrates that what matters is the **relations** each piece enters into with all the others, how the piece behaves vis-à-vis the other pieces.

Applied to language, this analogy has two implications. Firstly, it indicates that linguistic signs are not substance, but arbitrary forms: a particular sound combination is not naturally fixed to a particular object in the world, but the relationship is established by arbitrary social convention. Secondly, it indicates that the meaning of each sign, what defines it, is the relations each sign can enter into with other signs.

Relations between signs: the paradigmatic and syntagmatic axes

Saussure pointed out that the meaning of a sign must come from relations that it enters into with other signs. The two kinds of relations between linguistic signs, or rather the two **axes** along which we can look at relations, are the **syntagmatic axis**, which captures the relations of sequence or **chain** relations between signs, and the **paradigmatic axis**, which captures the relations of opposition or **choice** between signs. These axes of chain and choice are schematized in Figure 7.1.

Syntagmatic relations, relations along the axis of chain, are the relations by which signs can go together in sequences or structures, thus the relationship between one sign and the signs that can go before and after it. **Paradigmatic relations**, relations along the axis of choice, are the relations by which signs stand in opposition to other signs, thus the relationship between a sign and the other signs that might have occurred in its place.

In language we can define linguistic signs at each strata and rank of the linguistic system in terms of these two kinds of relations.

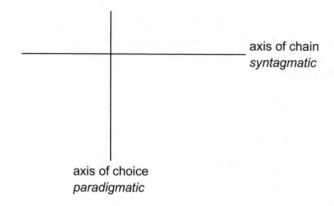

axis of chain
syntagmatic

axis of choice
paradigmatic

Figure 7.1   Axes of chain and choice

For example, at the phonological stratum, we can 'define' the phoneme /p/ in terms of its **syntagmatic relations,** i.e. the combinations it can enter into. So, we would enumerate such phonemic information as:

— that /p/ can proceed or follow any vowel;
— that within a syllable the liquids /l/ and /r/ are the only consonants which can follow it and /s/ the only one that can precede it.

Thus, part of the meaning of the phoneme /p/ comes from these syntagmatic possibilities. The second dimension of its meaning comes from its **paradigmatic relations:** the oppositions in which it stands in a given context. For example, in the phonological context of initial sound in the sequence /...it/, we would be able to determine that /p/ stands in opposition to the phonemes /b,t,l,h,s,n,w,z/ (since we can form the words /bit/, /tit/, /lit/, /hit/, /sit/, /nit/, /wit/, /zit/ and each means something different), but not /v/ (*vit), etc. Thus, the meaning of the phoneme /p/ is the sum of these two types of relations it enters into.

At the morphological level, the lowest rank in the lexico-grammatical stratum, we can apply exactly the same principles to determine the meaning of a morpheme. For example, the meaning of the morpheme *friend* is defined partly by its **syntagmatic** or combinatorial possibilities, which other morphemes, either bound morphemes (prefixes and suffixes) or free morphemes (other independent lexical items), it can combine with. We would find that the morpheme *friend* can combine with the morphemes -less (*friendless*), -ly (*friendly*), un- (*unfriendly*), be- (*befriend*), -ship (*friendship*), -liness (*unfriendliness*), but that it could not combine with the morphemes dis- (**disfriend*), -ation (**friendation*), sub- (**subfriend*), over- (**overfriend*), -ize (**friendize*), etc.

Thus, part of the meaning of *friend* is these syntagmatic relations. But its meaning also comes from its **paradigmatic** or oppositional relations: we would consider what morphemes could occur instead of the morpheme *friend*. Here we would find that *friend* has paradigmatic relations with *lecture, member, dictator, professor,* etc. in that they all contrast with one another in the environment -*ship* (*lectureship, membership, dictatorship, professorship,* etc.).

Moving up the grammatical rank scale, the meaning of clauses is also established relationally. For example, the meaning of the clause *the baby slept* is partly defined by the constituents that can occur after and before it:

Yesterday, due to fatigue <u>the baby slept</u> soundly all night in bed with his toys without dreaming.

where *the baby slept* can be combined with a large number of Circumstantial Adjuncts expressing different meanings of time, cause, location, accompaniment, manner. But the same clause could not combine with a Complement, an Attributive Complement, or an Adjunct expressing Beneficiary:

> *the baby slept / the night
> *the baby slept light
> *the baby slept to his mother

Thus, part of the meaning of our clause is the set of clause constituents with which it can possibly combine. However, the clause is also partly defined by the paradigmatic oppositions it enters into. This would involve listing clauses which could replace it and which would make a difference in meaning. Here the contrasts would involve different types of processes or actions that contrast with the action of sleeping:

> *The baby slept*   (physiological action)
> vs
> *The baby thought*   (mental action)
> *The baby hit*   (physical action)
> *The baby was*   (no action, just being)

Syntagmatic relations give **structures**: a sequence of ordered elements in linear arrangement. Paradigmatic relations, on the other hand, give **paradigms**. A paradigm is a set of oppositions, or choices, in a particular context. A common method used in learning foreign languages is to rote learn important paradigms in the language. For example, the paradigm of the French irregular verb *aller* has a familiar ring to those who have studied French:

> Je vais
> Tu vas
> Il va
> Nous allons
> Vous allez
> Ils vont

In previous chapters you have already been presented with a number of different paradigms, not of verbs but of clauses. For example, the following groups of clauses from Chapter Five constitute paradigms:

Set 1:

> The redback spider gave the captured beetle a poisonous bite.
> Did the redback spider give the captured beetle a poisonous bite?
> What did the redback spider give the captured beetle?
> Who gave the captured beetle a poisonous bite?
> Give a poisonous bite, redback spider!
> What a poisonous bite the redback spider gave the captured beetle!

Set 2:

> The redback spider gave the captured beetle a poisonous bite.
> It was the redback spider who gave the captured beetle a poisonous bite.

By the redback spider the captured beetle was given a poisonous bite.
A poisonous bite was what the redback spider gave the captured beetle.
To the captured beetle the redback spider gave a poisonous bite.

Set 3:

The redback spider gave the captured beetle a poisonous bite.
The redback spider bit the captured beetle with poison.
The redback spider sniffed the captured beetle.
The redback spider thought about biting the captured beetle.
The redback spider has a poisonous bite.
The redback spider is the most deadly Australian spider.

Each of these sets of clauses is a paradigm: a list of clauses which contrast in a particular way. It should now be possible for you to identify the first set of clauses as exemplifying a paradigm of Mood choices. Constructing such paradigms is the first step in identifying the paradigmatic relations between units.

Since, as Saussure (1959/66: 111) pointed out, 'language is only a system of pure values', the study of language involves establishing, at each level (so for each linguistic unit), the paradigmatic and syntagmatic relations which give linguistic signs their meaning. Linguistic approaches since Saussure have tended to give priority to one or other of these types of relations, with formal grammatical approaches tending to prioritize the description of syntagmatic relations (what elements from what classes can go next to each other in structures), while functional grammatical approaches tend to prioritize the description of paradigmatic relations (what functional constituents stand in opposition to each other).

We will see below that while the systemic approach does give theoretical priority to paradigmatic relations, its formalism through the system network captures both paradigmatic and syntagmatic relations.

MOOD revisited: syntagmatic and paradigmatic relations of Mood

In the previous chapter, we developed a description of the syntagmatic relations of the clause from the point of view of the possible combinations of Mood constituents that we find in different English clauses. Thus, a description such as:

Subject ^ Finite ^ Predicator ^ Complement ^ Adjunct

offers a syntagmatic definition of what a non-elliptical declarative 'means'. Thus, a statement of the structure of a clause is also a statement of its syntagmatic organization. So we are now able to define **structure** in more technical terms, as **the set of functional constituents in syntagmatic relation**.

However, applying Saussure's argument, we would need to also describe the paradigmatic relations between clause constituents if we are to have fully described what a declarative 'means'. In fact, in the previous chapter we did also describe paradigmatic relations. So, when we contrasted the formula:

Subject ^ Finite ^ Predicator ^ Complement ^ Adjunct

with the formulae:

Finite^Subject^Predicator^Complement^Adjunct	(polar interrogative)
WH-Complement^Finite^Subject	(WH-interrogative)
WH-Complement^Subject^Finite	(exclamative)
Predicator^Complement	(imperative)

what we were doing was describing the paradigmatic contrasts between the structure of clauses of different Moods. In Chapter Six our description was both i) syntagmatic: in describing how constituents go together linearly, in sequence, we presented a description of clause types in terms of their structure; and ii) paradigmatic: in describing how configurations of constituents differ from each other, we presented a description of clause types in terms of their oppositions.

In Chapter Six we used functionally labelled boxes to capture the syntagmatic structure of the clause. What was lacking from the previous chapter, however, was the formalism for presenting paradigmatic description, and the method for capturing the relationship between the syntagmatic and the paradigmatic.

Systems

The formalism used in the systemic model to capture paradigmatic relations is the **system**. The basic system consists of an entry condition and a set of two or more signs in opposition, of which one and only one must be chosen. The signs are called the **terms** in the system. A system is always read from left to right. See the basic system in System 7.4.

This system should be read as saying 'if the entry condition of *x* applies, then either *a* or *b* must be chosen'. This system is the kind we needed to represent the content of the traffic lights in Chapter One. See System 7.5.

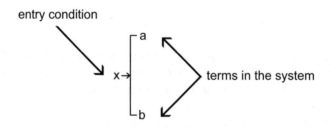

System 7.4   Basic system

System 7.5   Traffic lights as a system

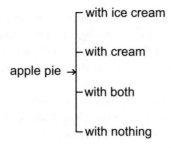

apple pie →
- with ice cream
- with cream
- with both
- with nothing

System 7.6   A non-binary system

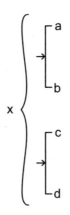

x {
- a
- b
- c
- d

System 7.7   Simultaneous choice

Systems do not have to consist of only two choices. For example, the system you might face when being offered your dessert could be as is shown in System 7.6.

Systems are usually more complex than this. Frequently systems involve simultaneous choice, which is indicated by the use of a curled bracket (see System 7.7).

This system should be read as saying 'if the entry condition of *x* is met, then you must choose either *a* or *b* AND either *c* or *d'*. The 'output' of the system, then, would be any of the following sets of features:

a + c
a + d
b + c
b + d

But not:

*a + b; or
*c + d

System 7.8 provides a concrete example of such a system.

So, you can choose either steak or fish, with either salad or vegetables, but you cannot choose both steak and fish, or both salad and vegetables.

Most semiotic systems cannot be described using only one system. Usually we find that choices lead to other choices: for example, having chosen vegetables, you may need to choose between carrots or courgettes. To capture further choices, we simply write further systems, applying the same conventions introduced above. For example, we can extend our simple system, as in System 7.9.

Here you must first choose either *a* or *b*. Then, if you choose *a* you must go on to choose between *m* or *n*; whereas if you choose *b* you must then choose between *y* or *z*.

Extending our more complex system might give us choices as in System 7.10.

Possible outputs from System 7.10 are as follows (only the terminal choices are listed):

m y
m z
m j
m k
n y
n z
n j
n k
p y
p z
p j
p k
q y
q z
q j
q k

A concrete example of an extended system network is provided in System 7.11.

You should be able to construct several alternative meals from this network.

The basic organizing concept of the system is that of **choice**. Each system in a system network represents a point at which a choice has to be made. The first choice that is made (from the system at the farthest left-hand side of the system network) is called the **least**

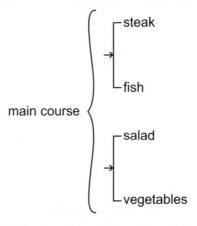

System 7.8   Example of simultaneous choice

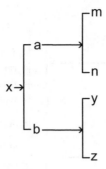

System 7.9   Extending the system in delicacy

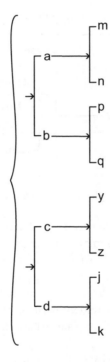

System 7.10   Simultaneous choice and increased delicacy

delicate choice. It is the first choice in logical priority that has to be made. As the network extends to the right, we say we are moving in **delicacy**, until we reach the final system (i.e. that at the extreme right-hand side of the network), which is called the **most delicate** system, in which the most delicate choices are made. In our dinner network above, the least delicate choice is between steak or fish and vegetables or salad. The most delicate choices are the choices we have to make between mashed or baked potatoes, the type of meat/fish and its method of preparation, and the type of vegetables.

As this example shows, the scale of delicacy refers to the *logical priority* among choices: before you can choose between mashed or baked potato, you must first have chosen potato rather than chips, which in turn means that you must first have chosen vegetables rather than salad.

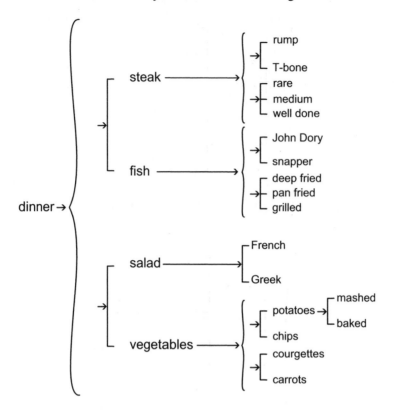

System 7.11 Example of an extended system network

A system network has nothing to do with time. A system does not capture the temporal sequence of choices. You may, for example, have gone in to the restaurant having already decided that you really want chips, and then once you're in the queue you decide you'd also like some mash, and then just as you get to the serving section you decide on fish. This real-time sequence is not represented in the network. Instead, what is captured in a system network is the logical structure of the system: what contrasts with what, for example the fact that at this particular restaurant, if you want to have chips you cannot also have mashed potato.

Having presented the basic conventions for reading and writing system networks, a linguistic system network is presented in System 7.12. It will take you only a moment to recognize what it describes.

The relationship between system and structure

The system network presented in System 7.12 captures the paradigmatic relations of Mood in the clause. However, as it stands it is incomplete. It may have occurred to you that the structural descriptions that most of Chapter Six dealt with seem to be missing. The system at the moment captures only the paradigmatic relations. A complete network, however, captures both paradigmatic and syntagmatic relations. The complete system network is presented in System 7.13.

The difference between this and the previous system is that in this system each choice is now expressed by a **realization**. We have added to the system **realization statements**,

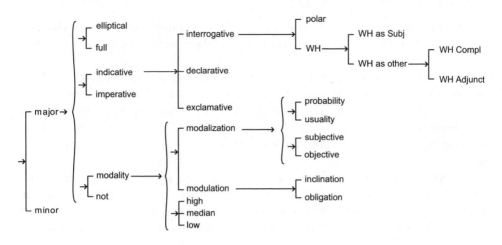

System 7.12 Linguistic network

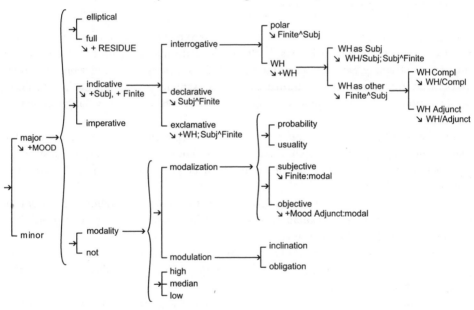

System 7.13 Mood network with realizations

in which we stipulate the output of the different choices made. You will note that the output of a linguistic system is a structural statement. These structural statements or realizations may involve specifying:

- the **presence** of a functional constituent (for example, choice of the feature *full* is realized by the presence of the structural element + RESIDUE)
- the **ordering** of functional constituents (for example, choice of the feature polar interrogative is realized by the ordering of the Finite constituent before the Subject, Finite^Subject)
- **conflation** of functional constituents (for example, choice of a WH-Complement interrogative is realized by the conflation of the WH element with the Complement element, WH/Compl)

- **specification** of the sub-class of particular constituents (for example, choice of Modalization involves selection of a Finite of the sub-class modal).

A complete system network involves organizing the choices into systems, and specifying how those choices are realized as structures. In this way a network captures both the paradigmatic and the syntagmatic relations of the clause. In the **systems** we are capturing the **paradigmatic** relations between configurations of constituents, the choices, while in the **realizations** we are capturing the **syntagmatic** relations between constituents, the structures.

In a network like this we are defining the meaning of the grammatical sign 'declarative clause', for example, both syntagmatically and paradigmatically. We are defining it both in terms of the structure it has (through the realization Subject^Finite, etc.), and in terms of what it is not (the other clause types with which it contrasts, such as interrogatives).

Priority of paradigmatic relations

The system network presented above is not only a convenient formalism for capturing syntagmatic and paradigmatic relations. It also makes a theoretical claim about the relative importance of syntagmatic and paradigmatic relations. The systemic functional approach gives theoretical priority to paradigmatic relations: systemicists take the notion of choice, or oppositions, to be of fundamental importance in understanding how language makes meanings.

In other words, we model language as choice. We represent language as a resource for making meanings by choosing. These paradigmatic choices are captured through systems. The consequences or output of the choices are the structures, captured through realization statements.

Since opposition is the primary category, the methodology for establishing systems is critical. This means we must explain how we determine when we have an opposition. That is, on what basis do we set up a system?

The answer is: when we find a difference in structure. Every choice in a system or system network is realized by a structure. We therefore only set up a system when we can identify differences in structure.

To illustrate this point, let us construct a system at the grammatical stratum, but this time at the rank of morpheme. The system we will construct is to describe the following paradigm of Subject personal pronouns in English:

I	*like Henry James*
you	*like Henry James*
he/she/it	*likes Henry James*
we	*like Henry James*
they	*like Henry James*

The system based on this paradigm is presented in System 7.14.

This example shows that a system is only set up when there is a structural reflex, i.e. a difference in structure. For example, although there is a real-world difference between talking to two or more people as opposed to talking to just one, since we have only one pronoun form (*you*), we do not in fact need to set up a singular vs plural choice for the second person pronoun.

This system also allows us to demonstrate one final system-writing convention. Although the system as it stands is perfectly correct (in that it captures the relevant oppositions), it is somewhat clumsy, as the singular/plural opposition has to be repeated at two different places. System 7.15 is an alternative drawing of this system.

This system uses two more types of bracketing to capture possible interrelations between choices from different systems. The square bracket is used to capture the 'or' relation: if first person *or* third person, then choose either singular or plural. The curly bracket is used to indicate the '**and**' relation: if both singular *and* third person, then either masculine, feminine or neuter. Both systems capture the same systemic contrasts. The difference is purely presentational.

Although systems are only set up when there is a structural difference, the scale of delicacy means that structures can be alike at one point, and then subsequently differentiated for a more delicate structural difference. For example, in Chapter Six we did not refer to any structural difference between:

Who	*is*	*Henry James?*
WH/Complement	Finite	Subject
RESIDUE	MOOD	

What	*is*	*Henry James?*
WH/Complement	Finite	Subject
RESIDUE	MOOD	

At this level of delicacy, both clauses have identical structural descriptions, in that the WH element is fused with the Complement and precedes the Finite and the Subject. However, if we were to take the analysis one step further in delicacy, we could capture this distinction between interrogatives which enquire about human actors (who-interrogatives) and those which enquire about non-human participants (what-interrogatives), with a realization statement specifying the sub-class of interrogative word to be chosen, as represented in System 7.16.

The systemic notation allows us to recognize that at a less delicate level, two structures share a structural realization, while at a more delicate level, they can be structurally differentiated. The degree of delicacy to which a network is developed will generally be determined by the purpose of the description.

Grammatical and semantic systems: links of pre-selection

To this point the only linguistic systems demonstrated have been from the grammatical stratum, from the ranks of clause and morpheme. However, systems are used to capture paradigms at all strata and ranks of language. System 7.17 is a familiar system from the semantic stratum.

This system, which slightly extends on the diagrammatic presentation of Chapter Six, states that any move in dialogue involves a choice between the speech roles of either

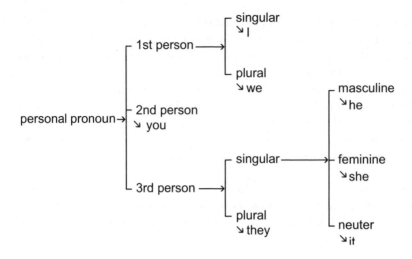

System 7.14   System of personal pronouns

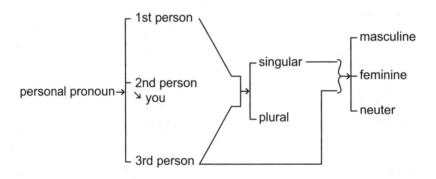

System 7.15   Alternative drawing of system of personal pronouns

giving or demanding, the commodities of either goods and services or information, and the exchange role of either initiating or responding. Several of the primary choices have then been more delicately described: e.g. offering goods and services may be speaker oriented (*May I get you a coffee?*) or addressee oriented (*Would you like a coffee?*); demanding goods and services can be done inclusively (*Let's read a book*) or exclusively (*Read it*); demanding information can be querying (*Who wrote it?*) or questioning (*Is it by Henry James?*); information involves a choice between opinion (*He should stop smoking*) or fact (*He quit last week*), and responding moves can be either supporting (*Yes, that's right*) or confronting (*No, you're wrong there*).

This network, like all the networks presented in this chapter, is still at a very indelicate level of description. For systemicists, 'doing systemic analysis' largely involves taking indelicate networks and extending them to the right in delicacy, through the analysis of the paradigms found in whatever data is being examined. For example, a systemic grammarian might take the Mood system and try to push the category of *minor clause* in delicacy, using a corpus of interactive dialogue to establish contrasts between different types of minor clauses, specifying more delicate systems and their realizations. A systemic discourse analyst might take the speech function choice of *opinion* and try to take this further in

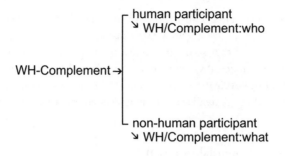

System 7.16   WH-complement system

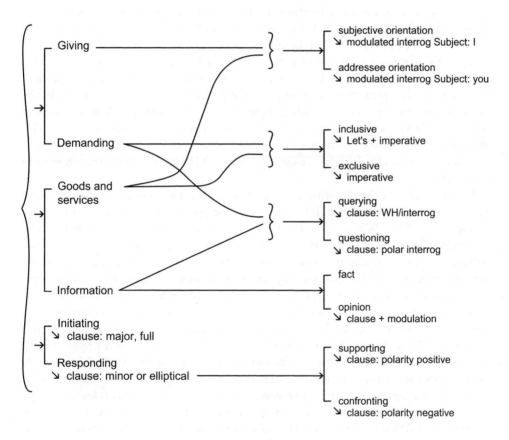

System 7.17   Speech function system (discourse-semantic stratum)

delicacy, asking what different sorts of opinions get expressed in a particular corpus and how (see Eggins and Slade 1997 for examples of speech function networks).

This last point raises the issue of what the realization statements are in a semantic system. As the speech function system above indicates, the realizations specified for semantic systems may not be structures as they were in the grammatical system. You will recall that the systemic model posits a relationship of realization between the different strata, i.e. semantics is realized through the lexico-grammar. The systemic notation makes clear what this means: choices made at the semantic level are realized through the **pre-selection** of features from grammatical systems. Thus, choice of the move *initiating* involves the pre-selection from the Mood system of *non-elliptical major clause*.

Although pre-selection means that some grammatical choices have already been made, this does not make lexico-grammatical systems redundant. For, although semantic systems may pre-select typical or **congruent** grammatical choices, other less typical, incongruent choices may be made, since they are available in the lexico-grammatical system.

Implications of the system: potential vs actual

By giving priority to paradigmatic relations in language systemicists represent language as a system for making meanings by choosing. By drawing systems we try to capture what choices speakers *could* make. We do this because it is only by knowing what someone *could* have meant that we can understand in full the meaning of what they *did* in fact mean.

This brings us back to a distinction mentioned in Chapter One, between what you *can* mean (linguistic **potential**) and what you *do* mean on any particular occasion (**actual**). System networks capture the **meaning potential** available to speakers. For example, the Mood system captures what you could possibly mean in an interaction. When we look at text, we study what speakers did actually mean, by describing the choices they did make. We can then explain that choice, work out 'what it means', by relating it back to the other possibilities the speaker had. So, we can ask 'Why did the speaker make that choice and not another one?'

For example, why does a person go to work as a teacher and say to his students '*I can hardly hear myself think in here*', while the same person goes home to his kids and says '*Stop making that racket!*'? Why did the speaker choose the declarative Mood rather than the imperative Mood? Or the imperative Mood rather than the declarative? The explanation will almost certainly lead us to explore dimensions of the context of situation, for if we look for our explanations only within the linguistic system, we will find ourselves going round in circles (e.g. he chose imperative because he didn't want to choose declarative, etc.).

Where we can begin to explain the choice is by considering the relationship between the social role the person was playing and the discourse roles to which this appears to give him access. We would find that in our culture the role of parent (with the tenor dimensions of unequal power, frequent contact and high affective involvement) gives access to the congruent realizations of commands (i.e. the choice of imperative), whereas the role of teacher (with unequal power, frequent contact but no affective involvement) leads to incongruent realizations, as the teacher finds ways to disguise the speech functional import of his command. Thus, systemic linguistics is oriented to asking questions about the relationship *between* potential and actual meaning choice. Such questions demand a functional approach, and demand that the explanations be sought outside language, in the social and cultural context.

This potential/actual orientation also gives us a framework within which it makes sense to compare different choices. In particular, it leads us to consider the **appropriacy** of linguistic choice. For example, spoken data would show us that society considers it quite appropriate for a parent to choose imperatives in addressing his young child, but generally inappropriate for the child to use imperatives to the parent. Again, we might or might not wish to explore the implications of social appropriacy.

Interpreting language as a system for making meanings in context by choosing gives us a way of asking the most interesting questions linguists can ask: why did a speaker make *that* choice, and not another? And we have a way of interpreting the choices speakers make not just as linguistic choices, but as social choices, a way which leads inevitably to uncovering the implicit, covert social conventions which make certain choices appropriate in one context but inappropriate in another.

Summary

Halliday provides a concise summary of the material that has been covered in this chapter:

> A system network is a theory of language as choice. It represents a language, or any part of a language, as a resource for making meaning by choosing. Each choice point in the network specifies:
>> 1) an environment or context: an entry condition or the choices already made
>> 2) a set of possibilities of which one is (to be) chosen
> The output of networks are structures. A structure is the realization of the sets(s) of features chosen in passing through the network. (Halliday 1985a: xxvii[2])

Having now covered the practical and theoretical aspects of systems, we will in the next chapter return to our functional description of the clause, using both system networks and functional box diagrams to describe how the clause is structured to encode in text the first component of ideational meaning, that of **experiential meaning**.

Notes

1. Culler (1976) provides a very accessible discussion of Saussure's ideas about language.
2. These paragraphs have been rewritten in Halliday 1994 and in Halliday and Matthiessen 2004, but I find the 1985a version more concise.

Chapter 8

The grammar of experiential meaning: TRANSITIVITY

Introduction

In Chapter Seven we explored the systemic modelling of meaning as choice, and the formalism by which paradigmatic relations are captured in systems. In this chapter, we return to the structural focus, while drawing on systemic notation to present the paradigmatic oppositions which give rise to structural differences. However, the semantic focus of this chapter and the next shifts to the organization of the clause to realize **ideational meanings**, meanings about how we represent reality in language. In the SFL account (see Halliday and Matthiessen 2004), the ideational strand of meaning in fact involves two components: that of **experiential meaning** in the clause (covered in this chapter), and that of the **logical meaning** between clauses in clause complexes (Chapter Nine).

Experiential meaning is expressed through the system of Transitivity or process type, with the choice of process implicating associated participant roles and configurations. Systemicists argue that the clause's experiential meaning is realized simultaneously with its interpersonal meaning, so that the description of Transitivity in the clause complements its simultaneous Mood description. While the Mood structure of the clause can be related to the contextual dimension of Tenor, Transitivity choices will be related to the dimension of Field, with the choice of process types and participant roles seen as realizing interactants' encoding of their experiential reality: the world of actions, relations, participants and circumstances that give content to their talk.

We will begin by returning to one of the implications of taking a functional approach to grammar: that nearly every constituent in a clause is playing more than one functional role at a time.

Simultaneous meanings in texts and clauses

Here to get us started is another excerpt from a conversation you have encountered in Chapter Six. We now know that the participants involved (Stephen, Simon, Diana, George, Margaret and Sue) are friends. We have seen from Chapter Six that in order to sustain a dialogue successfully, participants must keep negotiating, they must keep exchanging commodities, playing the roles of demander or giver, initiator or responder, as they either argue about information or transfer goods and services. As they interact, the Mood and Modality choices participants make express interpersonal meanings which indicate the role relationships between them. As you read this excerpt through, consider what other kinds of choices these participants are making in order to be able to achieve that exchange of interpersonal meanings. The division of the text into phases will be explained later, and can be ignored at this stage. Numbers in the left-hand column refer to turns at talk.

Text 8.1: Giving Blood[1]

————————————PHASE 1————————————

1	St	Do you give blood?
2	Si	Yea. Last time I gave blood I gave
3	St	There's nothing of you. How can you give blood?
4	Si	How much they take out of you?
5	Di	Oh an armful
6	St	Oh come on!
7	Si	How much? How much?
8	Di	I think a pint or whatever it is 800 um millimetres.
9	Si	The last time I gave blood was in Greece, right, where they pay you
10	St	Simon, isn't that where they put the needle in
11	G	Have you ever given blood, Stephen?
12	St	No
13	G	No you wouldn't
14	Di	I've done it 36 times. That's why I have all this scar tissue. I said 'Can you avoid the scar tissue?' And they said 'We like to get it into the vein'
15	St	. . . heroin don't they put the needle in there?
16	Di	I know I said 'I'm beginning to look like a junkie' and she said 'No, no, no junkies look a lot worse than that'
17	Si	How how did – have you given blood before?
18	Di	36 times
19	St	It makes me go all funny just thinking about it
20	G	You've never done it, obviously
21	St	Oh no
22	Di	No I do it because I had a daughter who when she was two days old needed blood transfusions cause she was getting sort of premature jaundice and things. This was in Geneva. And they rang me up on the Sat- this was Saturday night and said 'You've got to come in and have your blood tested against the donor's'. And there were these two wonderful Swiss men who'd left their dinner you know 8 o'clock at night and come in there to give blood to my daughter. And I was really impressed and you know I had to give blood to be tested to see if it

was compatible with theirs. And I had to deliver it to the clinic where she was. There was snow on the ground and everything. It was very exciting. And then I stayed up all night and watched this um operation taking place and fortunately her umbilical artery hadn't closed so because I mean all the other things would have been minute

23	S	So tiny, yea
24	Di	So they could actually do it through the umbilical artery or whatever. So I said 'OK', you know, 'be a blood donor after that'. But in Switzerland they give you a cognac. Here they give you tea and bikkies
25	Si	In Greece they give you nothing
26	M	They pay you, you said
27	Si	Yea they pay you
28	G	Oh well that's
29	Si	Oh they give you a cup of tea. Well they tell you they're taking a pint you know then they . . .

————————————————PHASE 2————————————————

30	Di	It doesn't hurt. They just put a little thing in and I mean 'cause I hate injections. I used to hate them
31	Si	Tell you what. When they drain a litre out of you – A pint you're laughing. They cop a litre out of you and it's like
32	Di	They can't take a litre out of somebody! It's too much
33	Si	You should believe me

————————————————PHASE 3————————————————

34	Di	How many pints of blood do you think you've got?
35	St	8
36	S	Yea
37	Di	8 – Between 8 and 9 isn't it? I mean depending on the size of you?
38	Si	A litre's not so big. Hang on. You get a litre of milk and it stands this tall
39	St	I have 9 because everyone else has 8
40	Si	You get a pint of milk and it stands this tall. The difference is
41	Di	You probably haven't got much more than 8. You're very skinny. And how long do you think it takes to be replaced?
42	St	About a day
43	S	A day, isn't it?
44	Di	No, no. God it's more than a day!

————————————————PHASE 4————————————————

45	Si	I'm telling you they took a litre out of me
46	S	So you walk round weak-kneed all this
47	Di	3 days. No I'm not weak at all. We're used to giving blood. No. It's the guys who faint. Women are fine
48	Si	'It's the guys who faint' holy shit!
49	Di	Course they do. Women are used to giving blood. They give blood once a month
50	Si	Women are used to giving blood!

─────────────────────PHASE 5─────────────────────

51	M	Do you want some more soup, Diana?
52	Di	Just a little bit
53	M	OK. I'll come – I'm just heating it so I'll take – George, more soup?
54	Di	I won't be a pig if no-one else
55	M	No I'm heating it up. George will
56	G	Yea, I'll have some more
57	M	Stephen, more soup?
58	St	Just a touch
59	M	Oh good
60	Di	Well I'll bring those out so you don't have to. Just give me a whistle

─────────────────────PHASE 6─────────────────────

61	Di	If you weigh under 50 kilos they take less
62	Si	Oh no believe me when you pay when they pay you some money they don't give a shit what you weigh, right, they just shoot it up. They wait till you turn green

─────────────────────PHASE 7─────────────────────

63	Di	You have to fill in all sorts of forms now about AIDS and stuff, you know. Like, do you think your partner is actually fucking fellows that kind of thing you know I mean

─────────────────────PHASE 8─────────────────────

64	Di	Cause there are women who go in there who are married and have no idea that their husbands are actually picking up little boys. And that's really the danger. There's no way those women can know
65	S	They're the real victims
66	Di	No well I mean they don't know that they may be giving blood and shouldn't be. That's terrible

─────────────────────PHASE 9─────────────────────

67	Si	I tell you what. I give my award for the most unfortunate female of the year, right, to the poor lady that starts a relationship with a guy, gets pregnant, right, and
68	(all)	(laughter)
69	Si	and he proposes marriage, right and they decide they'll get married in Israel, and so they book the flight
70	S	'Can you take my bag for me?'
71	G	Well at least she didn't get blown up, Simon
72	Si	And she – he hands her the bags and sweet as apple pie, right, she trips off to the airport. At the last minute there's a hitch and he can't make it, right. So he's going to meet her there and then I mean how would you feel?
73	G	She was a bit dumb
74	St	Why?
75	Di	Did this happen? Who are we talking about? What's going on?

With the benefit of Chapter Six, it is possible to suggest how interactants here are creating and clarifying their role relationships with each other. An analysis of the Mood choices here would show that, for example, we have Marg as hostess offering goods and services (*Do you want some more soup, Diana? . . . Stephen, more soup?*), with the other participants enacting linguistically their role as (gendered) guests, by accepting more or less directly, according to sex (Di *I won't be a pig if no-one else . . . Just a little bit* vs G *Yea, I'll have some more*). We see the continuation of the teasing relationship between the male participants, with George questioning (*Have you ever given blood, Stephen?*), only to criticize (*No you wouldn't*). We see also Diana assuming the role of entertainer/performer, as she produces an extended sequence of declarative clauses in telling the story about Geneva. These dimensions of the roles being played by the interactants can be made explicit through a Mood analysis of the clauses of the text.

However, at the same time as indicating and clarifying their relationships with each other, the participants in this interaction are talking *about* something. In fact, it would not be possible for them to create relationships without talking about something. Their talk has content, it makes representational or experiential meanings. We could summarize this experiential dimension of the text by giving it a title which captures the main topic of talk: **blood**. (At the end of this chapter we will return to consider the different ways in which this topic is explored in the talk.)

Thus we need to recognize that in order to take part in texts, participants must make not only interpersonal meanings but also experiential meanings. We must also recognize that these types of meanings are being made simultaneously: it is not that George asks a question (to demonstrate a role of seeker of information), and then starts to talk about blood. The question *is* about blood. Similarly, George cannot contradict Simon (thereby demonstrating the particular combative male relationship they have) without challenging something he has said. They must not only talk in a way that signals how each person feels about the others, but their talk must, necessarily, be about something.

This simultaneous encoding of experiential and interpersonal meanings is achieved through the simultaneous structuring of the clauses which together are making up the text. It is in describing how these layers of meaning can be expressed in clauses that we will be in a position to describe how these layers of meanings can be expressed in texts.

The metafunctions

In Chapter Five, Halliday's example of the role of Subject was used to demonstrate that each clause expresses not just one kind of meaning, but in fact three. To capture these different types of meaning, we differentiated between the three roles of Subject, Theme and Actor. Through the description of the Mood structure of the clause we elaborated on the constituent of Subject, and its associated functions. We could now analyse any clause from Text 8.1 above for these Mood constituents. For example, imagine Diana had said:

But	*George*	*in Switzer-land*	*they*	*give*		*you*	*a cognac.*
Adjunct: conjun	Adjunct: vocative	Adjunct: circ	Subject	Finite	Pred	Complement	Complement
		RESIDUE	MOOD			RESIDUE	

This analysis shows that the clause is structured as a non-elliptical declarative, directed at one particular interactant, with the arguability centred on *they* and their action of *giving*: the MOOD component of the clause. In addition, the speaker is presenting the message as a fact: there is neither modulation nor modalization in the clause. On the basis of our structural analysis, we are able therefore to predict possible (and impossible or unlikely) responding moves to this initiating declarative, and to suggest what semantic value the different responses would encode. Beyond stating that George is very likely to be the next speaker, we can predict what that next speaker might say:

do they? really?	– acknowledgement
no they don't	– contradiction
how do you know?	– challenge

Our structural analysis also tells us that the following responses are highly unlikely:

- should he?
- you don't have to
- thanks

Thus the Mood description of this clause allows us to see how it functions to enable an interaction to take place: by nominating George to respond, and by giving him some information to argue about.

However, such an analysis has not exhausted the meanings being made by the clause. For as well as making meanings about how the interaction is structured and its potential continuation, this clause is also a representation of experience, a packaging of content meaning. The clause is not just a giving of information: it is a giving of information **about something**. It is, for example, giving the information that in a certain place (*Switzerland*), some group of people (*they*) perform a fairly concrete action (*giving*) of an object (*cognac*) to someone who benefits (*you*). To capture these kinds of representational meanings, we would need to analyse the clause differently, using a different set of labels to capture the fact that constituents encode content meanings. Using, then, an alternative set of labels, we might describe this clause as:

But	George	*in Switzerland*	*they*	*give*	*you*	*a cognac.*
		Circumstance: location	Actor	Process: material	Beneficiary	Goal

While this structural description allows us to label clause constituents for their content roles, it now obscures the role of constituents in establishing interaction. We need to show both, for a constituent such as *they* is both offering the arguable participants on which the proposition depends (i.e. Subject), and also representing the participants involved in performing a certain kind of action. The clause is best described, then, as realizing two strands of meaning simultaneously:

But	*George*	*in Switzer-land*	*they*	*give*		*you*	*a cognac.*
Adjunct: conjun	Adjunct: vocative	Adjunct: circ	Subject	Finite	Predicator	Comple-ment	Comple-ment
		RESIDUE	MOOD			RESIDUE	
		Circumst-ance: location	Actor	Process: material		Benefic-iary	Goal

When we 'map' these two analyses on to each other, we see the demonstration of the semantic complexity of language referred to in Chapter Five: <u>that clause constituents very often play more than one functional role at a time.</u>

However, even this description has not exhausted the meanings this clause is making. For, as well as making meanings about the interaction, and the speaker's experience of reality, the clause is also making meanings about how this bit of information relates to other bits of information near it in the conversation. For example, the clause-initial *but* clearly suggests a relationship of contrast between this message and other messages; the initial placement of the vocative also indicates the priority given to managing the turn-taking system; and by placing the expression of location *in Switzerland* at the beginning rather than at the end of the clause, the speaker is seeking to highlight that chunk of information. As we will see in detail in Chapter Ten, by looking at what the speaker puts first in the clause we can capture the encoding of **textual** meanings. To do this, we need yet another set of functional labels, with Theme used to refer to the point of departure ('what I'm talking about') and Rheme to label the point of arrival ('what I'm telling you about it'). Our comprehensive analysis of the clause would now look like this:

But	*George*	*in Switzer-land*	*they*	*give*		*you*	*a cognac.*
Adjunct: conjun	Adjunct: vocative	Adjunct: circ	Subject	Finite	Predicator	Comple-ment	Comple-ment
		RESIDUE	MOOD			RESIDUE	
		Circumst-ance: location	Actor	Process:material		Benefic-iary	Goal
textual	interpersonal	topical					
THEME			RHEME				

As this example demonstrates, not *every* constituent is playing a role in each type of meaning. For example, the vocative *George* plays an important role in structuring the interaction, but no role in the content meanings being expressed (he is being talked *to*, not being talked *about*). Similarly, the conjunction *but* has no experiential function (it does not represent any referential entity), and it is also outside of the MOOD/RESIDUE structure (it is not arguable). It is, however, important in the Thematic strand, where it provides the textual link between this message and other messages. Other constituents (e.g. *they give you a cognac*) are not differentiated in the Thematic strand, but are all assigned the one label of Rheme.

However, the example also shows that most clause constituents are playing two and often three different functional roles. Each constituent is thus realizing a maximum of three types of meaning: a meaning about the interaction (an interpersonal meaning), a meaning about reality (an experiential meaning) and a meaning about the message (a textual meaning).

The practical implication of this recognition of semantic complexity is that we have to describe the structure of the clause <u>three times over</u>! Just describing the Mood structure is not enough. That only tells us about one strand of the clause's meaning. We will also need to describe the structure of the clause as a representation of experience (the concern of this chapter), and the structure of the clause as a message (Chapter Ten).

The fact that the clause is simultaneously structured in these three different, but essentially complementary ways was also demonstrated in Chapter Seven with the sets of paradigms about *the redback spider*. In each set of clauses only one type of meaning was varied, while the other strands of meaning were held constant.

These three types of meaning – the interpersonal, the ideational (with its two components of experiential and logical meaing) and the textual – are known as the **metafunctions** ('semantic functions'). What we are exploring in the grammatical chapters of this book is how each metafunction is realized through choices from major systems at the lexicogrammatical stratum, with the experiential metafunction realized through Transitivity choices, the interpersonal metafunction through Mood choices, and the textual metafunction through Theme choices.

Introduction to experiential meaning: the system of TRANSITIVITY

Chapter Six demonstrated two basic principles of functional grammatical analysis :

1. that it is not just *one* constituent that accounts for differences in meaning, but *configurations of functions*. In order to describe the structure of the clause as interaction, it was not enough just to label the MOOD element in each clause. We had to label a range of functional constituents (i.e. Mood, Residue, Subject, Finite, Complement, Adjuncts) <u>and</u> look at their possible configurations;
2. that there was one key system involved in interpersonal meaning: the system of Mood choice. The systems of Modality (Modalization and Modulation) were dependent on this Mood system.

When we look at the experiential metafunction, we are looking at the grammar of the clause as *representation*. As with the clause as exchange, we find there is one major system of grammatical choice involved in this kind of meaning. This is the system of **TRANSITIVITY**, or *process type*. The Transitivity system is presented in System 8.1, using the conventions presented in Chapter Seven.

The process type system is what underlies the differences in a paradigm such as:

Diana gave some blood.	[material]
Diana thought she should give blood.	[mental]
Diana said that giving blood is easy.	[verbal]
Diana dreamt of giving blood.	[behavioural]

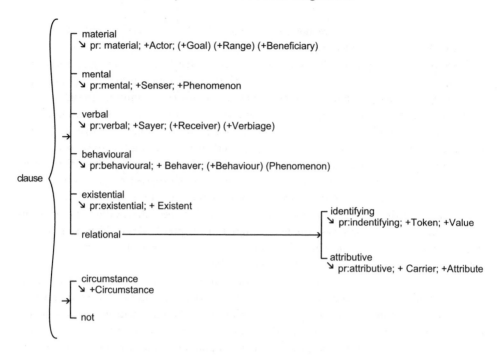

System 8.1 Transitivity

There is a reward for giving blood.   [existential]
Diana is a blood donor.   [relational]

The circumstantial system is what underlies differences between a simple clause, such as *Diana gave blood*, and an expanded clause such as 'Last year, in Geneva, *Diana gave blood voluntarily and without pain with her sister at the clinic*'.

Thus, there is one major system (process type) and one minor system (circumstantial) involved. However, as the realization statements show, the choice of process involves a particular configuration of participant roles. We will see that it is not enough only to describe the process type selected in each clause. Each process is associated with different participant roles, occurring in different configurations.

For example, the realization statements say that the choice of a material process involves choosing the associated roles of an Actor (obligatory), and optional elements such as a Goal, Range or Beneficiary, whereas the choice of a mental process will involve roles such as Senser and Phenomenon. So, in describing the grammar of the clause as representation we have not only to describe the differences between process types, but also the associated differences in functional participant roles, and the possible selection of circumstances.

In analysing transitivity structure in a clause we are concerned with describing three aspects of the clause:

1. the selection of a process: the process choice will be realized in the verbal group of the clause:
   Last year Diana <u>gave</u> blood.
2. the selection of participants: participants will be realized in the nominal groups:
   Last year <u>Diana</u> gave <u>blood</u>.

3. the selection of circumstances: circumstantial meanings are expressed through adverbial groups or prepositional phrases:

Last year Diana gave blood.

In the remainder of this chapter we will concentrate on describing the different types of processes and their associated configurations of participant roles.

Material processes

Consider the following clauses:

> Diana <u>has donated</u> blood 36 times.
> Diana <u>went</u> to Geneva.
> Diana <u>stayed up</u> all night.
> The Swiss men <u>left</u> their dinner.
> They <u>gave</u> Diana a cognac.

All these clauses are describing processes of *doing*, usually concrete, tangible actions. Processes of doing are what we call **material** processes. The basic meaning of material processes is that some entity does something, undertakes some action. This is the semantic <u>definition</u> of material processes.

One <u>identification</u> criterion for material processes is that they can be probed by asking: *What did x do?*

> *What has Diana done?*   *Diana has donated blood 36 times.*
> *What did Diana do?*   *Diana went to Geneva.*

The following clauses would not be material processes, because it is not possible to probe them in this way:

> There was an incentive to donate blood in Switzerland.
> • we can't ask 'what did there?'
> Diana is a blood donor.
> • we can't ask 'what did Diana do?' (the answer would have to be **She beed a blood donor*)

So, material processes are processes about doing, about action. Actions involve actors, or **participants**. Participants are realized by nominal groups. We can make an important distinction between the number of participants involved in the process:

> <u>Diana</u> went to Geneva.
> <u>Diana</u> stayed up all night.

In these examples we see that there is only one participant, one **Actor** or person doing the action (*Diana* in these clauses). But not all material processes have to involve only one participant:

> <u>Diana</u> has donated <u>blood</u> 36 times.
> <u>The Swiss men</u> left <u>their dinner</u>.
> <u>They</u> gave <u>Diana a cognac</u>.

As these examples show, while some material processes involve one participant only, others involve two, or even three. So we can make a distinction between:

1. processes in which there's only one participant: these processes are called **middle**, or **intransitive**. These are clauses in which 'someone does something', and are probed by asking 'what did x do?'
2. processes in which there are two (or more) participants: these are called **effective**, or **transitive**. These are clauses in which 'someone does something and the doing involves another entity'. Transitive clauses are probed by 'what did x do to y?'

Some effective or transitive processes (e.g. *give*) seem obligatorily to involve three participants. They are probed by 'what did x do to y to z?'

If you consider the following pairs of effective processes, you will notice that effective clauses can be either **active** or **passive**:

1. Active: probed by 'what did x do (to y)?'
    They tested my blood.
    She carried the bomb.
2. Passive: probed by 'what happened to y?' With the passive we can ask 'who by?'
    My blood was tested (by them).
    The bomb was carried onto the plane (by her).

The difference between active and passive clauses relates to whether the Actor role (the doer of the action) is conflated with the Mood function of Subject or not. In the active, the roles of Actor and Subject are mapped on to the same constituent. In the passive, however, the Subject is not also the Actor (see analysed examples below).

Direct participants in material processes: Actor and Goal

The two most frequent participants in material process clauses are the **Actor** and the **Goal**. **ACTOR**: the Actor is the constituent of the clause who does the deed or performs the action. When the clause only has one participant and is active, the participant will be ACTOR.

Diana	*went*	*to Geneva.*
Actor	Process:material	

So	*you*	*walk round*	*weak-kneed for 3 days.*
	Actor	Process:material	

GOAL: the Goal is that participant at whom the process is directed, to whom the action is extended. It is the participant treated in traditional grammar as the Direct Object, and it usually maps on to the Complement participant in the Mood analysis. The Goal is usually what becomes Subject in the passive.

They	avoided	the scar tissue.
Actor	Process:material	Goal

These two wonderful Swiss men	left	their dinner.
Actor	Process:material	Goal

There can only be one Goal per clause.

In the passive, the Goal becomes the Subject, and the Actor may be omitted.

active

They	tested	my blood	against the donors'.
Actor	Actor	Goal	

passive

My blood	was tested	against the donors'	(by them).
Goal	Process:material		(Actor)

active

She	carried	the bomb	onto the plane.
Actor	Process:material	Goal	

passive

The bomb	was carried	onto the plane	(by her).
Goal	Process		(Actor)

Goal vs range

Halliday (1994: 146–9)[2] makes an important, if sometimes difficult, distinction between a Goal and a related participant called a Range. Consider the following clauses:

> They did the transfusion.
> They transfused the blood.

These are processes of doing, and so we classify them as Material processes. Each involves two participants, but while *they* is clearly the Actor in both, the question is: what label should be attached to the second participant: *the transfusion, the blood?* While we might initially assume these participants should be called Goals, there is a problem in that they are not probed using the Goal probe of 'What did x do to y?'.

For example, it makes no sense to ask 'What did they do to the transfusion?', because the answer 'They did it' is redundant. Hence, in this case although we appear to have a separate participant (*transfusion*), it seems to be very closely tied to the verb: in *doing the transfusion* only one action took place.

Similarly, if we probe the second example with: 'What did they transfuse?', the answer must most certainly be 'the blood', because that is about the only thing that can be transfused.

Hence, in these two cases, there seems to be a closer relationship between the Process and the second participant than we found above between a Process and a Goal. Halliday calls these less independent participants **Ranges**, and he suggests that a Range specifies one of two things:

1. either it is a restatement or continuation of the process itself or
2. it expresses the extent or 'range' of the process.

Examples of Ranges which express the process itself include:

They	*ran*	*the race.*
Actor	Pr:material	Range

where *race* is really a restatement of the process *run*. You cannot have races unless you run them. So really the two participants are saying the same thing. Verbs like this can usually be collapsed into one single process, e.g. *raced*.

Other examples of process Ranges are what are called in traditional grammar cognate objects: for example, *do a dance, sing a song*. Here the object of the verb is derived directly from the verbal meaning itself, and again we can typically substitute just one verbal element: *dance, sing*.

The second type of Range is not cognate, but expresses the domain or extent of the process. For example:

They	*were playing*	*bridge/tennis/a game.*
Actor	Pr:material	Range/Range/Range

Halliday argues that constituents like *bridge* or *tennis* or *a game* are not fully autonomous participants since these games do not exist without the playing. They are just continuations of the process, expressing its range or domain. In these cases it is fairly easy to see that they are not Goals because they do not exist except through the process. The Range is really just another name for the process itself. Less obvious but similar Ranges occur in:

Have	*you*	*given*	*blood*	*before?*
	Actor	Pr:material	Pr:material	

Marg	*served*	*the dinner.*
Actor	Pr:material	Range

Although *blood* and *dinner* exist independently of the processes, we still find it hard to probe these participants with *do to* or *do with*. The second participant is just specifying the range or domain of process.

A third type of Range is that created by the use of dummy verbs, like *do, have, give, take, make*:

You	*just*	*give*	*me*	*a whistle.*
Actor		Process:material		Range

give	*a smile*
Pr:material	Range

have	*a bath*
make	*a mistake*
take	*a look*
Pr:material	Range

This is quite a common pattern to English, whereby the verb is emptied of its content, and the meaning expressed through the nominal Range constituent.

While it is not always easy to distinguish Goals from Ranges, Halliday (1994: 148) lists a number of tests which can be applied:

1. if the participant is a Range, you cannot (sensibly) probe with 'what did x do to y?'. Ranges cannot usually be probed by *do to* or *do with*, whereas Goals can.
2. a Range cannot be a personal pronoun
3. a Range cannot usually be modified by a possessive (e.g. **Just give me your whistle*)
4. Ranges are less likely to become Subjects than Goals. They often sound quite odd as Subjects, e.g. *The whistle wasn't given by you, was it? The blood was given by you, was it?*
5. a Range can often be realized as a prepositional phrase:
   I'm playing bridge.   *I'm playing Simon <u>at bridge</u>.*
   He plays the piano.   *He plays beautifully <u>on the piano</u>.*
   He does great whistles.   *He does great <u>at whistling</u>.*
6. Ranges using 'dummy verbs' can be 'collapsed' into one verb, e.g.
   give a whistle – whistle
   do a dance – dance
   give a lecture – lecture
7. Ranges cannot take attributes of result, i.e. an element which gives the outcome of the process

She	*cooked*	*dinner*	*to perfection/to a turn.*
Actor	Pr:material	Goal	Resultative attribute

but not

* She	*served*	*dinner*	*to perfection/to a turn.*
Actor	Pr:material	Goal	Resultative attribute

While it is not always easy to distinguish a Range from a Goal, the following examples may help to emphasize the distinction:

RANGE	**GOAL**
shoot a gun	shoot a kangaroo
kick a goal	kick the dog
serve dinner	serve the ball
give a smile	give a present
make a mistake	make a cake
take a bath	take a biscuit

Beneficiary

One further participant which may occur in a material process clause is the Beneficiary. Consider again the clause:

> But in Switzerland they give you a cognac.
> They gave blood to my daughter.

These clauses involve three participants, and in each case there is one participant who in some way could be said to benefit from the process: *you, my daughter.* Participants which benefit from the process are called Beneficiary.

There are 2 kinds of Beneficiary: a **Recipient** (the one **to** whom something is given), and a **Client** (the one **for** whom something is done).

Both Clients and Recipients may occur with or without prepositions, depending on their position in the clause. If you want to put them in final position in the clause, then it is necessary to use a preposition. For example:

Recipient: the one goods are given to

But	*in Switzerland*	*they*	*give*	*you*	*a cognac.*
		Actor	Pr:material	Recipient	Goal

But	*in Switzerland*	*they*	*give*	*a cognac*	*to you.*
		Actor	Pr:material	Goal	Recipient

Note that it is possible to get the Recipient as Subject of the clause, thus giving another variety of passive:

In Switzerland	you	are	given	a cognac.
Adj:circ	Subject	Finite	Predicator	Complement
RESIDUE . . .	MOOD		. . . RESIDUE	
	Recipient		Pr:material	Goal

Compare these two versions of the passive:
Recipient-passive

My daughter	was	given	blood.
Subject	Finite	Predicator	Complement
MOOD		RESIDUE	
Recipient		Pr:material	Range

Range-passive:

Blood	was	given	to my daughter.
Subject	Finite	Predicator	Adj:circ
MOOD		RESIDUE	
Range		Pr:material	Recipient

The constituent playing the Client role (the one the service is done for) may also appear with or without a preposition:

I	'll heat	you	up	some soup.
Actor	Pr:material . . .	Client	. . . Process	Goal

I	'll heat up	some soup	for you.
Actor	Pr:material	Goal	Client

Although less frequent than Recipient-passives, some Client-passives do occur:

Marg	cooked	dinner	for them all.
Actor	Pr:material	Goal	Client

Marg	cooked	them all	dinner.
Actor	Pr:material	Client	Goal

They	were	all	cooked	dinner	for	by Marg.
Client . . .		. . . Client	Pr:material	Goal		Actor

but not: * *You will be heated up some soup for.*

Circumstances

The last type of participant we need to look at for material process clauses is that of Circumstantials, which are realized by adverbial groups or prepositional phrases.

Circumstances can occur not only with material processes, but with <u>all</u> process types. They are presented here for convenience. System 8.2 indicates the different types of Circumstances we can find in clauses.

Circumstantials can best be identified by considering what probe is used to elicit them:

1. **extent**: how long? (duration); how far? (spatial distance)

I	*'ve given*	*blood*	*36 times.*
Actor	Pr:material	Goal	Circ:extent

I	*stayed up*	*all night.*
Actor	Pr:material	Circ:extent

2. **location**: when? (temporal); where? (spatial)

They	*rang*	*me*	*up*	*on the Saturday night.*
Actor	Pr:material . . .	Beneficiary	. . . Pr:material	Circ:location

I	*delivered*	*it*	*to the clinic where she was.*
Actor	Pr:material	Goal	Circ:location

3. **manner**: how? with what? (means); how? how . . .–ly (quality); what . . . like? (comparison)

So	*they*	*did*	*the transfusion*	*through the umbilical artery.*
	Actor	Pr:material	Range	Circ:manner

In Switzerland,	*unlike Greece,*	*they*	*give*	*you*	*a cognac.*
Circ:location	Circ:manner	Actor	Pr:material	Beneficiary	Goal

4. **cause**: why? (cause); what for? (reason); who? who for? (behalf)

My daughter	*survived*	*thanks to the two Swiss men.*
Actor	Pr:material	Circ:cause

She	carried	the bomb	for her boyfriend.
Actor	Pr:material	Goal	Circ:cause

5. **accompaniment**: with whom?

She	got	on the plane	with/without her boyfriend.
Actor	Pr:material	Circ:loc	Circ:accompaniment

6. **matter**: what about?

As for Greece,	they	give	you	nothing.
Circ:matter	Actor	Pr:material	Beneficiary	Goal

7. **role**: what as?

She	was travelling	to Israel	as a tourist.
Actor	Pr:material	Circ:location	Circ:role

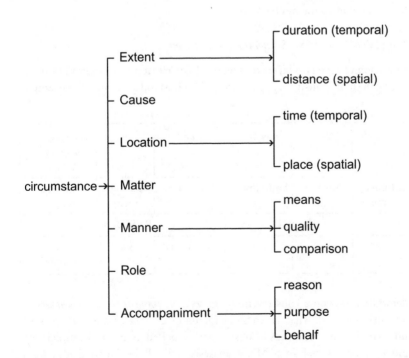

System 8.2   System of Circumstance

Causative constructions

In the description presented so far, we have seen that the role of Actor is that of the doer, the one who does or undertakes the action. It is also useful to identify a clausal participant of **Agent**: the one who initiates the action, the one who makes something happen. Typically the two roles of Agent and Actor are mapped onto the same constituent, since the Actor is the one who makes the action happen, and is therefore also the Agent:

non-causative: girlfriend = doer (Actor) + initiator (Agent)

His girlfriend	*carried*	*the bomb*	*onto the plane.*
Actor	Pr:material	Goal	Circ:loc

However, in **causative** constructions, the Agent is distinct from the Actor, with the Agent causing an Actor other than himself/herself to carry out the action. This usually involves using the causative process *make*:

He	*made*	*his girlfriend*	*carry*	*the bomb*	*onto the plane.*
Agent	Pr:causative	Actor	Pr:material	Goal	Circ:loc

They	*make*	*you*	*fill in*	*forms.*
Agent	Pr:causative	Actor	Pr:material	Range

As a general rule, the role of Agent will not be shown unless the clause is causative. Otherwise the single label of Actor can be used.

MOOD vs TRANSITIVITY ANALYSIS: simultaneous functions

We are now in a position to give two layers of structural description to all material process clauses, describing both their Transitivity structure and their Mood structure. For example:

And	*fortunately*	*they*	*could*	*do*	*it*	*through the umbilical artery.*
Adjunct: conjun	Adjunct: comment	Subject	Finite:mod	Predicator	Comple- ment	Adjunct: circ
		MOOD			RESIDUE	
		Actor		Pr:material	Goal	Circ: manner

As this clause demonstrates, some constituents (e.g. *they, it, through the umbilical artery*) have functions in both analyses. That is, these elements of the clause are making both interpersonal and experiential meanings. Constituents labelled Subject, Complement, Predicator, Adjunct:circumstantial in a Mood analysis will all be labelled also for a Transitivity role.

However, other constituents can be assigned constituent roles only for Mood (e.g. *could*). The explanation for this is that some constituents are really **in** the clause in order to express interpersonal meanings rather than experiential meanings. These are the constituents which would fall into the MOOD box in our Mood analysis, i.e. the Finite (modal or temporal elements, when not fused with the Predicator), Mood Adjuncts, realizations of Modalization and Modulation. These elements express meanings about how the interaction is being organized, and the writer/speaker's attitude towards the interaction. While they are rich in the interpersonal meanings they express, they are empty of experiential meaning, and do not get labelled for a transitivity role (since they do not play one).

Finally, some elements were observed to lie outside the Mood/Residue structure altogether (e.g. *and, fortunately*). These constituents also have no transitivity functions but (as we will see later) get into the clause in order to express textual meanings. Conjunctive, Continuity, Vocative and Comment Adjuncts will not be labelled for transitivity.

Mental processes

Consider the following clauses:

> I hate injections.
> She believed his excuses.
> I don't understand her letter.
> I don't know her name.
> They don't give a shit about it.

From clauses such as these, we see that people are not always talking about concrete processes of doing. We very often talk not about what we are doing, but about what we *think* or *feel*. Halliday calls processes which encode meanings of thinking or feeling **mental processes**.

We can recognize that these are different from material processes because it no longer makes sense to ask 'What did x do to y?'

> What did you do to the injection? *I hated it.*
> What did she do to his excuses? *She believed them.*
> What don't I do to her behaviour? *I don't understand it.*

With these clauses, it makes more sense to ask: 'what do you think/feel/know about x?'

> What you think about injections? *I hate them.*
> What did she think about his excuses? *She believed them.*

One thing, then, that makes mental processes look different from materials is that we probe them differently. When we probe, we find we are not asking about actions or doings in a tangible, physical sense, but about mental reactions: about thoughts, feelings, perceptions.

Halliday divides mental process verbs into three classes: **cognition** (verbs of thinking, knowing, understanding, for example *I don't <u>know</u> her name*), **affection** (verbs of liking, fearing, e.g. *I <u>hate</u> injections*), and **perception** (verbs of seeing, hearing, e.g. *Simon <u>heard</u> it on the news*).

The difference between the way we probe material and mental processes is one semantic reason for differentiating them. However, the main reasons why we want a different analysis are that mental processes behave differently grammatically from material processes in a number of ways, enumerated below.

1. **choice of unmarked present tense**: Halliday notes that one significant difference between mental and material processes is in their unmarked present tense. In a mental process, the unmarked present tense is the simple present:

> I hate injections.   Simon loves the soup.   She knows his name.

But in material processes, the unmarked present tense is the present continuous (the -ing form).

> Marg is heating the soup up.
> Diana is donating blood because of her experience in Geneva.

We only use the simple present with material processes if we wish to convey a special, marked meaning of habitual action:

> Marg heats the soup up (every day).
> Diana donates blood (every year).

This does not mean that mental processes never occur in the present continuous, or materials in the simple present. But there is a clear unmarked correlation which differentiates the two process types. The choice of another, marked present tense form carries an extra dimension of meaning. In fact there is a general association of mental processes with non-continuous tense. Even in the past tense it is much more common to get:

> She believed his excuses. (simple past)

than

> She was believing his excuses. (past continuous)

But it is in the present that the contrast is most marked.

2. **number of participants**: while material processes could have either one or two participants (they could be either middle or effective in voice), mental processes must always have two participants (except for the situation of projection, discussed below). There will always be two nominal-type participants associated with any mental process. Even if one participant is apparently absent, it will need to be retrieved from the context for the clause to make sense. For example *She believed* always implies *She believed something or someone*.

There is, then, no such thing as an intransitive mental process. All mental processes have two participants. This raises the question of what labels we should use for the participants in a mental process clause. One option is to keep using the labels of Actor, Goal, etc. that we identified for material processes. However, this recycling is rejected for two reasons:

>   i) firstly, since material processes are not probed as action processes, roles like Actor do not seem appropriate;

ii) secondly, different things can get to be participants in mental processes than in material process clauses.

This brings us to the third major difference between mental and material processes.
3. **nature of the active participant**: one participant in the mental process clause must be a **conscious human participant**. This participant is called the **Senser**. The Senser, who feels, thinks or perceives, must either be human or an anthropomorphized non-human. It must be a conscious being.

She	*believed*	*his excuses.*
Senser	Pr:mental	

I	hate	injections.
Senser	Pr:mental	

In contrast with material processes, then, we can say that as far as the active participant goes, the choice is more restricted for mentals than for materials. Any nominal can be Actor in a material process clause, but only conscious humans can be Sensers in mental processes.

When we turn to consider what label to apply to the second participant in a mental process, we find yet another difference between mental and material processes, for here the choice is far wider for mentals than materials.
4. **nature of the non-active participant**: Halliday labels the second participant in a mental process clause the **Phenomenon**. The Phenomenon is that which is thought, felt or perceived by the conscious Senser:

She	*believed*	*his excuses.*
Senser	Pr:mental	Phenomenon

Do	*you*	*want*	*more soup?*
	Senser	Pr:mental	Phenomenon

While these examples are reminiscent of Goals in material process clauses, Halliday demonstrates that in fact a far greater range of elements can be Phenomena in mental processes than can be Goals in materials. As well as the simple Phenomena of the type analysed above, Halliday also identifies two types of embedded Phenomena: Acts and Facts.

PHENOMENON: Acts

Acts occur with mental processes of perception: seeing, hearing, noticing, etc. An Act is realized by an imperfective non-finite clause acting as if it were a simple noun. For example:

I	*saw*	*{the operation taking place.}*
Senser	Pr:mental	Phenomenon:act

He	*felt*	*{the needle going in.}*
Senser	Pr:mental	Phenomenon:act

One test to determine an Act is that the word *that* cannot be inserted directly after the mental process:

> *I saw that the operation taking place.

A further test is that the embedded clause which realizes the Act can be turned into a simple 'thing' Phenomenon by rewording it as a (long) nominal group:

I *He*	*saw* *felt*	*the occurrence of the operation.* *the insertion of the needle.*
Senser	Pr:mental	Phenomenon

Notice that Acts cannot occur in material process clauses:

> *Marg cooked the soup heating up.
> *They tested my blood being good.

PHENOMENON: *Facts*

The second type of embedded Phenomenon is what Halliday calls a Fact Phenomenon. A Fact is an embedded clause, usually finite and usually introduced by a 'that', functioning as if it were a simple noun. It can be identified as a Fact-embedding because a Fact-noun can be inserted before the (explicit or implicit) *that* which introduces it:

She	*didn't realize*	*{that it was a bomb}.*
She	*didn't realize*	*{the fact that it was a bomb}.*
Senser	Pr:mental	Phenomenon

She	*regretted*	*{that they hadn't watched the operation}.*
She	*regretted*	*{the fact that they hadn't watched the operation}.*
Senser	Pr:mental	Phenomenon

Fact Phenomenon clauses can usually be reversed, using an active synonymous mental process verb while having the Fact-embedding as Subject (this pattern of reversibility is discussed below):

{The fact that it was a bomb}	*escaped*	*her.*
{The fact that they hadn't watched the operation}	*disappointed*	*her.*
Phenomenon	Pr:mental	Senser

As these examples show, Fact Phenomena are clauses implicitly post-modifying a Fact-noun, even though that noun may be implicit. Halliday (1994: 266–7) identifies four sub-classes of Fact-nouns:

   i) 'cases', e.g. fact, case, point, rule . . .
   ii) 'chances', e.g. chance, possibility, likelihood, probability, certainty . . .
   iii) 'proofs', e.g. proof, indication, implication, confirmation, demonstration . . .
   iv) 'needs', e.g. requirement, need, rule, obligation . . .

Note that Fact Phenomena cannot occur in material processes:

   * Marg cooked the fact that the dinner was ready.
   *The fact that the dinner was ready Marg . . . .
   * Marg cooked the news that the dinner was ready.

While it is important to appreciate how Facts and Acts make the Phenomenon category much broader than that of Goal in a material process, for most analytical purposes it is sufficient to label the constituent as 'Phenomenon'.

5. **reversibility**: the fifth major difference Halliday identifies between mental and material processes is the **reversibility** of many mental processes. Consider these pairs of mental process clauses:

A.	B.
I hate injections.	Injections piss me off.
She believed his excuses.	His excuses convinced her.
I don't understand her letter.	Her letter puzzles me.
I don't know her name.	Her name escapes me.
They don't give a shit about it.	It doesn't worry them.

Each A clause is very similar in meaning to its matching B clause. One analogy we might be tempted to make is with the active/passive distinction identified for transitive material processes. However, there is a major difference, in that **both** the clauses under A **and** those under B are active in voice, as can be seen by the fact that passives exist of both A clauses and B clauses:

A.	B.
Injections are hated (by me).	I am pissed off by injections.
His excuses were believed by her.	She was convinced by his excuses.
Her letter is not understood (by me).	I am puzzled by her letter.

The clauses can therefore not be explained as active/passive variants. In fact, what we are dealing with here is a reversibility, a kind of two-way process. This can be brought out by labelling our participant roles for both Transitivity and Mood functions:

active:

She	*believed*		*his excuses.*
Subject	Finite	Predicator	Complement
MOOD		RESIDUE	
Senser	Pr:mental		Phenomenon

His excuses	*convinced*		*her.*
Subject	Finite	Predicator	Complement
MOOD		RESIDUE	
Senser	Pr:mental		Phenomenon

passive:

His excuses	*were*	*believed*	*(by her).*
Subject	Finite	Predicator	(Adjunct:circ)
MOOD		RESIDUE	
Phenomenon		Pr:mental	(Senser)

She	*was*	*convinced*	*(by his excuses.)*
Subject	Finite	Predicator	(Adjunct:circ)
MOOD		RESIDUE	
Senser		Pr:mental	(Phenomenon)

The structural analysis shows us that we dealing with active, reversible synonyms, and not with simply active/passive pairs: we can express a mental process meaning as an active clause, with either the Senser or the Phenomenon as Subject. Similarly, we can express a mental process meaning as a passive clause with either the Senser or the Phenomenon as Subject. While not all mental process verbs exist as pairs, many do. This reversibility is another reason for distinguishing mentals from materials, for material processes do not form such pairs. For example, we cannot make the Goal of a material process clause the Subject while keeping the clause in the active voice:

> I'm heating up the soup.   *The soup's . . . me up. ???
> She carried the bags.   *The bags . . . her. ????

6. projection: the sixth major difference between mental and material processes is that most mental processes (except those of perception) can **project**. Material processes cannot project.

Projection was mentioned briefly in Chapter Five, where it was explained that the systemic interpretation of **clause complex relations** (how one clause relates to another) differs from that of many other grammatical approaches. As the clause complex is the subject of Chapter Nine, here I will just present a very brief outline, in order simply that this distinctive aspect of mental processes can be appreciated.

To facilitate explanations, here, first, are some examples of where one clause (typically the first) is a mental process which is **projecting** (the shaded boxes indicate a clause boundary):

So	I	thought			I	'd give	blood.
	Senser	Pr:mental			Actor	Pr:material	Range

So	I	thought		'Oh bugger	I	'll give	blood'.
	Senser	Pr:mental			Actor	Pr:material	Range

'He	will meet	me	in Israel'		she	believed.
Actor	Pr: material	Goal	Circ:loc		Senser	Pr:mental

He	decided		that	he	'd meet	her	in Israel.
Senser	Pr:mental			Actor	Pr:material	Goal	Circ:loc

'I	'll meet	her	in Israel'		he	decided.
Actor	Pr: material	Goal	Circ:loc		Senser	Pr:mental

He	decided		to meet	her	in Israel.
Senser	Pr:mental		Pr:material	Goal	Circ:loc

In each of the above examples we are dealing with two clauses. The relationship between the two clauses is a relationship by which one clause 'shoots out' or **projects** a second clause. Projection is one kind of what Halliday calls the **logical** relationships that can hold between adjacent clauses. Projection describes the relationship that you probably know by the terms *indirect* or *reported thought*, or *direct* or *quoted thought*. Mental process projection has to do with **quoting** or **reporting ideas**.

As we will see more clearly in Chapter Nine, the two clauses are not in a relationship of constituency: the projected clause is not an embedded constituent of the projecting clause. We can tell that it is not embedded within the first because:

i) it is a Finite clause (and so cannot be an Act)
*So I thought giving blood.
ii) it is not dependent on any Fact noun (and so cannot be a Fact)
*So I thought [the fact] that I'd give blood.
iii) it has its own clause structure, for both Transitivity and Mood (and therefore cannot be a simple noun Phenomenon):

So	I		thought		I	'd	go and give	blood.
Adj:conjun	Subject	Finite	Pred		Subject	Finite	Pred	Compl
	MOOD		RESIDUE		MOOD		RESIDUE	

We are therefore not dealing here with any kind of embedding or rank shift. Instead, we have a relationship of logical dependency between two units of the same rank, both clauses. They are two separate clauses; the first is a mental process but the second is in fact a material process clause.

Projection is just one of the different types of logical relationships that can bind adjacent clauses together. The **projecting** clause is the clause which contains the mental process verb, and it may occur before or after the **projected** clause. The two clauses which are in a projection relationship may be dependent upon each other or independent. If they are **dependent**, we have what you may call **reporting**; if **independent**, then **quoting**:

- 1st clause projects, 2nd clause is dependent (reporting)
  So I thought// I'd go and give blood.
- 1st clause projects, 2nd clause is independent (quoting)
  So I thought,// 'I'll go and give blood'.
- 2nd clause projects, 1st clause is dependent (reporting)
  I'd go and give blood,// I thought.
- 2nd clause projects, 1st clause is independent (quoting)
  'I'll go and give blood',// I thought.

When the projected clause is reporting, we can typically insert a *that*:

So I thought// [that] I'd go and give blood.

With quoting, no *that* can be inserted. Instead, the independence relation will be signalled either orthographically with quotation marks, or intonationally by a pause and voice quality change.

With most mental processes of cognition you can both report and quote, while with affection processes, only reporting is possible:

Simon	*wanted*		*to get*	*a cognac.*
Senser	Pr:mental		Pr:material	Goal

but not:

Simon wanted, //'To get a cognac'.

She	*was hoping*		*to get married*	*in Israel.*
Senser	Pr:mental		Pr:material	Circ:location

She	*was hoping*		*that*	*they*	*'d get married*	*in Israel.*
Senser	Pr:mental			Actor	Pr:material	Circ: location

This relationship of projection between clauses is particular to only two types of processes: mentals and, as we will see below, verbal processes. It is not possible with material processes:

*Marg was cooking that the soup was hot.
*'The soup is hot' Marg cooked.

As far as analysis is concerned, it is important to understand that with projection there are two clauses involved. Each clause needs to be analysed for its transitivity structure. Only the projecting clause will be a mental process (or verbal process). The projected clause can be of any process type: material, mental, verbal, existential, relational.

Circumstantials in mental process clauses

The full range of different Circumstantial elements can occur with mental processes as with materials:

Afterwards	*she*	*must have felt*	*a lot of pain.*
Circ: loc	Senser	Pr:mental	Phenomenon

I	*heard*	*that story*	*on the news.*
Senser	Pr:mental	Phenomenon	Circ:loc

Behavioural processes

The third process type is that of behavioural processes, exemplified in the following clauses:

Diana sighed loudly.
The poor woman cried for hours.
Simon sniffed the soup.

Halliday describes these processes semantically as a 'half-way house' between mental and material processes. That is, the meanings they realize are mid-way between materials on the one hand and mentals on the other. They are in part about action, but it is action that has to be experienced by a conscious being. Behaviourals are typically processes of physiological and psychological behaviour. For example:

breathe, cough, dream, frown, gawk, grimace, grin, laugh, look over, scowl, smile, sniff, snuffle, stare, taste, think on, watch . . .

Indicating their close relationship with mental processes, some behaviourals in fact contrast with mental process synonyms, e.g. *look at* is behavioural but *see* is mental, *listen to* is behavioural but *hear* is mental.

Not only are these types of verbs semantically a mix of material and mental, but grammatically they also fall mid-way between material and mental processes.

The majority of Behaviourals have only **one participant**. Behaviourals thus express a form of doing that does not usually extend to another participant. This one obligatory participant is called the **Behaver**, and is typically a conscious being (like the Senser in the mental process clause):

She	*sighed*	*with despair.*
Behaver	Pr:behavioural	Circ:manner

He	*coughed*	*loudly.*
Senser	Pr:behavioural	Circ:manner

Behaviourals can contain a second participant that is like a Range: a restatement of the process. This participant is called the **Behaviour**:

He	*smiled*	*a broad smile.*
Behaver	Pr:behavioural	Behaviour

If there is another participant which is not a restatement of the process, it is called a **Phenomenon**:

George	*sniffed*	*the soup.*
Behaver	Pr:behavioural	Phenomenon

Behavioural processes often occur with Circumstantial elements, particularly of manner and cause:

Simon	*laughed*	*at the girl's stupidity.*
Behaver	Pr:behavioural	Circ:cause

She	*was crying*	*with frustration.*
Behaver	Pr:behavioural	Circ:manner/cause

While behaviourals display many features of mental processes, the process functions more like one of 'doing' than one of 'thinking/feeling', etc. The evidence for this is that the unmarked present tense for behaviourals is the present continuous, as it is for materials.

present continuous tense (unmarked):	*I am watching the operation.*
	They're all listening to Simon's story.
present tense (marked):	*I watch the operation.*
	They listen to Simon's story.

Also like materials, behavioural processes cannot project, i.e. they cannot quote or report:

> *They're all listening [that] Simon's story . . .

So behaviourals, involving the role of a conscious being but being unable to project and taking present continuous tense, are half-way mixes both semantically and grammatically between mental and material processes.

Verbal processes

The following clauses are all examples of verbal processes:

> So I asked him a question.
> They tell you nothing.
> Simon told them a story.
> The Arab boyfriend told her a lot of rubbish.

As these examples show, verbal processes are processes of verbal action: *saying* and all its many synonyms, including symbolic exchanges of meaning such as in:

> My recipe says red wine.

A verbal process typically contains three participants: **Sayer**, **Receiver** and **Verbiage**. The **Sayer**, the participant responsible for the verbal process, does not have to be a conscious participant (although it typically is), but anything capable of putting out a signal. The **Receiver** is the one to whom the verbal process is directed: the Beneficiary of a verbal message, occurring with or without a preposition depending on position in the clause. The **Verbiage** is a nominalized statement of the verbal process: a noun expressing some kind of verbal behaviour (e.g. *statement, questions, retort, answer, story . . .*):

So	*I*	*asked*	*him*	*a question.*
	Sayer	Pr:verbal	Receiver	Verbiage

The Arab boyfriend	*told*	*her*	*a lot of rubbish.*
Sayer	Pr:verbal	Receiver	Verbiage

As with all process types, Circumstantials can occur in verbal processes. The commonest type is manner Circumstantials:

They	*'re talking*	*about the news.*
Sayer	Pr:verbal	Circ:manner

What	*are*	*they*	*talking*	*about?*
Circ:manner . . .		Sayer	Pr:verbal	. . . Circ:manner

Although many verbal processes occur with a nominal element, a Verbiage, it is a distinctive feature of verbal processes that they project. That is, like mental processes, verbals form a clause complex, projecting a second clause by either **quoting** or **reporting**. But whereas mental processes report or quote ideas, verbal processes quote or report speech (or 'locutions' in Halliday's terms). A relationship of interdependence between the two clauses gives quoting or **direct speech**, whereas a relationship of dependency between projected and projecting clause gives indirect or **reported speech**. The projecting clause may occur as first or second in the sequence. Analysis must describe the transitivity structure of both the projecting clause (the verbal process clause) and the projected clause (which may be any process type).

direct/quoted speech:

I	*said*		*'Can*	*you*	*avoid*	*the scar tissue?'*
Sayer	Pr:verbal			Actor	Pr:material	Goal

indirect/reported speech:

I	*asked*	*them*		*to avoid*	*the scar tissue.*
Sayer	Pr:verbal	Receiver		Pr:material	Goal

direct/quoted speech:

'They	*pay*	*you,'*		*you*	*said.*
Actor	Pr:material	Client		Sayer	Pr:verbal

indirect/reported speech:

You	*said*		*that*	*they*	*pay*	*you.*
Sayer	Pr:verbal			Actor	Pr:material	Client

The quoted or reported clause can be either a proposition (information) as in the above examples, or a proposal (goods and services), in which case the Mood element will often be ellipsed in the direct quotation, while modulation will be used in the indirect reporting.

direct/quoted:

He	*said*			*'Carry*	*the bags'.*
Subject	Finite	Predicator		Predicate	Complement
MOOD		RESIDUE		RESIDUE	
Sayer	Pr:verbal			Pr:material	Goal

indirect/reported:

He	said			she	should	carry	the bags.
Subject	Finite	Predicator		Subject	Fin:modul	Pred	Compl
MOOD		RESIDUE		MOOD		RESIDUE	
Sayer	Pr:verbal			Actor		Pr:mat	Goal

A reported clause may be either finite or non-finite:

He	demanded			that	she	carry		the bags.
Subject	Finite	Pred		Adj:conjun	Subj	Finite	Pred	Compl
MOOD		RESIDUE			MOOD		RESIDUE	
Sayer	Pr:verbal				Actor	Pr:material		Goal

He	commanded		her		to carry	the bags.
Subject	Finite	Predicator	Compl		Predicator	Compl
MOOD		RESIDUE			RESIDUE	
Sayer	Pr:verbal		Receiver		Pr:material	Goal

When speech is reported, it is usually introduced with a *that* clause, but note that this is not an embedded Fact clause, since we cannot introduce a Fact-noun:

> *She told me the fact that junkies look worse than that.
> *He said the fact that she should carry the bags.

More on projection in the next chapter.

From *action* to *being:* existential and relational processes

We have now described the structure of all the process types that have to do with actions or events of some kind. There remains a very large group of processes in English that do not encode action meanings at all, but instead encode meanings about *states of being*. For example:

> There were these two wonderful Swiss men.
> How many pints of blood are there in your body?
> She must have been really stupid.

There are two main types of these being processes: 1. **existential** processes, where things are simply stated to exist; and 2. **relational** processes, where things are stated to exist in relation to other things (are assigned attributes or identities). We will now examine the structure of these two process classes.

Existential processes

Existential processes represent experience by positing that 'there was/is something'. For example:

> There was snow on the ground.
> There were these two wonderful Swiss men.
> There's a hitch.

Existentials are easy to identify as the structure involves the use of the word *there*. *There*, when used in existential processes, has no representational meaning: it does not refer to a location. It is present in the clause merely because all English clauses require a Subject. It is important to distinguish between *there* used as an existential Subject, and *there* used as a Circumstance of location. While structural *there* is usually unstressed, circumstantial *there* is usually stressed and often carries an intonation contour:
structural *there*:

> There is a book on the table, and a bag on the chair.

circumstantial *there*:

> There is your book – on the table.

The structural *there* in an existential process does not receive any functional label, as it is not encoding any representational meaning. It is left unanalysed for Transitivity, although in Mood analysis it is of course assigned the Subject role.

Existential processes typically employ the verb *be* or synonyms such as *exist, arise, occur*. The only obligatory participant in an existential process which receives a functional label is called the **Existent**. This participant, which usually follows the *there is/there are* sequence, may be a phenomenon of any kind, and is often in fact an event (nominalized action), e.g. *There was a battle*. Circumstantial elements (particularly of location) are common in existential processes:

There	*was*	*snow*	*on the ground.*
	Pr:existential	Existent	Circ:location

There	*were*	*these two wonderful Swiss men.*
	Pr:existential	Existent

Should	*there*	*arise*	*any difficulties*
		Pr:exist	Existent

Relational processes

The category of Relational processes covers the many different ways in which *being* can be expressed in English clauses. Examples of the domain covered by relational processes are:

i) Di is a blood donor.
ii) The operation was in Geneva.
iii) The operation lasted one hour.
iv) The story was Diana's.
v) Diana has a daughter.
vi) Women are the brave ones.
vii) The best place to give blood is in Geneva.
viii) The operation took one hour.
ix) The bomb was her boyfriend's.
x) The bomb belonged to the boyfriend.

System 8.3 captures these contrasts.

As this is a rich and complex area of clause Transitivity, the discussion here can only provide an outline (see Halliday and Matthiessen 2004: 210–48 for further discussion). We will begin by clarifying the basic structural difference between Attributive and Identifying processes, exemplified initially for the *intensive* sub-type.

Intensive Attributive Processes

An intensive Relational process involves establishing a relationship between two terms, where the relationship is expressed by the verb *be* or a synonym.

In the **Attributive** sub-type, a quality, classification or descriptive epithet (**Attribute**) is assigned to a participant (**Carrier**). The Carrier is always realized by a noun or nominal group.

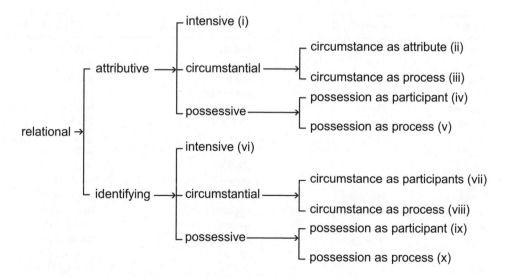

System 8.3   Relational processes

The meaning of an Attributive intensive is that *'x is a member of the class a'*. In this classification kind of attributive intensive, the Attribute is also a nominal group, typically an indefinite nominal (introduced by *a/an*).

Diana	*is*	*a talkative dinner guest.*
Carrier	Pr:intensive	Attribute

I	*won't be*	*a pig.*
Carrier	Pr:intensive	Attribute

In the descriptive attributive intensive, the Attribute is a quality or epithet ascribed to the Carrier, i.e. *'x carries the attribute a'*. In these attributive intensives, the Attribute is typically an adjective:

You	*are*	*very skinny.*
Carrier	Pr:intensive	Attribute

All the other things	*would have been*	*minute.*
Carrier	Pr:intensive	Attribute

Although the commonest intensive verb used is *be*, various attributive intensive synonyms exist. Some of these are listed and exemplified in Table 8.1.

The essential characteristic of the Attributive intensive (as indeed for all Attributive relationals) is that an Attributive clause is **not reversible**. This means that there is no

Table 8.1   Intensive Attributive verbs

VERB	CARRIER	Process:intensive	ATTRIBUTE
become	She	became	suspicious.
turn	He	turned	pale.
grow	She	grew	serious.
turn out	It	turned out	OK.
start out	She	started out	healthy.
end up	She	ended up	dead.
keep	She	kept	quiet.
stay		Stay	still.
remain		Remain	patient.
seem	It	seemed	unlikely.
sound	His story	sounded	suspicious.
appear	The luggage	appeared	harmless.
look	She	looked	jaundiced.
taste	The soup	tasted	wonderful.
smell	The soup	smells	fantastic.
feel	I	feel	funny.
stand	A litre of milk	stands	this tall.

passive form of the clause: the Subject can never conflate with the role of Attribute, but will always conflate with the role of Carrier. This is because Attributive intensives in fact contain only one independent nominal participant, the Carrier, with the Attribute functioning to encode the ascription assigned to the Carrier. For example, the following is not a passive version of the relevant clause, but merely involves the repositioning of the clause constituents, with the Subject (always the Carrier) moved to clause-final position:

Not weak at all	*am*	*I.*
Complement	Finite	Subject
RESIDUE	MOOD	
Attribute	Pr:intensive	Carrier

Even when the clause involves the inversion of the Subject and Finite, the Subject remains the Carrier:

A pig	*I*	*won't be!*
Complement	Subject	Finite
RESIDUE	MOOD	
Attribute	Carrier	Pr:intensive

Since the verb *to be* does not in fact have a passive form (we cannot say **Skinny is not been by you*), it is sometimes difficult to determine whether a *be*-clause is an Attributive or an Identifying intensive (we will see below that Identifying intensives <u>can</u> form passives). The test is to try to find a substitute for the *be* verb. If a possible substitute verb can be found from the list of Attributive intensive verbs given above, then it will be seen that the clause must be Attributive, as even with the substitute verb, the clause cannot be made passive:

original clause	***possible alternative***	***no passive***
You're skinny.	You've become skinny.	* Skinny is become by you.
I'm not weak at all.	I don't feel weak at all.	* Not weak at all is felt by me.
I won't be a pig.	I won't turn into a pig.	*A pig is not turned into by me.

Intensive Identifying processes

The intensive Identifying processes contrast with the Attributives both semantically and grammatically. Semantically, an Identifying clause is not about ascribing or classifying, but <u>defining</u>. The meaning of an identifying intensive is that '*x serves to define the identity of y*'. For example, in the clause:

You	*'re*	*the skinniest one here.*
Token	Pr:intensive	Value

you is identified as the 'holder' or 'occupant' of the identity or label of *skinniest one*.

Table 8.2   Intensive Identifying verbs

VERB	TOKEN	Pr:intensive	VALUE
equal	One plus two	equals	three.
add up to	One plus two	adds up to	three.
make	Manners	make	the man.
signify	Signing a contract	signifies	agreement.
mean	'Quantum leap'	means	a discrete jump.
define	The word 'exuberant'	defines	his style.
spell	C-A-T	spells	'cat'.
indicate	The presence of rust	indicates	moisture.
express	Her smile	expressed	pleasure.
suggest	His frown	suggested	annoyance.
act as	The commissioner	acts as	the mediator.
symbolize	An *	symbolizes	an unacceptable clause.
play	Robert de Niro	plays	Capone.
represent	The milk bottle	represents	one litre.
stand for	@	stands for	'at'.
refer to	'Quantum leap'	refers to	a sharp jump.
exemplify	His behaviour	exemplified	the typical terrorist.

Grammatically, defining involves two participants: a **Token** (that which stands for what is being defined) and a **Value** (that which defines). While the most frequently used Identifying intensive verb is *be*, other synonymous intensives are listed and exemplified in Table 8.2 above.

Both the Token and the Value are realized by nominal groups. Typically the nominal groups in Identifying intensives are definite, whereas in Attributives the Attribute is an indefinite nominal group, e.g. *the skinny one* (Identifying) vs *a skinny one* (Attributive). Because the Identifying clause contains two autonomous nominal participants, all Identifying clauses are reversible, i.e. they can form passives.

active:

You	*'re*	*the skinniest one here.*
Token	Pr:intensive	Value

passive:

The skinniest one here	*is*	*you.*
Value	Pr:intensive	Token

active:

Married women	*are*	*the real victims.*
Token	Pr:intensive	Value

passive:

The real victims	*are*	*married women.*
Value	Pr:intensive	Token

The reversibility of Identifying intensives raises the question of determining which 'side' of the clause is the Token and which the Value. This can be determined both semantically and grammatically. Halliday points out that semantically the Token will be a 'sign, name, form, holder or occupant' of a Value, which gives the 'meaning, referent, function, status or role' of the Token. The Token, then, is the nominal group which contains the 'name', and the Value is the nominal group which gives the classification. Often, semantic criteria will indicate immediately which part of the clause is Token or Value.

However, it is the grammatical test which determines role assignment. The test involves replacing the verb *to be* with one of the synonymous Identifying intensive verbs listed above, and then determining whether the resulting clause is active or passive, and which constituent is functioning as Subject. The correlation is that:

- TOKEN will always be Subject in an active clause
- VALUE will always be Subject in a passive clause.

For example, to determine which is Token and which Value, take the original clause:

You're the skinniest one here.

and substitute a possible synonymous verb:

= You represent the skinniest one here.

Determine whether this substitute clause is active or passive, and label the Subject role = active (no presence of be + past participle + by)

You	*represent*		*the skinniest one here.*
Subject	Finite	Predicator	Complement
MOOD		RESIDUE	

If active, then Subject must also be Token:

You	*represent*		*the skinniest one here.*
Token	Pr:intensive		Value
Subject	Finite	Predicator	Complement
MOOD		RESIDUE	

Check the analysis by forming the passive, where Subject will be Value:

The skinniest one here	*is*	*represented*	*by you.*
Subject	Finite	Predicator	Adj:circ
MOOD		RESIDUE	
Value		Pr:intensive	Token

In summary, this procedure involves:

   i) finding a substitute intensive verb (other than *be*)
  ii) analysing the clause for Mood to determine Subject
 iii) noting whether the clause is active or passive
 iv) applying the rule: Token is Subject in active; Value is Token in passive clause
  v) testing by changing active to passive or vice versa
 vi) establishing final analysis of original clause.

As a further example of applying this procedure, take the clause *Women aren't the weak ones.*

i) Women don't constitute the weak ones.
ii) *Women* is Subject

Women	*don't*	*constitute*	*the weak ones.*
Subject	Finite	Predicator	Complement
MOOD		RESIDUE	

iii) clause is active
iv) therefore, *women* is Token
v) passive:

The weak ones	*aren't*	*constituted*	*by women.*
Subject	Finite	Predicator	Complement
MOOD		RESIDUE	
Value		Pr:intensive	Token

vi) final analysis of original clause:

Women	*aren't*	*the weak ones.*
Subject	Finite	Complement
MOOD		RESIDUE
Token	Pr:intensive	Value

The verb substitution test can also be used to determine whether a given *be*-clause is Attributive or Identifying. If a possible verb substitute is one which cannot form a passive, then the clause must be Attributive. If the verb substituted can form a passive, then the clause is Identifying, and by labelling the Subject constituent you will be able to determine which constituent is Token and which Value.

For example, to determine whether the following clause is Attributive or Identifying:

Only people with 1993 badges are financial members.

First, find a verb to substitute for 'are':

Only people with 1993 badges	*represent*	*financial members.*
	constitute	
	symbolize	
* Only people with 1993 badges	*turn into*	*financial members.*
	seem	
	appear	

Test whether the selected substitute can form a passive or not:

Financial members are represented only by people with 1993 badges.

This shows that the clause is Identifying, and since the clause is active, it is possible to assign Token/Value labels to the original clause:

Only people with 1993 badges	*are*	*financial members.*
Subject	Finite	Complement
MOOD		RESIDUE
Token	Pr:intensive	Value

Other common sub-types of relationals: (1) Circumstantials

As well as the intensive relationals, two other types of relational processes, Circumstantial and Possessive, occur commonly, both as Attributive and Identifying processes.

Circumstantial relational processes encode meanings about the circumstantial dimensions discussed earlier: location, manner, cause . . ., etc. Circumstance, then, can be expressed in a clause either as a Circumstantial constituent in a material, mental, behavioural or verbal process, or through a relational process.

In the Attributive Circumstantial, the Circumstance is often expressed in the Attribute. While the verb remains intensive, the Attribute will be a prepositional phrase or an adverb of location, manner, cause, etc. We capture this by showing the conflation of the Attributive with the Circumstantial element:

The bomb	*was*	*in her luggage.*
Carrier	*Pr:intensive*	*Attribute/Circ:location*

As with all Attributive processes, these cannot form passives:

> *In her luggage was been by the bomb.

The Circumstantial meaning may also be encoded in the process itself, with the verb meaning '*is + circumstance*'. In this case, the process is specified as 'circumstantial':

The operation	*lasted*	*one hour.*
Carrier	Pr:circumstantial	Attribute

(where *lasted* = be + for one hour)

Di's narrative	*concerns*	*her daughter's operation.*
Carrier	Pr:circumstantial	Attribute

(where *concerns* = be + about)
Again, these Attributive processes are not reversible:

> *One hour was lasted by the operation.
> *Her daughter's operation was concerned by Di's narrative.

With Identifying Circumstantials, it is also possible to encode the circumstantial meaning within either the participants or the process.

When the circumstantial meaning is encoded through the participants, both the Token and the Value will be circumstantial elements of time, place, etc., while the verb remains intensive:

Yesterday	*was*	*the last time Di gave blood.*
Token/Circ:time	Pr:intensive	Value/Circ:time

The circumstance may also be expressed through the process, using verbs such as *take up, follow, cross, resemble, accompany*, etc. In these cases, the process is labelled as 'circumstantial':

The operation	*took*	*one hour.*
Token	Pr:circumstantial	Value

The terrorist	*accompanied*	*the young woman.*
Token	Pr:circumstantial	Value

A milk bottle	*holds*	*one litre of liquid.*
Token	Pr:circumstantial	Value

Being Identifying, these verbs form passives:

> One hour was taken up by the operation.
> The young woman was accompanied by the terrorist.
> One litre of liquid is held by a milk bottle.

Other relationals: (2) Possessives

Possessive processes encode meanings of ownership and possession between clausal participants. In Attributive Possessives, possession may be encoded through the participants (with the Attribute the possessor, and the process remaining intensive):

This	*is*	*yours.*
Carrier	Pr:intensive	Attribute/Possessor

Possession may also be encoded through the process, the commonest Attributive possessive verbs being *to have* and *to belong to*. Typically the Carrier will be Possessor:

I	*had*	*a daughter.*
You	*have*	*8 pints of blood.*
You	*'ve got*	*less blood than me.*
Carrier/possessor	Pr:possession	Attribute:possessed

But it is possible to have the Carrier as what is possessed:

The bomb	*belonged to*	*the boyfriend.*
Carrier/possessed	Pr:possession	Attribute/possessor

Attributive possessive processes are not reversible:

> *The boyfriend was belonged to by the bomb.

In Identifying possessives, possession may again be expressed either through the participants, or through the process. When possession is expressed through the participants, the intensive verb *to be* is used, with the Token and Value encoding the possessor and the possessed:

The bomb	*was*	*her boyfriend's.*
Token/Possessed	Pr:intensive	Value/Possessor

Her boyfriend's	*was*	*the bomb.*
Value/Possessor	Pr:intensive	Token/Possessed

The commonest Identifying possessive process is *to own*, which can form passives, so that either the Token or Value can be Subject:

Her boyfriend	*owned*	*the bomb.*
Token/Possessor	Pr:possessive	Value/Possessed

The bomb	*was owned by*	*her boyfriend.*
Value/Possessed	Pr:possessive	Token/Possessor

Causative relationals

A final type of relational process that needs to be mentioned briefly is the causative relational. Causative relational processes may occur with either Attributive or Identifying structures, with causation expressed either through a *make + be* (Process:intensive) structure, or, with Identifying relationals, through a causative process. As with the causative material processes we considered earlier, causatives involve an Agent in making or causing something. With Attributive relationals, an Agent (also called an Attributor) causes the Carrier to have an Attribute ascribed. For example:

The experience in Geneva	*made*	*Diana*	*(become)*	*a blood donor.*
Agent/Attributor	Pr:causative	Carrier	(Pr:intensive)	Attribute

The introduction of the causative process *make* as the Finite in these structures means that causative passives can be formed. Remember that the clause is still an Attributive one, however:

Diana	*was made*	*to become*	*a blood donor*	*by the experience.*
Carrier	Pr:causative	Pr:intensive	Attribute	Agent/Attributor

Note that the intensive process is often ellipsed from the clause:

Giving blood	*makes*	*you*	*weak.*
Agent/Attributor	Pr:causative	Carrier	Attribute

With the Identifying type, the Agent (or Assigner) makes the Token take a Value:

They	*made*	*Simon*	*the barman*	*for the night.*
Agent/Assigner	Pr:causative	Token	Value	Circ:extent

Note the analysis of the passive version of this clause:

Simon	*was made*	*the barman*	*for the night*	*(by them).*
Token	Pr:causative	Value	Circ:extent	(Agent/Assigner)

With Identifying clauses, the causative relationship between participants can also be expressed directly through a causative circumstantial verb. The common verbs are *result in, cause, produce*, etc. With these processes, the verb is a fusion of the intensive meanings *be* or *equal* and the expression of cause. The active/passive test can be used to determine the assignment of Token/Value labels. For example:

Donating blood	*results in/causes*	*weakness.*
Token	Pr:circumstantial	Value

Weakness	*caused by*	*donating blood.*
Token	Pr:circumstantial	Value

The meaning of transitivity

This chapter so far has reviewed the functional grammatical description of the Transitivity structure of English clauses. Clauses can be seen to select for a process type (material, mental, behavioural, verbal, existential, relational). The process type specifies the action, events or relationships between implicated participants (nominal constituents, functionally labelled according to the process type), and the processes may be situated circumstantially (for time, place, cause, etc.). Carrying out a Transitivity analysis involves determining the process type, participants and circumstances realized in any clause. Transitivity analysis offers a description of one of the structural strands of the clause. Each clause can also be analysed for its Mood structure.

It was stated at the beginning of this chapter that Transitivity patterns represent the encoding of experiential meanings: meanings about the world, about experience, about how we perceive and experience what is going on. By examining the Transitivity patterns in text, we can explain how the field of the situation is being constructed, i.e. we can describe 'what is being talked about' and how shifts in the field are achieved.

For example, with Text 8.1, the 'Blood' excerpt, our initial description of the field of the talk might be that the participants talk 'about blood and then about a news story'. A Transitivity analysis of the text, however, allows us to refine this description, and explain how the field both develops and shifts through a number of experiential phases.

Each of the phases (1–9) indicated in the transcript is identified according to the predominant process type being selected by participants, as the following summary of the Transitivity in each phase indicates.

Phase 1: material processes; predominantly *give*; with different individuals present as Actors. Circumstantial elements of time, extent, place. So this phase is 'about' everyone's individual experience of giving blood: who has/hasn't; where; when; how often.

(Diana's narrative is considered in detail below.)

Phase 2: mental and behavioural processes dominate here, with generalized *you* as participants. This phase reports what are presented as general statements about reactions to the actions described in phase 1.

Phase 3: relational processes dominate, with possessives in particular, and a shift between generalized *you* as Carrier/possessor and individual participants. Circumstantial expressions of extent (how many, how long) occur. This phase explores generalized possession of the commodity (blood) discussed in phases 1 and 2.

Phase 4: material and relational processes, a phase which establishes contrasts, with *we* (women) as Carriers in attributive processes (which positively evaluate), and *men* as Actors in (pejorative) material processes.

Phase 5: mental and relational processes, with individual participants as Sensers/Carriers. This phase explores participants' ascription of themselves and their wants/desires.

Phase 6: relational and mental processes, with generalized *you* and *they* as participants. In part a reiteration of previous discussion, hence the transitional nature of this phase.

Phase 7: material processes, with generalized *you* as Actor. Brief phase, introducing more substantial content of phase 8.

Phase 8: relational processes, notably identifying processes, with generic classes as participants (some women, etc.). Here participants construct their classification of the reality they are discussing: their taxonomy of people in relation to blood.

Phase 9: the beginning of a narrative phase.

Transitivity analysis is also useful in explaining the structuring of Diana's narrative about her daughter. The schematic structure of this short narrative is suggested below. Note that Diana's narrative achieves some of its suspense by beginning with a statement of the Complicating Action (the pivotal drama) of the event:

Abstract/Complication 1

> No I do it because I had a daughter who when she was two days old needed blood transfusions cause she was getting sort of premature jaundice and things.

Orientation 1

> This was in Geneva.

Complication 2

> And they rang me up on the Sat- this was Saturday night and said 'You've got to come in and have your blood tested against the donor's'.

Orientation 2

> And there were these two wonderful Swiss men who'd left their dinner you know 8 o'clock at night and come in there to give blood to my daughter.

Evaluation 1

> And I was really impressed

Complication 3

> and you know I had to give blood to be tested to see if it was compatible with theirs. And I had to deliver it to the clinic where she was.

Orientation 3

> There was snow on the ground and everything.

Evaluation 2

> It was very exciting.

Complication 4

> And then I stayed up all night and watched this um operation taking place

Resolution

> and fortunately her umbilical artery hadn't closed so because I mean all the other things would have been minute. So they could actually do it through the umbilical artery or whatever.

Evaluation 3

> So I said 'OK', you know, 'be a blood donor after that'.

Coda

> But in Switzerland they give you a cognac. Here they give you tea and bikkies

It is in the transitivity patterns of this short story that we find evidence in support of the generic structure. Each stage of the narrative can be associated with particular transitivity choices, summarized below:

Abstract/Complication 1
Material process; Diana as Actor.
Relational possessive process: Diana as possessor; Attributive processes: her daughter as Carrier; complicating situation as Attribute.

Orientation 1
Relational Circumstantial process; Carrier as 'the events'; Attribute as Circumstance:location (setting in place).

Complication 2
Material processes: 'they' as Actor; circumstance:location (time); Verbal process: they as Sayer; Material process: Diana as Actor.

Orientation 2
Existential process; Existent as critical subsidiary participants in story.

Evaluation 1
Attributive relational process; Diana as Carrier; Attribute: intensified evaluative adjective (past participle used adjectivally).

Complication 3
Material processes; Diana as Actor; Circumstances of cause and location.

Orientation 3
Existential process; Existent as physical phenomena (setting scene); Circumstance: location.

Evaluation 2
Relational process; Carrier: events in the story; Attribute: intensified attitudinal/evaluative adjective.

Complication 4
Material process, circumstance of extent; behavioural process with Phenomenon; Diana as Actor/Behaver.

Resolution
Relational attributive: body parts as Carrier; dimensions, etc. as Attribute;
Material process: 'they' as Actor; Circumstance:manner of body parts.

Evaluation 3
Verbal process; projecting relational attributive: Diana as Sayer and Carrier; Attribute: 'a blood donor' (personal attribution).

Coda
Circumstance of location (in Thematic position); material processes with three participants: Actor, Beneficiary, Goal; Actor: generic 'you'.

This analysis shows that the boundaries between each element of schematic structure relate to changes in transitivity choices. The Orientations are realized by Existential or Relational processes with circumstantial elements providing setting in time/place and introducing subsidiary participants. Evaluations are realized by relational attributive processes, involving attitudinal Attributes which encode Diana's reactions to the unfolding events. Diana's final Evaluation involves ascribing herself with the label of 'blood donor', both demonstrating the 'point' of the story (personal transformation), and reinforcing the lexical cohesive links with the talk immediately prior to the narrative.

Sustaining the dramatic interest of the narrative are the several stages of Complication, spread across the story. Complication stages are realized by material, verbal or behavioural process clauses in which Diana is the active participant. This transitivity choice clearly constructs the narrative as 'Diana's story', even though it is ostensibly *about* her daughter. The Resolution involves material processes blended with Attributive relationals. But while in the Complications the focal participants are both Diana and her daughter, in the Resolution the focus has moved to the doctors as participants.

The Coda blends material process choices of the Complication stages, but gives thematic prominence to Circumstantial choices common in Orientations. Note the significant variation in the number and nature of participants involved in the process: the story concludes with a shift from Diana as Actor to a generalized *they*, and the introduction of a Beneficiary, realized as a generalized *you*. This shift in participants (and also in tense, from past to present) signals the return to interaction, after the extended monologue, and frees up topic space for other conversationalists (they do not have to talk only about Diana and her daughter to be cohesive; they may now talk about places or about blood donating or about rewards, which is exactly what Simon does do).

Summary of transitivity

This brief discussion of the conversational excerpt illustrates how Transitivity patterns are the clausal realization of contextual choices. In selecting which process type to use, and what configuration of participants to express, participants are actively choosing to represent experience in a particular way. We explore this construction of field again in the final chapter, when we consider transitivity patterns in the three Crying Baby texts presented in Chapter One.

The experiential structure of the clause is just one of two components through which ideational meanings are expressed through language. In the next chapter we look at how the logico-semantic systems of the clause complex provide options that allow text creators to link individual clauses of experiential meaning together into ideationally coherent text.

Notes

1. This text is an excerpt from the 'Dinner at Stephen's' dinner party conversation (author's data).
2. In Halliday and Matthiessen (2004: 293), Range is introduced in conjunction with a complex discussion of the ergative analysis of the clause. For reasons of space and clarity, I limit my discussion to Halliday's earlier presentations of the Range function.

Chapter 9

The grammar of logical meaning:
CLAUSE COMPLEX

Introduction

In the previous chapter we explored experiential structure: the functional organization of the clause to express content through the transitivity systems of English. Experiential meaning is one component of what Halliday identifies as the ideational metafunction in language, the metafunction which expresses 'meanings about the world'. In this chapter we examine the second component of ideational meaning: the logical structure of the clause complex. After defining the clause complex, we will review the two systems of logical relations: that of **taxis** (or how two or more adjacent clauses are linked to each other through relations of dependency or interdependency) and **logico-semantics** (the types of meanings that allow adjacent clauses to project or expand on each other). We will see that the logical systems of the clause complex complement transitivity choices, allowing us to compose spontaneously complex clusters of experiential representations. Finally, we will also see how variations in the amount and types of logical relations realize differences in mode and genre.

What is a clause complex?

In Chapter Eight we looked in detail at the meanings Diana was making in her story about giving blood in Geneva. We saw that in turning life into text, Diana used Transitivity resources to set the scene (through relational and existential processes), narrate the events (through material processes), evaluate the dramatic experience (through attributive processes), and finally express the effect of the events on her continuing behaviour (through the identifying process of becoming a blood donor). To carry out our Transitivity analysis, we divided Diana's story into separate clauses. But in fact one of the distinctive skills Diana has as a story-teller is that she 'packages' her tale: she delivers her story in bursts of information, not as separate clauses. For example, she begins her story like this:

> Di $_{(i)}$No I do it $_{(ii)}$because I had a daughter $_{(iii \ldots)}$who $_{(iv)}$when she was 2 days old $_{(\ldots iii)}$needed blood transfusions $_{(v)}$cause she was getting sort of premature jaundice and things.

This opening burst by Diana in fact consists of five clauses (indicated by subscript numbers). In the transcript, I have shown this as one 'sentence': there's only one full stop. But of course people don't speak in sentences: Diana didn't reach the words 'jaundice and things' and then say 'full stop, new sentence', the way one of my old teachers used to do when she was giving us a dictation passage. But nor did Diana simply run on this chunk of five clauses into the next clause *This was in Geneva*. She also did not begin her story with a series of separate clauses, which might have gone something like this:

> Di No. I have a reason for giving blood. The reason is that my daughter needed blood transfusions. This happened when she was two days old. She was getting sort of premature jaundice and things. This was in Geneva.

Notice how much more stilted and formal this separate clause version sounds. If she'd begun in that way, Diana ran the risk of being interrupted before she'd had the chance to sweep us into the story and earn our permission to hold the floor.

What this example shows is that when we talk we often chain two or more clauses together in sequence. When we do this, we use markers to show the relationship between each clause (words like *because, when*), and we also use the spoken language systems of rhythm and intonation to signal to our listeners when we've reached the end of a clause sequence. As a participant present during Diana's story, and then later as the transcriber who turned Diana's talk into a written record, I heard a definite break or pause, along with a falling intonation, between the first five clauses and the clause about Geneva. In my transcription, I captured that with the use of full stops. In other words, I turned Diana's cluster of clauses into a sentence.

The sentence, with its punctuation conventions of initial capital and final full stop, is a unit derived from spoken language. In all cultures, spoken language exists as a fully functional system before the development of written language. Written language systems of orthography and punctuation are secondary systems, developed as people searched for ways to record talk in permanent forms. The full stop is the main orthographic symbol we use to capture a very significant grammatical and semantic boundary: it marks the end of a clause complex.

Clause complex is the term systemicists use for the grammatical and semantic unit formed when two or more clauses are linked together in certain systematic and meaningful ways. When we write clause complexes down, either from speech or composed in written language, we generally show clause complex boundaries with full stops. In other words, while the sentence is an orthographic unit of written language, the clause complex is a grammatical and semantic unit, and it is a unit that occurs in both spoken *and* written language. From now on, we will be using the term **clause complex** to refer to clause clusters of two or more clauses. We can use the term **clause simplex** to refer to single clause units (or sentences of only one clause).

Why analyse clause complexes?

I've already suggested that our Transitivity analysis, though it captured much about the structure and meanings of Diana's unfolding story, could not capture the significant dimension of its 'flow' or 'packaging' into grammatical units. We've seen that Diana *could* have chosen to package her opening turn as a set of separate clauses. She didn't. Similarly, as her story went on, she chose at some points to cluster clauses together into clause complexes (for example she links together (3i)*And they rang me up on the Sat-* (3ii)*this was Saturday night* (3iii)*and said* (3iv)*'You've got to come in* (3v)*and have your blood tested against the donor's'*), while at other times she chose to deliver just a single clause as a unit (e.g. *This was in Geneva*). Sometimes when Diana linked clauses she seemed to be linking events to each other. For example:

> (9i)And then I stayed up all night (9ii)and watched this um operation taking place (9iii)and fortunately her umbilical artery hadn't closed (9iv)so because I mean all the other things would have been minute

while at other times, she uses linking to package what she or other people said about the events (for example, (11i)*So I said* (11ii)*'OK', you know, 'be a blood donor after that'*).

Sometimes she seems to package together clauses which *could* have stood alone with only very minor grammatical changes (e.g. *And then I stayed up all night. And I watched this operation taking place. And fortunately her umbilical artery hadn't closed*), while at other times the linked clauses seem more closely dependent on other clauses (for example, we need to make greater changes to the clauses in her opening turn if we want to separate them).

Wherever there is choice, there is meaning. But what are the meanings being made here? To understand why speakers and writers choose clause complexes over clause simplexes, and choose particular *types* of clause complexes, we need to look in detail at the system of the clause complex in English. As we do this, we'll see that clause complex systems provide language users with structural resources to construe logical connections between experiential events. This system of logical meaning works alongside the experiential structures of Transitivity. Together, the logical and the experiential functions allow us to express ideational meanings as we turn life into text.

One further reason for looking at clause complex relations is that the categories of clause complex relations actually apply over other areas of the grammar as a whole: not just clauses but also groups and phrases form 'complexes', and they do so along the same principles as the clause. Understanding how the natural logic of English works to form clause complexes can thus help us understand the basic process of complexing: how language offers us the creative potential to 'blow out' or develop on the meaning in any grammatical unit. Although in this book there is not space to cover word, group and phrase structure, if you understand how complexing works in the clause, you will begin to recognize the same process and meanings happening at those other ranks.

The structure of clause complexes

To appreciate the difference between the structure of clauses and that of clause complexes, remember that when we analysed Mood and Transitivity, we took each clause and divided it into functional constituents, to which we attached labels that captured each constituent's contribution towards the structure as a whole. So the clause *And fortunately they could do it through the umbilical artery* can be analysed into both Mood and Transitivity constituents:

And	fortunately	they	could	do	it	through the umbilical artery.
Adjunct: conjun	Adjunct: comment	Subject	Finite:mod	Predicator	Complement	Adjunct:circ
		MOOD		RESIDUE		
		Actor	Pr:material		Goal	Circ:manner

But when we analyse clause complexes, we find we are dealing with a very different type of structure. Consider again Diana's opening burst:

> Di (i)No I do it (ii)because I had a daughter (iii . . .)who (iv)when she was 2 days old (. . . iii) needed blood transfusions (v)cause she was getting sort of premature jaundice and things.

With a clause complex like this, it's easy to demonstrate that we're not dealing with a finite, definable whole. After all, Diana could easily have extended her clause complex ad infinitum, for example:

> Di   No I do it because I had a daughter who needed a blood transfusion when she was two days old cause she was getting sort of premature jaundice and things and they thought she might die if she didn't get a transfusion within a few hours and so there were these two wonderful Swiss men who rushed in there and gave blood so that my daughter could have the transfusion and it was really exciting because . . .

While such a lengthy clause complex might be tiring for both speaker and listeners, there is absolutely nothing grammatically wrong with it. This suggests that clause complexes are formed on a different structural basis to clauses, and that's exactly what Halliday claims when he points out that the clause is a **multivariate** structure but the clause complex is a **univariate** one. These are two useful terms to understand when looking at language.

A **multivariate** structure is one where we can identify a complete whole which is made up of functionally distinct constituents, for example the clause which is (interpersonally) made up of a Subject, Finite, Predicator, Complement, Adjunct. Each element performs a distinct and different role in contributing to the meaning of the whole clause structure. Obligatory elements (such as Subject and Finite) can only occur once, otherwise we have by definition a new clause. Both Mood and Transitivity structures are multivariate, as are most generic structures, reviewed in Chapter Three.

In a **univariate** structure, on the other hand, we're dealing with a relationship between elements that are essentially the same and which can be chained together indefinitely. A clause complex is composed of one clause after another clause after another clause. Provided the links between the clauses make sense, we can go on and on and on. There is no final 'whole' that has to be constituted to ensure grammatical completeness. Univariate structures, then, are defined as iterative, recursive structures: the same type of unit simply gets repeated indefinitely.

But this does not mean that any sequence of adjacent clauses constitutes a well-formed clause complex. For example, imagine Diana had produced the following sequence of clauses without any breaks of rhythm and intonation between them:

> She was getting sort of premature jaundice and things this was in Geneva it was snowing everywhere I had to go in to give blood it was very exciting.

Here we have six clauses, each individually well-formed in terms of both Transitivity and Mood structure. But we don't have a clause complex because there are no indications of links between each clause. We are missing any conjunctions that could show us how one clause relates to the previous clauses. We simply have a running-on from one clause to another, a kind of breathless outpouring of individual clauses. While people sometimes speak like this at moments of great stress or excitement, most of the time clauses in a clause complex must be linked to each other explicitly, often with conjunctions or (in writing) with punctuation markers, for listeners to be able to process the information. But there's more to it than that. Consider now:

> She was getting sort of premature jaundice and things but rainfall is always heaviest in autumn so Jedda decided to buy the book after all.

Here again we have three clauses, each individually well-formed in terms of both Transitivity and Mood structure. But the clause complex is a nonsense: although we have linking words, the links don't make sense because there is no logical or coherent relationship between the ideational content of one clause and that of the next. We appear to be jumping from talking about one set of participants and processes to another. This incoherence should remind you of our examples of non-text in Chapter Two, but note that in the example we're dealing with now the incoherence is occurring *within* a single clause complex/sentence, rather than between sentences in a text. This shows us that clause complexes involve the *logical* chaining together of *experientially related* meanings. Let's look now at the systems that allow us to constitute logical, well-formed, coherent clause complexes.

Systems of the clause complex

Here first are the systems of clause complex relations in diagrammatic form, in System 9.1. This system network is saying that there are two systems involved in the formation of clause complexes:

1. **the tactic system**: this is the system that describes the type of interdependency relationship between clauses linked into a clause complex. The two options in this tactic system are **parataxis** (where clauses are related as equal, independent entities) and **hypotaxis** (where clauses relate to a main clause through a dependency relationship). Very roughly this corresponds to what some conventional grammars

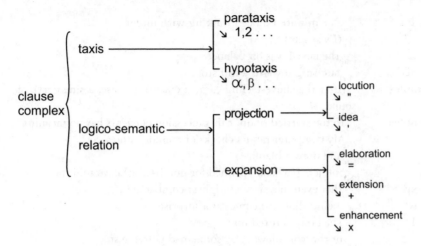

System 9.1   System of the clause complex

refer to as 'co-ordination' versus 'sub-ordination' relationships. We will see examples in a moment.

2. **the logico-semantic system**: this is the system that describes the specific type of meaning relationship between linked clauses. Again, there are two main options: clauses may be related through **projection** (where one clause is quoted or reported by another clause), or through **expansion** (where one clause develops or extends on the meanings of another). Projection offers two choices: **locution** (where what is projected is speech) and **idea** (where what is projected is thoughts). The system of expansion is one we have already met when looking at conjunction in Chapter Two. Expansion consists of three main options: **elaboration** (relations of restatement or equivalence); **extension** (relations of addition); and **enhancement** (relations of development).

To understand these systemic choices and how they work, we'll draw on Diana's story about giving blood, but also on some other texts. The first, Text 9.1, is another story text, this time a highly crafted written narrative of personal experience. It is the opening two sections from a non-fiction book called *Shot* written by Australian author Gail Bell. Sentence numbers are shown in ordinary numbers (1, 2, 3 . . .); clause numbers in roman numerals. Embedded clauses are shown in [[parentheses]]. At this stage, just ignore the hieroglyphics in the left-hand columns.

Text 9.1: *Shot*[1]

xβ	(1i)While walking home one dry moonless night in 1968
α	(1ii)I was shot in the back.
1	(2i)The experience was spectacularly new to me;
=2	(2ii)I had nothing [[to compare it with]], no neural circuitry [[to process similarities]], no language for the shock.
xβ	(3i)When the bullet struck
α	(3ii)I traveled forward an extra half-step,
xγ	(3iii)as if someone [[wielding a broom handle]] had given me a rude shove from behind.

1	1	(4i)One minute I'd been walking with intent
	x2	(4ii)(I was late),
+2	α	(4iii)the next I was off balance,
	xβ	(4iv)faltering towards a full stop.
clause simplex		(5)After the shove-feeling came a crackling noise, a sine curve of sound, *kerwump*.
clause simplex		(6)To the startled brain, this procession of events has no meaning.
1		(7i)My computer ran its checks of memory stores
+2		(7ii)and drew a blank.
α		(8i)Soldiers [[who are primed for gun battle]] have told me
"β	xβ	(8ii)that even in a state of highest combat alert[2],
	α	(8iii)being shot still comes as a surprise.
1	1	(9i)The body is lifted up
	+2	(9ii)or thrown sideways by some mad poltergeist,
+2		(9iii)and it is only with the return of conscious awareness that comprehension takes over from confusion[3].
xβ		(10i)When realization arrived for me
α		(10ii)it came hesitantly, like a messenger [[unsure of the address.]]
α		(11i)I used up valuable and dangerous seconds
xβ	α	(11ii)trying to work out
	'β	(11iii)what had happened.
1		(12i)The shooter,
<'2>		(12ii)I saw,
1		(12iii)was in a car fifteen metres away.
xβ		(13i)When that pulse of comprehension arrived,
α	1	(13ii)I turned
	x2	(13iii)and ran for my life.
		◊◊◊◊◊◊
clause simplex		(14)I didn't see my attacker's face.
1		(15i)I saw a car and a shape at the steering wheel,
=2	α	(15ii)only as much as the eye will register
	xβ 1	(15iii)when you swivel your neck
	x2	(15iv)and glance over your shoulder.
clause simplex		(16)From the shooter's vantage point, the target was a tall girl [[walking northwards into the darkness.]]
1		(17i)He saw the back of me,
+2		(17ii)I saw a glimpse of a shadow.
xβ		(18i)After the bang and before I ran – in that pause [[where visual contact might have been made but wasn't]] –
α		(18ii)the car remained ominously still.
clause simplex		(19)Speculation [[about what he was doing]] is a luxury for later, for now.
clause simplex		(20)Then, I had no thought, only reactions.
1		(21i)Now, I am harangued by questions:
=2		(21ii)Was he re-loading?
clause simplex		(22)Was the gun jammed?
α		(23i)Was he waiting
xβ	α	(23ii)to see

'β			(23iii)if I would fall down dead?
clause simplex			(24)Was he playing a game with complexities [[I couldn't begin to imagine]]?
clause simplex			(25)That pause was significant in other ways.
clause simplex			(26)For me it was the hiatus before an opera of panic and pain.
clause simplex			(27)For him, I can only guess.
xβ			(28i)As I ran away,
α	1		(28ii)he revved the motor of his car,
	x2		(28iii)spun gravel
	x3		(28iv)and sped out of sight.
1	1		(29i)I almost wrote
	"2		(29ii)'he gunned the car',
+2			(29iii)but it was me, the girl in the new maroon shoes, he gunned

By way of comparison, here now is the transcript of part of an interview I carried out with Gail Bell in preparation for writing a review of *Shot*. We began by talking about a shared interest, the practice of yoga. Again, ignore the analysis for now:

Text 9.2: interview with Gail Bell[4]

			SE: Has yoga brought you mental benefits, then?
α			GB: (1i)Yes, I think it has,
xβ			(1ii)for when I'm doing it.
1			(2i)But I am kind of naturally um
=2			(2ii)I seem to live in this state of hyperawareness.
1			(3i)So it's very easy for me to lapse into my former kind of intense that intense mode
x2	α		(3ii)so I really have to make a conscious effort
	xβ	1	(3iii)to switch off
		+2	(3iv)and get into that other space.
1	α		(4i)I really wish
	'β	1	(4ii)I could sit for an hour
		+2	(4iii)and stare out the window
x2			(4iv)but I don't have that facility.
			SE: So would you say you're always thinking?
clause simplex			GB: (5)Yea.
xβ			(6i)And even if I'm not focusing on anything in particular
α			(6ii)I seem to be intensely engaged at some level somewhere in my mind.
clause simplex			(7)It's very tiring.
clause simplex			(8)It engages the nervous system.
α	α		(9i)I suspect that
	<xβ>		(9ii)having now done quite a bit of research for *Shot*
'β			(9iii)that it's part of the greater spectrum of post-traumatic stress disorder.
1	α	1	(10i)So I'm sort of hypervigilant, you know,
		=2	(10ii)I'm always on the alert,
	xβ		(10iii)even though I wouldn't acknowledge that at a

				conscious level
+2	α			(10iv) but I think
	'β	α		(10v) at a deeper level it is a sort of hypervigilance
		=β		(10vi) that people with PTSD[5] seem to suffer from.
				SE: That must be useful for a writer, hyperawareness?
				GB: (11i) Yes, I think
α				
'β				(11ii) it is.
1				(12i) And it might be why
=2				(12ii) it might have contributed.
clause simplex				(13) It certainly makes me more alert.
1	xβ			(14i) I mean if I go out to restaurants or social events or anywhere really
	α	α		(14ii) I'm always very conscious
		'β	1	(14iii) of who's doing what where,
			+2	(14iv) and where everyone is in relation to me
x2	α			(14v) and I now realize
	'β	α		(14vi) that that scanning and vigilant behaviour relates to a vestige of the old trauma
		=β		(14vii) which is –
		=γ	α	(14viii) you know
			'β	(14ix) how old it is now.
1				(15i) But the parts of the mind hold on to that
x2	α			(15ii) and remain vigilant
	xβ			(15iii) long after they need to.
				SE: Forever, do you think?
α	α			(16i) I'm beginning to think
	'β			(16ii) it's forever, yes,
xβ	α			(16iii) the more people I speak to
	=β			(16iv) who are living with PTSD.
1	α			(17i) I think
	'β			(17ii) all that changes are your coping mechanisms,
+2				(17iii) and it's some days . . .
=3	1			(17iv) it's like having asthma or something
	=2	1		(17v) some days it's good
		+2		(17vi) and some days it's not good.
clause simplex				(18) And you go through cycles of coping and not coping.
1				(19i) And I have a very mild form
+2				(19ii) but I had some visitors here the other day.
1	α			(20i) An old school friend[6]
	=β			(20ii) whose husband was in Vietnam
+2	α			(20iii) and he's an extremely damaged man,
	=β			(20iv) as many vets are,
+3				(20v) and I was sort of watching him, almost in a clinical sense,
+4	α			(20vi) and I thought
	'β	α		(20vii) that we shared some mannerisms, he and I,

=β	α	(20viii)you know fiddling with our fingers quite a lot,
	+β	(20ix)and never really looking comfortable in your chair.
clause simplex		(21)I mean he much more than I do.
clause simplex		(22)I'm very good at disguising all of that.

Analysing clause complexes

The first thing we can note about both Texts 9.1 and 9.2 is that each contains some clause simplexes (sentences that consist of only one clause), and many clause complexes (sentences consisting of more than one clause). We will consider the effects of such alternations later; for now we'll just note that alternation is the common pattern in both spoken and written texts. We'll now concentrate on analysing how the clause complexes in texts are formed, beginning with the choice of taxis, and looking initially at two-clause complexes only.

Analysing taxis

The system of taxis captures the dependency, or independency, relationship between adjacent clauses. There are two options: **parataxis** or **hypotaxis**. Compare:

(17i)He saw the back of me, (17ii)I saw a glimpse of a shadow.

(1i)While walking home one dry moonless night in 1968 (1ii)I was shot in the back.

In the first example, the two pieces of information (what he saw, what I saw) are presented as being of equal weight. Neither is more important than the other; just two clauses, two parcels of experience, placed next to each other. Each *could* stand alone as a sentence:

He saw the back of me. I saw a glimpse of a shadow.

Although this would represent a difference in meaning, grammatically we do not have to make any changes to our two clauses for this to work.

But in the second example, one of our two clauses is structurally dependent on the other. Only one of the two clauses could stand alone in its current form: *I was shot in the back*. We cannot have a sentence that consists of:

*While walking home one dry moonless night in 1968.

This structural difference (which is the expression of a semantic difference) is what differentiates parataxis (a relationship between equals) from hypotaxis (a relationship between a dependent and its Head).

Parataxis

In parataxis, clauses relate to each other as equals. They are independent. This equality is reflected in the fact that each clause in a paratactic complex could usually stand alone as a complete sentence. Consider:

(2i)The experience was spectacularly new to me; (2ii)I had nothing to compare it with, no neural circuitry to process similarities, no language for the shock.

(17i)He saw the back of me, (17ii)I saw a glimpse of a shadow.

In both cases Bell presents the two clauses as two equal partners in a clause complex. She could also have written:

The experience was spectacularly new to me. I had nothing to compare it with, no neural circuitry to process similarities, no language for the shock.

He saw the back of me. I saw a glimpse of a shadow.

There is of course a difference in meaning between the clause complex and the clause simplex examples. Bell's choice to link the clauses into a paratactic clause complex creates a closer logico-semantic bond between them than the clause simplex option. The choice is part of what gives fluency to writing, as professional writers seek to capture some (but not all) of the flow that characterizes the spoken language.

At other points, Bell chooses to separate what could also be presented as a paratactic clause complex. For example:

(14)I didn't see my attacker's face. (15i)I saw a car and a shape at the steering wheel

This could just as easily have been presented as:

I didn't see my attacker's face; I saw a car and a shape at the steering wheel.

We will consider the effect of the choices Bell has made when we analyse the text as a whole later in the chapter.

As we've seen from these examples, clauses in a paratactic clause complex may be linked to each other simply by adjacency and punctuation. A comma, colon or semi-colon may be the only marker of the structural boundary between clauses, as in:

(17i)He saw the back of me, (17ii)I saw a glimpse of a shadow.

However, in spontaneous speech and less crafted prose, parataxis is commonly signalled also by an accompanying linking word or **conjunction**. For example, Bell could have written:

He saw the back of me, and I saw a glimpse of a shadow.
He saw the back of me, but I saw a glimpse of shadow.

Instead of using a semi-colon between clauses, in this next example Bell could have used the paratactic conjunction *so*:

The experience was spectacularly new to me, so I had nothing to compare it with, no neural circuitry to process similarities, no language for the shock.

Paratactic conjunctions express the logical relationship between two clauses of equal structural status. The commonest paratactic conjunctions are *and, or, so, yet, neither . . . nor, either*

. . . *or*. But there are others as well, as will become clear as we explore logico-semantic meaning in the section below.

Having said that with parataxis either clause could stand alone, there is just one qualifier to add. Consider:

(7i)My computer ran its checks of memory stores (7ii)and drew a blank.

This pair of clauses is a paratactic sequence, even though the second clause could not stand alone as a sentence as it is at the moment. You will realize from your knowledge of Mood structure that the second clause is missing a Subject element. The ellipsis of the Subject can only happen here because readers know to infer that the Subject of the second clause is the same as the Subject of the first clause (you cannot ellipse a Subject from an earlier clause complex, or one that has never been mentioned). The ellipsis of the Subject can be filled in to give:

My computer ran its checks of memory stores, and (it = my computer) drew a blank.

Once the ellipsis is filled in, you can see that each of these clauses is of equal structural status. Bell could have presented this as:

My computer ran its checks of memory stores. It drew a blank.

Since each clause in a paratactic clause complex is of equal status, the only variable is which occurs first. For example, compare:

(17i)He saw the back of me, (17ii)I saw a glimpse of a shadow.
I saw a glimpse of a shadow, he saw the back of me.

Structurally, there is no difference: in each case we have two independent clauses placed adjacent to each other. But of course there *is* a slight difference of meaning simply because the choice of the other order was always available. Bell's decision to place her attacker first is one way of expressing the power he was exercising in the situation.

Coding two-clause complexes

For easy presentation of clause complex analysis, each clause can be shown on a separate line, indented from the left. In the left-hand column we can then display a structural code that captures the relationship between clauses. To show paratactic relations, Halliday proposes a notation system where each paratactic clause in a complex is labelled with an ordinary number (1, 2, 3). Our initial analysis looks like this:

1   (17i)He saw the back of me,
2   (17ii)I saw a glimpse of a shadow

Here is another example from Text 9.1:

1   (2i)The experience was spectacularly new to me;
2   (2ii)I had nothing to compare it with, no neural circuitry to process similarities, no language for the shock.

And here is a paratactic pair from Text 9.2 (this is not the complete clause complex):

1 (15i)But the parts of the mind hold on to that
2 (15ii)and remain vigilant

Our notation in the left-hand column will grow more complicated as we add in multiple clause complexes and the system of logico-semantic relations, but first we need to consider hypotaxis.

Hypotaxis

In hypotaxis, clauses relate to each other in a modifying or dependency relationship. For example:

(1i)While walking home one dry moonless night in 1968 (1ii)I was shot in the back.

In this example there is one clause (the Head clause) which in these simple examples could stand alone as a sentence: *I was shot in the back*. But the other clause (the modifying or dependent clause) could not stand alone as a sentence (*while walking home one dry moonless night in 1968*). The two constitute a hypotactic clause complex. Note that changing the order of the clauses is quite possible (although it changes the effect of the sentence), but it does not change the structural dependency:

I was shot in the back while walking home one dry moonless night in 1968.

In this example, the clause beginning with *while* is still dependent on the main clause. Unlike paratactic clauses which can sometimes occur without explicit markers, almost all hypotactically dependent clauses are linked to their Head clause with explicit structural markers, either hypotactic conjunctions or relative pronouns (*who, which, that*). The exceptions are hypotactic clauses that are intrinsically structurally incomplete, such as non-finite clauses (see discussion below).

The most common **hypotactic conjunctions** include *if, while, because, when*. More will be given when we look at logico-semantic relations.

Halliday uses Greek letters (α, β, γ, δ . . .) to label hypotactic clauses, with α (the alpha symbol) reserved for the Head clause, wherever it occurs. The other Greek letters are then attached in sequential order. With two-clause complexes, this is not difficult. Compare:

α (1i)While walking home one dry moonless night in 1968
β (1ii)I was shot in the back.

β I was shot in the back
α while walking home one dry moonless night in 1968.

Recognizing hypotaxis/parataxis in two-clause complexes

To recognize the difference between parataxis and hypotaxis in two-clause complexes, it helps if you draw on the knowledge you have about the Mood structure of clauses. You should be able to appreciate that **non-finite clauses** (clauses which have not selected for the Mood component of Subject^Finite) are by structural necessity hypotactically dependent: a non-finite clause cannot stand alone because key elements of its Mood structure are realized only in the Head clause. For example, imagine Bell had written:

My computer ran its checks of memory stores, drawing a blank.

Here, the second clause in the complex is non-finite, depending on the Head clause for its Subject (<u>my computer</u>) and the tense component of the Finite (past tense). As the next example shows, the non-finite clause may appear before the Head clause:

Having been struck by the bullet, I traveled forward an extra half-step.

Note that with these non-finites we're not dealing simply with ellipsis of the Subject. Compare our earlier paratactic example with the non-finite variant:

My computer ran its checks of memory stores, and drew a blank.
– paratactic, both clauses finite
My computer ran its checks of memory stores, drawing a blank.
– hypotactic, main clause followed by non-finite clause

In the second, hypotactic non-finite pair, filling in the Subject does not make the clause structurally independent (**it drawing a blank*). Only a structural change to the verbal component (changing the non-finite form *drawing* to the finite form *drew*) will turn the second clause into a possible paratactic clause.

So, while all non-finite clauses are by definition hypotactic at this first level of coding, a **finite** clause may be either paratactic or hypotactic. Again, you can draw a relatively easy distinction between finite clauses that are structurally marked for dependency (and are therefore hypotactic, at least at the primary level of analysis) and those that are not (and are therefore likely to be paratactic). Dependency markers include:

1. relative pronouns: *who, which, that, whose*
2. hypotactic conjunctions: traditionally called 'subordinating conjunctions' exactly because they make the clause they introduce dependent on a main clause (*when, if, where, as, while, before, because, unless, although, even if* . . .)
3. verbal conjunctions: words like *supposing that, granted that, provided that, seeing that,* e.g. *Seeing that you don't agree/we'll postpone the decision.*
4. other markers of dependency, usually prepositional, such as *to* in non-finite clauses (*he revved the car/to get away*), *for* (*she paid the price/for walking home alone*)

By a process of elimination, then, you are left only with finite clauses which contain no explicit markers of dependency. Some of these clauses will be Head clauses in hypotactic complexes. To check, ask: does the clause have other clauses dependent upon it? If so you are looking at the alpha clause in a complex. If not, you are almost certainly looking at paratactically related clauses. Check for any markers of paratactic interdependency. These are:

- paratactic conjunctions: *and, but, so, neither . . . nor, either . . . or*
- punctuation marks: colon, semi-colon, comma

Table 9.1   Halliday's clause nexus (from Halliday and Matthiessen 2004: 376)

	Primary	Secondary
Parataxis	1 (initiating)	2 (continuing)
Hypotaxis	α (dominant)	β (dependent)

Remember that the deciding test is: if you fill in ellipsis (but do *not* convert non-finites to finites), can the clause stand alone as a structurally well-formed sentence?

Summary of taxis

A clause complex consists of two or more interdependent clauses. The interdependency may be either parataxis (equal status) or hypotaxis (dependency) or a combination of both. Each clause complex consists of a primary clause (the initiating clause in a paratactic pair, the Head clause in a hypotactic one) and then any secondary clauses which are interdependent on it. These principles are summarized in Table 9.1.

Halliday describes parataxis and hypotaxis as 'the two basic forms taken by logical relations in natural language' (1994: 224), and points out that we find tactic relations among other grammatical units. At the rank of phrases and groups we can recognize **paratactic phrase/group complexes**:

> Up the street, round the corner and next to the newsagent.
> – three prepositional phrases, paratactically related

and **hypotactic phrase/group complexes**, e.g. the Mood structure of the clause: a sequence of different functional constituents:

Was	*he*	*playing*	*a game?*
Finite	Subject	Predicator	Complement
MOOD		RESIDUE	

We can also recognize **nesting** (a type of structural layering) in word and phrase/group complexes:

> Salmon and cream cheese, mushroom and olives, or eggplant and tomatoes.
> – three paratactically related nominal groups, each consisting of two paratactically related nouns.

Using our indenting method, we could capture this as:

1	1	Salmon
	2	and cream cheese
2	1	mushroom
	2	and olives

3　1　or eggplant
　　2　and tomatoes

Text 9.1 displays several examples of complexing at group/phrase rank. A simple one is:

(19)Speculation about what he was doing is a luxury for later, for now.

Here, there are two prepositional phrases paratactically linked: *for later/for now*. Notice how using this phrase complexing allows Bell to make the contrastive meaning (then/now) in the same clause, instead of having to write:

Speculation about what he was doing is a luxury for later.
Speculation is for now.

Taxis vs embedding

Taxis is a basic language resource, then, for expanding units at any rank to make more meaning at that same rank. Taxis works on a univariate principle: the reiteration of units of the same functional role. Taxis thus contrasts with embedding, also called rank shift. We saw in Chapter Five how embedding allows us to pack more meaning into units, usually by packing a whole clause into a unit of a lower rank (e.g. as a group or within one constituent of a group). For example, in the following clause complexes from Text 9.1, Gail Bell also uses embedding (embedded constituents shown in [[ ]]):

(3i)When the bullet struck (3ii)I traveled forward an extra half-step, (3iii)as if someone [[wielding a broom handle]] had given me a rude shove from behind.
– non-finite clause embedded in the nominal group acting as Subject, as post-modifier of the noun 'someone'

(8i)Soldiers [[who are primed for gun battle]] have told me (8ii)that even in a state of highest combat alert, (8iii)being shot still comes as a surprise.
– finite relative clause embedded in the nominal group acting as Subject, as post-modifier of the noun 'soldiers'

Bell also uses embedding to pack more meaning into clause simplexes:

(19)Speculation [[about what he was doing]] is a luxury for later, for now.
– finite WH-clause embedded in a prepositional phrase, itself part of the nominal group acting as Subject of the clause
(24)Was he playing a game with complexities [[I couldn't begin to imagine?]]
– finite clause embedded in the nominal group acting as Complement, post-modifying the noun 'complexities'

While the principle behind taxis or complexing is expansion, the principle behind embedding is compression. Complexing is more dynamic: it requires little forward planning, as you can simply chain on another unit of the same type. Embedding is more static: it requires some forethought in the construction of the clause, because you have to be ready to pack the extra meanings in at the right slot. Not surprisingly, then, complexing is more characteristic of spontaneous, spoken language or informal written texts, while embedding associates more with formal, careful written text. Halliday suggests that:

> The clause complex is of particular interest in spoken language, because it represents the dynamic potential of the system – the ability to 'choreograph' very long and intricate patterns of semantic movement while maintaining a continuous flow of discourse that is coherent without being constructional. This kind of flow is very uncharacteristic of written language. (Halliday 1994: 224)

But most texts involve an intricate mix of both complexing and embedding, with the dynamic flow of taxis balancing the denser packing of rank shift. Here's just one example from Text 9.1 where Bell uses embedding, clause complexing and phrase/group complexing:

> (2i)The experience was spectacularly new to me; (2ii)I had nothing [[to compare it with]], no neural circuitry [[to process similarities]], no language for the shock.

Here we have two paratactically related clauses. The second clause contains three paratactically related nominal groups (*nothing to compare it with/no neural circuitry to process similarities/no language for the shock*), two of which contain embedded non-finite clauses post-modifying the main nouns. That makes for an awful lot of meaning in one sentence, but note how *apparently* simple the sentence is. It takes careful crafting to make such complexity sound spare.

To fill out this understanding of the meanings of the clause complex, we need to look at the second system in the logical structure of the clause, that of its logico-semantic relations.

The basic opposition: projection vs expansion

While taxis describes the type of interdependency between linked clauses, the system of logico-semantic relations describes the semantic relations, the ways in which clauses that are either independent or dependent build on the experiential meanings of the clauses they relate to.

At primary delicacy, the system of logico-semantics offers a choice between projection and expansion. In **projection**, one of the clauses indicates that someone or something said or thought something; any other clauses in the complex then express what the person or phenomenon said or thought. For example, Diana's story contains two examples where she directly quotes speech:

> (3i)And they rang me up on the Sat- (3ii)this was Saturday night (3iii)and said (3iv)'You've got to come in and have your blood tested against the donor's'.

> (11i)So I said (11ii)'OK', you know, 'be a blood donor after that'.

And in her interview with me, Gail Bell several time reported her thoughts to me:

> (16i)I'm beginning to think (16ii)it's forever, yes,

> (20vi)and I thought (20vii)that we shared some mannerisms, he and I,

In **expansion** the secondary clause builds on the meanings of the primary clause, developing them in several ways. For example:

(1i)While walking home one dry moonless night in 1968 (1ii)I was shot in the back.

Here, the dependent beta clause offers a temporal expansion of the bare statement made in the alpha clause. Bell uses this pattern frequently in Text 9.1:

(3i)When the bullet struck (3ii)I traveled forward an extra half-step, (3iii)as if someone wielding a broom handle had given me a rude shove from behind.

Here the central alpha clause (*I traveled forward an extra half-step*) is first expanded with a temporal clause (*when the bullet struck*), and then also expanded on with a clause expressing the manner of the events (*as if someone . . .*).

Through expanding clause complexes like these, Bell forces us to slow down and really notice, with her, the second-by-second impact of the shooting.

So projection and expansion are the two logical resources through which we can link one clause to another in sequence. Projection is the logico-semantics of quoting and reporting speech or thoughts, while expansion is the logico-semantics of developing on previous meanings. Most of the time it is not difficult to differentiate between projection and expansion: if the clause contains a verb of saying or thinking (or any of their many synonyms), you are probably looking at a projecting relationship. If no verb of saying or thinking is present in your clause, the relationship is likely to be expansion.

Knowing more about the categories of projection and expansion will also help you to identify and understand them.

The system of projection

When people write or talk, particularly when they're telling stories, they frequently want to tell us what was said or thought during the events they are relating. For example, to explain why she found herself donating blood in Geneva, Diana tells us:

(3i)And they rang me up on the Sat- (3ii)this was Saturday night (3iii)and said (3iv)'You've got to come in and have your blood tested against the donor's'.

In the second half of this four-clause complex, Diana quotes for us the words 'they' (presumably the hospital staff) said to her.

Similarly, in the opening of her story about her own shooting, Gail Bell relates her experience to that of others, by reporting what soldiers have told her:

(8i)Soldiers who are primed for gun battle have told me (8ii)that even in a state of highest combat alert, (8iii)being shot still comes as a surprise.

Both of these are examples of projection, where one clause anchors the complex by telling us who said or thought something, which is then linked to a quoting or reporting of what someone said or thought. Projection is thus a resource the grammar offers us for attributing words and ideas to their sources.

The system of projection involves the attribution of either locutions (what someone said) or ideas (what someone thought). The examples above are both projections of locutions, but in her interview with me Gail Bell also used projections with ideas, as she told me about her thoughts. Here are examples with just the projecting clause and its projected clause shown:

> (9i)I suspect that . . . (9iii)that it's part of the greater spectrum of post-traumatic stress disorder.

To *suspect* something is to think it without complete certainty.

> (16i)I'm beginning to think (16ii)it's forever, yes,
>
> (20vi)and I thought (20vii)that we shared some mannerisms, he and I,

In both these examples, the standard mental process verb *think* is used to project Gail's thoughts and opinions.

> . . . (14ii)I'm always very conscious (14iii)of who's doing what where, (14iv)and where everyone is in relation to me

In this example Gail doesn't use the verb *to think*, but *to be very conscious* is a mental process which here then projects what she thinks, which itself takes two clauses to unfold.

Halliday's notation uses a double quotation mark (") to indicate locution and a single quotation mark (') to show ideas.

As the system network (System 9.1) indicates, projection cross-selects for taxis. Thus we can have paratactic projection or hypotactic projection. Here are some simple two-clause complexes of each type, shown with the notation for projection:

Locution
Paratactic locution
i) Projecting clause first:
1   They said
"2   'You've got to have your blood tested'

ii) Projecting clause after projected clause
1   'You've got to have your blood tested,'
"2   they said

Hypotactic locution
α   They said
"β   that I had to have my blood tested against the donor's.

Idea
Paratactic idea
i) projecting clause first
1   I thought to myself
'2   'This is so exciting'.

ii) projected clause first

1	'This is so exciting,'
'2	I thought to myself

Hypotactic idea

α	I thought to myself
β	that it was so exciting.

As these examples show, in paratactic projection what someone thought or said is presented as if it were exactly their words or thoughts. We hear it 'live', so to speak. Traditional grammars usually refer to this as direct speech, but note that in the systemic analysis paratactic projection also includes direct thought.

Projection of locutions

In paratactic projection of locutions, the projecting clause is a verbal process, but a range of verbs can be used, including:

1. the verb *say*
2. verbs specific to different speech functions: i) statements (*tell, remark, observe, point out, report, announce*); ii) questions (*ask, demand, inquire, query*); iii) offers and commands (*suggest, offer, call, order, request, tell, propose, decide*)
3. verbs combining 'say' with some circumstantial element: *reply, explain, protest, continue, interrupt, warn*
4. verbs associated with speech having connotations of various kinds: *insist, complain, cry, shout, boast, murmur, stammer, blare, thunder, moan, yell, fuss*
5. verbs embodying some circumstantial or other semantic feature(s) such as *threaten, vow, urge, plead, warn, promise, agree*
6. verbal processes using verbs of writing: *write, note down, put*

Paratactic projection of locutions is common in fictional narratives, where characters must usually engage in dialogue with each other. Here are some examples from the *The BFG* excerpt by Roald Dahl, first presented in Chapter Two, with the projecting verb underlined:

	(13)Sophie took a small nibble.
1	(14i)'Uggggggggh!'
"2	(14ii)she <u>spluttered</u>.

1	(19i)'It tastes of frogskins!'
"2	(19ii)she <u>gasped</u>.

"1	(21i)'Worse than that!'
2	(21ii)<u>cried</u> the BFG,

1	(23i)'Do we really have to eat it?'
"2	(23ii)Sophie <u>said</u>.

> 1 $_{(28i)}$'Words,'
> <"2> $_{(28ii)}$he <u>said</u>
> 1 $_{(28i)}$'is oh such a twitch-tickling problem to me all my life.'

These examples show that Dahl's preferred style of dialogue is to present the projection first, followed by the projecting clause. He also prefers not to use the simple verb *say*, but to infuse the projecting verb with meanings about the manner in which something is said (*splutter, gasp, cry*), no doubt a strategy used to help his inexperienced readers correctly decode the attitudes and emotions of characters.

In hypotactic locution, what someone thought or said is re-packaged into an indirect form. This is the indirect speech of traditional grammar, but must also include indirect thought. A similar range of verbs is used to project hypotactically, but the projected clause(s) will be marked for dependency on the alpha projecting clause (usually by *that* or *WH* words), and changes to the tense and mood must be made. For example, note what happens if we convert Dahl's paratactic dialogue to hypotaxis. With *say* examples, the conversion is relatively easy. Note that we tend to move the projecting clause to first position, and we usually lose some of the 'colour' of direct speech:

> α   Sophie asked
> "β   whether they really had to eat it.

In the next example, the locution is split up and presented around the inserted projecting clause:

> "β   Words,
> <α>   he said,
> "β   had been a problem to him all his life.

When the verb is a colouring of *say*, hypotactic locution begins to sound forced:

> α   She gasped
> "β   that it tasted of frogskins.

> α   The BFG cried
> "β   that it was worse than that.

And when the locution is an expression of emotion, hypotaxis requires a rewording. *'Uggggggh!' she spluttered* needs to become:

> α   Sophie spluttered
> "β   that the taste was disgusting.

While hypotactic locution is less successful at bringing characters to life, it is more effective at summarizing the import of what someone said.

Of course, the same verbs that can be used to project can also be used in single clause structures as well. Compare these examples:

Single clause, verbal process	Projecting clause complex: paratactic	Projecting clause complex: hypotactic
She remarked scathingly on his new haircut.	*'Your new haircut is appalling,'* // *she remarked.*	*She remarked* // *that his new haircut was appalling.*
He threatened her with violence.	*'I'll kill you!'* // *he threatened.*	*He threatened that he would kill her.*
I'll put you down for Monday.	*'You'll do Monday,'* // *I'll put down.*	*I'll put down* // *that you'll do Monday.*

Projection of ideas

In projections of ideas, the projecting clause is typically a mental process. When what is being projected is information (what we thought, for example), the typical verbs used are mental processes of cognition: *know, believe, think, wonder, reflect, surmise, guess* (in the sense of calcuate mentally). But we can also project not what we *know* but what we *want, like, hope* or *fear*. Thus, some mental processes of reaction can also project:

α   I wish
'β   it had never happened to me.

Finally, we are not always simply recording our own mental activity, but sometimes urging other people to perform mental activity. For example, in the first Crying Baby text (Text 1.1 in Chapter One) we find:

α   Remember
'β   that babies get bored

Free indirect speech or free indirect discourse

One final type of projection occurs in third-person narration, where one character is used to 'focalize' the narration or a part of it. In free indirect discourse (FID), the narrator (who rationally, we know, is separate from the 3rd person character they are describing) slips into what seems to be the words and tone of the character. When FID is operating, the boundary between narrator and character becomes blurred. Look again at these sentences from Text 2.4, 'The Story of an Hour', from Chapter Two:

> (25)Now her bosom rose and fell tumultuously. (26i)She was beginning to recognize this thing that was approaching to possess her, (26ii)and she was striving to beat it back with her will – (26iii)as powerless as her two white slender hands would have been.
> (27i)When she abandoned herself (27ii)a little whispered word escaped her slightly parted lips. (28i)She said it over and over under her breath: (28ii)'free, free, free!' (29)The vacant stare and the look of terror that had followed it went from her eyes. (30)They stayed keen and bright. (31i)Her pulses beat fast, (31ii)and the coursing blood warmed and relaxed every inch of her body.

In this section of the text we have a strong sense of the presence of a narrator, through whose description we have access to Mrs Mallard's experiences. But as the emotions increase, the narrator seems to merge with Mrs Mallard herself:

₍₄₀₎And yet she had loved him – sometimes. ₍₄₁₎Often she had not. ₍₄₂₎What did it matter! _(43i)What could love, the unsolved mystery, count for in face of this possession of self-assertion _(43ii)which she suddenly recognized as the strongest impulse of her being!

We have here a strong impression that it is Mrs Mallard who is thinking/saying *'What did it matter! What could love . . .'* rather than an objective, external narrator. We could make this source explicit if we filled out these elliptical sentences:

> And yet she had loved him, she knew, sometimes.
> Often, she knew, she had not.
> What did it matter, thought Mrs Mallard
> What could love count for, she thought.

Both these filled-out versions and the elliptical versions Chopin uses are examples of FID. As Halliday points out, grammatically FID falls between paratactic and hypotactic projection:

> It has some of the features of each of the other two types. The structure is paratactic, so the projected clause has the form of an independent clause retaining the mood of the quoted form; but it is a report and not a quote, so time and person reference are shifted. (Halliday and Matthiessen 2004: 465)

For example, with *What could love count for, she thought* we have parataxis, but no markings of quotation and a tense shift in the quoted clause. You can see the difference if you compare *What could love count for* (FID) with *'What can love count for?' she thought* which would be normal paratactic projection of idea.

Narratologist Rimmon-Kenan (2003: 111–17) points out that because of FID's capacity to reproduce the idiolect of a character's speech or thought but within the narrator's reporting language, it is often used in stream of consciousness writing (what is sometimes called 'indirect interior monologue'). When FID comes into action, it is not always possible for the reader to determine who is thinking what, or what the source of the discourse is:

> FID enhances the bivocality or polyvocality of the text by bringing into play a plurality of speakers and attitudes . . . In cases of an ambiguity concerning the speaker, it also dramatizes the problematic relationships between any utterance and its origin. (Rimmon-Kenan 2003: 115)

Because sourcing is ambiguous, Rimmon-Kenan argues that FID can produce a 'double-edged effect':

> On the one hand, the presence of a narrator as distinct from the character may create an ironic distancing. On the other hand, the tinting of the narrator's speech with the character's language or mode of experience may promote an empathetic identification on the part of the reader. . . . Perhaps most interesting are cases of ambiguity, where the reader has no means of choosing between the ironic and the empathetic attitude. (Rimmon-Kenan 2003: 115)

While Kate Chopin is using FID empathetically (to encourage us to identify with the focalizing character and share her emotional experience), in writers like James Joyce FID is often used ironically (see, for example, his short story 'Araby' in *Dubliners*).

Projected ideas vs embedded facts

This is the point to remind you of one type of structure that looks like projection but isn't. This is the embedded Fact clauses, first discussed in Chapter Eight (Transitivity). Compare the following two examples involving mental processes:

> Diana thought that she should become a blood donor.
> Diana regretted that she'd become a blood donor.

The first is hypotactic idea and should be analysed as follows:

α	Diana thought
'β	that she should become a blood donor

But the second, in Halliday's analysis, is not. It is one clause, a mental process, analysed as follows:

Diana	*regretted*	*{{that she'd become a blood donor.}}*
Senser	Pr:mental	Phenomenon:fact

What is the difference between these two? Semantically, in the first we have a verb of cognition (*thought*), which construes its Senser (*Diana*) as capable of agentive mental activity. The outcome of her mental activity is a complete proposition, a clause in its own right. That projected clause cannot be analysed as an embedded constituent in the first clause because we cannot insert any of the Fact nouns before it:

> *Diana thought [the fact] that she should become a blood donor.

But in the second example, we have one of those reversible mental processes noted in Chapter Eight. We can construct a pair:

Diana	*regretted*		*{{that she'd become a blood donor.}}*
Senser	Pr:mental		Phenomenon:fact
Subject	Finite	Predicator	Complement
MOOD			RESIDUE

That she'd become a blood donor	*annoyed*		*Diana.*
Senser	Pr:mental		Phenomenon:fact
Subject	Finite	Predicator	Complement
MOOD			RESIDUE

This suggests that *that she'd become a blood donor* is not a projection but instead an embedded constituent of the clause, and we can confirm this by inserting the implicit Fact-noun:

Diana regretted [the fact] that she'd become a blood donor.

How can you identify these embedded 'facts'? There are several tests:
1. the type of projecting verb: mental processes of cognition usually project ideas, while mental processes of reaction (the reversible type) are usually followed by a Phenomenon:fact. That is, they do not project. You can recognize this sub-type of mental process because you can find a semantic match for the verb that allows you to form an active clause with the Phenomenon:fact made Subject. For example, *regret/annoy* constitute such a pair:

Diana	*regretted*	*{{that she'd become a blood donor.}}*
Subject/Senser		Phenomenon:fact

{{That she'd become a blood donor}}	*annoyed*	*Diana.*
Phenomenon:fact		Subject/Senser

2. you cannot form a single passive clause from a projecting clause complex:

*That she'd become a blood donor was thought by Diana.

3. if you're dealing with an embedded fact as Phenomenon, you can insert the Head noun 'the fact' after the mental process:

Diana regretted [the fact] that she'd become a blood donor.

But not

*Diana thought [the fact] that she'd become a blood donor.

The grammatical difference between projection and embedded Facts construes some mental processes as less agentive. Whereas we are in control (the grammar suggests) of processes of cognition, we almost undergo processes of reaction.

The system of expansion

While the projection system allows us to incorporate locutions and ideas into clause complexes, the system of expansion allows us to develop on the experiential meanings of a clause in three main ways: through **elaboration**, **extension** or **enhancement** of its meanings. As we saw in Chapter Two, elaboration is a relationship of restatement, extension is a relationship of addition or variation, and enhancement is, well, everything else (relations of time, space, cause, condition).

As we know from Chapter Two, the logico-semantic system of expansion is not confined to relationships in the clause complex. It also describes cohesive relations of conjunction.

But there are important differences between what we were doing in Chapter Two and what we're doing here.

In clause complex analysis, we analyse the **structural relationships between clauses within sentences**, while in conjunctive cohesion we analyse the **non-structural relationships between sentences within text**. Although the range of semantic relations turns out to be similar, the domain of clause complex relations is different from the domain of conjunctive cohesion.

Similarly, we find both overlap and difference in the markers of these logico-semantic relations. Many of the words which realize structural, clause complex relations are the same class of words (conjunctions) that we analysed in Chapter Two. Words like *so, but, that is, thus* can function both to link clauses into clause complexes, but also cohesively, to link sentences to other sentences. But when these words link clauses into clause complexes they are operating to create a structural relation. When they link sentences or even larger units of text such as paragraphs to other sentences/paragraphs etc., they are functioning non-structurally, as was explained in Chapter Two. There are also many words which function only to express structural relations between clauses and cannot function to create cohesive links.

There is no need to be confused or surprised to find logico-semantic relations of expansion appearing in two different types of analyses. In fact, Halliday suggests that because logico-semantic categories reflect the 'natural logic' of English, the semantic relations of expansion operate at many ranks and between many units of the lexico-grammar. He summarizes these different realizations of expansion in a table in Halliday and Matthiessen 2004: 598–9. Other systemicists have also found that logico-semantic categories provide powerful descriptions of a range of discourse phenomena (e.g. Eggins and Slade 1997, Martin and Rose 2003).

As mentioned in Chapter Two, Halliday proposes a clever notation for labelling each type of expansion relationship. The mathematical signs used are suggestive of the meanings expressed:

> **Elaboration**: signified by =
>
> **Extension**: signified by +
>
> **Enhancement**: signified by x

Halliday and Matthiessen (2004) and Martin *et al.* (1997) provide many pages of discussion and examples of all the expansion relations. Here I provide the minimum you will need to analyse and interpret each of these relation types.

Elaboration: =

In elaboration, one clause elaborates on the meaning of another by further specifying or describing it in one of three ways:
i) by **exposition**: 'in other words'. The secondary clause restates the core meaning of the primary clause in different words, to present it from another point of view, or perhaps just to reinforce the message. For example:

    1   (10i)So I'm sort of hypervigilant, you know,

    =2   (10ii)I'm always on the alert,

Typical conjunctions which make this relationship explicit are *or (rather), in other words, that is to say, i.e.* But in paratactic pairs there is often no conjunction used, with a comma or colon or tone boundary present. You can test for this relation by inserting 'that is' or 'I mean'.

ii) by **exemplification**: 'for example'. The secondary clause develops the meaning of the primary clause by becoming more specific about it, often citing an actual example:

> 1   She took the fastest route home;
> =2   she took the shortcut near the river.

Explicit conjunctions are *for example, for instance, in particular, e.g.*

iii) by **clarification**: 'to be precise'. The secondary clause clarifies the primary clause, backing it up with some form of explanation or explanatory comment. Typical conjunctions include *in fact, actually, indeed, at least, what I mean is.*

Here's a slightly more complex example:

> 1   (17iv) it's like having asthma or something
> =2 1   (17v)some days it's good
>   +2   (17vi)and some days it's not good.

Here, Bell sets up the simile in clause iv): that having PTSD is like having asthma. She then explains that claim by restating it in more precise terms, but the elaboration takes two clauses to achieve because it involves a contrast between *some days* and *other days*. Note how we use the indented coding to capture this nesting.

Common to all these types of elaboration is that the secondary clause does not introduce a new element of meaning, but rather provides a further characterization of a meaning that is already there, restating it, clarifying, refining it, or adding a descriptive attribute or comment. The = notation used to represent elaboration captures its meaning of 'restatement'.

Remember that expansion cross-selects with taxis, so that we can have paratactic elaboration or hypotactic elaboration. Compare:

> (2i)The experience was spectacularly new to me; (2ii)I had nothing to compare it with

> The experience was spectacularly new to me, being a completely unfamiliar sensation.

In the first example, we have our two independent clauses (parataxis) where the second clause more or less restates or rewords the meaning of the first clause. We could capture this by inserting an explicit conjunction *that is* or *I mean to say*. In the second example, a similar meaning is made, but now the second clause (a non-finite) is structurally dependent on the first clause, giving a hypotactic elaborating clause complex. Note that because the Subject of the non-finite clause must be assumed to be the same as Subject of the main clause (*the experience*), we must change the wording of the non-finite clause slightly. The following, though common in spoken language, is strictly speaking grammatically faulty, since the implied Subject of the second clause is now *I*:

> *The experience was spectacularly new to me, having nothing to compare it with.

Hypotactic elaboration is typically expressed through the structure that is known traditionally as the **non-defining relative clause**, either **finite** or **non-finite**. A non-defining relative clause adds a further characterization for something that is taken to be already fully specific. The domain of a non-defining relative may be a whole clause or any of its constituents. Three types of non-defining clauses are common:

1. *which* non-defining relative clauses, whose domain is either the whole of the primary clause or some part of it that is more than a nominal group:

> The experience changed my life, which is not surprising really.

> – here we have a non-defining relative clause elaborating on the whole of the previous clause. These are always structured $\alpha^\wedge\beta$.

2. *which, that, who, whose, that* relative clauses whose domain is a nominal group:

> The experience changed my life, which until then had been quite ordinary.

> – this is a non-defining relative clause elaborating on the nominal group *my life.*

There's an example of this type of structure in the middle of an intricate clause complex in Text 9.2:

> $_{(10v)}$at a deeper level it is a sort of hypervigilance $_{(10vi)}$that people with PTSD seem to suffer from.

Here the non-defining relative clause in (10vi) elaborates the nominal group *a sort of hypervigilance.*
   When the nominal group is non-final in the primary clause, the secondary clause is often enclosed so as to follow immediately after it, as in:

> The experience, which was spectacularly new to me, took me seconds to understand.

Here the structure is $\alpha^\wedge<\beta>^\wedge\alpha$, which can be shown as:

α	The experience,
$<=\beta>$	which was spectacularly new to me,
α	took me seconds to understand.

3. clauses with *which, when* or *where*, having as domain some expression of time or place:

α	She was shot quite late at night,
$=\beta$	which is when those suburban back streets are deserted.

Non-defining vs defining relative clauses

The only trick with non-defining relative clauses is not to confuse them with their close relative, the **defining relative clause**. The two are different in meaning and expression. Compare:

> ***non-defining relative clause***
>   The girl, who was wearing new maroon shoes, was shot in the back.

    – the non-defining relative clause elaborates on some descriptive detail about *the girl*

defining relative clause
    The girl who was wearing new maroon shoes was shot in the back.

    – this tells us which girl was shot: the one wearing the maroon shoes, not the one in the black shoes.

As these examples show, the non-defining relative clause is an expanding clause complex, but the defining relative clause is an embedded structure in the nominal group. In writing, the non-defining relative clause is marked off by punctuation (paired commas if it's inserted into the alpha clause, or a dash if it's appended at the end). Defining relative clauses are *not* separated by punctuation from the noun or nominal group they modify. These punctuation distinctions reflect the intonational differences we make in speech: non-defining relative clauses are usually produced on a separate tone group from the alpha clause; defining relative clauses share the same tone group.

Extension: +: is added to

The second type of expansion relation is that of extension. In extension, one clause extends the meaning of another by adding something new to it. Halliday identifies two main categories: **addition** and **variation**.

1. **Addition**: one process is simply joined on to another, with no implication of any causal or temporal relationship between them. The relationship is simply additive (*and*), negative addition (*nor*) or adversative (*but*). For example, when Di says:

    1     $_{(5i)}$And I was really impressed
    +2 $_{(5ii)}$and you know I had to give blood

she is simply joining on a second event telling us how she feels. Similarly, when Gail Bell says:

    1     $_{(15i)}$But the parts of the mind hold on to that
    +2 $_{(15ii)}$and remain vigilant

she is simply extending on her first clause. When she later says of PTSD:

    1     $_{(17v)}$some days it's good
    +2 $_{(17vi)}$and some days it's not good.

she is now adding a contrasting extension. She could just as easily have introduced the second clause with *but*.

2. **Variation**: one clause is represented as being in total or partial replacement of another. The meaning here, and common conjunctions, are *or, instead of* or *except for*. For example:

    1     $_{(9i)}$The body is lifted up
    +2 $_{(9ii)}$or thrown sideways by some mad poltergeist

All these examples of **paratactic extension** (shown as 1 + 2) are what traditional grammars often refer to as **co-ordination** of clauses.

Hypotactic extension (alpha + beta) expresses the same two meanings of either addition or variation, but the extending clause is dependent and may be finite or non-finite. If finite, hypotactic clauses of addition are introduced by *whereas, while*. For example, here's the analysis of a hypotactic variant of an earlier example:

> α   Some days it's good,
> +β while some days it's not good

Hypotactic extension, especially non-finite, is often introduced by a preposition or preposition group functioning conjunctively, e.g. *besides, apart from, instead of, other than, without.*

Enhancing: x: *is multiplied by*

The largest sub-category of expansion is enhancement. In this relation, one clause enhances the meaning of another by qualifying it in one of a number of possible ways: by reference to time, space, manner, cause or condition (including consequence). Note these meanings are similar to those expressed by Circumstances in the Transitivity structure of the clause. In fact enhancement can be thought of as a 'next step' in developing circumstantial meanings: if the circumstantial information is sufficiently important, it may be taken out of a single clause and expanded into an enhancing clause complex.

Again, enhancement can be either paratactic or hypotactic, and if hypotactic, either finite or non-finite. Halliday and Matthiessen (2004: 410–22) provides extensive examples and discussion of all the sub-types. Here I just present some examples of the principal sub-types, where possible taken from texts presented in Chapters One to Nine:

Temporal: when? at what time?
i) same time

> xβ Just when I feared we would have to turn back,
> α   I saw a light that looked like a fire.

ii) different time

> 1   At first I was proud to do it,
> x2 then nervous
> x3 and now I'm terrified.

Spatial: where? whereabouts?

> α   Donovan was hunting her,
> xβ wherever she might go.

Manner: how? in what way? by what means? like what?

> α   (63i)It was Brently Mallard who entered, a little travel-stained,
> xβ (63ii)composedly carrying his grip-sack and umbrella.

α	His gaze ran down her body,
xβ	lingering,
xγ	touching,
xδ	seeking

Causal

i) cause: reason

α	I ducked,
xβ	sending him over my back and into the fire.

ii) cause: purpose

xβ	(1i)Knowing that Mrs Mallard was afflicted with a heart trouble,
α	(1ii)great care was taken . . .

Conditional and Concessive

conditional:

α	A trip, reunion or important talk that you could not fit in last month will be more straightforward or enjoyable
xβ	if you wait until November.

xβ	If you don't wait until November,
α	you could find yourself in trouble.

concessive:

α	Nobody paid any attention to her,
xβ	despite her being in charge of the whole thing.

Analysing longer clause complexes: mixed taxis, nesting, ellipsis

As you will have realized by now, in real texts many clause complexes involve more than two clauses. Once a clause complex gets over two clauses, the possibilities arise for a switch in taxis and/or an interweaving of projection and expansion relations. Clauses can also be elliptical, and in spoken language sometimes abandoned or incomplete. When you analyse real clause complexes, it can help you to keep in mind three guiding principles:

1. if taxis changes, you'll need to recognize another layer of structure (i.e. another level of indenting in your analysis)
2. if projection occurs as well as expansion in the same clause complex, you'll need to recognize at least one more layer of structure
3. if taxis does *not* change, you need to test for nesting to determine whether you have a sequence of clauses at the same layer of structure or not.

In other words, with complexes that switch taxis, and which move between projection and expansion, we need to recognize nesting or 'internal bracketing'. We first came across internal bracketing in Chapter Five, where we saw structures like this:

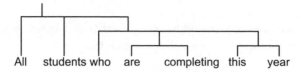

Here we noted that we need an extra bracket to show that [*who are completing this year*] belong together, and together function to fill one slot. Similarly, [*this year*] constitutes one group of words, distinct at this lower level from [are completing]. What we were recognizing then was that some constituents at word rank were more closely related to other adjacent constituents than they were to non-adjacent constituents at the same rank: *this* was more closely related to *year* than to *completing*.

The same principle applies with clause complexes: some clauses in the complex may be directly tied to an adjacent clause, together with which they are then in turn related to another clause. This is **nesting**.

Consider this clause complex:

(4i)One minute I'd been walking with intent (4ii)(I was late), (4iii)the next I was off balance, (4iv)faltering towards a full stop.

Four clauses, but it might strike you the clause complex falls logically into two parts, based on the contrast it sets up between *one minute* and *the next*:

One minute I'd been walking with intent (I was late)	the next I was off balance, faltering towards a full stop

Now you can see that each part of this two-part structure itself then subdivides into two. The clause *I was late* relates very closely to *One minute I'd been walking with intent*, in fact it's an enhancement of that clause (implied is *because I was late*), and is not directly related to the second part of the structure. Similarly, *faltering towards a full stop* is really tied to *the next I was off balance*, as a clarification of that, rather than having a direct tie to either of the first two clauses. Here's how we capture this nesting:

1	1	(4i)One minute I'd been walking with intent
	x2	(4ii)(I was late),
x2	α	(4iii)the next I was off balance
	=β	(4iv)faltering towards a full stop.

How can you figure this out in a more principled way? Well, you can apply exactly the same techniques you used to identify nested constituents in Chapter Five: movability and deletion.

The movability test

If you change the order around, what bits seem to need to move together? For example, to change the order here you'd get something like:

The second moment I was off balance, faltering towards a full stop, but the first moment I'd been walking with intent (I was late).

You don't get:

*The second moment I was off balance, (I was late), faltering towards a full stop, but the first moment I'd been walking with intent.

The deletion test

If you delete one element of structure, what else goes or stays? For example, if you try to delete *One minute I'd been walking with intent*, you'll find that what you're left with doesn't make sense:

*I was late, the next I was off balance, faltering towards a full stop.

You also can't say:

*One minute I'd been walking with intent (I was late), faltering towards a full stop.

But you can say:

One minute I'd been walking with intent, the next I was off balance, faltering towards a full stop.

And

One minute I'd been walking with intent (I was late), the next I was off balance.

So, your internal bracketing tests will show you the layers of structure you need to recognize in expanding clause complexes. The same tests work with projecting complexes. For example:

(8i)Soldiers [[who are primed for gun battle]] have told me (8ii)that even in a state of highest combat alert, (8iii)being shot still comes as a surprise.

You'll recognize that the first clause sets up a projection of locution (the verb *told*). Now ask: just what was she told? The answer is: all the rest of the clause complex. In other words, the locution itself consists of two clauses, and those two clauses are then more closely related to each other than each is to the projecting alpha clause. You can test that claim by trying to move each of the following clauses independently:

*That even in a state of highest combat alert, soldiers have told me being shot still comes as a surprise.
*Being shot still comes as a surprise soldiers have told me that even in a state of highest combat alert.

And you'll find that the only clause you can delete without problems is *that even in a state of highest combat alert*. Here's the way to capture the nested structure:

α		(8i)Soldiers [[who are primed for gun battle]] have told me
"β	xβ	(8ii)that even in a state of highest combat alert,
	α	(8iii)being shot still comes as a surprise.

You can now appreciate the basis for the shorthand principles suggested on page 284. After a couple of essential clarifications, I'll demonstrate these principles at work by coding some intricate clause complexes from Texts 9.1 and 9.2.

A note on and *and* but *and implicit conjunctions*

Although explicit conjunctions can help you to identify the type of logico-semantic relation operating, you need to realize that:

i) some conjunctions can express more than one logico-semantic meaning
ii) some logico-semantic categories are implied rather than expressed directly.

An obvious example of the first situation is the conjunction *but*, which can express either a meaning of extension or of enhancement. It can help to sort this out if you keep in mind the different sub-types of extension *but* can express, in contrast to its enhancing meaning. Drawing on Martin *et al.* (1997: 186–7), here's a guide:

Extending *but*
1. adversative (or contrasting) meaning: try substituting the conjunctions *in contrast, by contrast, on the other hand*:
example from Text 9.1:

in that pause where visual contact might have been made *but* wasn't

example from Text 1.3:

(31)Luckily I didn't have that with the second baby *but* the first one was that typical colicky sort of stuff from about five o'clock.

2. replacive: occurs with negative polarity structures. Trying substituting *instead, rather*:

It isn't that Gail Bell did anything to provoke the attack, *but* just that she was in the wrong place at the wrong time.

3. subtractive: meaning of *except*:

(29i)I almost wrote (29ii)'he gunned the car', (29iii)*but* it was me, the girl in the new maroon shoes, he gunned.

'As I am telling you before, I know exactly what words I am wanting to say, *but* somehow or other they is always getting squiff-squiddled around.'

If none of these alternatives seems right, you may be looking at an enhancing use of *but*.

4. enhancing *but*:

Martin *et al.* refer to this meaning as 'frustrated cause': *but* here indicates 'that a situation does not cause the effect it could be expected to have' (Martin *et al.* 1997: 186). Perhaps the closest gloss is *yet, despite all that*:

example from Text 1.1:

(2i)You feed him, (2ii)you change him, (2iii)you nurse him, (2iv)you try to settle him, (2v)*but* the minute you put him down (2vi)he starts to howl.

example from Text 1.2:

(8i)Counselling about normal crying may relieve guilt (8ii)and diminish concerns, (8iii)*but* for some the distress caused by the crying cannot be suppressed by logical reasoning.

Not only can one conjunction express a variety of logico-semantic relations, but sometimes the real logico-semantic relation between clauses is left implicit. We've seen how the paratactic elaboration relationship is frequently not expressed by a conjunction at all, but perhaps just by a punctuation or intonation marker. Slightly more confusing, though, are the times when the conjunction *and* is used in what are really enhancing logico-semantic complexes. For example:

(13i)When that pulse of comprehension arrived, (13ii)I turned (13iii)and ran for my life.

Although the conjunction *and* in (13iii) might lead you to code this as a relationship of extension, look more closely and you'll see that this is really an enhancing clause complex. Implicit 'behind' the *and* is the temporal meaning *then*: the logic connecting these two events/clauses is one of temporal sequence. The accurate analysis is in fact:

β		(13i)When that pulse of comprehension arrived,
α	1	(13ii)I turned
	x2	(13iii)and ran for my life.

In the following example, despite the different markers or absence of markers, we have a series of enhancing temporal relations:

xβ		(28i)As I ran away
α	1	(28ii)he revved the motor of his car,
	x2	(28iii)spun gravel
	x3	(28iv)and sped out of sight

Sorting out non-finites

Although non-finite clauses are by definition hypotactic, it is sometimes difficult to decide which type of expansion they express because they can express elaboration, extension or enhancement. The recommended procedure is to turn the non-finite clause into its most closely related finite form. The correspondence is then as follows:

1. if the finite form is a non-defining relative clause, the non-finite is elaborating;
2. if it is a co-ordinate clause (introduced by *and, but, or*), the non-finite is extending;
3. if it is an enhancing clause, the non-finite is enhancing.

For example, Roald Dahl is very fond of non-finite clauses in his descriptions of dialogue between characters. Here's one example:

(10i)'No, thank you,' (10ii)Sophie said, (10iii)backing away.

How do we code the non-finite clause *backing away*? If we turn it into a finite clause we get *as she backed away*, which is clearly an enhancing relation of time. So the correct analysis is:

1		(10i)'No, thank you,'
"2	α	(10ii)Sophie said,
	xβ	(10iii)backing away.

The next example is also clearly enhancing:

1		(21i)'Worse than that!'
"2	α	(21ii)cried the BFG,
	xβ	(21iii)roaring with laughter. (*as he roared with laughter*)

But in the next example the non-finite clause is less clear-cut: it could be glossed either as a relative clause (elaborating) or as a temporal enhancement:

(39i)'You do?' (39ii)cried the BFG, (39iii)suddenly brightening. (*who brightened suddenly* or *as he brightened suddenly*)

Dahl's repeated emphasis on temporal sequence in his dialogic passages suggests that the enhancing analysis is more convincing. But the following example from 'Fatal Alaska' (Text 2.5) is clearly elaborating:

α	My other companion was still in the plane,
=β	looking like it was he who had been attacked.

The change to a finite form here gives a non-defining relative clause: *My companion, who looked like it was he who had been attacked, was still in the plane.*

Least frequent are extending non-finites. Here is an analysed example:

+β	Instead of phoning her father for a lift
α	that night Gail Bell chose to walk home alone.

An equivalent finite form shows the extending relation: *While she usually phoned her father for a lift, that night Gail Bell chose to walk home alone.*

Where the taxis and logico-semantic link is unclear

Because spoken language is produced spontaneously, speakers sometimes grope for words, stumble, and then change their minds. For example:

> (9i)And then I stayed up all night (9ii)and watched this um operation taking place (9iii)and fortunately her umbilical artery hadn't closed (9iv)so because I mean all the other things would have been minute

In introducing her final clause Diana uses three different conjunctions: *so* (enhancing: cause/consequence), *because* (enhancing: cause), *I mean* (elaborating). Two (*so, I mean*) are paratactic, while *because* is hypotactic. How do you code this? There is no clear answer, but it's probably wisest to code according to the speaker's *final* choice, in this case *I mean*, paratactic elaboration:

> 1   (9i)And then I stayed up all night
> x2   (9ii)and watched this um operation taking place
> +3   (9iii)and fortunately her umbilical artery hadn't closed
> =4   (9iv)so because I mean all the other things would have been minute

Analysing intricate clause complexes

Let me now demonstrate these categories and principles of clause complex analysis by taking you step-by-step through four of the most elaborate clause complexes in Text 9.1, starting with the simplest:

Example 1:

> (9i)I suspect that (9ii)having now done quite a bit of research for *Shot* (9iii)that it's part of the greater spectrum of post-traumatic stress disorder.

You should notice right away that there's a mental process in (9i) so we're dealing with projection. But just what is projected? What Gail actually suspects is only (9iii), and clause (9ii) is a kind of aside, an insertion she slips in to justify what she's about to reveal. In a written version Gail might well have reordered the clauses:

> Having now done quite a bit of research for *Shot*, I suspect that it's part of the greater spectrum of post-traumatic stress disorder.

This reordering would make the logical relations more apparent: what we have is a non-finite dependent clause (*Having now done . . .*), hypotactically related to the Head clause (*I suspect*), which is a mental process clause projecting as an idea the final clause (*that it's part of . . .*). The relation between the non-finite and the Head clause is one of enhancement because the nearest finite equivalent would be *now that I have done . . .*, i.e. a relation of time. To capture these relations you need to show two levels of analysis:

> α   α   (9i)I suspect that
>   xβ   (9ii)having now done quite a bit of research for *Shot*

'β   (9iii)that it's part of the greater spectrum of post-traumatic stress disorder.

Example 2:

(14i)I mean if I go out to restaurants or social events or anywhere really (14ii)I'm always very conscious (14iii)of who's doing what where, (14iv)and where everyone is in relation to me (14v)and I now realize (14vi)that that scanning and vigilant behaviour relates to a vestige of the old trauma (14vii)which is – (14viii)you know how old it is now.

This one is very complex, involving both parataxis and hypotaxis, projection and expansion, and an incomplete clause (14vii). First, sort out the nesting: ask which clauses relate more closely than others? It can help to make explicit all the logical relations, by adding in any extra conjunctions (e.g. *If I go out to restaurants, then I'm always very conscious . . .*). Notice just what belongs with the 'then' part of the complex:

If I go out to restaurants or social events or anywhere really	(then) I'm always very conscious of who's doing what where, and where everyone is in relation to me

Next, work out the boundary and extent of the two projections:

I'm always very conscious	of who's doing what where, and where everyone is in relation to me [all of this is what she's conscious of]
and I now realize	that scanning and vigilant behaviour relates to a vestige of the old trauma which is – you know how old it is now [all of this is what she realizes]

Now you have a picture of the nesting or layering you have to capture in your complex. You know now that there have to be two main complexes in the far left-hand line, and that there will be at least one, probably two, further levels of indenting to tease apart the subsidiary relationships. Note any markers of dependency or independency (underline the *if* in 14i, the *that* in 14vi, the *which* in 14vii). Now start analysing from the top. Start in the far left-hand box, then move in a level every time you need to recognize a new layer. When you get to the incomplete clause (14vii), you'll need to decide if you think there's a change of taxis from (14vii) to (14viii). I'm suggesting no – that you treat (14viii) as hypotactic, like (14vii). Check the marginal notation on page 262 for my suggested analysis.

Example 3:

(17i)I think (17ii)all that changes are your coping mechanisms, (17iii)and it's some days . . . (17iv) it's like having asthma or something (17v)some days it's good (17vi)and some days it's not good.

Again we have to worry about the scope of the projection (ask: what exactly does she think?), and how to treat the incomplete clause (is it part of the projection?). There's really no way of resolving this – like many verbal acts, this one has an indeterminacy that causes no problem to the interactants at the time but can send analysts mad later. Here's what I suggest:

1	α		(17i)I think
	'β		(17ii)all that changes are your coping mechanisms,
+2			(17iii)and it's some days . . .
=3	1		(17iv)it's like having asthma or something
	=2	1	(17v)some days it's good
		+2	(17vi)and some days it's not good.

Note that I've suggested here that the projection ends after (17ii), but that the projected pair (17i and 17ii) are linked by expansion to the next clause. I've interpreted (17iv) as a restatement of the incomplete (17iii), which is then elaborated in a nested two-clause complex.

Example 4:

(20i)An old school friend (20ii)whose husband was in Vietnam (20iii)and he's an extremely damaged man, (20iv)as many vets are, (20v)and I was sort of watching him, almost in a clinical sense, (20vi)and I thought (20vii)that we shared some mannerisms, he and I, (20viii)you know fiddling with our fingers quite a lot, (20ix)and never really looking comfortable in your chair.

This one's a real challenge. To start with, you'll wonder why I've shown what looks like a nominal group only as a clause (20i). I'm reading this as an elliptical clause (=*I had an old school friend to dinner*), cohesively (but not tactically) related to the previous clause. The clause complex only makes sense if we assume that ellipsis, and since I had no trouble understanding Gail at the time, I assume I did 'read in' the ellipsis as she spoke:

1	α			(20i)An old school friend[6]
	=β			(20ii)whose husband was in Vietnam
+2	α			(20iii)and he's an extremely damaged man,
	=β			(20iv)as many vets are,
+3				(20v)and I was sort of watching him, almost in a clinical sense,
+4	α			(20vi)and I thought
	'β	α		(20vii)that we shared some mannerisms, he and I,
		=β	α	(20viii)you know fiddling with our fingers quite a lot,
			+β	(20ix)and never really looking comfortable in your chair.

One final characteristic of logical relations in intricate complexes needs to highlighted. It occurs in a sequence like the following, from Text 9.1:

1				(15i)I saw a car and a shape at the steering wheel,
=2	α			(15ii)only as much as the eye will register
		xβ	1	(15iii)when you swivel your neck
			x2	(15iv)and glance over your shoulder.

The structure here involves a first clause which is then elaborated on through restatement. We could make this explicit by inserting a conjunction and filling out the ellipsed Mood element at the start of clause (ii): *In other words I saw only as much as the eye will register. . .* Clauses (iii) – (iv) are all part of the elaboration (none can move independently), so we are dealing here with a nested structure. If you apply your tests, you'll see that the elliptical second clause (*only as much as the eye will register*) must be the alpha to the hypotactic enhancing sequence (iii): *when you swivel your neck.* Finally, the last two clauses constitute a paratactic pair (*you swivel your neck/and glance over your shoulder*). You may be uncomfortable calling (iii–iv) a paratactic pair because of the presence of *when* at the start of clause (iii). But if you think this through you'll realize that the *when* functions to tie the (iii–iv) pair back to clause (ii). It doesn't function to tie (iii) to (iv). The *and* does that. Once we've accounted for the structural role of *when*, we can cancel it out, as it were, when assessing the taxis of the following clause.

This is a general principle to keep in mind: each structural marker will be creating just one link. Once you've analysed that link, you can now ignore that marker and look at how the clause relates to other clauses. This explains why sometimes a clause that looks hypotactic (because it couldn't stand alone in its current form) can actually be part of a paratactic sequence: the hypotactic part of its structure has been used up linking it to one clause, so the rest of the clause can now be considered afresh when determining how it relates to the next adjacent clause.

Discussion of analysed texts

You are now in a position to understand the coding in the left-hand columns of Texts 9.1 and 9.2. Below are some tables that summarize the analytical results for each text.

The two texts have an almost identical ratio of words to sentences (14.7 for Text 9.1 and 14.6 for Text 9.2). But the dramatic differences are in the distribution of those words across sentences. While in the written Recount there are almost as many clause simplexes as clause complexes, in the spoken text almost three-quarters of the sentences are clause complexes. This gives further weight to the claim that spoken language tends to use the dynamic patterns of complexing more than written language does. This spoken/written difference is reinforced by the dramatic difference in the use of embedding: 9 instances

Table 9.2 Basic clause complex summary of Texts 9.1 and 9.2

	Text 9.1	Text 9.2
no. of words in text	429	323
no. of sentences in text	29	22
no. of clause simplexes	11 (37%)	6 (27%)
no. of clause complexes	18 (62%)	16 (72%)
no. of embedded clauses	9	0
no. of clause complexes of 2 clauses	8	6
no. of clause complexes of 3 clauses	7	2
no. of clause complexes of 4 clauses	3	3
no. of clause complexes >4 clauses	0	4

in Text 9.1 but none at all in the spoken text. This suggests that in careful literary text, even in an event-focused genre of Recount, the writer exploits the variety of resources the language offers for getting more meaning into the text.

We see also that while written text prefers less intricate clause complexes, the spoken text thrives on intricacy. In Text 9.2 two clause complexes contain 6 clauses, and two contain 9 clauses each! Thus it seems that the frequency and type of clause complexing is strongly related to mode difference.

Table 9.3 shows taxis in each text (note that because of layering, tactic relations will exceed clause complex numbers).

The tactic patterns show that in Text 9.1 hypotaxis and parataxis occur in almost equal proportions, but Text 9.2, the spoken text, uses significantly more hypotaxis than parataxis. This is largely because Text 9.2 makes significant use of hypotactic projection. These choices can be related to differences in the genres: Text 9.1, the Recount, expresses events, with just occasional ideas and locutions attributed to sources. By contrast, the Expository nature of the spoken text is realized through increased incorporation of sourced comments.

We get a clearer picture of why this sourcing is happening if we look at the final table, Table 9.4, which summarizes the types of logico-semantic relations in each text.

Note here the striking number of projected ideas in the spoken exposition and the complete absence of locution. Exposition, then, is about expressing thoughts, while in a Recount there is only modest expression of both ideas and locutions, with the focus instead of expressing the logical relation between events. A further difference is in the proportions of expansion relationships: while in Recount, most emphasis is on the 'external' logic through which events are related (through extension and enhancement), in Exposition there is a strong emphasis on the 'internal' or rhetorical relationship between pieces of information offered by the speaker.

Table 9.3   Taxis in Texts 9.1 and 9.2

Taxis		Text 9.1	Text 9.2
hypotaxis	projection	3	10
	expansion	11	14
	total	14	24
parataxis	projection	2	0
	expansion	13	16
	total	15	16

Table 9.4   Logico-semantic relations in Texts 9.1 and 9.2

		Text 9.1	Text 9.2
projection	locution	2	0
	idea	3	10
	total:projection	5	10
expansion	elaboration	3	12
	extension	6	11
	enhancement	17	11
	total:expansion	26	34

This comparison shows that patterns of clause complexing are particularly sensitive to the contextual dimensions of genre and mode. We will see more of this in discussion of the complex analysis of the Crying Baby texts in Chapter Eleven. You can view the clause complex analyses for all three Crying Baby texts in the Appendix.

Ideational = logical + experiential

In Chapters Eight and Nine we have looked at the two dimensions of ideational meaning. Through choices of Transitivity and Clause Complex, language users express experiential meanings about participants and processes, and link these logically into coherent, semantically sequenced packages. The successful negotiation of a text, however, involves more than just expressing sequences of content in text. The content must be expressed in a way which makes clear its relationship to prior text, and which signals to us which part of the text is more/less important to an understanding of the overall text. Clauses need to be structured in ways which enable interactants to interpret the speaker's priorities and direction. In the following chapter we will explore the grammatical means by which the message is 'enabled', when we examine the textual structure of the clause.

Notes

1. This excerpt is taken from *Shot* by Gail Bell (2003), Picador, pp. 3–4.
2. I'm interpreting this clause as elliptical: even [when they are in] a state of highest combat alert.
3. Theme predication combined with nominalization make this clause look more intricate that it is. Grammatically, we have one clause: *Comprehension takes over from confusion only with the return of conscious awareness.*
4. Interview carried out December 2003. My thanks to Gail Bell for permission to reproduce this excerpt.
5. PTSD stands for post-traumatic shock disorder.
6. Interpreted as elliptical: [I had] an old school friend [to dinner].

Chapter 10

The grammar of textual meaning: THEME

Introduction

In the previous chapters we have explored a functional-semantic approach to two strands of meaning in the clause. We have looked at how the clause is organized to express interpersonal meanings (through selections of Mood), and how it is organized to express ideational meanings (through selections of Transitivity and Logical Relations).

In this chapter we turn to examine the third simultaneous strand of meaning that enables texts to be negotiated: textual meaning. In describing the structural configurations by which the clause is organized as a message, we will recognize that one major system is involved, that of Theme, with a configuration of the clause into the two functional components of a Theme (point of departure for the message) and a Rheme (new information about the point of departure). We will see how the thematic structure of the clause mirrors the tripartite semantic structure of language, when we recognize textual, interpersonal and experiential (or topical) thematic elements.

After reviewing the realization of the systems in the Theme network, we will examine the contribution that Thematic organization makes to the cohesive development of text, explaining why Halliday (1974: 97) refers to the textual function of language as the 'enabling' function[1].

Metafunctional analysis and the textual strand of meaning

Material presented in previous chapters now permits us to explain in part how a single clause is making meanings. Take, for example, the final two clauses from Diana's story about her daughter's blood transfusion (presented in Chapter Eight):

> But in Switzerland they give you a cognac. Here they give you tea and bikkies.

We can now appreciate that these clause simplexes are making two types of meanings simultaneously. Firstly, the clauses are making meanings about the interaction. In this case, both clauses have the Mood structure of declaratives, and are therefore functioning as statements of information, which situate the listeners in the potential role of acknowledgers. No specific 'next speaker' is specified. The absence of modulation indicates that Diana is presenting us with what she is encoding as factual information, and the absence of modalization indicates that she considers herself certain of her facts.

At the same time, the clauses are expressing experiential meanings, realizing parallelism not only in their Mood choices but also in their Transitivity selections: each clause contains a Circumstance of location, an Actor (generalized *they*), the action process *give*, a Beneficiary (generic *you*) and a Goal.

If we consider for a moment the purpose, or the effect, of these clauses of Diana's, we will notice that they function to bring her short narrative to an end. They effectively signal the conclusion of extended monologue, and the potential resumption of a more interactive, turn-taking structure to the dialogue. They are in fact followed by rapid interactive talk. Neither the Mood nor the Transitivity descriptions of these clauses can explain fully how this pair of clauses achieves the status as Coda to the narrative.

However, we can bring out the contribution of these clauses by contrasting them with possible alternatives. For example:

original

> But in Switzerland they give you a cognac. Here they give you tea and bikkies.

alternatives

> But they give you a cognac in Switzerland. They give you tea and bikkies here.
> They give you a cognac in Switzerland, though. They give you tea and bikkies here.
> They give you a cognac in Switzerland, though. Here they give you tea and bikkies.
> But in Switzerland they give you a cognac. They give you tea and bikkies here.
> But they give you a cognac in Switzerland. They give you tea and bikkies here.

If you read each of these alternatives through, you will find that none of them has quite the same effect as Diana's original choice. They do not 'sound' quite as good, quite as conclusive, quite as neat, as the original pair. If you look closely, you will see that no new elements have been introduced into the alternatives. From the point of view of the Mood and Transitivity, the grammar of these clauses has not been changed: the clauses are still both unmodalized declaratives, still action process clauses with three participants and a circumstance.

This suggests that the variation we are observing is the realization of yet another strand of meaning. If you look closely, you will see that the only variation that has been made concerns the <u>order</u> of the constituents: elements that occur as the first constituents in the original have been moved to clause-final position, sometimes in both clauses, sometimes in just one of the pair. The effect of this simple reordering of the constituents is marked: the clauses lose something of their narrative effect.

This is the case even where parallelism in the order of constituents is maintained (i.e. where the same constituents are moved to the same position in both clauses). For example:

> But they give you a cognac in Switzerland. They give you tea and bikkies here.
> They give you a cognac in Switzerland, though. They give you tea and bikkies here.

Neither of these pairs is as effective as the original. Even more noticeable is when constituents have been repositioned in one clause but not the other (i.e. when there is no longer parallelism in the position of constituents). For example:

> They give you a cognac in Switzerland, though. Here they give you tea and bikkies.
> But in Switzerland they give you a cognac. They give you tea and bikkies here.
> But they give you a cognac in Switzerland. They give you tea and bikkies here.

The choice that Diana made in producing her original pair of clauses did not affect either the interpersonal or the experiential meanings she was making. What her skill as an oral narrator was sensitive to was the way in which **textual** meanings are made.

The textual metafunction, the third and final strand of meaning made in the clause, is described by Halliday (1974: 95, 97) as the 'relevance' or the 'enabling' metafunction. This is the level of organization of the clause which enables the clause to be packaged in ways which make it effective given its purpose and its context. For example, any of the alternatives given above would be quite acceptable English clauses – but none was quite as effective as Diana's original choice, because her original choice maximizes the realization of her purpose (to signal completion of the narrative) and chooses to emphasize a dimension of the context of her story which has been significant in its telling (the importance she had given earlier in her narrative to the location where the incident took place). Thus, the textual strand of meaning, while not adding new reality nor altering interpersonal dimensions of the clause, is concerned with the potential the clause offers for its constituents to be organized differently, to achieve different purposes.

As the examples discussed here have illustrated, textual meaning in English is expressed largely through the ordering of constituents. We will see below that it is what gets put first (and last) in an English clause that realizes textual choice. Other languages will express textual meanings differently (e.g. through the use of particles to signal the textual status of particular constituents). What does seem true, however, is that all languages will somehow encode textual meaning, since language users depend on signals which indicate the cohesive relations between the clause, its context and its purpose.

Two key systems enter into the expression of textual meaning in the clause: the system of Theme, and the system of Information Structure. However, since Information Structure (with its constituents of Given and New) is realized through intonation choices, it will not be treated in this book (you can read about Halliday's analysis of intonation in English, and Given/New structure in Halliday and Matthiessen 2004: 87–92). The only textual system we will examine here is that of Theme.

As we will see below, the system of Theme is realized through a structure in which the clause falls into just two main constituents: a Theme (the first part of the clause) and a Rheme. We will also see that we can identify different types of Themes, and that the choice of what gets to be Theme in an English clause contributes very significantly to the communicative effect of the message. But to understand these points, we need firstly to develop the description of the clause in its textual constituents.

THEME/RHEME: the system

The system network of textual meaning in the clause is given below in System 10.1.

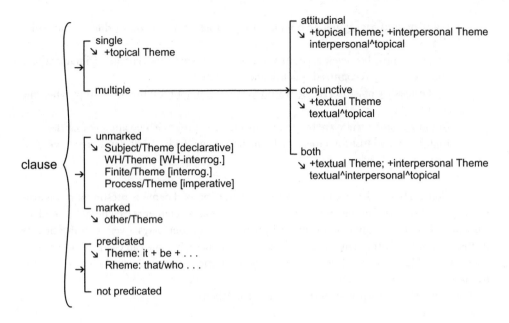

System 10.1 Theme

As this network shows, Theme involves three major systems: choice of type of Theme, choice of marked or unmarked Theme, and choice of predicated or unpredicated Theme. The realization statements indicate that the type of Theme is realized by the insertion of a particular type of constituent in Thematic position. Theme markedness depends on the conflation (mapping together) of the Theme constituent with different Mood and Transitivity constituents. Theme predication involves the use of an additional clausal element.

We will begin working through this network by presenting the two main constituents, Theme and Rheme.

THEME

Just as we did when discussing earlier functional constituents such as Subject and Finite, we will here distinguish between the definition of the constituent we call Theme and its identification.

The definition of Theme as given by Halliday and Matthiessen (2004: 64) is that it is the element which serves as 'the starting-point for the message: it is what the clause is going to be about'. Since we typically depart from places with which we are famliar, the Theme typically contains familiar, or 'given', information, i.e. information which has already been mentioned somewhere in the text or is familiar from the context.

The identification of Theme is based on order: Theme is the element which comes first in the clause. In the following clauses, taken from Text 1.2 (the second Crying Baby text given in Chapter One), the Theme has been underlined:

<u>The compelling sound of an infant's cry</u> makes it an effective distress signal.
<u>However, cries</u> are discomforting.

> Many reasons for crying are obvious, like hunger and discomfort due to heat, cold, illness, and lying position.
> These reasons, however, account for a relatively small percentage of infant crying and are usually recognized quickly and alleviated.
> In the absence of a discernible reason for the behaviour, crying often stops when the infant is held.
> In most infants, there are frequent episodes of crying with no apparent cause,
> Infants cry and fuss for a mean of 1¾ hr/day at age 2 wk, 2¾ hr/day at age 6 wk, and 1 hr/day at 12 wk.

As mentioned above, although the functional definition of Theme is presumed to be universally valid (i.e. all languages will recognize some clause elements as Theme), the identification criteria are only true for English, where word order plays a very significant role in the grammar. In other languages, for example Japanese, Theme can occur in other positions in the clause because there is a specific grammatical particle (*wa*) which can be used to mark it.

The only other constituent in the clause is the Rheme.

RHEME

The definition of the Rheme is that it is the part of the clause in which the Theme is developed. Since we typically depart from the familiar to head towards the unfamiliar, the Rheme typically contains unfamiliar, or 'new', information.

The identification criteria for the Rheme are simple: everything that is not the Theme is the Rheme. Thus, once you have identified the Theme in a clause, you have also identified the Rheme, which is just 'everything else'. The Rheme in the examples analysed above includes all the non-underlined constituents of the clause.

The boundary of Theme: types of Themes

Claiming that 'what comes first in the clause' is Theme raises the obvious question: just how much of what comes first in a clause counts as Theme? More technically, how many of the clause's constituents (which we are now able to identify through either a Mood or Transitivity analysis) belong in the Theme, and how many in the Rheme? In the examples above, you will note that Theme sometimes consists of just one grammatical constituent:

In most infants,	*there are frequent episodes of crying with no apparent cause,*
Adj:circ	
Circ:loc	

Infants	*cry and fuss for a mean of 1¾ hr/day at age 2 wk . . . .*
Subject	
Behaver	

whereas in other cases two constituents have been underlined as Theme:

However	*cries*	*are discomforting*
Adj:conjun	Subject	
	Carrier	

The same issue is raised by the clauses from Diana's narrative, considered earlier:

> <u>But in Switzerland</u> they give you a cognac. <u>Here</u> they give you tea and bikkies.

Here the indication of Theme may lead you to ask why, for example, the boundary is not *but*, since that can be recognized as one constituent (a Conjunctive, i.e. textual, Adjunct). Why is *they* not part of the Theme?, etc. These questions about the boundary between Theme and Rheme can be answered by examining the system of Types of Themes in the Theme network.

Reflecting the three-dimensional metafunctional structure of the clause, we can identify three different types of elements of clause structure that can get to be Theme: topical (or experiential) elements, interpersonal elements and textual elements. We will briefly examine each type of Theme, and explain the criteria for determining the Theme/Rheme boundary.

Topical Theme

When an element of the clause to which a Transitivity function can be assigned occurs in first position in a clause, we describe it as a **topical Theme**. For example:

In most infants	*there*	*are*	*frequent episodes of crying with no apparent cause.*
Circ:loc		Pr:existential	Existent
topical			
THEME	RHEME		

Infants	*cry and fuss*	*for a mean of 1¾ hr/day at age 2 wk . . .*
Behaver	Pr:behavioural	Circ:extent
topical		
THEME	RHEME	

I	*'ve given*	*blood*	*36 times.*
Actor	Pr:material	Range	Circ:extent
topical			
THEME	RHEME		

This	*was*	*in Geneva.*
Carrier	Pr:intensive	Attribute/Circ
topical		
THEME	RHEME	

In all these clauses, the first constituent in the clause is a constituent to which we can attach a transitivity role, such as Actor, Behaver, Senser or Circumstance.

An important principle to remember is that **every clause must contain one and only one topical Theme**. Once you have identified a topical Theme in a clause, you can consign all the remaining clause constituents to the Rheme role. It is this principle which allows us to determine the Theme/Rheme boundary in the following examples:

In Greece	*they*	*give*	*you*	*nothing.*
Circ:loc	Actor	Pr:material	Beneficiary	Goal
topical				
THEME	RHEME			

The first constituent is a Circumstance of location, and is therefore a topical Theme. All remaining constituents are therefore Rheme.

However,	*cries*	*are*	*discomforting.*
	Carrier	Pr:intensive	Attribute
	topical		
THEME		RHEME	

In this clause, the first constituent is a textual (Conjunctive) Adjunct, which does not receive any Transitivity role. The second constituent is a Carrier, and therefore a topical Theme. While *however* is therefore considered part of the Theme, all constituents after the topical Theme are part of the Rheme. (We will see below that *however* is a textual Theme.)

While clauses do very frequently begin with a single Transitivity constituent acting as Theme, it is also possible to get either interpersonal or textual elements in Thematic position.

Interpersonal Theme

When a constituent to which we would assign a Mood label (but not a Transitivity label) occurs at the beginning of a clause, we call it an interpersonal Theme. The constituents which can function as interpersonal Themes are the unfused Finite (in interrogative structures) and all four categories of Modal Adjuncts: Mood, Vocative, Polarity and Comment.

1. Finite (unfused) as interpersonal Theme

Do	*you*	*give*	*blood?*
Finite	Subject	Predicator	Complement
MOOD		RESIDUE	
	Actor	Pr:material	Goal
interpersonal	topical		
THEME		RHEME	

Do	*you*	*want*	*some more soup,*	*Diana?*
Finite	Subject	Predicator	Complement	Adjunct:vocative
MOOD		RESIDUE		
	Senser	Pr:mental	Phen	
interpersonal	topical			
THEME		RHEME		

Can	*you*	*take*	*my bag*	*for me?*
Finite	Subject	Predicator	Complement	Adj:circ
MOOD		RESIDUE		
interpersonal	topical			
THEME		RHEME		

2. Mood Adjuncts as Interpersonal Theme

I think	*they*	*take*		*a pint or whatever it is.*
Adj:mood	Subject	Finite	Predicator	Complement
MOOD			RESIDUE	
interpersonal	topical			
THEME		RHEME		

Maybe	*Stephen*	*could*	*help.*
Adj:mood	Subject	Finite	Predicator
MOOD			RESIDUE
interpersonal	topical		
THEME		RHEME	

Just	*give*	*me*	*a whistle.*
Adj:mood	Predicator	Complement	Complement
MOOD	RESIDUE		
interpersonal	topical		
THEME		RHEME	

3. Vocative Adjuncts as interpersonal Theme

Although not constituents of the MOOD element, Vocative Adjuncts contribute interpersonal meanings to the clause. Thus, Vocative Adjuncts, when they occur before the first topical Theme, are also classified as interpersonal Themes:

Simon,	*isn't*	*that*	*where they put the needle in?*
Adjunct:vocative	Finite	Subject	Complement
	MOOD		RESIDUE
interpersonal	interpersonal	topical	
THEME			RHEME

Stephen,	*do*	*you*	*want*	*more soup?*
Adj:vocative	Finite	Subject	Predicator	Complement
	MOOD		RESIDUE	
interpersonal	interpersonal	topical		
THEME			RHEME	

Note that when a vocative Adjunct occurs after a topical Theme, it is no longer part of the Theme, but becomes part of the Rheme:

Do	*you*	*want*	*some more soup,*	*Diana?*
Finite	Subject	Predicate	Complement	Adjunct:voc
MOOD		RESIDUE		
interpersonal	topical			
THEME		RHEME		

Remember that the rule is to identify one and only one topical Theme per clause. This means that if the clause begins with an interpersonal Theme, you must keep analysing until you have a topical element. Once you have identified one topical constituent, you can consign all remaining constituents to the Rheme role.

4. Polarity Adjuncts

You will remember from Chapter Six that the items *Yes* and *No* can function in two ways: either as a sub-category of Modal Adjuncts, when they stand in for an ellipsed MOOD constituent, or as Continuity Adjuncts, performing a textual role in the clause.

In cases where *yes* or *no* act interpersonally (i.e. as Polarity Adjuncts) they are analysed as interpersonal Themes. (Note that, due to the ellipsis which will accompany them, there will not be a following topical Theme.)

No/Yes
Adjunct:Polarity
MOOD
interpersonal
THEME

5. Comment Adjuncts

The category of Comment Adjuncts which we identified when looking at the Mood structure of the clause included adverbial expressions of attitude, where that attitude related to the entire clause. Where a comment Adjunct occurs before the first topical Theme, it is analysed as an interpersonal Theme.

Fortunately,	*the bomb*	*didn't*	*explode.*
Adjunct:comment	Subject	Finite	Predicator
	MOOD		RESIDUE
interpersonal	topical		
THEME		RHEME	

Textual Theme

The third clause constituent that can occur in Thematic position is the category of textual elements. These are elements which do not express any interpersonal or experiential meaning, but which are doing important cohesive work in relating the clause to its context. The two main types of textual elements which can get to be Theme are Continuity Adjuncts and Conjunctive Adjuncts.

1. Continuity Adjuncts as Theme

As we saw in Chapter Six, Continuity Adjuncts are words which are used in spoken dialogue to indicate that the speaker's contribution is somehow related to (continuous with) what a previous speaker has said in an earlier turn. The commonest continuity items are: *oh, well. Yea* and *no* are also continuity items when these are not used as stand-ins for clause ellipsis, but as the first item in a clause.

Oh	*they*	*give*		*you*	*a cup of tea.*
Adj:contin	Subject	Finite	Predicator	Complement	Complement
	MOOD		RESIDUE		
textual	topical				
THEME		RHEME			

No	*you*	*wouldn't.*
Adj:continuity	Subject	Finite
	MOOD	
textual	topical	
THEME		RHEME

2. Conjunctive Adjuncts as Theme

As we saw in Chapters Two and Nine, cohesive conjunctions are elements which serve to link sentences together. They were described as Conjunctive Adjuncts in our Mood analysis of the clause. I explained in Chapter Six that tactic conjunctions which are used to link clauses together within a clause complex will necessarily occur in first position in the clause (*and, but*), whereas cohesive conjunctions which link sentences to other sentences (e.g. *however, therefore*) may occur in other positions. Both kinds of conjunctions are described as textual Themes when they occur before the first topical Theme in a clause.

So	*they*	*could*	*actually*	*do*	*it*	*through the umbilical artery or whatever.*
Adj:conjun	Subject	Finite	Adj:mood	Pred	Compl	Adj:circ
	MOOD			RESIDUE		
textual	topical					
THEME		RHEME				

But	*in Switzerland*	*they*	*give*		*you*	*a cognac.*
Adj:conjun	Adj:circ	Subject	Finite	Predicator	Compl	Compl
	RESIDUE . . .	MOOD		. . . RESIDUE		
textual	topical					
THEME		RHEME				

and	*he*	*proposes*		*marriage*
Adj:conjun	Subject	Finite	Predicator	Complement
	MOOD		RESIDUE	
textual	topical			
THEME		RHEME		

Multiple Themes

While it is possible for a clause to realize only one Thematic element (in which case it must be a topical Theme), it is far more common for clauses to contain a sequence of Themes, with often several textual and/or interpersonal Themes occurring before the obligatory topical Theme:

No	*well*	*I mean*	*they*	*don't*	*know.*
Adj:contin	Adj:contin	Adj:conjun	Subject	Finite	Predicator
				MOOD	RESIDUE
textual	textual	textual	topical		
THEME				RHEME	

Well	*at least*	*she*	*didn't*	*get blown up,*	*Simon.*
Adj:contin	Adj:conjun	Subject	Finite	Predicator	Adj:voc
		MOOD		RESIDUE	
textual	textual	topical			
THEME		RHEME			

You will no doubt be wondering why the principle of one topical Theme per clause is suggested. This relates to a consideration of how much **choice** a writer/speaker has in deciding what to make Theme, which in turn relates to the notion of the **Thematic potential** of a clause.

Some elements, if they are to occur at all in the clause, <u>must</u> occur in initial position. For example, the conjunction *and* always occurs in clause initial position. Similarly, if the clause is to be an interrogative, the Finite element must go to the front of the clause to meet the structural demands of Mood. This means that elements like *and* and the Finite have not involved any choice about their positioning: once the particular meaning they need to make has to be expressed, those items simply must be placed in Theme position. This means that very little of the clause's Thematic potential has yet been used. With many textual elements, there is relatively little choice as to their position in the clause. With interpersonal elements, there may be slightly more choice (for example, a vocative may occur initially, finally or medially). These elements are then using up some of the clause's thematic potential: they involve meaningful choice, because we can recognize different possible positions. But still their mobility is limited.

When we consider experiential elements, however, we can see that these are the elements where there is maximum choice as to order. A clause which contains two participants, two circumstances and a process (e.g. *last week/ in the city/ Diana/blood/ donated*) can be realized in a large number of different orders:

i) Last week in the city Diana donated blood.

ii) Last week Diana donated blood in the city.

iii) Last week blood was donated by Diana in the city.
iv) Diana last week donated blood in the city.
v) In the city last week Diana donated blood.
vi) Blood was donated last week in the city by Diana.
vii) Donated last week was blood by Diana. (etc.)

While each clause is experientially and interpersonally equivalent, they are not inter-changeable. Some are more *marked* (less usual) than others, and each would be more or less appropriate in different contexts. For example, the first clause suggests the Orientation to a narrative (with the Thematic positioning of the location information). With the appropriate ellipsis operating, several of the variants would be appropriate responses to different clarification questions: e.g. ii) *What's Diana up to these days?*; vi) *What did you say she's been giving away?* The highly marked variant vii) suggests a commendation/announcement.

What this illustrates is that we have great freedom of choice in the positioning of topical clause elements, and it is for this reason that we consider the choice of WHICH topical element to put first in a clause to be the most significant choice in terms of the clause's thematic potential. Once that key decision about which of the Transitivity roles will occupy clause initial position has been made, the Thematic potential (our choice potential) is considered largely exhausted. Hence the principle that once we have identified one topical Theme in a clause, we consign all remaining constituents to the role of Rheme.

Thematic analysis, then, is relatively straightforward. Simply take each clause in a text and assign a label of interpersonal, textual or topical to the elements at the beginning. If the first element is a topical element, you call that THEME and all the rest of the clause RHEME. If other elements (interpersonal, textual) come before the topical element, you include them in the THEME, up to the end of the first topical element. Remember that THEME analysis is like MOOD, in that there are two layers of analysis to write: the level of 'topical', 'textual' or 'interpersonal', and the second level of THEME vs RHEME.

Since the boundary between Theme and Rheme is related to the realization of experiential and interpersonal constituents, Theme analysis is best undertaken *after* you have analysed the clause for its Mood and Transitivity structure.

Although the principles outlined here should be your overall guide, there are a few cases in which further comments are necessary. For example, there are a few situations where the 'one topical Theme' rule is not apparently followed. These particular cases can be dealt with by discussion of how Theme is analysed in different Mood classes and how we treat Theme in dependent clauses. We also need to consider what is meant by marked and unmarked Theme, and what is involved in a predicated Theme structure.

THEME and MOOD: analysing Theme in different Mood classes

1. declaratives
As we saw earlier, analysing Theme in declarative clauses is straightforward. Simply analyse the constituents to the point where one topical Theme is recognized, and label the remainder of the clause Rheme:

You	probably	haven't	got	much more than 8.
Subject	Adj:mood	Finite	Predicator	Complement
MOOD			RESIDUE	
Carrier			Pr:possessive	Attribute: possession
topical				
THEME	RHEME			

2. elliptical declaratives

Theme analysis of elliptical declaratives depends on determining which constituents have been ellipsed. Thus, it is necessary to 'fill out' the ellipsed constituents (in your mind only – there is no need to write them in), and then to consider what the Thematic analysis of the non-elliptical clause would have been. To fill out ellipsis you will of course have to refer to the context of the clause:

i) *A day, isn't it?* filled out:

It	takes		about a day	(for your blood to be replaced).
Subject	Finite	Predicator	Adj:circ	
MOOD		RESIDUE		
Token	Pr:circ		Value:circ	
topical				
THEME	RHEME			

The response is therefore analysed as Rheme.

ii) *Just a touch* =

I	'll	have	just a touch more soup.
Subject	Finite	Predicator	Complement
MOOD		RESIDUE	
Actor		Pr:material	Goal
topical			
THEME	RHEME		

So, *just a touch* is Rheme.

iii) No.
iv) Yes.

As pointed out earlier, in cases where *yes* or *no* appear on their own (i.e. not introducing a following clause), they are analysed as functioning as Polarity Adjuncts (standing in for an ellipsed clause). As exemplified above, they are therefore analysed as interpersonal Themes. **In this case there is NO topical Theme realized** (it has been ellipsed).

3. yes-no interrogatives

The analysis of polar interrogatives is straightforward, with the Finite (modalized or not), appearing before the Subject and functioning as an interpersonal Theme:

Can	I	get	you	some more?
Finite	Subject	Predicator	Complement	Complement
MOOD		RESIDUE		
interpersonal	topical			
THEME		RHEME		

Did	this	happen?
Finite	Subject	Predicator
MOOD		RESIDUE
interpersonal	topical	
THEME		RHEME

4. WH-interrogatives

In the Mood analysis of the clause, WH elements were seen to conflate with different constituents: Subject, Complement or Adjunct:circumstantial. As all these conflations involve a participant which plays a Transitivity role, WH elements which initiate questions will function as topical Themes:

How much	do	they	take out	of you?
WH/Adj:circ	Finite	Subject	Predicator	Adj:circ
RESIDUE . . .	MOOD		. . . RESIDUE	
Circ:extent		Actor	Pr:material	Circ:loc
topical				
THEME	RHEME			

When	did	he	give	her	the bomb?
WH/Adj:circ	Finite	Subject	Predicator	Complement	Complement
RESIDUE . . .	MOOD		. . . RESIDUE		
Circ:loc		Actor	Pr:material	Beneficiary	Goal
topical					
THEME	RHEME				

5. elliptical interrogatives

As with WH-interrogatives, in elliptical WH-interrogatives the WH element will always be a topical Theme. This is because the WH element, which must always occur in first position, is always fused with a clause constituent which plays a transitivity role (you can test this by filling out the ellipsis as we did with elliptical declaratives above):

Why? =

Why	*was*	*she*	*a bit dumb?*
WH/Adj:circ	Finite	Subject	Complement
RESIDUE . . .	MOOD		. . . RESIDUE
Circ:cause	Pr:intensive	Carrier	Attribute
topical			
THEME	RHEME		

6. imperatives

With imperatives, the Mood demands mean that often the Subject and Finite elements do not appear in the clause, which often begins with the Predicator. The Predicator is labelled for the Transitivity function of Process, and should therefore be treated as a topical Theme:

Pass	*me*	*the bowls,*	*Simon.*
Pr:material	Beneficiary	Goal	
topical			
THEME	RHEME		

Take	*this.*
Pr:material	Goal
topical	
THEME	RHEME

With *let's* imperatives, the *let* particle is analysed as Subject, takes a Transitivity role, and is therefore a topical Theme:

Let's	*have*	*some more soup.*
Subject	Predicator	Complement
MOOD	RESIDUE	
Actor	Pr:material	Goal
topical		
THEME	RHEME	

Imperatives involving *do* introduce an interpersonal Theme element before the topical Theme, which is the Process:

Do	*tell*	*me*	*about your daughter.*
Finite	Predicator	Complement	Adj:circ
MOOD	RESIDUE		
	Pr:verbal	Receiver	Circ:matter
interpersonal	topical		
THEME		RHEME	

7. minor clauses

As minor clauses carry neither Transitivity nor Mood labels, we do not consider that they have a Thematic structure. They can therefore be left unanalysed for Theme.

Oh good.
minor clause

Thanks a lot.
minor clause

8. Theme in exclamative clauses

With non-elliptical exclamatives, the WH element will always be a topical Theme, as is demonstrated by analysing it for Transitivity:

What a delicious soup	*this*	*is,*	*Marg!*
WH/Compl	Subject	Finite	Adj:vocative
RESIDUE	MOOD		
Attribute	Carrier	Pr:intensive	
topical			
THEME	RHEME		

With elliptical imperatives, the WH element should again be treated as topical Theme, on the basis that it would occupy Thematic position in the non-elliptical version:

How fantastic!
topical
THEME

= *How fantastic it was!*

Clauses which are intonationally exclamative but structurally minor clauses (e.g. *Oh dear!*, *Holy toledo!*) should be analysed as minor clauses (Theme-less).

9. reiterated Subject

In rapid conversational speech it is not uncommon to find the Subject of a clause mentioned twice. This often happens clause-initially, e.g.

Diana,	*she*	*'s*	*given*	*blood*	*36 times.*
Subject	Subject	Finite	Predicator	Complement	Adj:circ
MOOD			RESIDUE		

However, in some dialects the Subject may be first mentioned with a pronoun, and then reiterated in full at the end of the clause in a partial or complete Mood tag (i.e. with or without a reiteration of the Finite as well):

She	*'s*	*given*	*blood*	*36 times,*	*Diana*	*(has).*
Subject	Finite	Predicator	Compl	Adj:circ	Subject	(Finite)
MOOD		RESIDUE			MOOD	

Consistent with the principle being followed here, only the first mention of the Subject is analysed as Theme:

Diana,	*she's given blood 36 times.*
topical	
THEME	RHEME

She	*'s given blood 36 times, Diana (has).*
topical	
THEME	RHEME

Theme in existential processes

An exception to the rule that a topical Theme will always carry a Transitivity label is found in the case of existential processes. You will recall that these processes, which involve the structure *there is/there are*, are analysed for Transitivity as follows:

There	*was*	*a bomb*	*in her bag.*
	Pr:exist	Existent	Circ:loc

Although the *there* does not in fact receive a Transitivity label, it is nonetheless described as topical Theme:

There	*was*	*a bomb*	*in her bag.*
topical			
THEME	RHEME		

Theme in clause complexes

To this point, we have looked only at Theme in single, independent clauses – clause simplexes. In clause complexes, each clause will of course have its own Thematic structure, but Theme analysis is affected by the tactic status of each clause and so we briefly review Theme analysis in paratactic and hypotactic clause complexes.

Theme in paratactic clause complexes

In paratactic clause complexes, where we have two independent clauses, each clause is given an individual Thematic analysis:

You	*get a litre of milk*		*and*	*it*	*stands this tall.*
topical			textual	topical	
THEME	RHEME		THEME		RHEME

Well	*I*	*'ll bring those out*		*so*	*you*	*don't have to carry them.*
textual	topical			textual	topical	
THEME		RHEME		THEME		RHEME

We know from Chapter Nine that although paratactic clauses are often linked by conjunctions such as *then, and, so*, they may also occur without conjunctions, particularly if in a series:

the poor lady	*starts*		*a relation-ship*		*gets*	*married*		*decides*	*to go*	*home*
Sub	Fin	Pred	Compl		Fin	Pred	Compl		Fin	Pred	Adj: circ
MOOD	RESIDUE				MD	RESIDUE			MD	RESIDUE	

One common occurrence with paratactically related clauses is the omission of the Subject in the second and subsequent clause(s). In these cases, the ellipsed Subject is considered to have filled the role of topical Theme. The second clause is therefore shown as having no topical Theme:

they	*may be giving blood*		*and*	** (ellipsis of they)*	*shouldn't be*
topical			textual		
THEME	RHEME		THEME		RHEME

the poor lady	*starts a relationship,*		** (ellipsis of she)*	*gets married*		** (ellipsis of she)*	*decides to go home*
topical							
THEME	RHEME			RHEME			RHEME

Theme in hypotactic clause complexes

In hypotactically related clauses, what is of particular Thematic interest is the ordering of the main and dependent clauses. Either the dependent (β) clause may follow the main clause (α), as in:

I do it	*// because I had a daughter.*
α	β

or the main clause may be preceded by the dependent clause:

If you weight under 50 kilos	*// they take less.*
β	α

In the first case, the procedure for Theme analysis is as for independent clauses: simply analyse the Thematic structure of each clause separately:

I	*do it*		*because*	*I*	*had a daughter.*
topical			textual	topical	
THEME	RHEME		THEME		RHEME

However, when the dependent clause comes before the main clause, we consider that there are two levels of Thematic structure operating. Firstly, each of the constituent clauses has its own Thematic structure which should be analysed:

If	*you*	*weigh under 50 kilos*		*they*	*take less.*
textual	topical			topical	
THEME		RHEME		THEME	RHEME

At a second level, however, the entire dependent clause can be seen to be acting as Theme to the sentence. Again, the principle is that of choice: the speaker/writer exercised choice in placing the dependent clause first, and in doing so set up thematic expectations for the rest of the sentence (the dependent clause signals that a second clause will follow). To capture the fact that the dependent clause has been placed in Thematic position, the entire dependent clause is described as Theme to the sentence it occurs in:

If	*you*	*weigh under 50 kilos*		*they*	*take less.*
textual	topical			topical	
THEME		RHEME		THEME	RHEME
THEME				RHEME	

Linking clauses into hypotactic clause complexes sometimes involves the use of what we could call simply 'structural elements'. For example, Diana's narrative contains the following clause sequence:

I had a daughter // who . . . needed blood transfusions.

As we saw in Chapter Nine, this could have been packaged as two sentences:

I had a daughter. She needed blood transfusions.

However, greater pace and continuity is created by packaging the two clauses into one clause complex. The link is created in part through the use of the relative pronoun *who*. For the purposes of Theme analysis, structural elements like *who* should be analysed as a conflation (fusing) of topical meaning (*she*, the Carrier of the second clause) and a structural element:

I	*had a daughter*		*who*	*needed blood transfusions.*
topical			structural/topical	
THEME	RHEME		THEME	RHEME

Another common structural element is *which*:

She	*carried*	*the bags,*		*which*	*is*	*pretty stupid.*
Actor	Pr:material	Goal		Carrier	Pr:inten	Attribute
topical				structural/topical		
THEME	RHEME			THEME	RHEME	

Predicated THEME

One further Thematic pattern that occurs quite frequently in both spoken and written texts is that of Theme Predication. Compare the following clauses:

i) Diana has donated blood 36 times.
ii) It was Diana who had donated blood 36 times.
iii) It was the 36th time that Diana had donated blood.
iv) It was blood that Diana had donated for the 36th time.

In i) we have a simple clause with a Mood structure of Subject, Finite, Complement, Adjunct. There is a single topical element as Theme. Through her Thematic position, Diana is presented as 'given' information. The typical intonation pattern on this clause would make *36 times* carry the selection of tone, thereby signalling the Circumstance of extent as the 'new' information being offered by the clause. Such a textual organization of the clause would be quite appropriate in the context where we are already talking about *Diana* (and so she is 'given').

However, versions ii) to iv) illustrate that it is possible to shift the status of 'given' and 'new' information through a process of Theme Predication. This process is used when the speaker/writer wishes to give emphasis to a constituent that would otherwise be unemphasized, while maintaining the 'real' news, which is in the Rheme of the original clause. By moving a constituent away from the beginning of the clause it is possible for it to carry the intonation choice for the clause. It can thus be signalled as 'new' information, rather than 'given' information. Version ii) for example allows *Diana* to attract the stress and become 'news'. This would be an appropriate structural choice in a context where there was argument about just who had been donating blood.

Theme Predication involves introducing what is technically a second clause: the elements *it was* have their own Mood structure. At one level, then, the structure should be analysed as consisting of two separate clauses (the second dependent on the first):

clause ii)

It	*was Diana*		*who*	*had donated blood 36 times.*
topical			topical	
THEME	RHEME		THEME	RHEME

This analysis shows that by moving *Diana* to allow it to carry intonation and appear in the Rheme of the clause we are presenting *Diana* as 'news', with the empty structural *it* as the point of departure for the message. But in fact one of the effects of turning what is typically expressed as one clause into two is in a sense to set up the predicating clause *it was Diana* as Theme to the entire sentence. The point of departure for the message, then, is not just *it*, but is '*I'm going to tell you something about Diana that is news*'. The Thematic role of the predicating clause can be captured by a second level of analysis:

It	*was Diana*		*who*	*had donated blood 36 times.*
topical			topical	
THEME	RHEME		THEME	RHEME
THEME			RHEME	

Similarly with clause iii):

It	*was the 36th time*		*that*	*Diana*	*had donated blood.*
topical			structural	topical	
THEME	RHEME		THEME		RHEME
THEME			RHEME		

clause iv)

It	*was blood*		*that*	*Diana*	*had donated for the 36th time.*
topical			struct	topical	
THEME	RHEME		THEME		RHEME
THEME			RHEME		

Patterns of Theme choice: marked and unmarked theme

The final point we need to make about Theme is to explain the system in the Theme network that distinguishes between marked and unmarked Theme. The term *unmarked* simply means 'most typical/usual', while *marked* means 'atypical, unusual'. All things being equal, an unmarked choice will be made. When a marked choice is made, the speaker/writer is signalling that all things are *not* equal, that something in the context requires an atypical meaning to be made.

Theme markedness has to do with the relationship between the Mood and Theme structures of the clause: how the functional roles assigned to constituents in a Theme analysis conflate with the functional roles assigned to those same constituents in the Mood structure.

Unmarked Theme is when the constituent that is Theme is also playing one of the following roles:

- Subject (in a declarative clause)
- Finite (in an interrogative)
- Predicator (in an imperative)
- WH element (in a WH-interrogative).

In other words, unmarked Theme is when Theme conflates with the Mood structure constituent that typically occurs in first position in clauses of that Mood class. All the clauses listed in Table 10.1 contain examples of unmarked Thematic choice.

Table 10.1   Examples of unmarked Theme

example	role conflation	mood class
I'm heating the soup up.	Theme/Subject	declarative
Did this really happen?	Theme/Finite	polar interrogative
Where did she fly to?	Theme/WH element	WH-interrogative
Pass me the soup.	Theme/Predicator	imperative

Marked Theme, then, is when Theme conflates with any other constituent from the Mood system. The commonest type of marked Theme is Theme conflating with an Adjunct:circumstantial (which is not conflated with a WH element). For example, to return to Diana's couplet:

In Switzerland	*they*	*give*		*you*	*a cognac.*
Adj:circ	Subject	Finite	Predicator	Complement	Complement
RESIDUE . . .	MOOD		. . . RESIDUE		
topical					
THEME	RHEME				

Here	*they*		*give*	*you*	*tea and bikkies.*
Adj:circ	Subject	Finite	Predicator	Complement	Complement
RESIDUE . . .	MOOD		. . . RESIDUE		
topical					
THEME	RHEME				

In both clauses, the constituent that is Subject is **not** part of the Theme. Theme in these clauses is conflated with the Circumstantial Adjuncts *in Switzerland* and *here*.

One way of creating a marked Theme is to move a circumstantial element to Thematic position. Another common strategy is to repackage a constituent (e.g. an Actor) as a Circumstantial element (typically of matter). For example:

1. unmarked; Theme/Subject

Diana	*has*	*donated*	*blood*	*36 times.*
Subj	Finite	Predicator	Complement	Adj:circ
MOOD		RESIDUE		
Actor		Pr:material	Goal	Circ:extent
topical				
THEME	RHEME			

2. marked; Theme/Circ

As for Diana,	*she*	*has*	*donated*	*blood*	*36 times.*
Adj:circ	Subject	Finite	Predicator	Complement	Adj:circ
RESIDUE . . .	MOOD		. . . RESIDUE		
Circ:matter	Actor		Pr:material	Goal	Circ:extent
topical					
THEME	RHEME				

Theme Predication is another strategy for producing marked Themes: all predicated Themes are in some sense marked, since the Subject of the original clause is made Rheme in the predicated version. However, we can also identify degrees of markedness in the internal structure of the predicating '*it.* . . . .' clause. Compare, for example:

i) unmarked: Subject as Theme

Diana	*donated blood in the city.*
topical	
THEME	RHEME

ii) marked (predicated) but Subject *it* as Theme

It	*was in the city*		*that Diana donated blood.*
topical			
THEME	RHEME		

iii) highly marked: Circumstance as Theme

In the city	*it was*		*that Diana donated blood.*
topical			
THEME	RHEME		

Skilful writers and speakers choose marked Themes to add coherence and emphasis to their text. For example, part of what makes Diana's two clauses *But in Switzerland they give you a cognac. Here they give you tea and bikkies* effective in signalling finality is the parallel choice of marked Theme in each clause. The marked Themes indicate that these clauses, together, are doing something significantly different from immediately preceding clauses (they realize the final stage, Coda). The choice of a location Circumstance as marked Theme creates links with the very earliest stages of the narrative, while the contrastive Thematic emphasis on *in Switzerland* and *here* helps to bring the narrative back to the 'here and now'. The implications of choices between marked and unmarked Themes leads us to consider in general the contribution of Thematic structure to text.

Theme, textual meaning and mode

In the SFL analysis of language, patterns of Thematic choice are seen as realizing textual meanings, which in turn are the realization of Mode dimensions of the context of situation. Thus, Thematic choices realize meanings about the organization of the communicative event (how the text hangs together), and the experiential and interpersonal distance involved (how the text relates to its context). The Theme system contributes to the realization of such meanings by offering us choices about what meanings to prioritize in a text, what to package as familiar and what as new, what to make contrastive, etc.

In its role of organizing the message, the textual metafunction is in a sense parasitic upon both the ideational and the interpersonal strands of meanings. Textual choices alone cannot create text: the text would have no content, nor would it be possible to interact with it. Meanings cannot be prioritized until those meanings have themselves been chosen; thus we need to construct Transitivity structures by making experiential choices, and to segment and link those experiential choices through logical relations. And text cannot be reacted to until it is first structured to initiate interaction; thus, we need to construct Mood structures by making interpersonal choices.

But while both ideational and interpersonal meanings are essential to the creation of text, they are not in themselves sufficient. Without the textual systems, those experiential and interpersonal meanings could not be expressed in a coherent manner. Consider the following text, familiar to you in another version:

Text 10.1: modified Text 1.2

The compelling sound of an infant's cry makes it an effective distress signal and appropriate to the human infant's prolonged dependence on a caregiver. Parents may be alarmed and discomforted by cries, however. It is very difficult for many of them to listen to their infant's crying for even short periods of time. Hunger and discomfort due to heat, cold, illness, and lying position are some of the obvious reasons for crying. A relatively small percentage of infant crying however is accounted for by these reasons, and they are usually recognized quickly and alleviated. As for crying, this often stops when the infant is held, in the absence of a discernible reason for the behaviour. There are frequent episodes of crying with no apparent cause in most infants, and holding or other soothing techniques seem ineffective. A mean of 1¾ hr/day at age 2 wk, 2¾ hr/day at age 6 wk, and 1 hr/day at 12 wk is spent in crying and fussing by infants.

Guilt may be relieved and concerns diminished by counselling about normal crying. But the distress caused by the crying for some cannot be suppressed by logical reasoning. Respite from exposure to the crying may be necessary for these parents, to allow them to cope appropriately with their own distress. Fatigue and tension may result in inappropriate parental responses unless relief is given.

While we are certainly able to read and make sense of this text, the unmodified version of it (Text 1.2) is certainly easier to follow. The unmodified version is clearly a text about *crying babies*. While the modified version contains all the same information, the writer's focus is not clear: at some points it seems to be text about *crying babies*, at other times about *parents* and at still other times about negative emotions and physical conditions (*guilt, fatigue, tension*).

As you have no doubt realized, the only difference between the two texts is that in the modified version the Thematic structure has been scrambled. Neither the ideational nor the interpersonal meanings have been changed, yet by manipulating the order in which the constituents are realized, a simple text is made quite difficult to follow.

It is because it plays this essential semantic support role that Halliday refers to the textual metafunction as the **enabling** function of language. Textual choices, such as Theme, do not introduce new content or new interpersonal dimensions into a text. But textual choices are essential to the text's making sense. The most striking contribution of Thematic choices, then, is to the internal cohesion of the text: skilful use of Thematic selection results in a text which appears to 'hang together and make sense'.

Thematic patterns are most strongly influenced by the register variable of mode: when mode varies, we also see variation in Theme/Rheme structure. Since the key dimension to mode variation is the distinction between (interactive) spoken and (monologic) written language, we can expect to find that Thematic choice varies according to these mode values. If a text is to have not only cohesion but coherence, we will find different textual choices being made according to the text's position along the two mode continua.

We can uncover the contribution of Thematic choice to both the cohesion and the coherence of the text by examining the following main aspects:

1. What gets to be Theme, i.e. what kinds of Themes get used

Remembering that there is a choice between using or not using textual and interpersonal thematic elements, texts can vary in the extent to which they contain multiple Themes (textual and/or interpersonal and topical) or single Themes (topical only). This variation relates to the mode values of the text. If we compare, for example, the mode dimensions of the three Crying Baby texts from Chapter One, we can describe Text 1.2 as written to be read, and we saw in Chapter Three that it contains a high degree of nominalization; Text 1.3 is a conversational interaction, with very low nominalization; and Text 1.1 we noted fell somewhere between the two in that it uses much less nominalization than Text 1.2, but is clearly written monologue, unlike Text 1.3. Thematic patterns help to explain a further dimension to the differences between Texts 1.2 and 1.3, and also the intermediate mode of Text 1.1.

Thus, although Text 1.3 is a highly attitudinal text, with frequent use of intensifying Mood Adjuncts (e.g. *pretty, just*) and attitudinally loaded lexical items (e.g. *fantastic, good*), it contains very little modality. The only interpersonal Themes in the text are the obligatory structural Theme in the interrogative *Did your kids used to cry a lot?*, the Polarity Adjunct *Yea* which functions as an elliptical clause, and the reiterated comment Adjunct (e.g. *luckily*). It is only this latter interpersonal Theme which involves choice on the speaker's part, and her choice to thematize her evaluation of the early and later events creates cohesion between the two situations, as well as signposting how the speaker is evaluating (and wants us to evaluate) the events she describes.

By contrast, the Thematic structure of Text 1.1 contains two uses of the Mood Adjunct *perhaps* used Thematically. This is an example of an optional interpersonal Theme, since *perhaps* could have been moved to the Rheme if the writer required, and it gives prominence to the expressions of tentativity which run through the text, often realized through modal Finites (*might, could*). One obligatory interpersonal Theme is also used (e.g. *Is his cot an interesting place to be?*). This thematization of modality is one way in which Text 1.1 creates its 'approachable, fallible' style.

Text 1.2 contains no interpersonal Themes at all. Although meanings of modality and modulation are made in this text, they are not given Thematic status, but are realized through non-Thematic modal Finites (e.g. *may*). As the only Mood structure used is declarative, no obligatory interpersonal Themes are needed. This non-Thematization of modality, and non-use of Mood classes which invite interaction (such as interrogatives), is part of how Text 1.2 creates its authority and distance.

There are also differences in the combinations of topical and textual Themes. In Text 1.3 we find that topical Themes are frequently preceded by textual Themes, e.g. continuity items (*oh, yea*) or conjunctions linking paratactic clause complexes (*and, so, but*). In Text 1.1, the only textual Themes that occur are conjunctive, and (ignoring *and* which is frequent in all texts) the conjunctions used typically introduce hypotactic dependent clauses (*if, when*). In Text 1.2, on the other hand, conjunctions are not often Thematic. For example, the delayed *however* in *These reasons, however, account for a relatively small percentage . . .* places the conjunction in the Rheme. On the one occasion that a conjunction is used Thematically, it is a paratactic conjunction (*however*). Thus, the choice of what gets to be Theme shows variation according to the mode of the texts.

2. Choice of topical Theme

Since there will (almost) always be a topical Theme present in a clause, it is useful to look at what it is. In conversation, such as Text 1.3, we find that the overwhelming majority of topical Themes are personal pronouns or names (*you, he, I*). Where they are not personal pronouns, the topical Theme tends to be a brief nominal group, referring either to specific individuals (*your kids*) or containing a simple circumstantial expression (*the last time, in Switzerland*). By contrast, the topical Themes found in Text 1.2 are often lengthy nominal groups, often involving several nominalizations, linked through modification:

> The compelling sound of an infant's cry
> Many reasons for crying
> In the absence of a discernible reason for the behaviour

Where simple nominal groups are used, the Thematized nouns refer to classes of people, not to individuals (*infants, parents*).

In Text 1.1, we find a middle position. Many of the topical Themes are the personal pronoun *you*, used here generically since the actual *you* is of course not known. A small percentage of topical Themes are class names (*babies, parents*), but frequently we find *your baby* or *he*. Occasional nominalized topical Themes are used, but these generally remain short and contain only one nominalized element (*the most common reason baby cries, outside stimulation*). Most striking in this text, however, is the frequency with which we have dependent clauses as topical Themes to entire sentences:

> Even if he was just recently fed he might still be adapting to the pattern . . .
> When he was in the womb, nourishment came automatically and constantly.
> if he turns away from the nipple or teat, you can assume it's something else.

Hypotactic structures such as these allow the writer to maintain a very congruent style: rather than building up the lexical density of the text, the writer exploits the strategy of grammatical complexity. However, the Thematic position of the dependent clause indicates an amount of pre-planning that is less common in spoken than written language. Thus the text is able to 'sound' like written language, while remaining accessible by maintaining its closeness to the spoken language.

The patterns of topical Theme choice in these texts, then, relate to the mode variation between the texts. In face-to-face conversation, our point of departure for most of our messages is ourselves or those somehow connected with us. In academic or scholarly writing, the mode demands the Thematization of abstractions: we do not depart from our own experience, but from our considered generalizations about people, situations, causes. Text 1.1, then, reveals through its topical Themes one of the strategies it uses to meet the competing demands of being a written text that is supposed to have the accessibility of speech: topical Themes remain personal, but the planning of the text allows frequent construction of dependent clause Themes.

3. Markedness of Theme choices

As with the other systems of Thematic choice, the decision to make a marked element Theme frequently relates to Mode dimensions. As Text 1.3 suggests, marked Themes are relatively rare in casual conversation, occurring mainly at schematic structure boundaries in monologic chunks such as the Codas in oral narratives (as with Diana's clauses that we have considered repeatedly in this chapter). In Text 1.2, on the other hand, marked Themes are used frequently:

> i) In most infants, there are frequent episodes of crying with no apparent cause
> ii) For these parents, respite from exposure to the crying may be necessary
> iii) In the absence of a discernible reason for the behaviour crying often stops
> iv) Without relief, fatigue and tension may result in inappropriate parental responses

As these examples demonstrate, a range of Circumstantial elements get made Theme: location, behalf, manner, etc. One effect of these marked Themes is to allow generic classes to be made Theme without having to make them the Actors/Subjects in a clause, as in examples i) and ii). Alternatively, markedness allows nominalizations to become Thematic, as is the case with examples iii) and iv). This allows the cumulative 'compacting' of the text, as nominalized versions of prior information can become the point of departure for the writer's next piece of new information.

By contrast, Text 1.1 contains only two marked Themes in a substantially longer text:

> During the day, a baby sling helps you to deal with your chores . . .
> At night when you want to sleep you will need to take action . . .

Significantly, both deal with time, which indicates a similarity between their role in this text and their occurrence in narrative segments of conversation.

4. Method of development

A final, but very significant, contribution that Theme makes to the cohesion and coherence of a text has to do with how Thematic elements succeed each other. Three main patterns of Thematic development can be observed:

i) Theme reiteration: one basic way to keep a text focused (i.e. cohesive) is to simply reiterate an element. As we saw with lexical cohesion, repetition is an effective means of creating cohesion. Having the same participant made Theme on a regular basis provides the text with a clear focus. This kind of Thematic pattern, where the same element occurs regularly as Theme, occurs for short periods in Text 1.3, for example the repeated use of *they* as Theme when talking about the *classy ladies*. However, the dynamic and unplanned nature of conversation tends to lead to rapid Thematic shifts, although the shifting is between a limited range of items as we saw above.

Theme reiteration is exploited with greater complexity and consistency in Text 1.2, however, where *crying* manages to occur Thematically in almost all the Themes of the text. However, because many of the Themes involve lengthy nominalizations, *crying* gets made Thematic in association with other elements introduced by the writer (e.g. *reasons, counseling*, etc.). This has the effect of maintaining a strong topical focus in the text, while avoiding simple repetition.

A text in which the Theme never varied would not only be boring to read or listen to, but would indicate a text which is going nowhere. If Theme is our point of departure, constancy of Theme would mean we are always leaving from the same spot, and that the 'new' information introduced in the Rhemes would not be being followed up. This explains the use of complex, nominalized Themes in written texts such as Text 1.2.

Text 1.1 again strikes a middle path, with the first and second paragraphs reiterating the same Themes, but in this case a simple, personal pronoun Theme (*you, he*), while the subsequent paragraphs reveal extensive Thematic shifts.

Thematic shifting can be achieved either 'accidentally', with the new Theme coming from outside the text, or cohesively, in which case we can describe it as **Thematic progression**. There are two main kinds of Thematic progression patterns: the zig-zag, and the multiple themes.

ii) the zig-zag pattern: in this pattern, an element which is introduced in the Rheme in clause 1 gets promoted to become the Theme of clause 2. This pattern is diagrammed in Figure 10.1.

In Text 1.3, it is the zig-zag pattern which allows *these two women*, introduced in the Rheme of a hypotactic clause pair, to become Theme for the following few clauses:

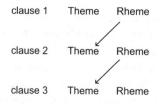

Figure 10.1   The zig-zag pattern of Thematic development

> And as we sat on the foreshore of this Vaucluse area these two women came down
> and they'd both been working . . . etc.

It is also the strategy by which *the baby* can become Theme again:

> and so I just handed the baby to them
> and LUCKILY he kept on crying

This zig-zag pattern is also illustrated in Text 1.1, when *hunger* leads to feeding, nourishment, etc. as Thematic elements:

> The most common reason baby cries is hunger.
> Even if he was just recently fed, he might still be adapting to the pattern . . .

Text 1.2 also uses the zig-zag strategy, but the situation is more complex. Take the sequence:

> These reasons, however, account for a relatively small percentage of infant crying
> and are usually recognized quickly and alleviated.
> In the absence of a discernible reason for the behaviour, crying often stops . . .

The Thematic element *In the absence of a discernible reason for the behaviour* comes in part from the Rheme of the preceding clause, but it also builds on the Themes and Rhemes of all the prior clauses. The noun *reason* sends us back to the Theme of the previous clause, which in turn comes from the earlier clause *Many reasons for crying are obvious, like hunger and discomfort due to heat, cold, illness, and lying position.*

The zig-zag pattern achieves cohesion in the text by building on newly introduced information. This gives the text a sense of cumulative development which may be absent in the repeated Theme pattern.

iii) the multiple-Rheme pattern: in this pattern, the Theme of one clause introduces a number of different pieces of information, each of which is then picked up and made Theme in subsequent clauses, as shown diagrammatically in Figure 10.2.

An example of this method of development is illustrated in Text 1.1, where the elements *relax and settle him* provide the Thematic content of *rocking, wrapping up, outside stimulation*, etc. in the subsequent clauses.

This multiple-Rheme pattern is also common in longer expository texts. We could construct a fourth Crying Baby text using such a pattern:

> The three main reasons babies cry are hunger, cold, and illness.
> Hunger can be determined by considering when the baby was last fed.
> Babies feel cold more acutely than we do and the smaller the baby, the more warmly
> it should be wrapped up.
> Finally, sickness or pain may also be signalled by crying . . .

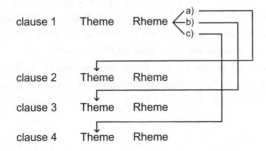

Figure 10.2   The multiple-Rheme pattern of Thematic development

As this example suggests, the multiple-Rheme pattern often provides the underlying organizing principle for a text, with both the zig-zag and theme reiteration strategies being used for elaborating on each of the main thematic points.

Like the other aspects of Theme choice, the use of Thematic patterns can also be related to mode. Spoken language reveals the least 'planned' method of development, with short segments of Theme reiteration followed by rapid Thematic shifts, often achieved by speakers simply dipping into the permanent pool of available conversational Themes: *you, I, he/she, we, they*. In monologic segments such as narratives, Thematic choice is likely to draw on the zig-zag strategy, as we saw in Text 1.3. Written texts will in general use Thematic progression strategies more frequently. Thus, both the zig-zag and the multiple-Theme patterns will be common. Nominalization also makes the Theme reiteration pattern a powerful means of creating cohesion in written text. Overall, a carefully written text will not surprise us with its Thematic choice: what gets to be Theme will come from somewhere in the nearby text.

Theme and levels of textual structure

This chapter has illustrated that the Theme/Rheme structure of the clause is an essential component in the construction of cohesive, coherent text. However, the implications of Theme go beyond the clause, in that the Theme/Rheme structure of the clause can be seen as merely the micro-level realization of textual organization. Martin (1992a) has led SFL explorations of how similar patterns of 'waves of information' operate across higher units of text. Martin and Rose (2003) devote one chapter to what they call **periodicity** or **information flow**. There they explore not only how Theme orients the reader to what is the point of departure for each clause, but also how the **hyperTheme**, or topic sentence, predicts what will happen in paragraphs or phases of longer texts. Above this, patterns of **macroTheme** are also indentified across larger phases of discourse. Martin and Rose establish a 'hierarchy of periodicity', or layering of textual organization, showing that skilful writers and speakers use these different levels of textual structure to continually re-orient the reader's expectations for the direction of the unfolding text.

Recognition of this hierarchy of textual organization underlines the systemic claim that the textual is the **enabling** metafunction: without structures such as Theme, there could be no text. The essential contribution made by textual meaning is to actualize a range of different textual structures which operate at all levels of the text, and whose function is to enable the ideational and interpersonal meanings we have chosen to make to be realized in a cohesive and coherent text.

Although there are many other aspects of systemic-functional grammar that we have not had space to describe, such as the grammar of phrases and groups and the systems of rhythm and intonation, this chapter completes the presentation of new material. You are now equipped with the analytic skills and technical vocabulary to enable you to analyse text, any text, and to talk about the grammatical patterns you find as the expression of semantic choices, which are in turn the realization of contextual dimensions.

In the final chapter we will look briefly at how these systemic tools can be applied to uncover and explain patterns in texts, by discussing the results of comprehensive analyses of the Crying Baby texts first presented in Chapter One.

Note

1.   For a more extensive discussion of Theme, see Halliday and Matthiessen 2004: Chapter 3.

Chapter 11

Explaining text: applying SFL

Introduction

This chapter begins by summarizing the model that has been presented in this book, and then offers a demonstration of how a systemic approach can be applied in text analysis. The demonstration involves presenting the results of the comprehensive lexico-grammatical and cohesive analyses of the three Crying Baby texts (Texts 1.1, 1.2 and 1.3 introduced in Chapter One). I will show how systemic analyses enable us to make explicit how the texts are alike and different, and to relate those patterns to the cultural and situational contexts of which they are the realization. The analyses of Texts 1.1, 1.2 and 1.3 can be found in the Appendix.

Summary of the model

Chapters One to Ten have outlined a model of language as a functional-semantic resource: language is modelled as networks of interconnected linguistic systems from which we choose in order to make the meanings we need to make to achieve our communicative purposes. The product of a sequence of choices is a text, and the choices realized in text are themselves the realization of contextual dimensions, including specific situational configurations of field, mode and tenor (register), cultural conventions (genre) and ideological positions. Language is thus modelled not just as a resource embedded in a social and cultural context, but as a resource through whose use we are continually constructing, maintaining and defining what constitutes appropriate meanings in possible contexts in our culture.

Language itself has been interpreted as a three-level semiotic system, where the semantic unit, the text, unified through cohesive patterns, is the locus of choices in ideational, textual and interpersonal meaning. These semantic choices, themselves derived from the need to express context in language, are in turn realized through lexico-grammatical choices, with each semantic dimension relating in a predictable and systematic way to choices from the four simultaneous systems of grammatical structure, Mood, Transitivity,

Clause Complex and Theme. The multiple structural description of the clause allows us to describe how language makes meanings simultaneously.

The essential distinguishing characteristic of the SFL model is that it sets up a realizational relationship extending all the way from the most abstract levels of context (ideology) through to the very concrete words, structures, sounds and graphology of text. This realization relationship, captured in various diagrams throughout the book, can be read in both a predictive and a deductive direction. That is, given the specification of context, we can predict with reasonable accuracy the linguistic choices which will characterize a text, its most typical realizational patterns. And, given a text, the actualization of linguistic choices, we can deduce the context within which it was produced and of which it is a realization.

As well as presenting a theoretical account of the model, this book has also introduced the following descriptive techniques:

i) cohesive analysis: a brief outline of analyses for patterns of reference, lexical relations and conjunctive relations were provided in Chapter Two
ii) grammatical analysis: Chapters Six, Eight, Nine and Ten presented an overview of the semantic and grammatical criteria for identifying the principal functional clause constituents which realize the Mood, Transitivity, Logico-semantic and Theme structures of the clause.

For reasons of space, theoretical concepts have not been treated in depth, and only major descriptive techniques have been covered. In the more specialized systemic works (e.g. Halliday and Hasan 1976, Halliday and Matthiessen 1999, 2004, Martin 1992a, Martin *et al.* 1997, Martin and Rose 2003, Matthiessen 1995) you will find more substantial accounts of concepts such as realization, delicacy, system, metafunction, etc., as well as details of a wide range of analytical techniques for each stratum, including:

i) other cohesive analyses: e.g. ellipsis and substitution, and cohesive harmony (cf. Hasan 1984, 1985b: 89–94);
ii) other lexico-grammatical analyses: nominal group, verbal group, prepositional phrase at group rank, and logico-semantic relations at all ranks.

The analytical techniques presented in this book were chosen on the basis that a description of the Mood, Transitivity, Clause Complex, Theme, reference, conjunctive and lexical relations of a text provides a reasonably thorough account of how the text is structured to make meanings in context. The remaining sections of this chapter consider just how these analytical resources can be applied to the text analysis task.

Systemic text analysis

You will recall from Chapter One that of the many possible applications of systemic linguistics, the most general one adopted as the framework for this book was that of explaining 'why a text means what it does'. Two pairs of terms can be used to clarify the aims and scope of systemic text analysis. Firstly, we can contrast the *interpretation* with the *explanation* of text. And secondly, we can recognize a distinction between the *understanding* of a text and its *evaluation*.

Traditional approaches to the study of literary texts model text analysis as an *interpretive* activity. Students learn to read a text and try to argue about what meanings they think the writer was making in the text. From a systemic perspective, however, text analysis is not an interpretive but an *explanatory* activity: 'The linguistic analysis of text is not an interpretation of that text; it is an explanation' (Halliday and Hasan 1976: 327). While the interpretation of a text would aim to uncover and state *what* a text means, the systemic analysis of a text aims to uncover and state *how* a text means. But in fact there is no dichotomy between these terms. Given that a functional-semantic perspective defines the meaning of any linguistic item (morpheme, clause, text) as that item's function in a context of use, it follows that in the very process of demonstrating *how* a text means, we are also in fact laying bare *what* a text means.

A second important distinction needs to be made between *understanding* a text and *evaluating* a text. Halliday (1994: xv) represents this distinction as one of two levels of analysis, with the lower of the two levels, that of **understanding**, involving the use of linguistic analysis to show 'how, and why, the text means what it does'. As he points out, this level of understanding 'should always be attainable', given an appropriate functional grammar of text as an analytical tool.

Halliday suggests that a more ambitious goal in text analysis is to be able to contribute an **evaluation** of the text. That is:

> the linguistic analysis may enable one to say why the text is, or is not, an effective text for its own purposes – in what respects it succeeds and in what respects it fails, or is less successful. (Halliday 1994: xv)

Halliday argues that this goal is more difficult to attain because:

> It requires an interpretation not only of the text itself but also of its context (context of situation, context of culture), and of the systematic relationship between context and text. (Halliday 1994: xv)

It is through the realizational relationships established between each metafunction and a grammatical system, and between the tripartite functional organization of language and the tripartite construction of register, between cultural context and the schematic structure of text, that a systemic model offers an effective tool for exploring this higher level of text analysis.

The explanatory and evaluative power of the model can be illustrated by the following discussion of the three Crying Baby texts.

Analysis of the Crying Baby texts

The analysis of the Crying Baby texts is an exercise in contrastive text analysis. Contrastive analysis involves taking texts which are similar in some respects but different in others. Contrastive analysis offers a relatively easy way in to tackling text analysis because it provides some picture of how an actual text is but one realization from a total potential. Patterns of linguistic choice are more easily identified and explained when seen in contrast with other texts exhibiting patterns that realize other possible choices.

A useful first step in undertaking text analysis is to problematize the texts by asking just what is interesting about them. This interest may arise from 'above' (i.e. because of the context that is realized in the text) or from 'below' (i.e. because of specific linguistic features being used). For example, interest in the Crying Baby texts may arise from either focus. From context, we may consider that Texts 1.1, 1.2 and 1.3 are of interest because they are texts which seem to be about the same thing, and yet they talk about it in very different ways. The 'problem' is to use text analysis techniques to explain both how the texts are similar (in what linguistic respects), and how they are different.

Our interest in the texts might equally well arise from 'below', as we might note lexicogrammatical or cohesive differences between the texts, such as for example that Texts 1.1 and 1.2 seem to use very different sorts of words in talking about crying babies. Here, the problem is to use text analysis techniques to specify the nature of that variation, and then to relate it to different ways of talking about the topic.

These very general statements of interest in the texts can then be made more specific in order to give the analytical task greater focus. For example, the general observation of 'differences' between the texts can be developed by observing that while both Texts 1.1 and 1.2 are written texts, Text 1.1 seems much 'friendlier' and less 'formal' than Text 1.2. How is that impression conveyed? And how does the spontaneity of the spoken Text 1.3 affect the way the topic of crying babies gets talked about?, etc.

To this point, the texts have been approached in non-technical terms. The same problems could now be restated technically, with reference to dimensions such as genre, register, cohesion and lexico-grammar. Taking some of the problems raised by a contextual interest in the texts, we could develop the following technical linguistic questions to explore:

- What linguistic evidence is there for claiming that Texts 1.1, 1.2 and 1.3 share a common field?
- What linguistic evidence is there for claiming that Texts 1.1 and 1.2 establish different tenor relationships with their readers?
- What is the relationship between differences in tenor and the mode shift that sets Text 1.3 apart from Texts 1.1 and 1.2?
- To what extent can Texts 1.1 and 1.2 be described as being of the same genre?
- How is the generic structure of the written texts different from that of the spoken text? That is, what impact do variables of tenor and mode have on generic choice and realization?

Where interest arises from lexico-grammatical or cohesive features, questions can also be rephrased technically. For example:

- Is there a difference in the way modalization and modulation are used in the texts? (focusing on lexico-grammar)
- Is there any evidence for claiming that one text is more or less cohesive than any other? (focusing on cohesive resources)

The statement of a dimension (or, more commonly, dimensions) of interest in the texts facilitates decisions about which analyses to undertake, for time does not usually allow a comprehensive analysis. In a comprehensive text analysis, the text would be analysed for all cohesive systems (reference, conjunction, lexical cohesion, conversational structure, ellipsis and substitution . . .) and for grammatical patterns, at least at clause rank (Mood, Transitivity, Theme, Logical Relations . . .), perhaps also at group rank (structure of nominal, verbal, prepositional phrases . . .), with both function and class labelling applied.

It is obvious that such exhaustive analysis of a text will demand considerable time and effort. What is less obvious is that it may produce information which is not particularly relevant to resolving the problem identified as interesting. For example, to explore differences in field between the texts, an analysis of modality may not be particularly revealing.

A more pragmatic approach, then, is to perform selective text analysis. Here the text is analysed only partially, with the systemic functional model being used to predict which analyses are likely to be rewarding in light of the specific text problem(s) identified.

For example, in order to determine whether Texts 1.1, 1.2 and 1.3 in fact share a common field, the model would predict that the following analyses should be undertaken:

- cohesive: lexical relations, conjunctive relations
- lexico-grammatical: Transitivity and Clause Complex

Similarly, to explore differences in mode, the most relevant analyses would be:

- cohesive: reference, conjunction
- lexico-grammar: Theme

Texts where tenor is of interest would first be analysed for Mood and conversational structure.

This is not to say that other analyses would not be undertaken, but that priority could be given to the analyses predicted by the model as 'at risk' given the context. It may be that in analysing one of these 'at risk' dimensions, it becomes obvious that another system is implicated. For example, it will be suggested below that while one way in which Text 1.1 creates a less formal tenor than Text 1.2 has to do with Mood selections, the informality of 1.1 is also the result of its use of a more spoken mode than Text 1.2 (although both texts are of course written texts). It is therefore necessary to describe how choices in Clause Complex, reference and conjunction realize a more spoken text, and how this in turn realizes a less formal tenor.

Interest in the use of a particular linguistic resource in a text will of course point directly towards an initial analysis. However, while the particular analysis indicated provides a starting point, analysis should be broadened to take in other systems which the model predicts realize the kind of meaning under focus. For example, interest in differences between the types of words used in Texts 1.1, 1.2 and 1.3 would indicate that an analysis of lexical cohesion should be undertaken. However, in order to get a complete picture of how field is constructed in the texts, this lexical description should be accompanied by analysis of Transitivity and Clause Complex relations, since these linguistic systems together contribute to realizing ideational meanings in the text.

The higher the contextual dimension involved in the problem, the greater the number of analyses 'at risk'. For example, interest in generic variation between two texts will almost certainly involve analysis of a number of systems, since genre is realized through configurations of all the register variables, which means all the cohesive and lexico-grammatical systems are likely to be influenced.

In order to provide a reasonably comprehensive demonstration of how the various concepts and systems presented in this book can be applied in text analysis, the analysis of the Crying Baby texts was undertaken with the following very broad questions in mind:

- In what respects are the three texts alike, and in what respects different?

- How can these similarities and differences be related to the register variables of field, mode and tenor, and to genre?

Texts 1.1, 1.2 and 1.3 have been analysed for all the following systems, according to the categories and methods set out in this book:

- Mood
- Transitivity
- Logical relations (clause complex)
- Theme
- Conjunctive relations
- Reference
- Lexical relations
- Schematic Structure

These analyses, presented in a compact form, can be found in the Appendix, accompanied by a key to each analysis.

In the following sections the results of these analyses will be discussed, beginning with the lexico-grammatical analyses. While a detailed clause-by-clause discussion of an analysed text can be highly revealing (see, for example, Halliday's analysis in the Appendix to Halliday 1994: 368–91, unfortunately not retained in Halliday and Matthiessen 2004), considerations of space here force the aggregation and tabulation of results. While this approach is more brutal, it will be seen that it is very effective in highlighting different patterns in texts. It can thus still provide substantial explanatory accounts of the texts, while avoiding one of the potential traps of sequential discussion, that of it degenerating into no more than a commentary on a text.

Throughout the discussion the linguistic patterns identified will be related to context, as the language patterns of course provide evidence to address questions concerning the similarity and difference in register variables.

Lexico-grammatical analyses of the texts

Mood analysis

All ranking and embedded clauses in each text were analysed for Mood according to the description presented in Chapter Six. Categories which did not occur in the data (e.g. Adjunct:vocative) are not listed in the key which precedes the analysis in the Appendix, and will not be further discussed.

Table 11.1 summarizes the results of the analysis of Mood class, showing figures for ranking (non-embedded) clauses only. Mood classes are only listed if at least one example occurred in one text.

As this table shows, Text 1.2 uses only one Mood type, the full (non-elliptical) declarative, a pattern which is not unsurprising in the written mode where feedback between writer and reader is not possible. However, while Text 1.1 is also written, it does select twice from outside the declarative Mood, with one imperative and one elliptical WH-interrogative realized. Each of these choices contributes significantly to the meanings being made in the text.

The imperative clause functions as a single congruent indication that the text is doing more than simply giving information, or, rather, that the information it gives has the

Table 11.1   Mood in the Crying Baby texts

Mood class	MOOD (ranking clauses only)		
	Text 1.1	Text 1.2	Text 1.3
full declarative	67	22	34
elliptical declarative	0	0	14
full polar interrogative	1	0	1
elliptical polar interrogative	0	0	1
full WH-interrogative	0	0	3
elliptical WH-interrogative	1	0	2
imperative	1	0	0
minor	0	0	2
abandoned/incomplete	0	0	3
total ranking clauses	70	22	60

potential to be packaged as a goods and service. That is, this imperative signals clearly that we should read the information as 'advice'. As the writer's role as 'adviser' is typically construed as one of unequal power (the writer, having greater knowledge, is in a position of 'expert', while the reader needs help), the tenor of the task has the potential to create boundaries, rather than solidarity, between writer and reader. If the writer therefore wishes to maintain a less distant relationship than her role as adviser might generically imply, other strategies must be mobilized in the text.

One way in which the formality of the expert's role is minimized in Text 1.1 is the use of the elliptical interrogative, which has the effect of creating a 'rhetorical' interactive context. Thus, while there is in fact no dialogue possible between writer and reader, the interrogative allows the text to seem interactive, dividing it into two parts: a question stage (up to sentence 3) and then an answer stage (from sentence 3 to the end). This creates an impression of dialogue, and therefore reduces the distance between reader and writer. Contributing to this effect is the choice of the pronoun *you* (i.e. the reader-parent) as Subject in the question stage, thus giving the text a reason for existing: you, the parent, are constructed as having asked the 'expert' the question 'Why?'. Therefore, of course, the expert will answer your question.

The (real) dialogic mode of Text 1.3 is indicated by its high use of elliptical structures, and the presence of minor and abandoned clauses. These Mood choices also establish speaker S in the role of questioner, while C takes the role of respondent. Although these roles are differentiated, the initial power difference they suggest (that S is in charge of the direction of the talk) is undermined in the latter part of the text, where C in fact takes the floor for a sustained period. The second half of the text is largely non-elliptical declaratives. This shift in roles, from C as respondent to C as giver of information, accompanied by the frequent overlaps and shared laughter, indicates that the tenor is an informal one.

The dominance of full declaratives in all three texts indicates that the texts share a common focus on the giving of information. However, the patterns of modality in the texts provide evidence to support the claim that there is a difference between the type of information being offered in Texts 1.1 and 1.2 (i.e. advice), and that offered in 1.3.

Table 11.2 indicates the frequency with which modality and polarity are expressed through verbal constituents of the clause (Mood Adjuncts are considered later).

As these results show, Text 1.3 has the lowest use of modality, with Text 1.1 using the highest amount, and Text 1.2 falling in between. In all cases, the use of modalization

Table 11.2   Modality and polarity in the Crying Baby texts

	MODALITY and POLARITY (expressed through verbal constituents of Finite, Predicator)		
Type	Text 1.1	Text 1.2	Text 1.3
modalization	18	5	5
modulation	5	2	1
negation	2	0	5
ranking clauses	70	22	60

dominates over modulation, but this difference is most marked in Text 1.3. In both Texts 1.1 and 1.2 the ratio of modalization to modulation is approximately the same.

These findings suggest that there is a difference between the information being given in Text 1.3 and that given in the other two texts. Whereas Texts 1.1 and 1.2 offer 'advice' (information about modulated actions, modalized since it cannot be assumed to be relevant to all potential advisees), Text 1.3 offers personal experience. Since personal experience is a domain over which a speaker possesses certain knowledge, and which does not involve getting other people to do things, the level of modality is low.

The higher use of modalization in Text 1.1 over Text 1.2 can be explained as part of the way the writer creates a less authoritative, more suggestive tenor, by balancing the power inequality inherent in the modulations. These results are complemented by a consideration of Adjuncts in the texts. Table 11.3 tabulates the use of Adjuncts in each text.

The results show that in both Texts 1.2 and 1.3 the number of Adjuncts exceeds the number of ranking clauses, while in Text 1.1 it is slightly less. Thus, a considerable proportion of the meanings made in these two texts are made as non-core, non-arguable information. This can be interpreted as a strategy by which the writer's/speaker's authority is created and protected: much of what is written/said is non-arguable by the reader. While in Text 1.3 the information may well not be arguable, since the listener presumably cannot dispute the veracity of the speaker's account of her experience, in Text 1.2 the packaging of meaning into Adjuncts suggests that the writer is making it more difficult for readers to dispute his claims.

In addition, a relatively high number of Circumstantial Adjuncts occur in Text 1.2: almost the same proportion as in the other much longer texts. This high specification of

Table 11.3   Types of Adjuncts in the Crying Baby texts

	ADJUNCTS		
Type of Adjunct	Text 1.1	Text 1.2	Text 1.3
Circumstantial	19	15	20
Mood	11	2	11
Comment	0	0	2
Polarity	0	0	1
Conjunctive	28	9	22
Continuity	0	0	22
Total Adjuncts	58	26	78
Ranking clauses	70	22	60

Table 11.4   Categories of Mood Adjuncts in the texts

	MODALITY (verbal and Adjunctive realizations)		
	Text 1.1	Text 1.2	Text 1.3
modalization (verbal)	17	5	5
modulation	4	2	0
Mood Adjunct: usuality	5	0	3
Mood Adjunct: probability	4	0	0
Mood Adjunct: intensification	4	0	8
total expressions of Modality	34	7	16
total ranking clauses	70	22	60

Circumstantial meaning will be considered in the discussion of Transitivity (below). While having fewer Adjuncts, however, Text 1.1 has a high proportion of Mood Adjuncts, again indicating that the grammar is used to temper the advice given. The high proportion of continuity Adjuncts in Text 1.3 is to be expected in informal face-to-face talk, while the high proportion of Conjunctive Adjuncts in Text 1.2 also indicates the more rhetorical organization of this formal, written text.

In order to gain a clearer picture of Modality in the texts, Table 11.4 above tabulates realizations of Modality verbally and in Adjuncts, with Mood Adjuncts divided into the categories of probability, usuality and intensification.

This table confirms that Text 1.1 makes the greatest use of modality. It also indicates that where modality is used in Text 1.3, it is most frequently used to express intensification (*really, just*, etc.), and is never used to express probability. In Text 1.2, by contrast, all expressions of modality are made through verbal elements of the clause. This preference for the *subjective* expression of modality indicates that the arguability of propositions will centre around the degree of modality (high, median, low). The effect of this appears to be to make the writer sound cautious, balanced, and 'academic'. Rash assertions are not made.

Text 1.1, in contrast, makes frequent use of *objective* modality, using Mood Adjuncts to reinforce the meanings made subjectively through the verbal modality realizations. However, whereas the verbal modalities were largely of probability, the Adjuncts express all three categories. While the usuality Adjuncts indicate that the advice offered is qualified in terms of usuality, the probability Adjuncts temper the relevance of the advice to each reader, and the high frequency of intensification Adjuncts again gives the text a less formal, more conversational tone.

Transitivity analysis

The process type and participant configurations of each clause (both ranking and embedded clauses) are shown in the Appendix. Table 11.5 below presents the total number of clauses of each process type in each text.

As this table shows, material processes are dominant in all texts. This indicates that all three texts are centrally concerned with actions and events and the participants who carry them out. However, the proportion of material processes to other process types is highest in Texts 1.1 and 1.3. Those texts, then, are predominantly about tangible, physical

Table 11.5   Transitivity in the Crying Baby texts

Process type	TRANSITIVITY		
	Text 1.1	Text 1.2	Text 1.3
material	34	8	19
mental	11	4	4
verbal	2	0	1
behavioural	14	3	3
existential	0	1	4
relational: attributive	20	6	10
relational: identifying	5	3	3
relational: possessive	0	0	2
causative	4	3	0
total no. of processes	90	28	46

actions. The presence of existentials in Text 1.3 suggests that these actions are sometimes framed as taking place within settings which are asserted simply as existing, while existentials are never chosen in Text 1.1.

Table 11.5 also shows that Text 1.1 uses a high proportion of behavioural processes. These processes construct the baby as a physiologically-dominated participant, whereas the higher proportion of mental processes in Text 1.2 suggest that conscious cognition, rather than bodily behaviour, is the text's concern. Texts 1.1 and 1.2 each contain roughly equal proportions of relational processes, although the attributives dominate the relational category in Text 1.1. This indicates that Text 1.1 is more descriptive than Text 1.2, which is just as much concerned with defining as describing participants.

Significantly, almost the same number of causative processes are used in the very brief Text 1.2 as in the much longer Text 1.1, while there are no causatives at all in Text 1.3. This provides evidence of the difference in purpose between the texts, with Texts 1.1 and 1.2 constructing a field to do with reasons and explanations, while Text 1.3 constructs a field of events and happenings. (See the discussion of generic structure below.)

Table 11.6 presents numbers for each type of Circumstantial element in the texts.

As this table shows, and as was noted above in the discussion of Adjuncts, Text 1.2 has a high number of Circumstances in proportion to its length. Part of the function of these circumstantial elements appears to be to deflect arguability from certain participants.

Table 11.6   Circumstances in the Crying Baby texts

Type	CIRCUMSTANCES		
	Text 1.1	Text 1.2	Text 1.3
location	11	2	10
extent	1	2	3
manner	4	5	0
role	0	0	1
cause	1	3	0
total	17	12	14
no. of ranking clauses	70	22	60

However, Circumstances also function to increase the experiential content of the text, as they add specificity to the information given. This frequency of Circumstantial detail, then, contributes to boosting the experiential density of the text, and complements other strategies used to make this text very written in mode (see the discussion of nominalization in this text in Chapter Four).

While in Text 1.1 and 1.3 the dominant circumstance is that of location, in Text 1.2 this role is shared by circumstances of manner and cause. Neither of these types occurs at all in Text 1.3, while manner is the second most frequent type realized in Text 1.1. While Text 1.3, then, concentrates on situating events in time and space, noting where, when and for how long they took place, Text 1.1 is concerned with where, when and how behaviours occurred, and Text 1.2 with how and why things are the way they are, and what caused them to be that way. These emerging ideational similarities and differences between the texts are further complemented by clause complex analysis.

Clause complex analysis

Table 11.7 displays the results of clause complex analysis for each text.

This table shows a difference in the proportion of words to sentences: 16.7 in Text 1.1, 22.8 in Text 1.2 and 7.7 in Text 1.3. That is, Text 1.3 spreads its words over a larger number of sentences than either of the other two texts, while Text 1.2 is the 'densest' in packing its words into sentences. This confirms an expected mode difference, with Text 1.3 the 'most spoken' and Text 1.2 the 'most written' of the texts. There is also a marked difference between the use of clause complex resources, with Text 1.3, the interactive text, using much less complexing (only 25 per cent) than either of the other texts. At first sight this would appear to go against our expectations of spoken language (where we've seen intricate clause complexes occurring, e.g. in Text 9.2). But in fact what we're seeing here is the competitive turn-taking environment of casual talk, which is very different from the authorized monologic mode of an interview. Text 1.3, then, shows that interactants generally only get the conversational space to produce single clauses, unless they negotiate the right to hold the floor, for example when they want to tell a story.

Table 11.7 also shows that Text 1.1 contains the most intricate clause complexes, suggesting again that this is one way in which it creates a more spoken mode. In fact, its clause complexes are much *more* dynamic and intricate than those in the face-to-face casual

Table 11.7   Basic clause complex summary of the Crying Baby texts

	CLAUSE COMPLEXES		
	Text 1.1	Text 1.2	Text 1.3
no. of words in text	451	228	332
no. of sentences in text	27	10	43
no. of ranking clauses	70	22	60
no. of clause simplexes	7	3	32
no. of clause complexes	20 (74%)	7 (70%)	11 (25%)
no. of embedded clauses	4	2	2
no. of clause complexes of 2 clauses	9	3	7
no. of clause complexes of 3 clauses	4	3	3
no. of clause complexes of 4 clauses	4	1	1
no. of clause complexes >4 clauses	3	0	0

Table 11.8   Taxis in the Crying Baby texts

Taxis		Text 1.1	Text 1.2	Text 1.3
hypotaxis	projection	8	1	4
	expansion	13	5	4
	total	21	6	8
parataxis	projection	0	0	1
	expansion	16	6	7
	total	16	6	8

conversation, which suggests that the magazine writer really is working very hard to sound as 'chatty' as possible.

Above is Table 11.8, showing taxis in each text (note that because of layering, tactic relations will exceed clause complex numbers).

This table shows that while Texts 1.2 and 1.3 use almost even proportions of hypotaxis to parataxis, Text 1.1 heavily favours hypotaxis, and with projection only uses hypotaxis. I interpret this as one way this text balances its 'chattiness' with its written mode. Hypotaxis is generally more common in written text because dependency relations require more care by the writer to construct and more effort by readers to interpret than parataxis. The hierarchic organization of information demanded by hypotaxis also offers the writer a resource for offering readers a more closely controlled logic between events. So Text 1.1 achieves something akin to the rapid flow of spoken language through its relatively high use of intricate complexes, but it takes advantage of the time realities of writing to structure these clause complexes carefully, thereby guiding readers closely in how to interpret the logical relations between experiential information provided by the text.

The fact that projection is least popular in Text 1.2 suggests that this is a text which constructs itself as an authority and so has no need to source comments to others. The conversational text does have some room for reported projections, not surprising in narrative where at least Evaluation stages typically involve the sourcing of reactions to the Complications.

The next table, Table 11.9, shows the sub-categories of projection and expansion (again, numbers exceed clause complexes because each relation is counted separately).

This table shows that projection in all texts is usually of ideas, with the low number of locutions perhaps explained by the topic of all the texts: the crying babies are not at speaking age, and so *their* locutions cannot be incorporated into the texts. Enhancement is the clear preference in expansion, showing that the focus in all three texts is on the sequential

Table 11.9   Logico-semantic relations in the Crying Baby texts

		Text 1.1	Text 1.2	Text 1.3
projection	locution	0	0	1
	idea	8	1	4
	total:projection	8	1	5
expansion	elaboration	2	1	3
	extension	10	4	2
	enhancement	23	6	6
	total:expansion	35	11	11

and causal relations between events. In sum, the Clause Complex relations both complement and fill out the ideational picture that emerged from our Transitivity analyses discussed above: all three texts are concerned with showing the temporal and causal logic that links experiential events; but while Text 1.1 does this as much through paratactic association of events suggested to be of *equal* relevance, Text 1.2 exploits more the hierarchic logic of hypotaxis, which in Text 1.1 is the clearly dominant logic imposed on events. These differences in the way experiential events are packaged are further elucidated by looking at patterns of Theme in each text.

Theme analysis

The analysis of Theme in all ranking clauses is shown in the Appendix. Where a dependent clause preceded its main clause, a double Theme analysis was given. Table 11.10 summarizes the findings of the Theme analysis.

As this table shows, marked Themes (where Theme does not conflate with Subject) are most common in Text 1.2. This would appear to be one realization of a careful written mode, in which the writer has planned the rhetorical development of the text to allow the foregrounding of Circumstantial information. Note here the interaction of Theme, Mood and Transitivity choices: the Circumstantial elements which occur as marked Themes encode familiar ('given') information, but information that is expressed as a non-arguable Adjunct in the clause.

Interpersonal Themes do not occur in Text 1.2 at all, while there are equal numbers in the other two texts. Again, this complements the results of the Mood analysis above, as this choice to make interpersonal elements Thematic contributes to realizing the less authoritarian tenor of Texts 1.1 and 1.3.

One striking feature of Text 1.1 is its use of dependent clauses as Themes. We've seen that this text makes high use of hypotaxis, setting up dependency relations between clauses. This then allows the choice between placing the dependent clause *after* the main clause (unmarked) or positioning it first (marked). This exploitation of the marked choice contributes to making Text 1.1 appear more spoken, as the frequent use of dependent clauses in Thematic position contributes to neutralizing the distinction between spoken and written language. Since clause complexes are more common in spoken language, while single clause sentences are frequent in written language, the presence of clause complexes suggests a spoken mode. However, by positioning the dependent clause first, the writer gives the text a degree of Thematic planning not common in spoken language. Text 1.2 adopts a more consistently written mode, both by having fewer clauses per sentence (i.e. fewer clause complexes), and by achieving its rhetorical organization through Thematizing highly nominalized Circumstantial constituents.

Table 11.10   THEME in the Crying Baby texts

	THEME		
Category	Text 1.1	Text 1.2	Text 1.3
marked	5	6	4
interpersonal element as Theme	3	0	5
dependent clause as Theme	6	0	1
ranking clause	70	22	60

Lexico-grammatical characterizations of the texts

One further lexico-grammatical dimension significant in differentiating these texts has already been discussed in Chapter Four, where it was pointed out that there is a very high degree of nominalization in Text 1.2, compared to the very low use of nominalization in Text 1.1. The unpacking of the nominalizations in Text 1.2, presented in Chapter Four, indicated that these nominalizations are accompanied by a decrease in the grammatical intricacy of the text, and an increase in the omission of Agent/Actors of processes.

Incorporating this feature along with the results of the separate analyses discussed above, an abbreviated lexico-grammatical characterization of each of the texts is presented in Table 11.11.

As this table shows, Text 1.1 is oriented towards making meanings about behaviours, and both material and physical actions, with some concern with the causation of those processes. Events are situated in time and place, and the manner of their performance is described. The text uses an interactive Mood choice (elliptical interrogative) to create the sense of a dialogue. The informality of speech is also created through the frequent use of intensification Adjuncts, the use of clause complexes, and infrequent nominalization. However, the text's response to the demands of the written mode involves using hypotaxis and thematizing dependent clauses.

Text 1.2 is oriented towards making meanings about actions and identity, and is concerned to explain why things are what they are, and how they came to be that way. The text creates a formal, authoritarian tenor by making human participants merely Adjuncts to the clause, in which nominalized abstractions feature as Subjects. The text makes only measured (modalized/modulated) claims, and avoids any direct interaction with the reader, who is not posited as Subject.

Table 11.11   Lexico-grammatical summary of the Crying Baby texts

LEXICO-GRAMMATICAL CHARACTERIZATION			
System	Text 1.1	Text 1.2	Text 1.3

Mood	+ declaratives
	+ single examples of
	  other mood clauses
	+ reader (you) as Subject
	+ modalization
	+ Mood Adjuncts
		+ full declaratives only
		+ nominalizations as
		  Subject
		+ Circumstantial
		  Adjuncts
		+ Conjunctive Adjuncts
		+ modalization in Finite
			+ elliptical declaratives,
			  interrogatives, minor,
			  abandoned
			+ Mood Adjuncts:
			  intensification

Transitivity	+ behavioural + attributive + causative + location + manner	+ mental + relational + causative + manner + cause	+ material + mental + existential + location + extent
Clause Complex	+ hypotaxis + projection + enhancement + 3+ complexes	+ complexes - projection + enhancement	+ simplexes + parataxis + enhancement
Theme	+ dependent clause as Theme	+ marked	unmarked

Text 1.3 is oriented towards meanings about actions, situated in time and place, and whose occurrence the speaker is certain of. Speakers change, as do their roles. The text exhibits features typical of spoken interactive talk, such as continuity items and rapid clause simplexes before the narrative section of the text.

Thus, the lexico-grammatical description of each text allows us to specify in some detail both how the texts are alike and different, and the effect of the different patterns observed. The results of these analyses can be complemented by considering the cohesive patterns in each text.

Cohesive analysis of the texts

The cohesive analyses of Text 1.1, 1.2 and 1.3 are presented in the Appendix, with a key accompanying each analysis.

Conjunctive cohesion

The conjunctive relations in each text were analysed, and the results are tabulated in Table 11.12.

As this table shows, Text 1.1 has little explicit conjunctive structure – much of the logical organization of the text has been achieved through clause complexes rather than through cohesive resources. Where used, however, the dominant conjunctive category is elaboration, suggesting that this text is concerned not so much with explaining by stating causes and consequences, but explaining by restating information in another way. As elaboration is an internal (rhetorical) conjunctive relation, its frequent use is one indication of written mode.

Text 1.2 reveals a more even implicit/explicit distribution, indicating some forward planning of the logical structure, as would be expected in a written text. With the major conjunctive category being enhancing, the text is constructed to offer advice in terms largely of cause and consequence.

In Text 1.3 we see that explicit conjunctions exceed implicits, with the most frequent conjunctive relation being addition. While other conjunctive categories are used, the analysis indicates that the text is mainly organized to extend: simply to give more information.

Reference

Reference chains for each text appear in the Appendix. Table 11.13 summarizes the main findings of the Reference analysis.

Table 11.12   Conjunctive relations in the Crying Baby texts

	CONJUNCTION		
Type	Text 1.1	Text 1.2	Text 1.3
elaborating	11	1	8
extending	6	0	9
enhancing	5	5	5
implicit	21	4	9
explicit	1	2	13
number of sentences	27	10	44

Table 11.13   Reference chains in the Crying Baby texts

REFERENCE CHAINS			
Feature	Text 1.1	Text 1.2	Text 1.3
number of head items	15	7	13
number of major participant chains (3+ items)	3	2	6
head items of 3 longest chains (no. of items in chains)	you (22) a baby who won't stop crying (37) babies get bored (3)	parents (6) normal crying (3)	your kids (13) your <u>kids</u> (15) these two women (7)
homophoric	6	1	5
exophoric	1	0	2
cataphoric	0	0	0
esphoric	5	1	0
bridging	0	1	0
number of sentences	27	10	44

As this table shows, there is little difference in the number of reference chains per text when length of text is taken into account. However, Text 1.3 indicates a more diverse number of participants. Both Texts 1.1 and 1.2 show a clear focus, with only a couple of major chains developed in each text. However, while the major participants in Text 1.1 are *you* (the addressed reader/parent) and *the baby*, Text 1.2 tracks *parents* and the nominalized process *crying*. Thus, while the participants in Text 1.1 are both particular and personal, in 1.3 they are generic (the class of parents) and abstractions.

The participants in Text 1.3 are closer in kind to Text 1.1, being both personal and specific. Thus, the reference pattern of Text 1.1 is similar to a spoken mode in that its participants are personal and specific, but more like a written mode in that only a small number of participants are developed consistently.

As far as the categories of retrieval are concerned, both Text 1.1 and 1.3 draw more heavily on retrieval from cultural and situational context than does Text 1.2, which is largely context-independent. This again indicates that Text 1.1 has certain characteristics of a spoken mode. However, to complete the blending of features it exemplifies, note the high number of esphoric retrievals in Text 1.1: as esphoric reference is text-internal, this is a type of reference more common in written mode. Again, the reference patterns show that Text 1.1 achieves a blending of spoken and written mode choices.

Lexical cohesion

The analysis of lexical relations in each text appears in the Appendix. The results of this analysis have been tabulated in Table 11.14.

Most noticeable from this table is the relatively high lexical content of Text 1.2: it contains almost as many lexical strings as the very much longer spoken text. In addition, most of these strings are major strings (consisting of four or more lexical items), so that despite the differences in length, Texts 1.1 and 1.2 each contain the same number of major strings. The figures for Text 1.3, on the other hand, indicate that many of the lexical strings are short, suggesting that this text has a less sustained focus on topic than either of the written texts.

Table 11.14 Lexical strings in the Crying Baby texts

	LEXICAL COHESION		
Feature	Text 1.1	Text 1.2	Text 1.3
number of strings (2+ items)	20	13	14
number of major strings (4+ items)	10	10	7
lexical items in strings/ all words in text	104/453	96/229	66/343
head items of longest strings (no. of words in string)	baby (12) grumpy (15) crying (10)	sound (15) distress (10) infant (9) effective (12) periods of time (15)	kids (7) tedious (8) houseboat (5) a lot (12) techniques (7)
meronymy	7	0	5
expectancy	2	0	6
number of sentences	27	10	44

This evidence of contrastive lexical density is reinforced by the figures for the number of lexical items in strings as a proportion of all words in a text. Here we see that a very high proportion of the words in Text 1.2 enter into strings, thus indicating a tightness of focus and careful selection of lexical items. In Text 1.3, however, there is a marked difference, with a very low proportion of the words used encoding cohesively related lexical items. Text 1.1 strikes a middle position between these two, with a relatively low proportion.

The three longest strings in Text 1.1 contrast noticeably with those in Text 1.2. While Text 1.1 develops around a key participant (*baby*) by describing its attributes (*moods*) and behaviour (*crying*), in Text 1.2 the *infant* is a less central string than those of the *sounds* it makes, the *time* it makes them for, and *effective* means for stopping it making them! In Text 1.3 the longest string has to do with the frequency of events and an attitudinal assessment of them (*tedious*, etc.), while the participants and settings occupy fewer lexical items.

While in all texts the vast majority of lexical relations are of superordination (and very often of repetition), meronymy is not uncommon in Text 1.1, as the baby and its parts are discussed. Text 1.2, on the other hand, is concerned with classification and not with composition.

The dominance of nominal resources in encoding ideational meanings in Text 1.2 is suggested by the absence of expectancy relations, which are relatively frequent in Text 1.3.

Cohesive characterization of the texts

Taken together, the patterns in the texts allow for the characterization of the texts as presented in Table 11.15.

As this table shows, Text 1.2 is concerned with causal relations involving generic participants or nominalized processes. It has very tight lexical cohesion, through which it is focused on the time infants cry for and the effectiveness of different methods used by parents for responding to the noise they make.

Text 1.3 develops by adding or contrasting information. It relies on cultural context for interpretation of key participants, including retrieval of the focal personal participants of *you* and *your kids*. Lexical cohesion is not dense, with many relations being of the expectancy

Table 11.15   Cohesive characterizations of the Crying Baby texts

	COHESIVE CHARACTERIZATION		
System	Text 1.1	Text 1.2	Text 1.3
conjunction	+ elaboration	+ enhancing (cause)	+ extending
reference	+ homophoric + esphoric + personal (*you*) + individual baby (*he*)	+ generic (*parents*) + nominalization (*crying*)	+ homophoric + personal (*you*) + individual (*your kids,* *the women*)
lexical cohesion	+ many major strings baby's behaviour mood	+ % words in strings + many major strings time and effective alleviation of distressing sound	+ expectancy quality of time with kids

kind, relating verbal and nominal elements of the text. It develops a focus on the quality of time with the speaker's kids.

Text 1.1 has features in common with both Text 1.2 and 1.3. Like Text 1.3, it traces the activities of individual human participants, and relies at times on cultural context for retrieval of referent identities. Its lexical cohesion is not as dense as 1.2, but not as diverse as Text 1.3. Its focus is on the baby's behaviour, parts and moods. Unlike both Texts 1.2 and 1.3, this text develops mainly through elaboration.

Register analysis of the texts

The information obtained from the detailed analyses of the texts can now be interpreted as the realization of contextual dimensions, enabling a summarized register description to be presented in Table 11.16 below.

This contrastive register description of the texts is based on the combined lexico-grammatical and cohesion evidence presented above. That evidence has now allowed us to specify similarities and differences between the texts at this contextual level. It permits two possible groupings of the texts in terms of which texts are 'more like' each other for different register dimensions.

Field analysis suggests a surprising similarity in field between Texts 1.2 and 1.3. Unlike Text 1.1, which deals with the behaviour and moods of the baby, Texts 1.2 and 1.3 construct the field from the perspective of the parents: what they do and how effective or tedious the experiences are for them. Thus, while in a general sense all the texts do share a common field of 'crying babies', linguistic analysis permits this to be more narrowly described, thus differentiating the way each text approaches, and thereby constructs, that field.

However, while 1.2 and 1.3 may be closer in field, Text 1.2 stands apart when mode and tenor are considered. It has a highly formal, authoritarian tenor, and constructs itself as a reflective text, written by an impersonal writer to be read by an unknown, distant reader. At the other extreme, the language of Text 1.3 indicates and reinforces a relationship of friendship between interactants in face-to-face contact. Text 1.1 falls mid-way between these two extremes. While the writer must of necessity present the text as largely context-independent, she seeks to minimize the formality and distance inherent in writing by incorporating

Table 11.16 Register description of the texts

	REGISTER DESCRIPTION of the texts		
Register variable	Text 1.1	Text 1.2	Text 1.3
field	clarifying what babies do, how they behave, how to describe their moods	explaining how, why and for whom crying causes distress and how to alleviate it effectively	adding judgements about techniques and actions for handling babies who cry
mode	blend of spoken and written mode; low interpersonal distance; moderate experiential distance	written-to-be-read; high interpersonal and experiential distance	spoken face-to-face; begins in interactive mode, becomes monologic
tenor	relatively informal; unequal power between expert and advisee minimized to construct non-authoritarian solidarity	formal; unequal power between expert and advisee maximized to construct authoritarian, academic distance	informal; equal power between friends exploited to enable alternation of roles: elicitor becomes listener, respondent becomes narrator

features of a spoken interactive mode. While the writer must take up the role of expert, she seeks to minimize the power difference and alienation this typically implies.

The generic analysis of the texts adds a further dimension to our understanding of how these texts are making meanings.

Generic structure in the texts

Simply asking what the overall purpose of each text is enabled us to suggest, as early as Chapter One, the generic categories to which each text might belong. No detailed analysis was necessary to claim that while Texts 1.1 and 1.2 are both kinds of Explanation texts, Text 1.3 functions to exchange experience, in part through the telling of a story. However, the grammatical and cohesive evidence provided by the analyses presented above can be used both to support these generic labels and to determine the (boundaries of the) schematic structure in each of the texts.

As the generic structure analyses presented in the Appendix show, Texts 1.1 and 1.2 can indeed both be analysed as examples of the Explanation of Problematic Behaviour genre, with a basic structure:

Statement of Problem ^ Explanation ^ Suggested Alleviating Action ^ Outlook

or

SP ^ EX^ SAA ^ OL

The detailed schematic structure analysis also indicates that the Explanation and Suggested Alleviating Action stages are recursive, and that Text 1.1 contains an additional optional stage, here labelled Morale Booster (MB).

A linear statement of the schematic structure for each text will be given, followed by a brief discussion of (i) the function of each stage, and (ii) its realizational correlates.

Text 1.1

The linear description of the schematic structure of this text is:

$$SP \wedge EX_1 \wedge SAA_1 \wedge EX_2 \wedge SAA_2 \wedge EX_3 \wedge SAA_3 \wedge SAA_4 \wedge SAA_5 \wedge SAA_6 \wedge SAA_7 \wedge EX_4 \wedge SAA_8 \wedge SAA_9 \wedge OL \wedge MB$$

Statement of Problem (SP)

This stage provides the introduction to the text, framing the subsequent stages of the text in terms of a problem (behaviour) which will be addressed by examining its causes.

The key realizations in this stage are: (i) negative evaluation of a behaviour (i.e. some behaviour or event is described as undesirable), and (ii) an expression of causation (i.e. there is an indication that the particular behaviour is describable in causal terms).

In Text 1.1, the negative evaluation is realized principally through the use of the negative mental process *despair* in the first sentence. This sentence also realizes cause, through the causative verb *drive*. That the remainder of the text will function to explain the causes of this negative situation is realized through the elliptical causal Adjunct: *why?*

Explanation (EX)

Explanation stages function to provide possible reasons for the behaviour negatively evaluated as problematic.

In Text 1.1 the function of the first Explanation stage is realized explicitly, through the use of the nominalized causal noun *reason*, a word reiterated in Explanation 4. Explanation 2 is indicated partly by the boundary signal in the SAA_1 stage which immediately precedes it, *you can assume it's something else*, which sets up what comes next to be read as that 'something else'. Sentence 8 is also a possible answer to the 'why?' question of the SP. Explanations are typically relational processes: identifying if the noun *reason* is used, or attributive if it is not, with the performer of the problem behaviour (*the baby*) as Carrier, and the explanation encoded in the Attribute (*lonely, bored . . .*).

Suggested Alleviating Action (SAA)

This is the core 'advice' stage of the genre, as it functions to offer the reader alternative ways of avoiding or alleviating the negative behaviour identified in the SP and explained causally in the EX stages.

SAA stages are realized as largely material processes in which the reader is encoded as Actor. These processes are situated in time, and there is frequently specification as to the manner in which the processes should be carried out. Modalization is high, since the advice offered in one stage is (a) only one of a number of possible actions that will be suggested in the text, and therefore (b) not guaranteed to work.

Outlook (OL)

This stage functions to forecast the future, once the problematic behaviour has been addressed. As the outlook in Text 1.1 is a positive one, it has been labelled as 'improvements to come'.

In Text 1.1, the positive attitude of the outlook is encoded from both the baby's perspective (he will be more able to do some things) and the reader/parents (you will be better at doing some things). The outlook is encoded in mental processes, indicating that the future holds not just action but reflection.

Morale Booster (MB)

This stage, which is optional, functions to provide support and encouragement to those faced with the problematic behaviour. It does this by being positive both about the behaviour, and about the people who have to deal with that behaviour.

In Text 1.1 it is realized through two identifying processes where the Value is positively loaded for attitude. The first identifying process defines the problematic behaviour in a positive light (it is *communication with you*), and the second defines the reader/parent in a positive light (as *the most important people*).

As the linear structure of Text 1.1 shows, this text offers far more advice than explanations: there are 9 SAS stages, to only 4 EX stages. This suggests that the text is more practical in orientation, concerned more to help than to explain exhaustively. This is in contrast to the structure of Text 1.2.

Text 1.2

The linear structure of this text is:

$$SP \wedge EX_1 \wedge EX_2 \wedge EX_3 \wedge SAA_1 \wedge SAA_2 \wedge OL$$

As can be seen from this, Text 1.2 offers more explanations than advice. This suggests that the more 'academic' approach to the field requires more emphasis on causes, and less on alleviation.

The SP stage in Text 1.2 is realized through an initial causative process, just as in Text 1.1. Negative lexis as Attributes is also used.

The EX stages all involve the nominalization *reason*, and its similarly nominalized partner, *cause*. Identifying processes dominate.

The SAA stages are realized by both material and mental processes. The material processes are heavily nominalized, with the reader/student as deleted Actor (counselling by doctors) and Agent (doctors can make parents spend time elsewhere). The parents are encoded as Sensers in mental processes (suppressing reasoning/coping).

The OL stage in Text 1.2 is decidedly negative, in contrast to Text 1.2. To capture this negative perspective, it has been given the sub-label 'warning'.

The negative perspective is realized through both negative lexis and a switch in the role of Actors. The formal negative adjective *inappropriate* is attached to the nominalized actions of parents: they are now Actors performing very undesirable behaviours, no longer Sensers *coping appropriately*. The doctors are still the implicit Agents, and it is their lack of action (in not providing respite, etc.) that is held up as potentially causally responsible for the negative actions of the parents.

Note that the Outlook of Text 1.2 could itself become the topic of another Explanation of Problematic Behaviour text: the actions of the parents foreshadowed in the Outlook could be Statements of Problems in texts for social workers, psychologists or judicial authorities.

Thus, Texts 1.1 and 1.2 are examples of the same genre, although that genre is realized through slightly different register configurations, illustrating the point made in Chapter Two that genre is a more abstract contextual level than register. However, the genre is not unaffected by the register values, as the different schematic structures of the two texts indicate. While the frequency of the SAA stage in Text 1.2 indicates its more pragmatic construction of the field, the negative OL stage in Text 1.3 indicates its more distant and authoritarian relationship with the reader than the solidarity created through the positive OL stage in Text 1.1.

Text 1.3

This interactive text clearly has a very different generic classification. In fact it is only the latter part of the text that can be described through a constituent schematic structure. The first part of the text can be described as a conversational exchange, and in the Appendix these interactive sections have been divided into exchanges, with speech function labels assigned to indicate the function of each part of the exchange. These labels indicate that the interaction begins as a question^answer sequence, with two interrogative exchanges initiated by S. Answers are provided by C, although not in strict sequence, since sentence 7 continues to answer the questions in the first exchange, while sentence 8 answers the question of the second exchange.

The exchange structure continues until sentences 20–21, which constitute a minimal generic structure of Topic ^ Comment. This schematic structure fragment seems to foreshadow the narrative to come, although it is not rich enough in interest to lead to a lengthy text. The narrative which begins in sentence 31 is in fact produced within the interactive structure: it is offered as an answer to S's continuing questions. This illustrates a common tendency for conversational interactions to drift into narratives and then back out into interactive talk (see, for example, the 'Geneva' story presented in Chapter Eight). The linear description of the schematic structure of the narrative is:

Abstract ^ Orientation1 ^ Complication1 ^ Orientation2 ^ Complication2 ^ Evaluation1 ^ Complication3 ^ Resolution ^ Evaluation2 ^ Coda

It can be seen from this that the text follows classic narrative structure. There is repetition of the Orientation stage towards the beginning of the text, as the speaker appears to consider that her first Orientation has not given sufficient time/place detail to contextualize the story. The Complications gradually increase in seriousness, and an Evaluation is provided of both early Complications and of the outcome of the successful Resolution.

As the stages of the narrative genre have already been discussed at other points in the book, only the realizations here will be briefly reviewed.

Abstract
Framed with the Comment Adjunct *luckily*, a narrative is foreshadowed with the contrastive reference between *the second baby* and *the first one*. The detail encoded in the Circumstance of time *from about five o'clock* also has a narrative sound to it.

Orientation 1
With permission to narrate granted by the *Hmm* of the listener, C establishes the setting for the story, realizing details of time and place through Circumstantial elements. The Mental process of *remember* with the narrator as Senser projects the narrative as personal experience.

Complications 1 and 2
The first Complication stage is realized by a Behavioural process with *the baby* as Behaver, and an Attributive process with *the parents* as Carrier. This establishes the baby not so much

as an Actor in the story, but rather as a precipitator of events in which the parents and their responses will figure. The Attributive process suggests the emotional interest and intensity of the narrative. The second Complication stage is more typically realized by material and verbal processes, with the main Actors/participants now encoded as *the parents* and *the classy ladies*. The stages are linked through implicit temporal conjunctive relations.

Evaluation 1
The key realization here is the expression of narrator attitude. The first Evaluation stage provides an interpersonally coloured clarification of what has just been said in the early Complication stage. The conjunction *you know* signals this as an elaboration, and the negative process *take over*, plus the intensification in *really*, indicates the speaker's attitude. The second Evaluation stage involves an Attributive process, with a highly positive attitudinal Attribute describing the narrator's response, setting up an effective contrast between the Evaluation of the ladies' behaviour and that of the baby.

Complication 3
Like the earlier Complication stages, this final Complication is realized through a material process, with the narrator as Actor. However, the causal relation set up (*and so I just handed the baby to them*) indicates that here is the pivotal drama of this story. We will need a Resolution now to move forward.

Resolution
In the Resolution stage there is a return to the baby as Behaver in a Behavioural process, followed by a material process with the *ladies* as Actors. The counter-expectations set up by the final Complication are signalled as resolved here through the implicit contrastive conjunctive relation *but*. Repetition of the comment adjunct *luckily* creates cohesion with the Abstract, and also foreshadows the emotional judgement made in the second Evaluation.

Coda
The switch back to a Material process, with *the ladies* as Actors, differentiates the Coda from the preceding Evaluation, and finalizes the ladies' role in the story. Although the narrative is not brought into the present, as was achieved through the Coda of the Geneva narrative (e.g. *here they give you tea and bikkies*), the finality of the story is effectively implied by the verb *handed back*, which appears to terminate the expected sequence of events: the baby has come home to roost – or squawk!

What makes this narrative particularly interesting (for the listener) is that the Complication shows the narrator/mother in a negative light: she is a mother who (willingly) gives her child away to strangers! The story is thus told as much at the narrator's own expense as at that of the two classy ladies. That the narrative is an effective entertainment text is indicated by the listener's spontaneous laughter, occurring both after the Complication has been revealed, after the Resolution, and following the Coda.

Integration: ideology in the texts

It is at the level of ideology, the most abstract context to which reference will be made, that the discrete findings of the various analyses can be most coherently integrated. As ideology impacts on each of the levels of context, and through them is realized in linguistic choices, the linguistic evidence from all the preceding analyses can be used to make explicit what positions, biases and interpretations are encoded in the texts.

The impact of ideology on field relates to how the text encodes such ideational meanings as who initiates, what the kinds of actions/events are, who responds to those actions, and how.

In Text 1.1 babies act by behaving, and parents react by thinking about it and then taking concrete steps; thus, babies behave in certain ways because those are the ways their bodies are programmed to behave. There is nothing extraordinary or mysterious or devious in it. And parents can take control by undertaking specific, practical actions. The text thus encodes an ideology of 'coping' with natural behaviour sequences.

In Text 1.2, on the other hand, when babies do act it is for statistical reasons. Babies' behaviour is defined as causing a problem for parents. And the parents need help in overcoming this problem. Here, then, we see an ideology of non-coping, justifying professional intervention to avoid negative actions that parents may undertake if not helped.

In Text 1.3 babies precipitate action and emotional sequences for parents. The ideology encoded here is that the function of babies' behaviour is personal growth for parents!

The impact of ideology on tenor relates to how the text encodes such interpersonal meanings as how the writer relates to the reader, how typical/likely/intense experiences are and who is the core participant being argued about.

In Text 1.1, we see that when an expert sets out to talk to parents, a friendly tenor has been adopted, by simulating an interactive, more spoken mode. The ideology here, then, is that 'ordinary' people need to be talked to in a personal, conversational way. In Text 1.2, on the other hand, we see that when the audience is trainee specialists, a distant, academic tenor is created. The ideological implications of this are that future experts should be trained to be distant and impersonal, an interactive style which they may well carry into their face-to-face encounters with the infants and parents they treat. In Text 1.3, the relationship of friend-to-friend supports the intrusion of intensity into interaction.

The impact of ideology on mode relates to how the text encodes such textual meanings as what information is taken as 'given' and what is not, and what distance is constructed between reader and writer and between writer and event.

In the choice of a highly nominalized mode in Text 1.2 we see the ideological implications that, when writing for trainee specialists, there is a need to induct them into the formal written mode, dealing with abstractions and generalizations. This kind of writing is teaching them how to see people and situations as representatives of groups, not individuals with discrete life histories and funny stories to tell.

While Text 1.1 also sees parents as a group, its focus is on typifying the baby's behaviour, rather than that of the parents, which is left more open. Statements such as *it's up to you* in fact indicate how carefully parents are left ungrouped.

Text 1.3 makes no attempt to claim experience as anything but that: personal experience. But typicality is encoded in terms of usuality. Thus, there is a generalizing not about participants or their behaviour, but about the frequency with which things may happen in a particular way.

At the level of genre, we can recognize that in some respects all three of the Crying Baby texts have a common purpose: to impart information for the benefit of the reader/listener. Ideology impacts here by indicating which genre will be chosen to achieve that imparting, and by influencing its schematic structure.

Thus, in the choice of the Explanation genre rather than the Narrative, we see the ideological implications that 'real' learning should take place via explicit objectification and generalization of information, whereas 'casual' learning takes place by sharing unique, personal experience. One kind of learning is the highly valued written kind; the other the highly powerful, but usually undervalued, spoken kind.

Ideology is also realized in the choice between the warning Outlook or the Improvements one. Text 1.1 constructs the position that parents need to be encouraged and empowered (or they may end up doing the terrible actions mentioned in Text 1.2), while Text 1.2 states that trainee medical personnel need to be warned in order to impress on them their responsibilities. In the narrative, the mother chooses not to evaluate the baby (who is never directly criticized, or held to blame), but both the classy women and the mother are taken down a notch. While the message of Text 1.1 could be summarized as 'you can do it', and Text 1.2 'watch out or you'll get in trouble for what they do', in Text 1.3 the message is 'you have to be able to laugh at yourself'.

Evaluation of texts

The discussion of the analyses presented above illustrates how a systemic approach can be used to gain an understanding of how the three Crying Baby texts make the meanings that they do. Although Halliday suggests that the understanding and the evaluation of texts are at two different levels, it does seem that in seeking to make explicit an understanding of how the texts work we are also inevitably led to make some evaluations of the texts. But, anchored as it is in an integrated model of context and language, the systemic evaluation of a text involves assessing the text on its own terms, as more or less effective in achieving its purpose for the audience for whom it was intended.

In this respect, we could suggest that Texts 1.1 and 1.3 appear more effective than Text 1.2. Text 1.3 elicits considerable laughter, an indication it is well received. It both informs and entertains, and it does so in a way that does not exploit the baby or disempower the parents.

Text 1.1 contains many practical suggestions expressed in very direct, accessible language, with an appealing degree of warmth towards both babies and parents giving the text an empathy which makes its suggestions more likely to be taken up.

However, Text 1.2 is more worrying: many of its readers may not be able to unpack the nominalizations involved. Readers may miss the implications of themselves as implicit Agents (it is they who must do the counselling, provide the respite), and therefore may miss the responsibility which is being attributed to them. Readers may be inclined to assume that the distance and formality of this text offers an example of the kind of behaviour that is considered appropriate with parents and babies. They may construe the text as indicating that babies' behaviour does not need to be understood so long as it falls within statistical norms. They may construe the class of parents as potential abusers. For reasons such as these, we might question whether this way of writing is really the most appropriate, effective way of training people to understand, empathize with and provide practical support for people struggling to cope with the natural behaviour of babies.

Conclusion: from life to text

The analysis of the Crying Baby texts demonstrates that detailed lexico-grammatical and cohesive analyses can shed light on how texts make meanings, where those meanings come from, and some of the implications they may carry with them. The close-up linguistic analysis of three very ordinary texts has illustrated that the texts are rich in meanings: they make not just meanings about what goes on and why, but also meanings about relationships and attitudes, and meanings about distance and proximity. By relating specific linguistic choices to the construction and reflection of situational, cultural and ideological contexts, these three texts have been shown to encode meanings about such far-reaching dimensions as ways of talking to parents, the experience of parenthood, the responsibility of the medical professional and the expected behaviour of 'good' mothers.

As this chapter and the book have shown, a systemic approach requires the detailed, close-up examination of patterns of language. It involves the use of a technical meta-language, which gives precise ways of identifying and talking about different cohesive patterns. It requires an investment of time and effort by the analyst, as learning to carry out linguistic analyses of any kind is a skill that must be worked at. Life is short, and if your background is not in functional linguistics, or even in linguistics at all, you may quite legitimately ask: why bother? Why not take other approaches to text which, superficially at least, seem less arduous and certainly involve less technicality and exactitude?

A functional linguistic approach is demanding because its ultimate goal is very different from that of other approaches to text. Functional linguistic analysis is not about offering a range of possible readings of texts, supported by carefully selected excerpts. It is about dealing with entire texts in their authentic form in their actual contexts of social life. And it is about explaining them, accounting for what they are doing and how they achieve that in the culture.

As Halliday suggests, the real value of a systemic functional approach to language is that:

> when we interpret language in these (functional-semantic) terms we may cast some light on the baffling problem of how it is that the most ordinary uses of language, in the most everyday situations, so effectively transmit the social structure, the values, the systems of knowledge, all the deepest and most pervasive patterns of the culture. With a functional perspective on language, we can begin to appreciate how this is done. (Halliday 1973: 45)

At issue in all linguistic analysis is the process by which lived or imagined experience is turned into text. Text is not life – it is life mediated through the symbolic system of language. I hope this book has shown you how SFL analysis can help us understand something of the process by which we live much of our lives at one remove – as texts.

Appendix

Analyses of the Crying Baby texts

A1. Clause analyses

Each text is analysed three times: the first time for Mood; the second time for Transitivity and Theme; the third time for clause complexing. Keys are presented for each analysis. The texts have been divided into clauses, with embedded clauses [[shown within double brackets]]. These are analysed for Mood and Transitivity, but not for Theme. Inserted clauses, indicated by three dots . . . at beginning and end, have been repositioned at the end of the clause they were inserted in where this facilitates analysis. Three dots within a clause indicate the place from which an inserted clause has been removed. Double slashed lines // indicate clause boundaries within embedded clauses.

A1.1. Mood analysis

Key:
S = Subject, F = Finite, Fn = negative, Fms = modalized, Fml = modulated
P = Predicator, Pml = modulated Predicator, Pms = modalized Predicator, F/P = fused Finite and Predicator
C = Complement, Ca = attributive Complement
A = Adjunct, Ac = circumstantial, Am = mood, Ao = comment, Ap = polarity, Av = vocative, Aj = conjunctive, At = continuity
WH = WH element, WH/S, WH/C, WHAc = fused WH element
mn = minor clause
MOOD element of ranking (non-embedded) clauses is shown in **bold**

Text 1.1

1.**A baby** [[who (S) won't (Fn) stop crying (P)]] **(S) can** (Fml) drive (P) anyone (C) to despair (P). 2i.**You (S) feed** (F/P) him (C), 2ii.**you (S) change** (F/P) him (C), 2iii.**you (S) nurse** (F/P) him (C), 2iv.**you (S) try** (F) to settle (P) him (C), 2v.but (Aj) the minute (Ac) **you (S) put** (F/P) him (C) down (Ac) 2vi.**he (S) starts** (F) to howl (P). 3.**Why?** (WH/Ac) 4.**The most common reason** [[baby (S) cries (F/P)]] **(S) is** (F) hunger (C). 5i.Even if (Aj) **he (S) was** (F) just (Am) recently (Ac) fed (P) 5ii.**he**

(S) **might (Fms) still (Am)** be adapting to (P) the pattern [[of sucking (P) // until (Aj) his tummy (S) is (F) full (Ca) // and (Aj) feeling (P) satisfied (Ca) // until (Aj) it (S) empties (F/P) again (Ac)]] (C). 6i.When (Aj) **he (S) was (F)** in the womb (Ac) 6ii.**nourishment (S) came (F/P)** automatically and constantly (Ac). 7i.Offer (P) food (C) first (Ac); 7ii.if (Aj) **he (S) turns (F/P)** away (Ac) from the nipple or teat (Ac) 7iii. **you (S) can (Fms)** assume (P) 7iv.**it (S) 's (F)** something else (C). 8i.**It happens (Am)** that (Aj) **babies (S) go (F/P)** through grumpy, miserable stages (Ac) 8ii.when (Aj) **they (S) just (Am) want (F/P)** 8iii.to tell (P) everyone (C) 8iv.how unhappy (WH/C) **they (S) feel (F/P)**. 9i.**Perhaps (Am) his digestion (S) feels (F/P)** uncomfortable (Ca) 9ii.or (Aj) **his limbs (S) are (F)** twitching (P). 10i.If (Aj) **you (S) can't (Fml)** find (P) any specific source of discomfort such as a wet nappy or strong light in his eyes (C), 10ii.**he (S) could (Fms) just (Am)** be having (P) a grizzle (C). 11.**Perhaps (Am) he (S) 's (F) just (Am)** lonely (Ca). 12i.During the day (Ac), **a baby sling (S) helps (F/P)** you (C) to deal with (P) your chores (C) 12ii. and (Aj) keep (P) baby (C) happy (Ca). 13i.At night (Ac) . . . **you (S) will (Fms)** need to take (Pml) action (C) 13iv.to relax (P) and settle (P) him (C). 13ii . . . when (Aj) **you (S) want (F/P)** 13iii.to sleep (P) . . . 14i.**Rocking (S) helps (F/P)**, 14ii.but (Aj) if (Aj) **your baby (S) is (F)** in the mood [[to cry (P)]] (Ac) 14iii.**you (S) will (Fms)** probably (Am) find (P) 14iv.**he (S) 'll (Fms)** start up (P) again (Ac) 14v.when (Aj) **you (S) put (F/P)** him (C) back (P) in the cot (Ac). 15i.**[[Wrapping baby up (P) snugly (Ac)]] (S) helps (F)** to make (P) him (C) feel (P) secure (Ca) 15ii.and (Aj) **stops (F)** him (C) from jerking about (P) 15iii.**which (S) can (Fms)** unsettle (P) him (C). 16i.**Outside stimulation (S) is (F)** cut down (P) 16ii.and (Aj) **he (S) will (Fms)** lose (P) tension (C). 17i.**Gentle noise (S) might (Fms)** soothe (P) him (C) off [[to sleep (P)]] (Ca) – a radio played softly, a recording of a heartbeat, traffic noise – 17ii.**even the noise of the washing machine (S) is (F)** effective! (Ca) 18i.**Some parents (S) use (F/P)** dummies (C) – 18ii.**it (S) 's (F)** up to you (Ca) – 18iii.and (Aj) **you (S) might (Fms)** find (P) 18iv. **your baby (S) settles (F/P)** 18v.sucking (P) a dummy (C). 19i.'**Sucky' babies (S) might (Fms)** be able to find (Pml) their thumbs and fists (C) 19ii.to have (P) a good suck (C). 20i.Remember (P) 20ii. that (At) **babies (S) get (F/P)** bored (Ca) 20iii.so (Aj) when (Aj) **he (S) is (F)** having (P) a real grizzle (C) 20iv.**this (S) could (Fms)** be (P) the reason (C). 21.**Is (F) his cot (S)** an interesting place [[to be (P)]] (C)? 22.**Coloured posters and mobiles (S) give (F/P)** him something [[to watch (P)]] (C). 23i.**You (S) could (Fms)** maybe (Am) tire (P) him (C) out (P) 23ii.by (Aj) taking (P) him (C) for a walk . . . or a ride in the car (Ac) – 23iii.not always practical (Ca) in the middle of the night (Ac). 24i.**A change of scene and some fresh air (S) will (Fms)** often (Am) work (P) wonders (C) – 24ii.**even a walk around the garden (S) may (Fms)** be (P) enough (Ca). 25i.As (Aj) **baby (S) gets (F/P)** older (Ca) 25ii.**he (S) will (Fms)** be more able to communicate (Pml) his feelings (C) 25iii.and (Aj) **you (S) will (Fms)** be (P) better [[at judging (P) the problem (C)]] (Ca). 26i.Although (Aj) **you (S) might (Fms)** be (P) at your wit's end (Ca), 26ii.remember (P) 26iii.that (Aj) **crying (S) is (F)** communication with you, his parents (C). 27.And (Aj) **you (S) are (F)** the most important people in your baby's life (C).

TEXT 1.2

1.**The compelling sound of an infant's cry (S) makes (F/P)** it (C) an effective distress signal and appropriate to the human infant's prolonged dependence on a caregiver (Ca). 2i.However (Aj), **cries (S) are (F)** discomforting (Ca) 2ii.and (Aj) **may (Fms)** be (P) alarming (Ca) to parents (Ac), 2iii.**many of whom (S) find (F/P)** 2iv.**it (S)** very difficult (Ca) [[to listen to (P) their infant's crying (C) for even short periods of time (Ac)]] (C). 3.**Many reasons for crying (S) are (F)** obvious (C), like hunger and discomfort due to heat, cold, illness, and lying position (S). 4i.**These reasons (S)**, however (Aj), **account for (F/P)** a relatively small percentage of infant crying (C) 4ii.and (Aj) **are (F) usually (Am)** recognized (P) quickly (Ac) 4iii.and (Aj) alleviated (P). 5i.In the absence of a discernible reason for the behaviour (Ac), **crying (S) often (Am) stops (F/P)** 5ii. when (Aj) **the infant (S) is (F)** held (P). 6i.In most infants (Ac), **there (S) are (F)** frequent episodes of crying with no apparent cause (C), 6ii.and (Aj) **holding or other soothing techniques (S) seem (F/P)** ineffective (Ca). 7.**Infants (S) cry (F/P) and fuss (F/P)** for a mean of 1¾ hr/day at age 2 wk, 2¾ hr/day at age 6 wk, and 1 hr/day at 12 wk (Ac). 8i.**Counselling about normal crying (S) may (Fms)** relieve (P) guilt (C) 8ii.and (Aj) diminish (P) concerns (C), 8iii.but (Aj) for some (Ac) **the distress [[caused (P) by the crying (Ac)]] (S) cannot (Fml)** be suppressed (P) by logical reasoning (Ac). 9i. For these parents (Ac), **respite from exposure to the crying (S) may (Fms)** be (P) necessary (Ca) 9ii.to allow (Pml) them (C) to cope (P) appropriately (Ac) with their own distress (Ac). 10i.Without relief (Ac), **fatigue and tension (S) may (Fms)** result in (P) inappropriate parental responses 10ii. such as leaving (P) the infant (C) in the house (Ac) alone (Ac) 10iii.or abusing (P) the infant (C).

TEXT 1.3

1.**Did (F) your kids (S)** used to cry (Pms) a lot (Ac)? 2.When (Aj) **they (S) were (F)** little (Ca)? 3.**Yea (Ap).** 4.Well (At) == what (WH/C) **did (F) you (S)** do (P)? 5.== **still (Am) do (F)** 6.Yea? (At) [laughs] 7.Oh (At) pretty tedious (Ca) at times (Ac) yea (At). 8.**There (S) were (F)** all sorts of techniques == Leonard Cohen (C) 9.== Like (Aj) what (WH/C) [laughs] 10.Yea (At) **I (S) used (Fms)** to use (P) . . . 11.**What (S) 's (F)** that American guy [[that (S) did (F) 'Georgia on your mind' (C)]] (C)? 12.Oh (At) yea (At) 13.== **Jim – James Taylor (S)** 14.== **James Taylor (S)** 15.Yea (At) yea (At). 16.**He (S) was (F)** pretty good (Ca). 17.Yea (At). 18i.No (At) **Leonard Cohen (S) 's (F)** good (Ca) 18ii.cause (Aj) **it (S) 's (F) just (Am)** so monotonous (Ca). 19.And (Aj) **there (S) 's (F) only (Am)** four chords (C). 20i.And (Aj) ah (At) **we (S) used (Fms)** to have (P) holidays (C) . . . on a houseboat (C) 20ii . . . when (Aj) **we (S) only (Am) had (F)** one kid (C) . . . 21.And (Aj) **that (S) was (F)** fantastic (C) **just (Am) the rocking motion of the houseboat (S)** 22.Mmm (mn) 23.Mmm (mn) 24.**Were (F) there (S) ever (Am)** times (C) . . . 25i.Like (Aj) **I (S) remember (F/P)** times (C) 25ii.when (Aj) **I (S) couldn't (Fms)** work out (P) 25iii. what the hell (WH/C) **it (S) was (F)**. 26.**There (S) just (Am) didn't (Fn)** seem to be (P) anything == [[you (S) could (Fms) do (P)]] (C). 27.== No reason or (C) . . . 28.Yea (At). 29.Yea (At) every night between six and ten (Ac) 30.Yea (At) yea (At). 31i.Luckily (Ao) **I (S) didn't (Fn)** have (P) that (C) with the second baby (Ac) 31ii.but (Aj) **the first one (S) was (F)** that typical colicky sort of stuff (C) from about five o'clock (Ac). 32.Hmm (mn) 33i.**I (S) remember (F/P)** 33ii. one day (Ac) going (P) for a um walk (Ac) along the harbour (Ac) – 33iii.one of those you know harbour routes [[that (S) had (F) been opened up (P)]] (Ac). 34i.And (Aj) um (At) **he (S) started (F)** kicking up (P) from about five o'clock (Ac) 34ii.and (Aj) **we (S)**

were (F) getting (P) panic stricken (Ca). 35i.**I (S) had** (F) him (C) in one of those um front strap things (Ac) you know (At) sling things (Ac) 35ii.ah (At) cause (Aj) **that (S) use** (Fms) to work (P) wonders (C) **from time to time** (Am) 35iii.but (Aj) **it (S) wasn't** (Fn) working (P) this time (Ac). 36i.And (Aj) as (Aj) **we (S) sat** (F/P) on the foreshore (Ac) of this Vaucluse area (Ac) 36ii.**these two women (S) came** (F/P) down (Ac) 36iii.and (Aj) **they (S) 'd** (F) both (S) been working (P) as um governesses or something like that (Ac) – 36iv.very very classy ladies (Ca). 37i.And (Aj) **they (S) said** (F/P) 37ii.'Oh (At) **what (WH/S) 's** (F) wrong with the baby (Ac)? 38.**He (S) 's** (F) got (P) colic (C)?' 39i.You know (At), **they (S) really** (Am) wanted (F/P) 39ii.to take over (P). 40.Yea (At) 41.And (Aj) so (Aj) **I (S) just** (Am) handed (F/P) the baby (C) to them (Ac). 42i.And (Aj) LUCKILY (Ao) **he (S) kept** (F) on crying (P) – 42ii.**they (S) couldn't** (Fnml) stop (P) him (C) 43.So (Aj) **I (S) was** (F) **really** (Am) delighted (Ca). 44.**They (S) handed back** (F/P) this hideous little red wreck of a thing (C).

A1.2. Transitivity and Theme analysis

Key:

P = Process, Pm = material, Pme = mental, Pb = behavioural, Pv = verbal, Pe = existential, Pi = intensive, Pcc = circumstantial, Pp = possessive, Pc = causative
A = Actor, G = Goal, B = Beneficiary, R = Range
S = Senser, Ph = Phenomenon
Sy = Sayer, Rv = Receiver, Vb = Verbiage
Be = Behaver, Bh = Behaviour
X = Existent
T = Token, V = Value, Cr = Carrier, At = Attribute
Pr = possessor, Pd = possessed
C = Circumstance, Cl = location, Cx = extent, Cm = manner, Cc = cause, Ca = accompaniment, Ct = matter, Co = role
Ag = Agent
Theme is <u>underlined</u>
textual Theme: in *italics*
interpersonal Theme: in CAPITALS
topical Theme: in **bold**
dependent clause as Theme: **whole clause in bold**

Text 1.1

1.<u>**A baby [[who (Be) won't stop crying (Pb)]]**</u> (Ag) can drive (Pc) anyone (S) to despair (Pme). 2i.<u>**You**</u> (A) feed (Pm) him (G), 2ii.<u>**you**</u> (A) change (Pm) him (G), 2iii.<u>**you**</u> (A) nurse (Pm) him (G), 2iv.<u>**you**</u> (A) try to settle (Pm) him (G), 2v.<u>*but* **the minute**</u> (A) you (A) put (Pm) him (G) down (Pm) 2vi.<u>**he**</u> (Be) starts to howl (Pb). 3.<u>**Why**</u>? (Cc) 4.<u>**The most common reason [[baby (Be) cries (Pb)]]**</u> (V) is (Pi) hunger (T). 5i.<u>*Even if* **he (G) was just recently (Cl) fed (Pm)**</u> 5ii.<u>**he**</u> (Be) might still be adapting to (Pb) the pattern [[of sucking (Pm) // until his tummy (Cr) is (Pi) full (At) // and feeling (Pi) satisfied (At) // until it (A) empties (Pm) again (Cl)]] (Ph). 6i.<u>*When* **he (Cr) was (Pi) in the womb (AtCl)**</u> 6ii.<u>**nourishment (A)**</u> came (Pm) automatically and constantly (Cm). 7i.<u>**Offer**</u> (Pm) food (G) first (Cl); 7ii.<u>*if* he</u>

(A) turns away (Pm) from the nipple or teat (Cl) 7iii.**you (S)** can assume (Pme) 7iv.**it (V)** 's (Pi) something else (T). 8i.**IT HAPPENS** *that* **babies** (A) go through (Pm) grumpy, miserable stages (R) 8ii.*when* **they** (S) just want (Pme) 8iii.**to tell** (Pv) everyone (Rv) 8iv.**how unhappy (At)** they (Cr) feel (Pi). 9i.**PERHAPS his diges-tion (Cr)** feels (Pi) uncomfortable (At) 9ii.*or* **his limbs (Be)** are twitching (Pb). 10i.**If you (S) can't find (Pme) any specific source of discomfort such as a wet nappy or strong light in his eyes (Ph),** 10ii.**he (Be)** could just be having (Pb) a grizzle (Bh). 11.**PERHAPS he (Cr)** 's (Pi) just lonely (At). 12i.**During the day (Cl),** a baby sling (Ag) helps (Pm) you (A) to deal with (Pm) your chores (G) 12ii.*and* keep (Pc) baby (Cr) happy (At). 13i.**At night** (Cl) . . . you (A) will need to take (Pm) action (R) 13iv.to relax (Pm) and settle (Pm) him (G). 13ii . . . *when* **you (S)** want (Pme) 13iii. to sleep (Pb) . . . 14i.**Rocking (A)** helps (Pm), 14ii.*but if* **your baby (Cr)** is (Pi) in the mood [[to cry (Pb)]] (At) 14iii.**you** (S) will probably find (Pme) 14iv.**he (Be)** 'll start up (Pb) again (Cx) 14v.*when* **you** (A) put (Pm) him (G) back (Pm) in the cot (Cl). 15i.**[[Wrapping (Pm) baby (G) up (Pm) snugly (Cm)]] (Ag)** helps to make (Pc) him (Cr) feel (Pi) secure (At) 15ii.*and* stops (Pc) him (Be) from jerking about (Pb) 15iii.**which (A)** can unsettle (Pm) him (G). 16i.**Outside stim-ulation (G)** is cut down (Pm) 16ii.*and* **he (A)** will lose (Pm) tension (R). 17i.**Gentle noise** (Ag) might soothe (Pc) him (Be) off to sleep (Pb) – a radio played softly, a recording of a heartbeat, traffic noise – 17ii.**even the noise of the washing machine** (Cr) is (Pi) effective (At)! 18i.**Some parents (A)** use (Pm) dummies (G) – 18ii.**it (Cr)** 's (Pi) up to you (At) – 18iii.*and* **you** (S) might find (Pme) 18iv. **your baby** (Be) settles (Pb) 18v.**sucking** (Pm) a dummy (G).19i.**'Sucky' babies (S)** might be able to find (Pme) their thumbs and fists (Ph) 19ii.**to have (Pm)** a good suck (R). 20i.**Remember** (Pme) 20ii.*that* **babies (Cr)** get (Pi) bored (At) 20iii.*so* **when he (Be) is having (Pb) a real grizzle (Bh)** 20iv.**this (T)** could be (Pi) the reason (V). 21.**IS (Pi) his cot (Cr)** an interesting place [[to be (Pi)]] (At)? 22.**Coloured posters and mobiles** (A) give (Pm) him (B) something [[to watch (Pb)]] (G). 23i.**You** (A) could maybe tire (Pm) him (G) out (Pm) 23ii.*by* **taking** (Pm) him (G) for a walk . . . or a ride in the car (Cl) – 23iii.**not always practical (At)** in the middle of the night (Cl). 24i.**A change of scene and some fresh air (A)** will often work (Pm) wonders (R) – 24ii.**even a walk around the garden (Cr)** may be (Pi) enough (At). 25i.**As baby (Cr) gets (Pi) older (At)** 25ii.**he (Cr)** will be (Pi) more able [[to communicate (Pv) his feelings (Vb)]] (At) 25iii.*and* **you** (Cr) will be (Pi) better [[at judging (Pme) the problem (Ph)]] (At). 26i.**Although you (Cr) might be (Pi) at your wit's end (At),** 26ii.**remember** (Pme) 26iii.*that* **crying (T)** is (Pi) communication with you, his parents (V). 27.*And* **you** (T) are (Pi) the most important people in your baby's life (V).

TEXT 1.2

1.**The compelling sound of an infant's cry (Ag)** makes (Pc) it (T) an effective dis-tress signal and appropriate to the human infant's prolonged dependence on a care-giver (V). 2i.*However,* **cries (Cr)** are (Pi) discomforting (At) 2ii.*and* may be (Pi) alarming (At) to parents (B), 2iii.**many of whom** (S) find (Pme) 2iv.it (Cr) very dif-ficult (At) [[to listen to (Pb) their infant's crying (Ph) for even short periods of time (Cx)]] (Cr). 3.**Many reasons for crying** (Cr) are (Pi) obvious, like hunger and dis-comfort due to heat, cold, illness, and lying position (At). 4i.**These reasons (T),** however, account for (Pi) a relatively small percentage of infant crying (V) 4ii.<u>*and*</u> are usually recognised (Pme) quickly (Cm) 4iii.<u>*and*</u> alleviated (Pm). 5i.<u>**In the absence of a discernible reason for the behaviour (Cm)**</u>, <u>**crying**</u> (A) often stops (Pm) 5ii.<u>**when the infant (G)**</u> is held (Pm). 6i.<u>**In most infants (Cl)**</u>, there are (Px) frequent episodes of crying (X) with no apparent cause (Cc), 6ii.<u>*and* **holding or other soothing techniques (Cr)**</u> seem (Pi) ineffective (At). 7.<u>**Infants (Be)**</u> cry (Pbh) and fuss (Pbh) for a mean of 1¾ hr/day at age 2 wk, 2¾ hr/day at age 6 wk, and 1 hr/day at 12 wk (Cx). 8i.<u>**Counselling about normal crying (A)**</u> may relieve (Pm) guilt (G) 8ii.<u>*and*</u> diminish (Pm) concerns (G), 8iii.<u>*but* **for some (Cc)**</u> the distress [[caused (Pc) by the crying (Ag)]] (G) cannot be suppressed (Pm) by logical reasoning (A). 9i.<u>**For these parents (Cc)**</u>, respite from exposure to the crying (Cr) may be (Pi) necessary (At) 9ii.<u>**to allow**</u> them (S) to cope (Pme) appropriately (Cm) with (Pme) their own distress (Ph). 10i.<u>**Without relief (Cm)**</u>, fatigue and tension (T) may result in (Pc) inappropriate parental responses 10ii.<u>*such as* **leaving**</u> (Pm) the infant (G) in the house (Cl) alone (Cm) 10iii.<u>*or* **abusing**</u> (Pm) the infant (G).

TEXT 1.3

1.<u>**DID your kids**</u> (Be) used to cry (Pb) a lot (Cx)? 2.<u>*When* **they**</u> (Cr) were (Pi) little (At)? 3.<u>**YEA**</u> 4.<u>*Well* == **what**</u> did you (A) do (Pm)? 5.== still do 6.Yea? [laughs] 7.<u>*Oh* **pretty tedious**</u> (At) at times yea. 8.<u>**There**</u> were (Px) all sorts of techniques (X) == Leonard Cohen 9.== *Like* what [laughs] 10.<u>**Yea I (A)**</u> used to use (Pm) . . . 11.<u>**What (T)**</u> 's (Pi) that American guy [[that (A) did (Pm) 'Georgia on your mind' (G)]] (V)? 12.<u>**Oh** yea</u> 13.== <u>**Jim – James Taylor (T)**</u> 14.== <u>**James Taylor**</u> (T) 15.<u>*Yea yea*</u>. 16.<u>**He (Cr)**</u> was (Pi) pretty good (At). 17.<u>**Yea**</u>. 18i.<u>**No Leonard Cohen (Cr)**</u> 's (Pi) good (At) 18ii.<u>*cause* **it (Cr)**</u> 's (Pi) just so monotonous (At). 19.<u>*And* **there's**</u> (Px) only four chords (X). 20i.<u>*And ah* **we**</u> (A) used to have (Pm) holidays (R) . . . on a houseboat (Cl) 20ii. . . . <u>*when* **we**</u> (Cr/Pr) only had (Pp) one kid (At/Pd) . . . 21.<u>*And* **that**</u> (Cr) was (Pi) fantastic (At) just the rocking motion of the houseboat (Cr) 22.Mmm 23.Mmm 24.<u>**WERE**</u> (Px) there ever times (X) . . . 25i.<u>*Like* **I**</u> (S) remember (Pme) times (Ph) 25ii.<u>*when* **I**</u> (S) couldn't work out (Pm) 25iii.<u>**what the hell (At)**</u> it (Cr) was (Pi). 26.<u>**There**</u> just didn't seem to be (Px) anything == [[you (A) could do (Pm)]] (X) 27.== No reason or . . . 28.<u>*Yea*</u> 29.<u>*Yea* **every night**</u> (Cx) between six and ten (Cl) 30.<u>*Yea yea*</u>. 31i.<u>**LUCKILY I**</u> (A) didn't have (Pm) that (G) with the second baby (Cl) 31ii.<u>*but* **the first one**</u> (Cr) was (Pi) that typical colicky sort of stuff (At) from about five o'clock (Cl). 32.Hmm 33i.<u>**I (S)**</u> remember (Pme) 33ii.<u>**one day**</u> (Cl) going for (Pm) a um walk (R) along the harbour (Cl) – 33iii.<u>**one of those**</u> you know harbour routes [[that (G) had been opened up (Pm)]]. 34i.<u>*And* **um he (Be)**</u> started kicking up (Pb) from about five o'clock (Cl) 34ii.<u>*and* **we**</u> (Cr) were getting (Pi) panic stricken (At). 35i.<u>**I**</u> (A) had (Pm) him (G) in one of those um front strap things you know sling things (Cl) 35ii.<u>*ah cause* **that (A)**</u> use to work (Pm) wonders (R) from time to time (Cx) 35iii.<u>*but* **it (A)**</u> wasn't working (Pm) this time (Cl). 36i.<u>***And as* we (A) sat (Pm) on the foreshore of this Vaucluse area (Cl)**</u> 36ii.<u>**these two women (A)**</u> came down (Pm) 36iii.<u>*and* **they (A)**</u> 'd both been working (Pm) as um governesses or something like that (Crl) – 36iv.very very classy ladies. 37i.<u>*And* **they**</u> (Sy) said (Pv) 37ii. '<u>*Oh* **what (Cr)**</u> 's (Pi) wrong with the baby (At)? 38.<u>**He (Cr/Pr)**</u> 's got (Pp) colic (At/Pd)?' 39i.<u>*You know*, **they (S)**</u> really wanted (Pme) 39ii.to take over (Pm). 40.<u>**Yea**</u> 41.<u>*And so* **I (A)**</u> just handed (Pm) the baby (G) to them (B) 42i.*And* LUCKILY **he** (Be) kept on crying (Pb) – 42ii.**they** (A) couldn't stop (Pm) him (G). 43.*So* **I (S)** was really delighted (Pme). 44.**They** (A) handed back (Pm) this hideous little red wreck of a thing (G).

A1.3. Clause Complex Analysis

[[embedded clauses]], [ellipsed elements]
1, 2, 3: parataxis, α β γ: hypotaxis
" locution, ' idea, = elaboration, + extension, x enhancement

Text 1.1

clause simplex			(1)A baby who won't stop crying can drive anyone to despair.
1			(2i)You feed him,
+2			(2ii)you change him,
+3			(2iii)you nurse him,
+4			(2iv)you try to settle him,
+5	xβ		(2v)but the minute you put him down
	α		(2vi)he starts to howl.
clause simplex			(3)Why?
clause simplex			(4)The most common reason [[baby cries]] is hunger.
xβ			(5i)Even if he was just recently fed
α			(5ii)he might still be adapting to the pattern [[of sucking // until his tummy is full // and feeling satisfied // until it empties again.]]
xβ			(6i)When he was in the womb
α			(6ii)nourishment came automatically and constantly.
1			(7i)Offer food first;
x2	xβ		(7ii)if he turns away from the nipple or teat
	α	α	(7iii)you can assume
		'β	(7iv)it's something else.
α			(8i)It happens that babies go through grumpy, miserable stages
xβ	α		(8ii)when they just want
	'β	α	(8iii)to tell everyone
		'β	(8iv)how unhappy they feel.
1			(9i)Perhaps his digestion feels uncomfortable
+2			(9ii)or his limbs are twitching.
xβ			(10i)If you can't find any specific source of discomfort such as a wet nappy or strong light in his eyes,
α			(10ii)he could just be having a grizzle.
clause simplex			(11)Perhaps he's just lonely.
1			(12i)During the day, a baby sling helps you to deal with your chores
x2			(12ii)and keep baby happy.
α			(13i)At night
<xβ>	α		(13ii)when you want
	'β		(13iii)to sleep

α				(13iv)you will need to take action
xγ				(13v)to relax and settle him.
1				(14i)Rocking helps,
x2	xβ			(14ii)but if your baby is in the mood to cry
	α	α		(14iii)you will probably find
		'β	α	(14iv)he'll start up again
			xβ	(14v)when you put him back in the cot.
1				(15i)[[Wrapping baby up snugly]] helps to make him feel secure
+2	α			(15ii)and stops him from jerking about
	=β			(15iii)which can unsettle him.
1				(16i)Outside stimulation is cut down
x2				(16ii)and he will lose tension.
1				(17i)Gentle noise might soothe him off to sleep – a radio [[played softly]], a recording of a heartbeat, traffic noise –
+2				(17ii)even the noise of the washing machine is effective!
1	1			(18i)Some parents use dummies –
	=2			(18ii)it's up to you –
+2	α			(18iii)and you might find
	'β	α		(18iv)your baby settles
		xβ		(18v)sucking a dummy.
α				(19i)'Sucky' babies might be able to find their thumbs and fists
xβ				(19ii)to have a good suck.
1	α			(20i)Remember
	'β			(20ii)that babies get bored
x2	xβ			(20iii)so when he is having a real grizzle
	α			(20iv)this could be the reason.
clause simplex				(21)Is his cot an interesting place to be?
clause simplex				(22)Coloured posters and mobiles give him something to watch.
α				(23i)You could maybe tire him out
xβ				(23ii)by taking him for a walk . . . or a ride in the car –
xγ				(23iii)[although this is] not always practical in the middle of the night.
1				(24i)A change of scene and some fresh air will often work wonders –
+2				(24ii)even a walk around the garden may be enough.
xβ				(25i)As baby gets older
α	1			(25ii)he will be more able to communicate his feelings
	+2			(25iii)and you will be better [[at judging the problem.]]
xβ				(26i)Although you might be at your wit's end,
α	α			(26ii)remember
	'β			(26iii)that crying is communication with you, his parents.
clause simplex				(27)And you are the most important people in your baby's life.

Text 1.2

clause simplex	(1)The compelling sound of an infant's cry makes it an effective distress signal and appropriate to the human infant's prolonged dependence on a caregiver.
1	(2i)However, cries are discomforting
+2 α	(2ii)and may be alarming to parents,
xβ α	(2iii)many of whom find
'β	(2iv)it [to be] very difficult [[to listen to their infant's crying for even short periods of time.]]
clause simplex	(3)Many reasons for crying are obvious, like hunger and discomfort due to heat, cold, illness, and lying position.
1	(4i)These reasons, however, account for a relatively small percentage of infant crying
x2	(4ii)and are usually recognised quickly
x3	(4iii)and alleviated.
α	(5i)In the absence of a discernible reason for the behaviour, crying often stops
xβ	(5ii)when the infant is held.
1	(6i)In most infants, there are frequent episodes of crying with no apparent cause,
+2	(6ii)and holding or other soothing techniques seem ineffective.
clause simplex	(7)Infants cry and fuss for a mean of 1¾ hr/day at age 2 wk, 2¾ hr/day at age 6 wk, and 1 hr/day at 12 wk.
1	(8i)Counselling about normal crying may relieve guilt
+2	(8ii)and diminish concerns,
x3	(8iii)but for some the distress [[caused by the crying]] cannot be suppressed by logical reasoning.
α	(9i)For these parents, respite from exposure to the crying may be necessary
xβ	(9ii)to allow them to cope appropriately with their own distress.
α	(10i)Without relief, fatigue and tension may result in inappropriate parental responses
=β α	(10ii)such as leaving the infant in the house alone
+β	(10iii)or abusing the infant.

Text 1.3

clause simplex	(1)Did your kids used to cry a lot?
clause simplex	(2)When they were little?
clause simplex	(3)Yea
clause simplex	(4)Well = = what did you do?
clause simplex	(5)= = still do
clause simplex	(6)Yea? [laughs]
clause simplex	(7)Oh pretty tedious at times yea.
clause simplex	(8)There were all sorts of techniques = = Leonard Cohen
clause simplex	(9)= = Like what [laughs]
clause simplex	(10)Yea I used to use . . .

clause simplex	(11)What's that American guy [[that did 'Georgia on your mind'?]]
clause simplex	(12)Oh yea
clause simplex	(13)== Jim – James Taylor
clause simplex	(14)== James Taylor
clause simplex	(15)Yea yea.
clause simplex	(16)He was pretty good.
clause simplex	(17)Yea.
α	(18i)No Leonard Cohen's good
xβ	(18ii)cause it's just so monotonous.
clause simplex	(19)And there's only four chords.
α	(20i)And ah we used to have holidays
xβ	(20ii)when we only had one kid on a houseboat.
clause simplex	(21)And that was fantastic just the rocking motion of the houseboat
clause simplex	(22)Mmm
clause simplex	(23)Mmm
clause simplex	(24)Were there ever times . . .
α	(25i)Like I remember times
'β α	(25ii)when I couldn't work out
'β	(25iii)what the hell it was.
clause simplex	(26)There just didn't seem to be anything == [[you could do]]
clause simplex	(27)== No reason or . . .
clause simplex	(28)Yea
clause simplex	(29)Yea every night between six and ten
clause simplex	(30)Yea yea.
1	(31i)Luckily I didn't have that with the second baby
+2	(31ii)but the first one was that typical colicky sort of stuff from about five o'clock.
clause simplex	(32)Hmm
α	(33i)I remember
'β 1	(33ii)one day going for a um walk along the harbour
=2	(33iii)[it was] one of those you know harbour routes [[that had been opened up.]]
1	(34i)And um he started kicking up from about five o'clock
x2	(34ii)and we were getting panic stricken.
α	(35i)I had him in one of those um front strap things you know sling things
xβ 1	(35ii)ah cause that use to work wonders from time to time
x2	(35iii)but it wasn't working this time.
xβ	(36i)And as we sat on the foreshore of this Vaucluse area
α 1	(36ii)these two women came down
+2 1	(36iii)and they'd both been working as um governesses or something like that –
=2	(36iv)[they were] very, very classy ladies.
1	(37i)And they said
"2	(37ii)'Oh what's wrong with baby?

clause simplex	(38)He's got colic?'
α	(39i)You know, they really wanted
'β	(39ii)to take over.
clause simplex	(40)Yea
clause simplex	(41)And so I just handed the baby to them
1	(42i)And LUCKILY he kept on crying –
=2	(42ii)they couldn't stop him.
clause simplex	(43)So I was really delighted.
clause simplex	(44)They handed back this hideous little red wreck of a thing.

A2. Cohesion analyses

The numbers in these analyses refer to the sentence numbers only.

A2.1. Conjunction

Key:
= elaborating
+ extending
x enhancing
Explicit conjunctions are given
Implicit conjunctions are lexicalized (in parentheses)

Text 1.1

1 x (because) 2 4=5 (i.e.) 5x6 (because) 6x7 (so) 7=8 (e.g.) 8+9 (or) 9x10 (however) 10=11 (e.g.) 12+13 (but) 13=14 (e.g.) 13=15 (e.g.) 13=16 (e.g.)13=17 (e.g.) 13=18 (e.g.) 18+19 (moreover) 19+20 (but) 20=21 (i.e.) 21=22 (e.g.) 22+23 (or) 23=24 (e.g.) 25x26 (so) 25+26 and

Text 1.2

1x2 however 3x4 however 5x6 (however) 6=7 (e.g.) 8x9 (so) 9x10 (since)

Text 1.3

1=2 (i.e.) 8=9 like 8=18 (i.e.) 18+=19 and (i.e.) 19+20 and 20+x21 and (so) 24+25 like 25=26 (i.e.) 26=27 (i.e.) 31=33 (e.g.) 33+34 and 35+36 and 36+x37 and (then) 37=38 you know 38+x40 and so 40+41 and 41x42 so 42x43 (so/when)

A2.2. Reference

Ties are anaphoric unless otherwise indicated with the following keys:
C: cataphoric S: esphoric P: comparative L: locational B: bridging
H: homophoric X: exophoric

Text 1.1

(2) you (X) – you – you – you – you – (7) you – (10) you – (12) you – (13) you – you – (14) your baby – you – you – (18) you – you – your baby – (23) you – (25) you – (26) you – you – (27) you – your baby

(1) a baby who won't stop crying – (2) him – him – him – him – him – he – (4) baby – he – he – his – (6) he – (7) he – (8) babies – they – they– (9) his digestion – (10) he – (11) he – (12) baby – (13) him – (14) he – him – (15) baby – him – him – him – (16) he – (17) him – (20) babies – he – (21) his cot – (23) him – (25) baby – he – his feelings – (26) his parents

(5) the pattern – of sucking until . . . (S)

(7) the nipple or teat (H)

(14) the mood – to cry (S)

(14) the cot (H)

(17) the noise – of the washing machine (S)

(17) the washing machine (H)

(20) babies get bored – this – the reason

(23) the car (H)

(23) the middle of the night (S)

(23) the night (H)

(24) the garden (H)

(1–24) – (25) the problem

(27) the most important people in your baby's life (S)

Text 1.2

(1) compelling sound – it

(2) parents – their infant's crying – (8) some – (9) these parents – them – their own distress

(3) many reasons for crying – (4) these reasons

(8) the distress – caused by the crying (S)

(8) normal crying – (8) the crying – (9) the crying

(10) the house (H)

(9) these parents – (10) the infant (B)

Text 1.3

(1) your kids (X) – (4) you – (10) I – (20) we – we – (31) I – (33) I – (34) we – (35) I – (36) we – (41) I – (43) I

(10) I – (25) I – I

(1) your kids (X) – (2) they – (20) one kid – (31) the second baby – the first one – (34) he – (35) him – (37) the baby – he – (41) the baby – (42) he – him – (43) this hideous little red wreck of a thing

(14) James Taylor (H) – (16) he

(18) Leonard Cohen (H) – it

(20) holidays on a houseboat – (21) that

(20) a houseboat – (21) the houseboat

(25–26) – (31) that – that typical colicky sort of stuff

(32) the harbour (H) – one of those harbour routes – that had been opened up (S)

(35) one of those front strap things (H) – that – it

(36) the foreshore – of this Vaucluse area (S)

(36) this Vaucluse area (H)

(36) these two women – they – (37) they – (38) they – (40) them – (41) they – (43) they

A2.3. Lexical Relations

Ties are superordination unless otherwise indicated, with:
X: expectancy
C: Composition

Text 1.1

(1) baby – (4) baby – (8) babies – (12) baby – baby – (14) baby – (15) baby – (18) baby – (19) babies – (20) babies – (25) baby – (26) baby

(5) tummy – (6) womb (C) – (7) nipple (C) – teat – (9) digestion (C) – limbs (C) – (10) eyes (C) – (19) thumbs (C) – fists (C)

(3) hunger – (6) nourishment – food

(5) full – satisfied – empties

(8) grumpy – miserable – unhappy – (9) uncomfortable – (10) discomfort – (11) lonely – (12) happy – (15) secure – lose tension – (20) bored – (21) interesting – (23) practical – (25) more able – better – (26) at your wit's end

(1) despair – (8) stages – (10) grizzle – (14) mood – (16) tension – (20) grizzle – (25) feelings

(2) feed – change – put down – (5) fed – sucking

(2) change – (10) nappy (X)

(12) day – (13) night – (23) middle of the night (C)

(9) twitching – (15) jerking about – unsettle – (16) stimulation

(16) cut down – lose

(17) noise – gentle (X)

(1) crying – (10) having a grizzle – (17) noise – radio – recording – noise – (20) having a grizzle – (26) crying

(18) dummies – dummy

(18) dummies – sucking (X)

(13) sleep – (23) tire out

(14) cot – (21) cot

(7) assume – (10) find – (14) find – (18) find – (19) find – (22) watch – (25) communicate – judging

(13) relax – settle – (14) rocking – (15) wrapping up – (17) soothe – (18) sucking – (19) sucky

(1) crying – (2) howl – (4) cries – (8) tell – (10) having a grizzle – (14) to cry – start up – (20) having a real grizzle – (25) communicate – (26) crying

Text 1.2

(1) sound – cry – signal – (2) cries – crying – (3) crying – (4) crying – (5) behaviour – crying – (6) crying – (7) cry – (8) crying – crying – (9) crying

(7) cry – fuss (X)

(2) discomforting – alarming – difficult

(3) lying – (5) held – (6) holding – soothing

(1) distress – (3) hunger – discomfort – illness – (8) guilt – concerns – distress – (9) distress – (10) fatigue – tension

(3) heat – cold

(4) alleviated – (8) counselling – relieve – diminish – suppressed – (9) respite – (10) relief

(1) infant – human infant – (2) infant – (4) infant – (5) infant – (6) infants – (7) infants – (10) infant – infant

(1) caregiver – (2) parents – (9) parents – (10) parental

(1) effective – appropriate – (2) discomforting – alarming – difficult – (3) obvious – (5) discernible – (6) apparent – ineffective – (9) necessary – appropriately – (10) inappropriate

(1) prolonged – (2) short – (4) small – (6) frequent

(2) periods of time – (6) episodes – (7) hour (C) – day (C) – age (C) – week (C) – hour (C) – day (C) – age (C) – week (C) – hour (C) – day (C) – week (C)

(4) percentage – (7) mean

(3) reasons – (4) reasons – (5) reason – (6) cause – techniques – (8) logical reasoning – (10) responses

(9) cope – (10) leaving alone – abusing

Text 1.3

(1) kids – (20) kid – (31) baby – (36) women – ladies – (37) baby – (41) baby

(2) little – (43) little

(7) tedious – (15) good – (18) good – monotonous – (21) fantastic – (34) panic stricken – (43) delighted – (44) hideous

(44) hideous – wreck (X)

(1) cry – (34) kicking up – (42) crying –

(34) started – (39) take over – (42) kept on – stop

(31) colicky sort of stuff – (37) wrong with the baby – (38) got colic

(36) Vaucluse – classy (X)

(20) houseboat – (21) houseboat – (33) harbour (X) – harbour – (36) foreshore – Vaucluse area

(33) walk – (36) sat – came down

(41) handed – (44) handed back

(37) baby – (38) got colic (X)

(1) a lot – (7) at times – (35) from time to time

(24) times – (25) times – (29) night – six (C) – ten (C) – (31) five o'clock (C) – (33) day (C) – (34) five o'clock (C)

(8) techniques – (25) work out (X) – (27) reason (X) – (35) work wonders (X) – working – (36) working – governesses (X)

(7) Leonard Cohen – (11) American guy – (13) James Taylor – (14) James Taylor – (18) Leonard Cohen

A3. Generic Analysis

In the following analysis, each text has been assigned to a genre, and divided into functionally labelled stages.

Text 1.1

Genre: Explanation of Problematic Behaviour

Statement of Problem

1. A baby who won't stop crying can drive anyone to despair. 2. You feed him, you change him, you nurse him, you try to settle him, but the minute you put him down he starts to howl. 3. Why?

Explanation 1

4. The most common reason baby cries is hunger. 5. Even if he was just recently fed he might still be adapting to the pattern of sucking until his tummy is full and feeling satisfied until it empties again. 6. When he was in the womb nourishment came automatically and constantly.

Suggested Alleviating Action 1

7. Offer food first; if he turns away from the nipple or teat you can assume it's something else.

Explanation 2

8. It happens that babies go through grumpy, miserable stages when they just want to tell everyone how unhappy they feel. 9. Perhaps his digestion feels uncomfortable or his limbs are twitching.

Suggested Alleviating Action 2

10. If you can't find any specific source of discomfort such as a wet nappy or strong light in his eyes, he could just be having a grizzle.

Explanation 3

11. Perhaps he's just lonely.

Suggested Alleviating Action 3

12. During the day, a baby sling helps you to deal with your chores and keep baby happy.

Suggested Alleviating Action 4

13. At night when you want to sleep you will need to take action to relax and settle him. 14. Rocking helps, but if your baby is in the mood to cry you will probably find he'll start up again when you put him back in the cot.

Suggested Alleviating Action 5

15. Wrapping baby up snugly helps to make him feel secure and stops him from jerking about which can unsettle him.

Suggested Alleviating Action 6

16. Outside stimulation is cut down and he will lose tension. 17. Gentle noise might soothe him off to sleep – a radio played softly, a recording of a heartbeat, traffic noise – even the noise of the washing machine is effective!

Suggested Alleviating Action 7

18. Some parents use dummies – it's up to you – and you might find your baby settles sucking a dummy. 19. 'Sucky' babies might be able to find their thumbs and fists to have a good suck.

Explanation 4

20. Remember that babies get bored so when he is having a real grizzle this could be the reason. 21. Is his cot an interesting place to be?

Suggested Alleviating Action 8

22. Coloured posters and mobiles give him something to watch.

Suggested Alleviating Action 9

23. You could maybe tire him out by taking him for a walk . . . or a ride in the car – not always practical in the middle of the night. 24. A change of scene and some fresh air will often work wonders – even a walk around the garden may be enough.

Outlook: improvements to come

25. As baby gets older he will be more able to communicate his feelings and you will be better at judging the problem.

Morale Booster

26. Although you might be at your wit's end, remember that crying is communication with you, his parents. 27. And you are the most important people in your baby's life.

TEXT 1.2

Genre: Explanation of Problematic Behaviour

Statement of Problem

1. The compelling sound of an infant's cry makes it an effective distress signal and appropriate to the human infant's prolonged dependence on a caregiver. 2. However, cries are discomforting and may be alarming to parents, many of whom find it very difficult to listen to their infant's crying for even short periods of time.

Explanation 1

3. Many reasons for crying are obvious, like hunger and discomfort due to heat, cold, illness, and lying position. 4. These reasons, however, account for a relatively small percentage of infant crying and are usually recognised quickly and alleviated.

Explanation 2

5. In the absence of a discernible reason for the behaviour, crying often stops when the infant is held.

Explanation 3

6. In most infants, there are frequent episodes of crying with no apparent cause, and holding or other soothing techniques seem ineffective. 7. Infants cry and fuss for a mean of 1¾ hr/day at age 2 wk, 2¾ hr/day at age 6 wk, and 1 hr/day at 12 wk.

Suggested Alleviating Action 1

8. Counselling about normal crying may relieve guilt and diminish concerns, but for some the distress caused by the crying cannot be suppressed by logical reasoning.

Suggested Alleviating Action 2

9. For these parents, respite from exposure to the crying may be necessary to allow them to cope appropriately with their own distress.

Outlook: warning

10. Without relief, fatigue and tension may result in inappropriate parental responses such as leaving the infant in the house alone or abusing the infant.

TEXT 1.3

Genre: conversational exchange, including Topic/Comment and Narrative of personal experience genres

Exchange 1

question	S	1. Did your kids used to cry a lot?
question		2. When they were little?
answer	C	3. Yea

Exchange 2

question	S	4. Well = = what did you do?
answer	C	5. = = still do
acknowledge	S	6. Yea? [laughs]
answer	C	7. Oh pretty tedious at times yea.
answer		8. There were all sorts of techniques = = Leonard Cohen
tracking	S	9. = = Like what [laughs]

Exchange 3

statement		10. Yea I used to use . . .
tracking		11. What's that American guy that did 'Georgia on your mind'?
response	C	12. Oh yea
statement	S	13. == Jim – James Taylor
acknowledge	C	14. == James Taylor
follow-up	S	15. Yea yea.

Exchange 4

statement		16. He was pretty good
agree	C	17. Yea.

Exchange 5

statement		18. No Leonard Cohen's good cause it's just so monotonous
acknowledge	S	[laughs]
statement	C	19. And there's only four chords.

Topic^Comment

statement: Topic		20. And ah we used to have holidays when we only had one kid on a houseboat.
statement: Comment		21. And that was fantastic just the rocking motion of the houseboat
acknowledge	S	22. Mmm
follow-up	C	23. Mmm

Exchange 6

question	S	24. Were there ever times . . . 25. Like I remember times when I couldn't work out what the hell it was. 26. There just didn't seem to be anything == you could do
acknowledge	C	27. == No reason or . . .
acknowledge		28. Yea
answer	S	29. Yea every night between six and ten
agree	C	30. Yea yea.

Exchange 7/Narrative

answer: **Abstract**		31. Luckily I didn't have that with the second baby but the first one was that typical colicky sort of stuff from about five o'clock.
acknowledge	S	32. Hmm
Orientation 1	C	33. I remember one day going for a um walk along the harbour – one of those you know harbour routes that had been opened up.
Complication 1		34. And um he started kicking up from about five o'clock and we were getting panic stricken.
Orientation 2		35. I had him in one of those um front strap things you know sling things ah cause that use to work wonders from time to time but it wasn't working this time.
Complication 2		36. And as we sat on the foreshore of of this Vaucluse area these two women came down and

they'd both been working as um governesses or something like that – very very classy ladies. 37. And they said 'Oh what's wrong with the baby? 38. He's got colic?'

Evaluation 1		39. You know, they really wanted to take over
	S	40. Yea
Complication 3	C	41. And so I just handed the baby to them
	S	[laughs]
Resolution	C	42. And LUCKILY he kept on crying – they couldn't stop him
	S	[laughs]
Evaluation 2	C	43. So I was really delighted.
Coda		44. They handed back this hideous little red wreck of a thing
		[laughter]

References

Allerton, D. J. (1979) *Essentials of Grammatical Theory*. London: Routledge and Kegan Paul.

Armstrong, E. M. (1991) The potential of cohesion analysis in the analysis and treatment of aphasic discourse. *Clinical Linguistics & Phonetics*, 5(1), 39–51.

Atkinson, J. M. and Heritage, J. (eds) (1984) *Structures of Social Action: Studies in Conversation Analysis*. Cambridge: CUP.

Bakhtin, M. (1994) Speech Genres. In P. Morris (ed.) *The Bakhtin Reader: Selected Writings of Bakhtin, Medvedev, Voloshinov*. London: Edward Arnold.

Bateman, J., Matthiessen, C. M. I. M., Nanri, K. and Zeng, L. (1991) Multilingual text generation: an architecture based on functional typology. *International Conference on Current Issues in Computational Linguistics, Penang, Malaysia*.

Belsey, C. (2002) *Critical Practice*, 2nd edition. London: Routledge, New Accent Series.

Benson, J. D. and Greaves, W. S. (1981) Field of Discourse: theory and application. *Applied Linguistics*, 2(1), 45–55.

Benson, J. D. and Greaves, W. S. (eds) (1985) *Systemic Perspectives on Discourse, Vol. 1: Selected Theoretical Papers from the 9th International Systemic Workshop*. Norwood, NJ: Ablex.

Benson, J. D. and Greaves, W. S. (eds) (1988) *Systemic Functional Approaches to Discourse*. Norwood, NJ:Ablex.

Benson, J. D., Cummings, M. J. and Greaves, W. S. (eds) (1988) *Linguistics in a Systemic Perspective*. Amsterdam: Benjamins (= *Current Issues in Linguistics Theory*, 39).

Berger, P. and Luckmann, T. (1966) *The Social Construction of Reality: A Treatise in the Sociology of Knowledge*. New York: Doubleday.

Bernstein, B. (1971) *Class, Codes and Control 1: Theoretical Studies towards a Sociology of Language*. London: Routledge.

Bernstein, B. (1973) (ed.) *Class, Codes and Control 2: Applied Studies towards a Sociology of Language*. London: Routledge.

Bernstein, B. (1977) *Class, Codes and Control 3: Towards a Theory of Educational Transmissions*. London: Routledge.

Bernstein, B. (1990) *Class, Codes and Control 4: The Structuring of Pedagogic Discourse*. London: Routledge.

Berry, M. (1977a) *Introduction to Systemic Linguistics: 1, Structures and Systems*. London: Batsford.

Berry, M. (1977b) *Introduction to Systemic Linguistics: 2, Levels and Links*. London: Batsford.

Berry, M. (1981) Systemic Linguistics and Discourse Analysis: a multi-layered approach to exchange structure. In M. C. Coulthard and M. Montgomery (eds) *Studies in Discourse Analysis*. London: Routledge and Kegan Paul.

Biber, D. (1986) Spoken and Written Textual Dimensions in English: resolving the contradictory findings. *Language*, 62(2), 384–414.

Bloor, T. and Bloor, M. (1995) *The Functional Analysis of English: A Hallidayan Approach*. London: Arnold. Co-published New York: Oxford University Press.

Brown, P. and Levinson, S. (1978) Universals in Language Usage: politeness phenomena. In E. Goody (ed.) *Social Markers in Speech*. Cambridge: CUP, 56–311.

Brown, R. and Gilman, A. (1960) The Pronouns of Power and Solidarity. In T. Sebeok (ed.) *Style in Language*. Cambridge, MA: MIT Press, 253–76.

Burton, D. (1980) *Dialogue and Discourse*. London: Routledge and Kegan Paul.

Burton, D. (1981) Analysing Spoken Discourse. In M. Coulthard and M. Montgomery (eds). *Studies in Discourse Analysis*. London: Routledge and Kegan Paul, 146–57.

Butler, C. S. (1985) *Systemic Linguistics: Theory and Applications*. London: Batsford.

Butler, C. S. (1987) Communicative Function and Semantics. In M. A. K. Halliday and R. P. Fawcett (eds) *New Developments in Systemic Linguistics Vol. 1: Theory and Description*. London: Pinter, 212–29.

Butler, C. S. (1988) Politeness and the Semantics of Modalised Directives in English. In Benson *et al.* 119–54.

Butt, D., Fahey, R., Feez, S., Spinks, S. and Yallop, C. (2001) *Using Functional Grammar: An Explorer's Guide*, 2nd edition. Sydney: National Centre for English Language Teaching and Research, Macquarie University.

Carter, R. and Nash, W. (1990) *Seeing Through Language: A Guide to Styles of English Writing*. London: Basil Blackwell.

Chafe, W. (ed.) (1980) *The Pear Stories: Cognitive, Cultural and Linguistic Aspects of Narrative Production*. Norwood, NJ: Ablex.

Christie, F. (ed.) (1988) *Social Processes in Education: Proceedings of the First Australian Systemic Network Conference, Deakin University, January 1990*. Darwin: Centre for Studies of Language in Education, Northern Territory University.

Christie, F. (1991a) First and second-order registers in education. In Ventola 1991: 235–58.

Christie, F. (ed.) (1991b) *Literacy in Social Processes: Papers from the Inaugural Australian Systemic Functional Linguistics Conference* held at Deakin University, January 1990. Darwin: Centre for Studies of Language in Education, Northern Territory University.

Christie, F. (ed.) (1999) *Pedagogy and the Shaping of Consciousness: Linguistic and Social Processes in the Workplace and School*. London: Cassell.

Christie, F. (2002) *Classroom Discourse Analysis*. London: Continuum.

Christie, F. and Martin, J. R. (eds) (1997) *Genre and Institutions: Social Processes in the Workplace and School*. London: Cassell.

Cloran, C. (1989) Learning through Language: the social construction of gender. In Hasan and Martin 1989: 111–51.

Culler, J. (1976) *Saussure*. London: Fontana, Fontana Modern Masters Series.

Culler, J. (1997) *Literary Theory: A Very Short Introduction*. London: OUP.

Downing, A. and Locke, P. (1992) *A University Course in English Grammar*. UK: Prentice Hall.

Droga, L. and Humphrey, S. (2003) *Grammar and Meaning: An Introduction for Primary Teachers*. Berry, NSW: Target Texts.

Eggins, S. (1990) Keeping the Conversation Going: a systemic functional analysis of conversational structure in casual sustained talk. PhD thesis, Linguistics Department, University of Sydney.

Eggins, S. (2000) Researching Everyday Talk. In L. Unsworth (ed.) *Researching Language in Schools and Communities: Functional Linguistic Perspectives*. London: Cassell, Open Linguistics Series, 130–51.

Eggins, S. [in preparation] Genre Hybridity and Semantic Ambivalence in the *Harry Potter* Series.

Eggins, S. and Iedema, R. (1997) Difference without diversity: semantic orientation and ideology in competing women's magazines. In R. Wodak (ed.) *Gender and Discourse*. London: Sage, 165–96.

Eggins, S. and Martin, J. R. (1997) Genres and Registers of Discourse. In T.A. van Dijk (ed.) *Discourse as Structure and Process*. Vol. 1 in Discourse Studies: A Multidisciplinary Introduction. London: Sage, 230–56.

Eggins, S. and Slade, D. (1997/2004) *Analysing Casual Conversation*. London: Cassell. Reprinted 2004 by Equinox, London.

Eggins, S., Wignell, P. and Martin, J. R. (1992) The discourse of history: distancing the recoverable past. In M. Ghadessy (ed.) *Register Analysis: Theory & Practice*. London: Pinter. (First published as Working Papers in Linguistics, No. 5., Linguistics Department, University of Sydney.)

Fairclough, N. (1989) *Language and Power*. London: Longman Language and Social Life.

Fairclough, N. (1992) *Discourse and Social Change*. Cambridge: Polity Press.

Fawcett, R. (1980) *Cognitive Linguistics and Social Interaction: Towards an Integrated Model of a Systemic Functional Grammar and the Other Components of an Interacting Mind*. Heidelberg: Julius Groos.

Fawcett, R. (1988a) The English Personal Pronouns: an exercise in linguistic theory. In J. D. Benson, M. J. Cummings and W. S. Greaves (eds) *Linguistics in a Systemic Perspective*. Amsterdam: Benjamins (= *Current Issues in Linguistic Theory*, 39), 185–220.

Fawcett, R. (1988b) What Makes a 'Good' System Network Good? – Four Pairs of Concepts for Such Evaluation. In Benson and Greaves 1988: 1–28.

Fawcett, R. P., van der Mije, A. and van Wissen, C. (1988) Towards a Systemic Flowchart Model for Discourse Structure. In R. P. Fawcett and D. Young (eds) 1988: 116–43.

Fawcett, R. P. and Young, D. (eds) (1988) *New Developments in Systemic Linguistics, Vol. 2: Theory and Application*, London: Pinter.

Firth, J. R. (1935) The Technique of Semantics. *Transactions of the Philological Society* (reprinted in J. R. Firth (1957), 177–89).

Firth, J. R. (1950) Personality and Language in Society. In Firth 1957: 177–89.

Firth, J. R. (1951) Modes of Meaning. In Firth 1957: 190–215.

Firth, J. R. (1957) *Papers in Linguistics 1934–1951*. London: OUP.

Fowler, R., Hodge, B., Kress, G. and Trew, T. (1979) *Language and Control*. London: Routledge and Kegan Paul.

Fries, C. (1981) On the Status of Theme in English: Arguments from Discourse. *Forum Linguisticum*, 6(1), 1–38. (Republished in J. S. Petöfi and E. Sözer (eds) (1983) *Micro and Macro Connexity of Texts*. Hamburg: Helmut Buske Verlag, 116–52.)

Ghadessy, M. (ed.) (1993) *Register Analysis: Theory & Practice*. London: Pinter.

Gregory, M. (1967) Aspects of Varieties Differentiation. *Journal of Linguistics*, 3, 177–98.

Gregory, M. (1985) Towards Communication Linguistics: a framework. In J. D. Benson and W. S. Greaves (eds) *Systemic Perspectives on Discourse, Vol. 1: Selected Theoretical Papers from the 9th International Systemic Workshop*. Norwood, NJ: Ablex, 119–34.

Gregory, M. (1988) Generic Situation and Register. In J. D. Benson, M. J. Cummings and W. S. Greaves (eds) *Linguistics in a Systemic Perspective*. Amsterdam: Benjamins (= *Current Issues in Linguistic Theory*, 39), 301–29.

Gumperz, J. (1968) The speech community. In *International Encyclopedia of the Social Sciences*. New York: Macmillan.

Gumperz, J. (1971) *Language in Social Groups: Essays Selected and Introduced by Anwar S. Dil*. Stanford, CA: Stanford University Press.

Gumperz, J. (1982a) *Discourse Strategies*. Cambridge: CUP.

Gumperz, J. (ed.) (1982b) *Language and Social Identity*. Cambridge: CUP.

Halliday, M. A. K. (1973) *Explorations in the Functions of Language*. London: Edward Arnold.

Halliday, M. A. K. (1974) Interview with M. A. K. Halliday. In H. Parret (ed.) *Discussing Language*. The Hague: Mouton (Janua Linguarum Series Maior, 93), 81–120. (Extracts reprinted in Halliday 1978.)

Halliday, M. A. K. (1975) *Learning How to Mean: Explorations in the Development of Language*. London: Edward Arnold (*Explorations in Language Study*).

Halliday, M. A. K. (1977) *Aims and Perspectives in Linguistics*. Sydney: Applied Linguistics Association of Australia Occasional Papers No. 1.

Halliday, M. A. K. (1978) *Language as Social Semiotic*. London: Edward Arnold.

Halliday, M. A. K. (1984) Language as Code and Language as Behaviour: a systemic-functional interpretation of the nature and ontogenesis of dialogue. In R. Fawcett, M. A. K. Halliday, S. M. Lamb and A. Makkai (eds) *The Semiotics of Language and Culture, Vol. 1: Language as Social Semiotic*. London: Pinter, 3–35.

Halliday, M. A. K. (1985a) *An Introduction to Functional Grammar.* London: Edward Arnold.

Halliday, M. A. K. (1985b) *Spoken and Written Language.* Geelong, Vic.: Deakin University Press (republished by OUP, 1989).

Halliday, M. A. K. (1985c) Part A. of *Language, Text and Context.* Geelong, Vic.: Deakin University Press (republished by OUP, 1989).

Halliday, M. A. K. and Hasan, R. (1976) *Cohesion in English.* London: Longman.

Halliday, M. A. K. and Hasan, R. (1985) *Language, Text and Context.* Geelong, Vic.: Deakin University Press (republished by OUP, 1989).

Halliday, M. A. K. and Matthiessen, C. M. I. M. (1999) *Construing Experience Through Meaning – A Language-based Approach to Cognition.* London: Cassell.

Halliday, M. A. K. and Matthiessen, C. M. I. M. (2004) *An Introduction to Functional Grammar,* 3rd edition. London: Edward Arnold.

Halliday, M. A. K. and Webster, J. (2002a) *On Grammar. Collected Works of MAK Halliday, Vol. 1.* Edited by Jonathan Webster. London: Continuum.

Halliday, M. A. K. and Webster, J. (2002b) *Linguistic Studies of Text and Discourse. Collected Works of MAK Halliday, Vol. 2.* Edited by Jonathan Webster. London: Continuum.

Halliday, M. A. K. and Webster, J. (2003a) *On Language and Linguistics. Collected Works of MAK Halliday, Vol. 3.* Edited by Jonathan Webster. London: Continuum.

Halliday, M. A. K. and Webster, J. (2003b) *The Language of Early Childhood. Collected Works of MAK Halliday, Vol. 4.* Edited by Jonathan Webster. London: Continuum.

Hasan, R. (1977) Text in the Systemic-Functional Model. In W. Dressler (ed.) *Current Trends in Textlinguistics.* Berlin: Walter de Gruyter, 228–46.

Hasan, R. (1979) On the Notion of Text. In J. S. Petöfi (ed.) *Text vs Sentence: Basic Questions of Textlinguistics.* Hamburg: Helmut Buske (Papers in Textlinguistics, 20 (2)), 369–90.

Hasan, R. (1984) Coherence and cohesive harmony. In J. Flood (ed.) *Understanding Reading Comprehension.* Newark, DE: IRA.

Hasan, R. (1985a) The Structure of a Text. In Halliday and Hasan 1985, 70–96.

Hasan, R. (1985b) The Texture of a Text. In Halliday and Hasan 1985, 70–96.

Hasan, R. (1985c) *Linguistics, Language and Verbal Art.* Geelong, Vic.: Deakin University Press (republished by OUP, 1989).

Hasan, R. (1986) The Ontogenesis of Ideology: an interpretation of mother–child talk. In T. Threadgold, E. Grosz, G. Kress and M. A. K. Halliday (eds), *Language, Semiotics, Ideology.* Sydney: Sydney Association for Studies in Society and Culture, 125–46.

Hasan, R. (1988) Language in the Processes of Socialisation: home and school. In L. Gerot, J. Oldenburg and T. van Leeuwen (eds) *Language and Socialisation: Home and School.* Proceedings from the Working Conference on Language in Education, Macquarie University, 17–21 November 1986. Sydney: Macquarie University, 36–96.

Hasan, R. and Cloran, C. (1990) Semantic Variation: a sociolinguistic interpretation of everyday talk between mothers and children. In J. Gibbons, H. Nicholas and M. A. K. Halliday (eds) *Learning, Keeping and Using Language: Selected Papers from the 8th World Congress of Applied Linguistics.* Amsterdam: Benjamins, 67–99.

Hasan, R. and Martin, J. R. (eds) (1989) *Language Development: Learning Language, Learning Culture.* Norwood, NJ: Ablex (*Meaning and Choice in Language: Studies for Michael Halliday*).

Hunt, P. (ed.) (2001) *Children's Literature: An Anthology 1801–1902.* London: Blackwell.

Hymes, D. H. (1962/74) The Ethnography of Speaking. In B. G. Blount (ed.) *Language, Culture and Society.* Cambridge, MA: Winthrop, 189–223.

Hymes, D. H. (1964/72) Towards Ethnographies of Communication: The Analysis of Communicative Events. In P. P. Giglioli (ed.) *Language and Social Context.* Harmondsworth: Penguin, 21–44.

Hymes, D. (ed.) (1964) *Language in Culture and Society: A Reader in Linguistics and Anthropology.* New York: Harper & Row.

Hymes, D. (1971) Competence and performance in linguistic theory. In R. Huxley and E. Ingram (eds) *Language Acquisition: Models and Methods.* London: Academic Press.

Hymes, D. (ed.) (1972) *Directions in Sociolinguistics: The Ethnography of Communication*. New York: Holt, Rinehart & Winston.

Iedema, R. (2003) *Discourses of Post-Bureaucratic Organization*. Philadelphia: Benjamins, Document Design Companion Series 5.

Iedema, R., Feez, S. and White, O. (1994) *Media Literacy (Write It Right Literacy in Industry Project: Stage Two)*. Sydney: Metropolitan East Region's Disadvantaged Schools Program.

Joia, A. de and Stenton, A. (1980) *Terms in Systemic Linguistics: A Guide to Halliday*. London: Batsford Academic.

Kress, G. (ed.) (1976) *Halliday: System and Function in Language*. Lardan: OUP.

Kress, G. (1985) *Linguistic Processes in Socio-cultural Practice*. Geelong, Vic.: Deakin University Press (republished by OUP, 1989).

Kress, G. (ed.) (1988) *Communication and Culture: An Introduction*. Sydney: New South Wales University Press.

Kress, G. and Hodge, B. (1979) *Language as Ideology*. London: Routledge and Kegan Paul.

Kress, G. and Hodge, R. (1988) *Social Semiotics*. London: Polity.

Kress, G. and van Leeuwen, T. (1990) *Reading Images*. Geelong, Vic.: Deakin University Press (Sociocultural Aspects of Language and Education).

Kress, G. and van Leeuwen, T. (1996) *Reading Images: The Grammar of Visual Design*. London: Routledge.

Kress, G. and van Leeuwen, T. (2001) *Multimodal Discourse: The Modes and Media of Contemporary Communication*. London: Edward Arnold.

Labov, W. (1972a) *Language in the Inner City*. Philadelphia: Pennsylvania University Press, 354–96.

Labov, W. (1972b) *Sociolinguistic Patterns*. Philadelphia: Pennsylvania University Press.

Labov, W. and Fanshel, D. (1977) *Therapeutic Discourse: Psychotherapy as Conversation*. New York: Academic Press.

Labov, W. and Waletzky, J. (1967) Narrative Analysis. In J. Helm (ed.) *Essays on the Verbal and Visual Arts. (Proceedings of the 1966 Spring Meeting of the American Ethnological Society)*. Seattle: University of Washington Press, 12–44.

Lemke, J. (1985) Ideology, Intertextuality and the Notion of Register. In J. D. Benson and W. S. Greaves (eds) *Systemic Perspectives on Discourse, Vol. 1: Selected Theoretical Papers from the 9th International Systemic Workshop*. Norwood, NJ: Ablex, 275–94.

Macken, M. and Rothery, J. (1991) *A Model for Literacy in Subject Learning*. Sydney: Disadvantaged Schools Program (DSP).

Macken-Horarik, M. and Martin, J. R. (eds) *Negotiating Heteroglossia: Social Perspectives on Evaluation*. Special Issue of *Text*, 23,2.

Malcolm, K. (1985) Communication Linguistics: a sample analysis. In J. D. Benson and W. S. Greaves (eds) *Systemic Perspectives on Discourse, Vol. 1: Selected Theoretical Papers from the 9th International Systemic Workshop*. Norwood, NJ: Ablex, 136–51.

Malcolm, K. (1987) Alternative Approaches to Casual Conversation in Linguistic Description. *Occasional Papers in Systemic Linguistics*, 1. Nottingham: Department of English, University of Nottingham, 111–34.

Malinowski, B. (1923/46) The Problem of Meaning in Primitive Languages. Supplement I to C. K. Ogden and I. A. Richards *The Meaning of Meaning* (8th edition, 1946). New York: Harcourt Brace & World, 296–336.

Malinowski, B. (1935) *Coral Gardens and their Magic, a Study of the Methods of Tilling the Soil and of Agricultural Rites in the Trobriand Islands*. Vol. 2. *The Language of Magic and Gardening*. London: Allen and Unwin.

Mann, W. and Thompson, S. (1986) *Rhetorical Structure Theory: Description and Construction of Text Structures*. Paper presented at the Third International Workshop on Text Generation, August 1986, Nijmegen, Netherlands. Published by The Information Sciences Institute Reprint Series, University of Southern California.

Martin, J. R. (1983) CONJUNCTION: the logic of English text. In J. S. Petöfi and E. Sözer (eds) *Micro and Macro Connexity of Texts*. Hamburg: Helmut Buske Verlag (Papers in Textlinguistics, 45), 1–72.

Martin, J. R. (1984) Language, Register and Genre. In F. Christie (ed.) *Children Writing: A Reader*. Geelong, Vic.: Deakin University Press, 21–9.

Martin, J. R. (1985a) *Factual Writing: Exploring and Challenging Social Reality*. Geelong, Vic.: Deakin University Press (republished by OUP, 1989).

Martin, J. R. (1985b) Process and Text: two aspects of semiosis. In Benson and Greaves 1985, 248–74.

Martin, J. R. (1992a) *English Text: System and Structure*. Amsterdam: Benjamins.

Martin, J. R. (1992b) *Macro-genres: The Ecology of the Page*. Mimeo. Sydney: Dept of Linguistics, University of Sydney.

Martin, J. R., Matthiessen, C. and Painter, C. (1997) *Working with Functional Grammar*. London: Edward Arnold.

Martin, J. R. and Rose, D. (2003) *Working with Discourse*. London: Continuum.

Martin, J. R. and Wodak, R. (eds) (2003) *Re/reading the past: Critical and Functional Perspectives on Time and Value*. Amsterdam: Benjamins.

Martinec, R. (2000) Rhythm in multimodal texts. *Leonardo*, 33 (4), 289–97.

Matthiessen, C. M. I. M. (1993) Register in the Round. In M. Ghadessy, 1993, 221–92.

Matthiessen, C. M. I. M. (1995) *Lexico-grammatical Cartography: English Systems*. Tokyo: International Language Sciences Publishers.

Nesbitt, C. and Plum, G. (1988) Probabilities in a Systemic-Functional Grammar: the clause complex in English. In R. P. Fawcett and D. Young (eds) *New Developments in Systemic Linguistics, Vol. 2: Theory and Application*. London: Pinter, 6–38.

O'Toole, M. (1989) Semiotic systems in painting and poetry. In M. Falchikov, C. Pike and R. Russell (eds) *A Festschrift for Dennis Ward*. Nottingham: Astra Press.

O'Toole, M. (1994) *The Language of Displayed Art*. London: Leicester University Press.

Painter, C. (1984) *Into the Mother Tongue: A Case Study of Early Language Development*. London: Pinter.

Painter, C. (1985) *Learning the Mother Tongue*. Geelong, Vic.: Deakin University Press (republished by OUP, 1989).

Painter, C. (1998) *Learning through Language in Early Childhood*. London: Cassell.

Poynton, C. (1984) Names as vocatives: forms and functions. *Nottingham Linguistics Circular 13* (Special Issue on Systemic Linguistics), 1–34.

Poynton, C. (1985) *Language and Gender: Making the Difference*. Geelong, Vic.: Deakin University Press.

Poynton, C. (1990) *Address and the Semiotics of Social Relations: A Systemic-functional Account of Address Forms and Practices in Australian English*. PhD Thesis, Department of Linguistics, University of Sydney.

Radway, J. (1991) *Reading the Romance: Women, Patriarchy and Popular Literature*, 2nd edition. Chapel Hill, NC: University of North Carolina Press

Ravelli, L. (1985) *Metaphor, Mode and Complexity: An Exploration of Co-varying Patterns*. BA Hons Thesis, Department of Linguistics, University of Sydney.

Rimmon-Kenan, S. (2003) *Narrative Fiction: Contemporary Poetics*, 2nd edition. London: Routledge.

Rothery, J. (1984) The development of genres – primary to junior secondary school. In F. Christie (ed.) *Children Writing: Study Guide* (ECT418 Language Studies). Geelong, Vic.: Deakin University Press.

Rothery, J. (1986a) Let's teach children to write. *Working Papers in Linguistics 4* (Writing Project Report). Sydney: Department of Linguistics, University of Sydney.

Rothery, J. (1986b) Teaching writing in the primary school: A genre-based approach to the development of writing abilities. *Working Papers in Linguistics 4* (Writing Project Report). Sydney: Department of Linguistics, University of Sydney.

Rothery, J. (1989) Learning about language. In R. Hasan and J. R. Martin (eds) *Language Development: Learning Language, Learning Culture* (Meaning and Choice in Language: Studies for Michael Halliday). Norwood, NJ: Ablex, 199–256.

Rothery, J. (1990) *Story Writing in Primary School: Assessing Narrative Type Genres*. PhD Thesis, Department of Linguistics, University of Sydney.

Rothery, J. (1991) *Developing Critical Literacy: An Analysis of the Writing Task in a Year 10 Reference Test*. Sydney: DSP.

Sacks, H., Schegloff, E. and Jefferson, G. (1974) A Simplest Systematics for the Organization of Turn-taking for Conversation. *Language*, 50(4).

Saussure, F. de (1959/66) *Course in General Linguistics*. Edited by Charles Bally and Albert Sechehaye. New York: McGraw-Hill.

Schegloff, E. A. (1981) Discourse as an interactional achievement: some uses of 'Uh huh' and other things that come between sentences. In D. Tannen (ed.) *Analyzing Discourse: Text and Talk*. Washington, DC: Georgetown University Press, 71–93.

Schegloff, E. A. and Sacks, H. (1973/74) Opening up Closings. *Semiotica*, 7(4), 289–327 (reprinted in R. Turner 1974 *Ethnomethodology: Selected Readings*. Harmondsworth: Penguin).

Schiffren, D. (1987) *Discourse Markers*. Cambridge: CUP.

Shklovsky, V. (1992) Art as Technique. In P. Rice and P. Waugh *Modern Literary Theory: A Reader*, 2nd edition. London: Edward Arnold.

Simon-Vandenbergen, A. M., Taverniers, M. and Ravelli, L. J. (eds) (2003) *Grammatical Metaphor: Views from Systemic Functional Linguistics*. Amsterdam: Benjamins.

Sinclair, J. McH. and Coulthard, R. M. (1975) *Towards an Analysis of Discourse: The English used by Teachers and Pupils*. London: OUP.

Tannen, D. (1980) A Comparative Analysis of Oral Narrative Strategies: Athenian Greek and American English. In W. Chafe (ed.) *The Pear Stories: Cognitive, Cultural and Linguistic Aspects of Narrative Production*. Norwood, NJ: Ablex, 51–87.

Tannen, D. (1989) *Talking Voices: Repetition, Dialogue and Imagery in Conversational Discourse*. Cambridge: CUP.

Tannen, D. (1990) *You Just Don't Understand*. London: Virago.

Tannen, D. (1991) *Conversational Style: Analyzing Talk Among Friends*. Norwood, NJ: Ablex.

Teich, E. (1999) *Systemic Functional Grammar in Natural Language Generation: Linguistic Description and Computational Representation*. London: Continuum.

Thibault, P. (1991) *Social Semiotics as Praxis: Text, Social Meaning Making and Nabakov's 'Ada'*. Minneapolis: University of Minnesota Press.

Thompson, G. (2004) *Introducing Functional Grammar*, 2nd edition. London: Edward Arnold.

Threadgold, T. (1986) Semiotics, ideology, language. In Threadgold, Grosz, Kress and Halliday 1986, 15–59.

Threadgold, T. (1988) The Genre Debate. *Southern Review* 21(3), 315–30.

Threadgold, T., Grosz, E., Kress, G. and Halliday, M. A. K. (eds) (1986) *Language, Semiotics, Ideology*. Sydney: Sydney Association for Studies in Society and Culture (= Sydney Studies in Society and Culture, 3).

Toolan, M. (ed.) (2002a–2002d) *Critical Discourse Analysis: Critical Concepts in Linguistics Vols I–IV*. London: Routledge.

Unsworth, L. (ed.) (2000) *Researching Language in Schools and Communities: Functional Linguistic Perspectives*. London: Cassell.

Ure, J. (1971) Lexical density and register differentiation. In G. E. Perren and J. L. M. Trim (eds) *Applications of Linguistics: Selected Papers of the 2nd International Congress of Applied Linguistics, Cambridge 1969*. Cambridge: CUP.

Ure, J. and Ellis, J. (1977) Register in Descriptive Linguistics and Linguistic Sociology. In O. Uribe-Villas *Issues in Sociolinguistics*. The Hague: Mouton, 197–243.

van Dijk, T. (1977) *Text and Context: Explorations in the Semantics and Pragmatics of Discourse*. London: Longman.

van Leeuwen, T. (1999) *Speech, Music, Sound*. London: Macmillan.

Ventola, E. (1987) *The Structure of Social Interaction: A Systemic Approach to the Semiotics of Service Encounters*. London: Pinter.

Ventola, E. (1988) The Logical Relations in Exchanges. In J. D. Benson and W. S. Greaves (eds) *Systemic Functional Approaches to Discourse*. Norwood, NJ: Ablex, 51–72.

Ventola, E. (ed.) (1991) *Functional and Systemic Linguistics: Approaches and Uses*. Berlin and New York: Mouton de Gruyter.

White, P. (2002) Death, disruption and the moral order: the narrative impulse in mass-media 'hard news' reporting. In M. Toolan, (ed.) *Critical Discourse Analysis: Critical Concepts in Linguistics Vol III*. London: Routledge.

Wignell, P., Martin, J. R. and Eggins, S. (1987) The Discourse of Geography: ordering and explaining the experiential world. *Writing Project: Report 1987* (*Working Papers in Linguistics 5*). Sydney: Department of Linguistics, University of Sydney (republished in *Linguistics and Education*, 1(4), 1990: 359–92).

Index